FIELDING
TRAVEL GUIDES

FIELDING'S ALASKA CRUISES AND THE INSIDE PASSAGE

Fielding Titles

Fielding's Alaska Cruises and the Inside Passage
Fielding's Asia's Top Dive Sites
Fielding's Amazon
Fielding's Australia
Fielding's Bahamas
Fielding's Baja
Fielding's Bermuda
Fielding's Birding Indonesia
Fielding's Borneo
Fielding's Budget Europe
Fielding's Caribbean
Fielding's Caribbean Cruises
Fielding's Disney World and Orlando Area Theme Parks
Fielding's Diving Indonesia
Fielding's Eastern Caribbean
Fielding's England
Fielding's Europe
Fielding's European Cruises
Fielding's Far East
Fielding's France
Fielding's Freewheelin' USA
Fielding's Kenya
Fielding's Hawaii
Fielding's Italy
Fielding's Las Vegas Agenda
Fielding's London Agenda
Fielding's Los Angeles
Fielding's Malaysia and Singapore
Fielding's Mexico
Fielding's New Orleans Agenda
Fielding's New York Agenda
Fielding's New Zealand
Fielding's Paradors, Pousadas and Charming Villages of Spain and Portugal
Fielding's Paris Agenda
Fielding's Portugal
Fielding's Rome Agenda
Fielding's San Diego Agenda
Fielding's Southeast Asia
Fielding's Southern Vietnam on Two Wheels
Fielding's Spain
Fielding's Surfing Indonesia
Fielding's Sydney Agenda
Fielding's Thailand, Cambodia, Laos and Myanmar
Fielding's Vietnam
Fielding's Western Caribbean
Fielding's The World's Most Dangerous Places
Fielding's Worldwide Cruises

FIELDING'S ALASKA CRUISES AND THE INSIDE PASSAGE

Shirley Slater
and
Harry Basch

Fielding Worldwide, Inc.
308 South Catalina Avenue
Redondo Beach, California 90277 U.S.A.

Fielding's Alaska Cruises and the Inside Passage
Published by Fielding Worldwide, Inc.
Text Copyright ©1997 FWI
Icons & Illustrations Copyright ©1997 FWI
Photo Copyrights ©1997 to Individual Photographers

FIELDING WORLDWIDE INC.

PUBLISHER AND CEO	Robert Young Pelton
GENERAL MANAGER	John Guillebeaux
MARKETING DIRECTOR	Paul T. Snapp
OPERATIONS DIRECTOR	George Posanke
ELECTRONIC PUBLISHING DIRECTOR	Larry E. Hart
PUBLIC RELATIONS DIRECTOR	Beverly Riess
ACCOUNT SERVICES MANAGER	Shawn Potter
PROJECT MANAGER	Chris Snyder

EDITORS

Amanda Knoles	Linda Charlton
Catherine Bruhn	Reed Parsell

PRODUCTION

Jebbie LaVoie	Alfredo Mercado
Martin Mancha	Ramses Reynoso
Craig South	

COVER DESIGNED BY	Digital Artists, Inc.
COVER PHOTOGRAPHERS—Front cover	Norwegian Cruise Line
Back cover	Norwegian Cruise Line
INSIDE PHOTOS	Harry Basch, Shirley Slater, Special Expeditions, Glacier Bay Tours and Cruises, Quark Expeditions, Alaska Sightseeing/Cruise West
AUTHORS' PHOTO	Patricia Viamontes

Inquiries should be addressed to: Fielding Worldwide, Inc., 308 South Catalina
Ave., Redondo Beach, California 90277 U.S.A., Telephone *(310) 372-4474*,
Facsimile *(310) 376-8064*, 8:30 a.m.–5:30 p.m. Pacific Standard Time.
Web site: http://www.fieldingtravel.com
e-mail: fielding@fieldingtravel.com

ISBN 1-56952-068-2

Printed in the United States of America

DEDICATION

To those pioneers of Alaska tourism who paved the way—men such as Charles B. "Chuck" West, founder of Westours; Stanley McDonald, founder of Princess Cruises; and new, young entrepreneurs such as Gary Odle and Brent Hobday, founders of Alaska Highway Cruises.

What they're saying about Fielding's Worldwide Cruises

"Lots of tips and inside information on each ship ... valuable beginner's information on the cruise life and choosing a cruise. Very detailed."

—Los Angeles Times

"Whereas the term 'expert' is thrown about with abandon, when it comes to travel writing, these two are the real deal. Harry and Shirley are cruise experts."

—Salt Lake City Tribune

"Slater and Basch ... probably are the top consumer writers about passenger ships.... You can trust them to tell the truth....It's fun and very informative."

—New Orleans Times-Picayune

"... a fresh sea breeze blowing in cruise guidebooks ... a witty, pithy departure from the norm ..."

—Vacations Magazine

"... insightful, always independent, frequently witty and occasionally irreverent personal reviews..."

—Cruise and Vacation Views

"This entertaining and useful guide will make even the most hardened landlubber want to set sail. Slater and Basch have redefined cruise guide books."

—Paul Lasley & Elizabeth Harriman, ON TRAVEL RADIO

"If you have space for only one cruise guidebook in your library, it should be this one."

—Cruise Travel Magazine

"This year the bookstores are being flooded with guides to cruising. One of the best is Fielding's Guide to Worldwide Cruises, *simply because the authors, Shirley Slater and Harry Basch, have sailed on more than 200 vessels and know the inside scoop on what makes ships and lines different."*

—Boston Globe

"... a very fresh approach to the subject ... much more colorful, lively and interesting than cruise guides from the past ..."

—Lawrence J. Frommer, travel agent consultant and cruise specialist

"Shirley Slater and Harry Basch are 'the travel agent's travel agent,' as far as cruise information is concerned ... they are frank and upfront as to what the public wants to hear."

—Duke Butler, president, Spur of the Moment Cruises

"If a useful, accurate and entertaining cruise guide can be compiled—and I have never been convinced it could—Shirley Slater and Harry Basch have brought it off for Fielding. Five star plus is no more, replaced by a point of view, a fresh layout and, yes, some wit. Bravo!"

—John Maxtone-Graham, marine historian and author of *The Only Way to Cross* and *Liners to the Sun*

Letter from the Publisher

Fielding invented the cruise guide 18 years ago. Back then people wondered why people would sail around in circles instead of crossing the oceans in style. Today cruising is a growth industry and a way for the adventurous to the complacent to see the world. Today, Fielding travel guides are still written by experienced travelers for experienced travelers. Our authors carry on Fielding's reputation for delivering travel experiences with a sense of discovery and style.

Authors Harry Basch and Shirley Slater have personally been aboard all the ships reviewed in *Fielding's Alaska Cruises* and have taken more than 200 cruises during the past 15 years. Their vast cruise experience will provide you with valuable insider information, enabling you to choose the perfect cruise.

Today the concept of independent travel has never been bigger. Our policy of *brutal honesty* and a highly personal point of view has never changed; it just seems the travel world has caught up with us.

Enjoy your cruise adventures with Harry, Shirley and Fielding.

RYP

Robert Young Pelton
Publisher and CEO
Fielding Worldwide, Inc.

ABOUT THE
AUTHORS

Harry Basch and Shirley Slater

Called by the *Chicago Sun-Times* "America's premier cruise specialists," Shirley Slater and Harry Basch are an award-winning husband-and-wife travel writing and photography team whose work has been published internationally since 1976. For more than a decade, they have been the world's most widely read cruise experts.

Slater and Basch are authors of *Fielding's Worldwide Cruises 1997* and *Fielding's European Cruises*. They are editors of Fielding's *Cruise Insider*, a quarterly news-and-reviews journal about the cruise industry, as well as authors of Fielding's *Freewheelin' USA* and the monthly newsletter *Shirley and Harry's RV Adventures*.

As contributing editors for the trade magazine *Cruise & Vacation Views*, their monthly ship reviews are read throughout the travel agent community. They have also written ship reviews for trade publications *Travel Weekly*, *TravelAge* and *ASTA Agency Management* magazine.

Their syndicated column "Cruise Views" has appeared regularly in the *Los Angeles Times* and other major newspapers for 15 years. They have also contributed to magazines such as *Bon Appétit, Vogue, Modern Maturity, Travel & Leisure, Islands, Travel Holiday*, as well as various auto club and inflight publications.

For the 2 million subscribers to Prodigy Computer Services, they have created six editions of an annual Ski Guide, two Cruise Guides and two Caribbean Ports of Call Guide. Slater is also the author of *The Passport Guide to Switzerland*.

At the 60th World Travel Congress in Hamburg, Germany, in 1990 the couple was awarded the prestigious Melva C. Pederson Award from the American Society of Travel Agents for "extraordinary journalistic achievement in the field of travel," the third time the award was given and the first time it was awarded to freelance writers.

They also received the 1995 award for distinguished RV writing for their *Fielding's Freewheelin' USA*.

FOREWORD

When we were very young (if that were ever possible), we lived in Europe for several years, traveling on the cheap but always willing to splurge whenever we could afford it on the best of something. Our guidebook and bible, text and verse, was Temple Fielding's *Europe* guide, because it was the only guidebook that made us laugh, gave us a sense of fun and was absolutely honest—we literally couldn't afford to make any wrong choices.

In this cruise guide, we go back to the basics, to Temple Fielding and his philosophy of always telling the reader honestly but with style, verve and an occasional grumpy touch, about the best and worst of travel.

If we also occasionally sound a little curmudgeonly, it's only because we've been "being there and doing that" for the past 20 years all over the world as full-time professional travel writers and photographers, tallying up along the way 175 countries and more than 200 cruises aboard virtually everything that floats.

This is a book we've always wanted to write. We hope you like it.

—Shirley Slater and Harry Basch

Fielding Rating Icons

The Fielding Rating Icons are highly personal and awarded to help the besieged traveler choose from among the dizzying array of activities, attractions, hotels, restaurants and sights. The awarding of an icon denotes unusual or exceptional qualities in the relevant category.

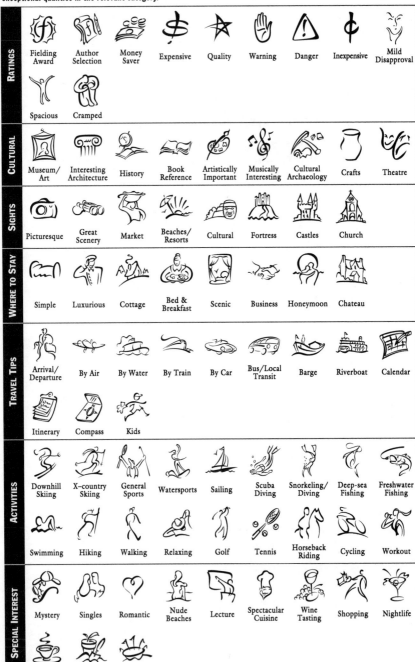

RATINGS: Fielding Award, Author Selection, Money Saver, Expensive, Quality, Warning, Danger, Inexpensive, Mild Disapproval, Spacious, Cramped

CULTURAL: Museum/Art, Interesting Architecture, History, Book Reference, Artistically Important, Musically Interesting, Cultural Archaeology, Crafts, Theatre

SIGHTS: Picturesque, Great Scenery, Market, Beaches/Resorts, Cultural, Fortress, Castles, Church

WHERE TO STAY: Simple, Luxurious, Cottage, Bed & Breakfast, Scenic, Business, Honeymoon, Chateau

TRAVEL TIPS: Arrival/Departure, By Air, By Water, By Train, By Car, Bus/Local Transit, Barge, Riverboat, Calendar, Itinerary, Compass, Kids

ACTIVITIES: Downhill Skiing, X-country Skiing, General Sports, Watersports, Sailing, Scuba Diving, Snorkeling/Diving, Deep-sea Fishing, Freshwater Fishing, Swimming, Hiking, Walking, Relaxing, Golf, Tennis, Horseback Riding, Cycling, Workout

SPECIAL INTEREST: Mystery, Singles, Romantic, Nude Beaches, Lecture, Spectacular Cuisine, Wine Tasting, Shopping, Nightlife, Cafe Stops, Gardening, Pro Sports

TABLE OF CONTENTS

LIST OF MAPS

Legend

Essentials

🏨 Hotel
🛏 Youth Hostel
✕ Restaurant
Ⓢ Bank
Ⓒ Telephone
ⓘ Tourist Info.
➕ Hospital
🍺 Pub / Bar
✉ Post Office
Ⓟ Parking
Ⓣ Taxi
Ⓢ Subway
Ⓜ Metro
Ⓜ Market
Ⓢ Shopping
Ⓒ Cinema
Theatre
✈ Int'l Airport
✚ Regional Airport
★ Police Station
⚖ Courthouse
🏛 Gov't. Building

■ Attraction
Military Airbase
Army Base
Naval base
Fort
University
School

Historical

∴ Archeological Site
✕✕ Battleground
Castle
Monument
Museum
Ruin
Shipwreck

Religious

✝ Church
Buddhist Temple
Hindu Temple
Mosque
Pagoda
Synagogue

Activities

Beach
▲ Campground
Picnic Area
Golf Course
Boat Launch
Diving
Fishing
Water Skiing
Snow Skiing
Bird Sanctuary
Wildlife Sanctuary
Park
Park Headquarters
Mine
Lighthouse
Windmill
⚓ Cruise Port
View
Stadium
Building
Zoo
Garden

Physical

— — — — · International Boundary	🚶🚶 Hiking Trail
– · – · – · – County / Regional Boundary	Dirt Road
PARIS ⊙ National Capital	┼┼┼┼┼┼ Railroad
Montego Bay • State / Parish Capital	**RR** Railroad Station
Los Angeles ● Major City	Ferry Route
Quy Nhon ○ Town / Village	▲ Mountain Peak
═(5)═ Motorway / Freeway	Lake
(163) Highway	River
Primary Road	◖ Cave
Secondary Road	Coral Reef
— — — — Subway	Waterfall
— 🚲 — Biking Routed	Hot Spring

©FWI 1995

SEEING ALASKA BY SEA

Alaska has a way of catching the imagination and snagging it with imagined vistas of untamed space stretched out as far as the eye can see.

Everyone says, "Someday I'll visit Alaska," but what they don't understand is, once is only the beginning. You can go back to Alaska and Western Canada time after time, and it's never the same way twice.

But the best way to see it, especially for a first time, is by sea. As someone once said about 50 million Frenchmen, half a million Americans can't be wrong. That's roughly the number who visited Alaska and Western Canada by cruise ship in the summer of 1996.

The popularity of the 49th state as a cruise destination has grown tremendously in the past 30 years since a fledgling Princess Cruises started offering summer sailings to Alaska in 1967.

With 34,000 miles of coastline, Alaska is ideally visited by ship, particularly if more adventurous visitors want to add on some flightseeing hops or an RV driving tour into the vast, remote interior. The additional bonus of visiting two of Canada's loveliest cities, Vancouver and Victoria, plus optional overland jaunts into the Yukon, British Columbia and Alberta, make this a more-than-once-in-a-lifetime destination.

Alaska cruise ships come in all shapes and sizes, from a 49-passenger catamaran (Glacier Bay Tours & Cruises' *Executive Explorer*) to sleek megaships carrying nearly 2000 passengers (Princess Cruises' dazzling new *Sun Princess* and *Dawn Princess*).

On small ships it's easier to meet fellow passengers and to get in closer to glaciers, small ports and islands. Larger ships usually offer more activities and diversions, everything from spas and gymnasiums to casinos, first-run films and full-fledged musical shows, as well as a smoother, more stable ride.

While most cruise ships concentrate on the popular, seven-day Inside Passage or Gulf of Alaska itineraries, a few venture farther afield. So if you think you've been-there-done-that, consider one of the Arctic expeditions—a cruise to the remote, bird-filled islands of the Bering Sea and Russian Far East, a transit across the legendary Northwest Passage at the top of the world, a sail around the southern tip of Greenland or even a journey by ice-breaker to the geographic North Pole.

Vancouver is home port for most scheduled Alaska cruises, but passengers can sail from other West Coast ports on some departures—from San Francisco, Seattle, Ketchikan, Juneau, Seward, Whittier, Anchorage and Dutch Harbor—even Hokkaido, Japan. Some travelers like several lazy days at sea to unwind before the first ports of call, while others want to begin their cruise right in the middle of the action for the optimum number of shore excursions in the least amount of time.

It's easy to arrange add-on overland extensions to Denali National Park and Mount McKinley, Fairbanks, the Canadian Rockies or the Yukon, or to take a few extra days of vacation before or after the cruise in the arrival or departure city.

You can even book a combination cruise and RV driving tour, and all you need to bring is a driver's license and personal wardrobe—the vehicle is furnished and ready to roll.

What's an Alaska cruise like?

It's for looking and listening—hearing peeps from colonies of black-winged kittiwakes, exchanging solemn, curious stares with a harbor seal floating by on an ice floe, spotting a nesting bald eagle high in an old-growth conifer.

You'll spend more time standing on deck or on your cabin's veranda than stretching out to get suntanned—although don't expect constant Arctic chills. Sometimes it's warm and sunny, even in Ketchikan, traditionally the rainiest city in the continental United States.

The weather is likely to be milder than you expect, but wildly unpredictable, alternating randomly among cool drizzle, misty overcast and dazzling sunshine, sometimes all in one day.

North of the Arctic Circle, you may encounter some below-freezing summer temperatures, but in the southeastern Panhandle the temperature seldom goes below 45 or 50 degrees during the cruise season, and thermometers during warm spells hover in the 80s or even 90s.

In fact, the only problem about the tremendous popularity of cruising in Alaska, according to one travel agent, is that some of the ships are getting so big they carry more passengers than the population of the towns they're visiting.

SHIPS BY ALPHABETICAL LISTING

The Ratings

When the *Fielding Worldwide Guide to Cruises* first began in 1981, the late Antoinette DeLand initiated the rating system of stars that has always been associated with this guide. We have decided to simplify the system somewhat by eliminating all the pluses but adding an extra star.

The present authors have been aboard all the ships rated with black stars and anchors in the following pages, and the **black star ratings** reflect our personal opinion of the ship and the cruise experience it offers.

White stars represent ships that are in transition from one company to another, which we have been aboard in the vessel's earlier life, or new vessels that are sister ships to existing, already inspected vessels due to come on line in the near future.

Anchor ratings were created by the publishers to reflect a cruise experience that was enriching and rewarding aboard an adventure, expedition, river or coastal vessel where the pleasure of the journey far exceeds the physical quality of the cruise vessel. A few ocean going ships that offer expedition and educational sailings will carry both star and anchor ratings.

Unrated ships are those the authors have not been aboard in the ship's present incarnation.

★★★★★★	The ultimate cruise experience
★★★★★	A very special cruise experience
★★★★	A high quality cruise experience
★★★	An average cruise experience
★★	If you're on a budget and not fussy
★	A sinking ship

Ship	Rating	Page
Century	★★★★★	245
Crown Majesty	★★★★	320
Crown Princess	★★★★★	344
Crystal Harmony	★★★★★★	267
Crystal Symphony	★★★★★★	267
Dawn Princess	☆☆☆☆☆	361
Ecstasy	★★★★★	226
Executive Explorer	⚓⚓⚓⚓	279
Fantasy	★★★★★	226
Fascination	★★★★★	226

Ship	Rating	Page
Galaxy	☆☆☆☆☆	245
Hanseatic	★★★★★, ♨♨♨♨♨	370
Horizon	★★★★★	250
Imagination	★★★★★	226
Inspiration	★★★★★	226
Legend of the Seas	★★★★★	380
Nieuw Amsterdam	★★★★	304
Noordam	★★★★	304
Regal Princess	★★★★★	344
Rhapsody of the Seas	☆☆☆☆☆	380
Rotterdam	★★★★★	310
Ryndam	★★★★★	299
Sea Bird	★★, ♨♨♨♨	412
Sea Lion	★★, ♨♨♨♨	412
Seabourn Legend	★★★★★★	393
Sensation	★★★★★	226
Sky Princess	★★★★	350
Spirit of '98	♨♨♨♨♨	213
Spirit of Alaska	♨♨♨♨	196
Spirit of Columbia	♨♨♨♨	196
Spirit of Discovery	♨♨♨	201
Spirit of Endeavour	♨♨♨♨♨	205
Spirit of Glacier Bay	♨♨♨♨	209
Star Princess	★★★★	356
Statendam	★★★★★	299
Sun Princess	★★★★★	361
Tropicale	★★★	233
Universe Explorer	★★, ♨♨♨	420
Veendam	★★★★★	299
Wilderness Adventurer	♨♨♨	283
Wilderness Explorer	♨♨♨	287
Windward	★★★★★	331
World Discoverer	★★★, ♨♨♨♨♨	403
Yorktown Clipper	♨♨♨♨♨	258
Zenith	★★★★★	250

SHIPS BY RATING

The Ratings

When the *Fielding Worldwide Guide to Cruises* first began in 1981, the late Antoinette DeLand initiated the rating system of stars that has always been associated with this guide. We have decided to simplify the system somewhat by eliminating all the pluses but adding an extra star.

The present authors have been aboard all the ships rated with black stars and anchors in the following pages, and the **black star ratings** reflect our personal opinion of the ship and the cruise experience it offers.

White stars represent ships that are in transition from one company to another, which we have been aboard in the vessel's earlier life, or new vessels that are sister ships to existing, already inspected vessels due to come on line in the near future.

Anchor ratings were created by the publishers to reflect a cruise experience that was enriching and rewarding aboard an adventure, expedition, river or coastal vessel where the pleasure of the journey far exceeds the physical quality of the cruise vessel. A few ocean going ships that offer expedition and educational sailings will carry both star and anchor ratings.

Unrated ships are those the authors have not been aboard in the ship's present incarnation.

★ ★ ★ ★ ★ ★	The ultimate cruise experience
★ ★ ★ ★ ★	A very special cruise experience
★ ★ ★ ★	A high quality cruise experience
★ ★ ★	An average cruise experience
★ ★	If you're on a budget and not fussy
★	A sinking ship

Rating	Ship	Page
★ ★ ★ ★ ★ ★	*Crystal Harmony*	267
★ ★ ★ ★ ★ ★	*Crystal Symphony*	267
★ ★ ★ ★ ★ ★	*Seabourn Legend*	393
★ ★ ★ ★ ★	*Century*	245
★ ★ ★ ★ ★	*Crown Princess*	344
☆ ☆ ☆ ☆ ☆	*Dawn Princess*	361
★ ★ ★ ★ ★	*Ecstasy*	226
★ ★ ★ ★ ★	*Fantasy*	226
★ ★ ★ ★ ★	*Fascination*	226
☆ ☆ ☆ ☆ ☆	*Galaxy*	245

Rating	Ship	Page
★★★★★	Horizon	250
★★★★★	Imagination	226
★★★★★	Inspiration	226
★★★★★	Legend of the Seas	380
★★★★★	Regal Princess	344
☆☆☆☆☆	Rhapsody of the Seas	380
★★★★★	Rotterdam	310
★★★★★	Ryndam	299
★★★★★	Sensation	226
★★★★★	Statendam	299
★★★★★	Sun Princess	361
★★★★★	Veendam	299
★★★★★	Windward	331
★★★★★	Zenith	250
★★★★★, ⚓⚓⚓⚓⚓	Hanseatic	370
★★★★	Crown Majesty	320
★★★★	Nieuw Amsterdam	304
★★★★	Noordam	304
★★★★	Sky Princess	350
★★★★	Star Princess	356
★★★	Tropicale	233
★★★, ⚓⚓⚓⚓⚓	World Discoverer	403
★★, ⚓⚓⚓⚓	Sea Bird	412
★★, ⚓⚓⚓⚓	Sea Lion	412
★★, ⚓⚓⚓	Universe Explorer	420
⚓⚓⚓⚓⚓	Spirit of '98	213
⚓⚓⚓⚓⚓	Spirit of Endeavour	205
⚓⚓⚓⚓⚓	Yorktown Clipper	258
⚓⚓⚓⚓	Executive Explorer	279
⚓⚓⚓⚓	Spirit of Alaska	196
⚓⚓⚓⚓	Spirit of Columbia	196
⚓⚓⚓⚓	Spirit of Glacier Bay	209
⚓⚓⚓	Spirit of Discovery	201
⚓⚓⚓	Wilderness Adventurer	283
⚓⚓⚓	Wilderness Explorer	287

CRUISE LINE CONTACTS

Company	Phone	Website
Alaska Sightseeing/Cruise West	(800) 426-7702	
Carnival Cruise Line	(800) 327-9501	http://www.carnival.com
Celebrity Cruises	(800) 437-3111	http://celebrity-cruises.com
Clipper Cruise Line	(800) 325-0010	
Crystal Cruises	(800) 446-6620	
Glacier Bay Tours and Cruises	(800) 451-5952	
Holland America Line	(800) 426-0327	http://www.hollandamerica.com
Marine Expeditions	(800) 263-9147	
Norwegian Cruise Line	(800) 327-7030	http://www.ncl.com/ncl
Princess Cruises	(800) LOVEBOAT	http://www.awcv.com/princess.html
Quark Expeditions	(800) 356-5699	
Radisson Seven Seas Cruises	(800) 333-3333	http://www.ten-io.com/clia/radisson/index.html
Royal Caribbean Cruises Ltd.	(800) 327-6700	http://www.royalcaribbean.com/main.html
Seabourn Cruise Line	(800) 929-4747	
Society Expeditions	(800) 548-8669	
Special Expeditions	(800) 348-2358	
Windstar Cruises	(800) 258-7245	http://www.windstarcruises.com
World Explorer Cruises	(800) 854-3835	http://www.wecruise.com
Zegrahm Expeditions	(206) 285-4000	

A NOTE ABOUT
THE STARS

The first thing you will probably notice as you leaf through *Fielding's Alaska Cruises* is a change in the rating system. The famous Five-Stars-Plus has been retired, and the pluses as well phased out of the ship ratings, a victim of their own built-in waffling.

When the system was originally initiated, ships were simpler and the top-ranked vessels somewhat less sophisticated in food, service and cabin amenities. As ships improved, the star ratings started pushing the envelope, everyone crowding the top and hardly anyone back at the average or beginning.

Now you'll find a **One-to-Six** Star rating system reflecting a much wider range of cruise offerings in the marketplace than ever before in history. Herewith, we proudly introduce the **Six-Star cruise ships in Alaska**, offering the best cruise ship experiences in the world.

Crystal Symphony's
SIX-STAR SERVICE
TO ALASKA.
SOME PEOPLE STILL
CHART THE SEA
by the stars.

1997 12-DAY ALASKA CRUISES
SAILING ROUND-TRIP FROM SAN FRANCISCO

Journey to the land of grandeur on board the newest, large luxury ship at sea, Crystal Symphony. From the Golden Gate Bridge in San Francisco to the majestic iceburgs in Glacier Bay, we offer you the finest amenities of both land and sea. Like gracious European service, private verandas in most staterooms, world renowned entertainment, and Six-Star dining including our two specialty restaurants, Jade Garden and Prego. All in all, the experience is quite stellar. To reserve your stateroom, call your travel agent. Or call 1-800-820-6663 for a free brochure.
The Most Glorious Ships at Sea

Yorktown Clipper, Misty Fjords, Alaska

THE BEST IN ALASKA
★★★★★★
The Six-Star Ships in Alaska

The Top Cruise Experiences in Alaska

Ultra-deluxe vessels with sophisticated cuisine, excellent service, far-reaching and imaginative itineraries, and a highly satisfying overall cruise experience.

★★★★★
The Five-Star Ships

Stylish, comfortable ships, each vessel or class with its own distinct personality catering to a variety of different audiences with a high overall quality in its price range.

* *Sensation*	**Carnival Cruise Lines**	*page 226*
Statendam	**Holland America Line**	*page 299*
Sun Princess	**Princess Cruises**	*page 361*
Veendam	**Holland America Line**	*page 299*
Windward	**Norwegian Cruise Line**	*page 331*

* *One of these ships is likely to cruise Alaska in 1998.*

Best Buys in Alaska

Celebrity	*Galaxy* *Horizon*	Offering excellent cruise ship food and service in handsome, tasteful surroundings at a good value, **the best large-ship buy afloat**.
Norwegian Cruise Line	*Windward*	Well-designed ship with a feeling of **intimate spaces in sophisticated surroundings** for young to middle-aged couples and singles.
Holland America Line	*Fleet*	**The most beautiful traditional cruise ships at sea**, a solid value for the money with tasty, imaginatively served food and warm friendly service, classy and classic.
Princess Cruises	*Dawn Princess* *Sun Princess*	**Gorgeous, glamorous and gracious**, these big beauties have everything a typical cruiser could want.
Royal Caribbean Cruise Ltd.	*Legend of the Seas* *Rhapsody of the Seas*	An **outstanding cruise experience** for first-time cruisers because of a tactful and caring staff that make you feel at ease.
Alaska Sightseeing/ Cruise West	*Spirit of '98*	A replica turn-of-the-century coastal steamer with **an all-American staff and home-cooked cuisine**, giving a great close-up look at Alaska and the Northwest.
Clipper Cruises	*Yorktown Clipper*	A yacht-like small ship that explores offbeat areas of Alaska **where the big ships don't go**.

Best Alaska Ships for Families with Kids

Holland America Line *Fleet*   Offers kids their own exclusive ranger programs and targets special family shore activities.

Princess Cruises   *Sky Princess*   Big, comfortable playroom, kiddy pool and well-trained counselors.

Going to Extremes: Top Adventure Vessels

Radisson Seven Seas Cruises   *Bremen (on certain sailings)*   The former *Frontier Spirit*, a purpose-built new expedition ship that goes from the Arctic to the Antarctic and points in between.

Hanseatic   Newest and most elegant of the expeditioners with music at teatime and the probable speed record for the Northwest Passage transit.

Marine Expeditions   *Fleet*   Small and simple Russian and Estonian icebreakers take passengers through the Arctic and Antarctic.

Quark Expeditions   *Kapitans Dranitsyn, Khlebnikov et al*   Russian icebreakers that crunch their way around the Antarctic or up to the North Pole.

Society Expeditions   *World Discoverer*   Another expedition champion that has garnered a lot of records on its worldwide wandering.

Outer Space: The Sweetest Suites at Sea

Crystal	*Crystal Symphony*	Two Crystal Penthouses, separate living rooms, dining area, large private veranda, big walk-in closets, extra guest half-bath, wet bar, Jacuzzi tub, lovely cabinetry.
Royal Caribbean Cruise Ltd.	*Legend of the Seas* *Rhapsody of the Seas*	The Royal Suite has a huge white piano dominating one corner of a spacious living room, green marble compartmented bathroom, wet bar, long private veranda, full entertainment center—drop-dead gorgeous.
Holland America	*Ryndam* *Statendam* *Veendam*	A single huge owner's suite on each ship has a wide private veranda, separate living room, dining room and bedroom, huge walk-in closet, compartmented bath, butler pantry to have meals prepared in suite.
Princess Cruises	*Dawn Princess* *Sun Princess*	Big elegant marble bathrooms, wide veranda, light, bright and airy, handsomely furnished, living room, dining table with four chairs, TV/VCR, mini-refrigerator.

Best Ships for Singles

Females Under 30	**Carnival Cruise Lines**	These ships attract a lot of single guys under 30, especially in Alaska.
30-50	**Royal Caribbean Cruise Line**	A good mainstream place to meet.
Women 50-up	**World Explorer**	Dancing hosts, lecturers, some live music and come-as-you-are dress codes.
Men 50-up	**World Explorer**	Try being a dancing host. See Everything You Ever Wanted to Know About Social Hosts, page 44.

The Best Cruise Lines For Buffets

Holland America Line	Consistently the best day-in, day-out Lido food service.
Celebrity Cruises	The prettiest arrangements and most convenient layouts, plus wine by the glass on a rolling cart.
Crystal Cruises	Outstanding special theme buffets and great deck grills.
Princess Cruises	24-hour buffet service on *Sun Princess* and *Dawn Princess*.

Best Spas in Alaska

Celebrity	*Galaxy*	The most innovative health, beauty and fitness center afloat.
Norwegian Cruise Line	*Windward*	Spacious spa with sauna, massage and fitness center.
Royal Caribbean Cruise Ltd.	*Legend of the Seas and Rhapsody of the Seas*	**The Solariums**, with a glass canopy-covered pool, water jets, Roman marble everywhere.

Best Alternative Restaurants

An alternative restaurant is an option to dine occasionally somewhere other than the ship's regular dining rooms, where you usually have assigned seating.

Crystal Cruises	*Crystal Symphony*	**Prego Restaurant**, Italian and very elegant.
Crystal Cruises	*Crystal Harmony*	**Kyoto Restaurant**, austere and Oriental, with spare decor and clean but simple dishes.
Princess Cruises	*Dawn Princess Sun Princess*	Verdi's Pizzeria with baked-to-order pizza.

Best Cruise Entertainment in Alaska

Princess Cruises	**The new "Mystique,"** a sensational production set under the sea with 23 performers, including nine acrobats, has scenery that "grows" in front of your eyes. It's a knockout.
Crystal Cruises	**Elegantly costumed** shows set a new high for class acts.
Norwegian Cruise Line	Offers **well-performed Broadway shows** such as "Will Rogers Follies," "Dreamgirls," "Grease," "George M" and "Pirates of Penzance" on the stages of its ships.

Good Ships for First-Timers and Why

Budget

World Explorer Cruises	*Universe Explorer*	Clean, comfortable vintage vessel with great itinerary.
Carnival Cruise Lines	*Tropicale*	A lot of pizazz for the price.

Moderate

Royal Caribbean Cruise Ltd.	*Legend of the Seas Rhapsody of the Seas*	Offers top-drawer surroundings, excellent entertainment and good food and service with tactful attention to first-timers.
Norwegian Cruise Line	*Windward*	Dive-in and onboard sports programs, themed dinners and costume evenings on all ships add energy and direction to the overall experience.

Splurge

Seabourn Cruise Line	*Seabourn Legend*	Top-drawer luxury cabins, food and service for people accustomed to the best.

Best Alaska Ships for Disabled Passengers

Celebrity Cruises	*Fleet*
Holland America	*Fleet*
Princess Cruises	*Fleet*
Royal Caribbean Cruise Ltd.	*Legend of the Seas, Rhapsody of the Seas*

INTRODUCTION: LOOK WHO'S AFLOAT

At twilight aboard the Rotterdam, this romantic couple at the rail might be shipboard companions of Noel Coward.

> "Why do the wrong people travel, travel, travel
> And the right people stay at home?"

Noel Coward song lyrics

Even the late Noel Coward, the most urbane and unflappable cruise passenger one can imagine, probably would have been rendered speechless at who and what's afloat these days.

On the decks he frequented, there were no earphone-wearing joggers or aerobics classes, just stately promenaders (the kind who nod only after being properly introduced) or dozing readers wrapped in steamer rugs. Certainly nobody ever requested a no-smoking table or a low-calorie lunch.

Coward definitely would have raised an eyebrow at cruise-ship dress codes allowing gentlemen to appear at dinner not only without black tie but without any tie or jacket at all. And he hardly could have imagined couples stealing away after dinner to screen a video in their cabin instead of dancing cheek to cheek to the ship's orchestra.

Suddenly four million Americans a year were going down to the sea in ships. And they weren't all wealthy retirees and they weren't all looking for love and attention. They were all ages, from all economic groups, singles, honeymoon couples, working couples on a budget, families with small children, grandparents with grandchildren.

We've been on cruises with—

- Amanda at two and Amy at 86

- High rollers and bingo buffs

- A fitness nut who found out she could cruise on a spa ship cheaper than going to a famous spa for a week

- Surfers, divers and joggers who run their daily mileage on deck from Bora Bora to Bequia

- A septuagenarian learning to operate a computer

- A purple-haired teen-aged punk rocker who spent more time on the deck than in the disco

- Bird watchers, whale watchers and girl watchers

- Women competing to see who could stuff the most ping pong balls into their bikinis

- A tycoon who has a stretch limousine waiting to take him sightseeing in every port

- An accountant who celebrated his 50th birthday by cruising to both the Arctic and Antarctic within the same year

- Best-selling novelists and supermarket checkers, retired teachers and circus owners, movie stars and mechanics—and none of them have ever been boring—or bored.

To Cruise or Not To Cruise

A girl never really looks as well as she does on board a steamship, or even a yacht.

Anita Loos, "Gentlemen Prefer Blondes," 1925

Life aboard cruise ships used to be thought of as a sedentary vacation for the very old and very rich, who reclined on wooden deck chairs reading books and sipping bouillon when they weren't wearing tuxedos and eating caviar.

Then along came the slick TV version, based on the premise that all a lovelorn individual had to do was get on board the "Love Boat" and the captain and his meddlesome staff would make everything smooth sailing. All problems would be settled, true love would triumph and, since the ship never seemed to move, no one's hairdo would even get mussed.

The real world of cruising today is volatile, ephemeral, constantly changing as lines are acquired, new ships come into service and old ships are retired or sold down the river into ignominious retirement as hotels or casinos.

Cruise lines are selling you a dream. And anyone old enough to remember the days of radio knows that the images the aural programs created in the mind were stronger, more dramatic and more compelling than the pallid stuff that came along later on TV. The power of your dream, your imagination, creates a challenge that the cruise industry is trying to meet. Sometimes they do, sometimes they don't.

Getting Real

TV commercials and brochures about cruises all promise the glamourous life.

TV commercials and glossy color brochures about cruises all promise the same thing—an unexcelled excursion into the glamourous life, with romantic evenings, a perfect tan, six or eight gourmet meals a day, and intermittent forays into picturesque and exotic ports of call where the sun always shines, the shopping is splendid and the natives are friendly and photogenic.

Oddly enough, more often than not, it works out that way.

But based on some of the complaints we've had from readers over the years, several of them signed up for a cruise that should have been advertised more like this:

"You'll have fun aboard the friendly, 30-year-old *SS Rustbottom*, which failed her last five sanitation inspections in spite of heavily spiking the drinking water with chlorine....Our bottom-of-the-line cabins are so small you have to take turns getting dressed inside, and our menus are created by a Miami-based computer programmed to give you the maximum number of calories for the lowest possible cost....Our inexperienced and incompetent staff could not care less about your comfort or pleasure, and the residents of our popular ports of call make their livelihoods by harassing you in the streets to purchase their overpriced souvenirs."

What are some of the things that make passengers angry?

First and foremost seem to be promises the passenger felt were implied in the brochure or claimed were actually made by the travel agent prior to the trip. Ambiguous terms like "first class," "deluxe," "elegance"—and, of course, the ever-popular "five-star-plus," the monster created by earlier editions of these guides—typical hyperbole churned out by ad agency copywriters who may never have been aboard the ship—are echoed bitterly by disappointed letter-writers who expected something grander than they received.

Some expectations appear unrealistic to more experienced cruisers—24-hour room service does not necessarily mean hot four-course meals are served in the cabin at 3 a.m., for instance, and no cruise-savvy travel agent would promise clients they could spend the entire disembarkation and turnaround day aboard the ship in their cabin until time to catch their evening flight home.

One of our favorite reader complaint letters was from a female attorney celebrating her 40th birthday on her first cruise. The ship was one of the former Royal Viking Line vessels, always top of the line in food and service, but the attorney was suing to have the price of her cruise refunded because at breakfast every morning the waiters persisted in offering her a silver tray of pastries despite the fact that she had told them she was on a diet.

Hey lady, get a life!

Take a Vacation from Vacations

The real pleasure of a cruise is not having to do anything you don't want to do.

At some point in every traveler's life, there comes a moment, bittersweet as the end of a love affair, when the vacation is over, the workaday world is looming and there's nothing you need worse than a vacation to recover from your vacation.

Next time, maybe you should take a cruise.

Cruise lines spend a lot of time and money telling us about the unending procession of meals and the nonstop fun and games, when the real pleasure of a cruise is not having to do anything you don't want to do—except attend the obligatory lifeboat drill at the beginning of the cruise.

No packing and unpacking to move from one hotel to another, no cars to rent or trains to catch, no lunchtime arguments about which restaurant or picnic spot looks more appealing, no bungled hotel reservations on a weary midnight arrival in Budapest because a convention of Bulgarians came to town.

Coming back to your ship after a day ashore is like coming home. Your waiter knows how you like your breakfast eggs, your steward knows what time you go to dinner so he can turn your bed down and put a chocolate on your pillow.

A travel agency that specializes in cruises can help you select the ship and itinerary that's best for you, as long as you make your wishes and your budget considerations clear to them. Don't just ask for a Alaska cruise and take whichever one is mentioned first. Ships and ports of call vary tremendously, and everybody loses if you don't enjoy yourself.

Take the right cruise, and you'll come home rested and happy. Of course, you will be expecting to be served breakfast in bed the first few days home, and you'll miss finding that good-night chocolate on your pillow.

DID YOU KNOW?

"I rather wished that I had gone first class," Evelyn Waugh wrote about sailing from Port Said aboard P&O's Ranchi in 1929. "It's not that my fellow passengers were not every bit as nice as the Port Said residents had told me they would be, but that there were so many of them."

Future Trends

Passengers on today's cruise ships are far from sedentary, with deck games, gyms, spas and aerobics classes always available.

If we can believe present trends, passengers of the future are going to be healthy, wealthy and wise.

Healthy, because virtually every ship menu afloat is offering low-calorie, low-fat and vegetarian options; because more and more cruise lines are banning smoking in their dining rooms and show lounges; and because well-equipped fitness centers and aerobics classes are as common as casinos. We're also seeing more stringent inspections of water and air conditioning systems and tougher restrictions on food handlers.

Wealthy (well, at least less poor), because money-saving early booking discounts that let you cut costs from the published brochure rate are in effect closer and closer to sailing time; no matter how late you book, have your travel agent check to see if you qualify. Frequent cruisers can qualify for free cruises with accrued cruise days from Cunard, and Seabourn passengers in the line's WorldFare program may purchase blocks of 45 to 120 cruise days at a reduced price and use them on any cruises over a period of three years.

Wise in the ways of the world, because there is more of it to see by ship than at any time in recent history.

Fear of Cruising

Cruises along Alaska's sheltered Inside Passage almost always keep you in sight of land.

A lot of people who think nothing of buying a package coach tour to a foreign country, driving the car across the continent or booking a week at a resort hotel on the recommendation of a casual friend over lunch, shy away from the idea of taking a cruise. Why?

Here's what they tell the pollsters:

Six Common Excuses

1. "Stuck in the middle of an ocean somewhere? I might get bored or feel trapped."

2. "I'm scared I'd get seasick."

3. "I can't plan my vacations that far in advance."

4. "I'd feel uncomfortable—I wouldn't know what to wear or how much to tip or which cabins were good."

5. "I'm afraid of gaining weight with all that food around."

6. "What if I don't like the ship? Then I've wasted my whole vacation."

Six Quick Answers

1. Forget about the ocean if you don't want to go out on one. Alaska cruises that depart from Vancouver travel the Inside Passage through some of the most spectacular scenery on earth and never out of sight of land. The same is true aboard paddlewheelers on the Mississippi River, yachtlike luxury ships in the Intracoastal Waterway or friendly, low-key vessels on the St. Lawrence, along the Columbia or in the San Juan Islands. As for boredom, most first-time cruisers claim they need a vacation when they get home from a cruise because they're exhausted from the non-stop activity.

2. If your previous seagoing experience is limited to sailboats, fishing boats or a hitch in the Navy, modern cruise ships equipped with stabilizers that eliminate much of the rolling motion may surprise you. Fewer than five percent of the passengers on any cruise complain of motion sickness; medications are readily available on board if you're bothered by *mal de mer*.
(See Scoping Out Seasickness and Sidestepping Seasickness, page 448.)

3. If there's one thing there's plenty of, baby, it's cruise ship cabins. A good travel agent can book you on almost any ship for any destination on short notice—sometimes with a deep discount.

4. If you're bugged by the unfamiliar, a cruise is the least complicated vacation you'll ever have to deal with; it all comes in one neat prepaid package. You don't need a special wardrobe for cruises; chances are, everything you need is already in your closet. (See Eleven Tips to Lighten Your Luggage, page 438.) Tipping suggestions are spelled out on board toward the end of the sailing (also, see Tipping, page 453) and there's a checklist on what to look for in a cabin.
(See Choosing A Cabin on page 32.)

5. Every ship offers a variety of seafoods, salads, fruits and vegetables, along with low-calorie, low-fat dishes. Some offer full spa menus. Even on small ships you'll find exercise classes and a full array of gym facilities. You could come back home in better shape than when you left. As for temptation, repeat after us—"Just because I paid for it doesn't mean I have to eat it all."
(See How to Avoid Pigging Out at Sea, page 37.)

6. Selecting the right ship is the biggest single decision you'll have to make. Don't let anyone tell you all cruises are alike—they're not—or that Brand X Cruise Line is "the best" because there's not one single "best." The best cruise for you is the one you'll enjoy the most.
(See Choosing A Cruise, page 31 and How To Read A Brochure, page 28, below.)

DID YOU KNOW?

Some 15 years ago when we first began writing our cruise column, a brusque California businessman planning his first cruise called us. He said he'd asked three travel agents which was the best cruise line–the first said Princess, the second said Carnival, the third said Sitmar (now defunct). So he called us to find out which of those three was the best. When we tried to counter by finding out something about him and what kind of cruise experience he was seeking, he screamed angrily into the phone, "I knew it! You don't know any more about it than those travel agents!" And he hung up.

The New Cruisers

More and more young singles and couples are discovering cruises as a fun and affordable mini-vacation.

A funny thing happened to ocean liners on the way to the 21st century— they got democratized.

The great and famous ships that carried royalty, heads of state, the Astors and the Glorias (Swanson and Vanderbilt) in first-class luxury, relegating to second and third class all other passengers from potato-famine Irish immigrants to '50s college students, have turned into one-class cruise ships where everyone on board is equal, more or less.

Meanwhile, the transatlantic jumbo jets that hastened the demise of ocean liners have become almost a parody of the old class system themselves, fawning over first-class passengers with sofa-sized seats and full-length beds, personal video monitors and champagne and caviar, and cramming everyone else into steerage, where bodies are jackknifed into tortuous positions, babies cry all night and unidentifiable foods in plastic compartments are slapped down at intervals on wobbly trays.

Even a decade ago, the change was apparent, as cruise lines began to notice the huge numbers of first-timer cruisers aboard. Carnival's president, Bob Dickinson, then vice president of sales and marketing, pointed out in 1985 that 70 to 75 percent of all his line's passengers were first-time cruisers. "We don't think we're in the cruise business; we're in the vacation business." He went on to predict—correctly—that Carnival would have a 10-ship fleet by 1995.

A lucrative and previously untapped new market was discovered— couples and singles from the world of young, upwardly mobile professionals; baby boomers with income and leisure time for longer vacations; blue-collar and clerical workers who appreciated one up-front, all-inclusive ticket price for a vacation as luxurious as any they could find at a land-based resort and often less expensive.

In contrast to the retired and/or wealthy passengers who make up the rosters on around-the-world cruises, the new cruise passengers are looking for mini-vacations at sea, comparing a cruise to a holiday spent in Nassau, Palm Springs, Las Vegas or Atlantic City.

You'll get the picture the minute you step aboard a cruise ship these days. Hardly a ship leaves dock without announcing a party for singles within a day or two of sailing, and guest hosts are on board many vessels expressly to dance, play bridge and socialize with unattached women.

If you're one of the new cruise passengers, you can count on more and more variety in the world of cruises. The day is not far off when you'll be able to cruise anywhere you wish for the length of time you prefer at a price you can afford, not once in a lifetime but once or twice a year.

Anatomy of a Cruise Ship: A Curmudgeon's Guide

The funnel or stack is where the cruise line displays its logo and sends out its combustion gases; never sit downwind of the funnel without checking for soot.

The Basics

- **FUNNELS** or **STACKS** are where the cruise line displays its logo, such as Princess Cruises' sea witch with flowing hair or Costa Cruises' blue-and-yellow C or Celebrity's big white X, Greek for Chi or C. The stack also carries away the ship's combustion gases and occasional bursts of black smoke. When wearing white pants, never sit in a deck chair downwind of the funnel without checking first for soot.

- **GANGWAYS** are the external stairways or ramps leading to the ship from the shore. They are also the place where the ship's photographers take pictures of passengers embarking or disembarking in every port, thereby creating a traffic jam in both directions.

- **LIFEBOATS** are the orange and white vessels that hang outside your cabin window blocking your view if your travel agent doesn't know how to read a deck plan. Some lines, such as Crystal and Princess, point out in their brochures where a cabin view is partly or entirely obstructed and reduce the price accordingly. Some lines, however, sketch the boats in on the deck plan but fail to point out or reduce the price on partially obstructed views. And still other lines fail to indicate the lifeboats at all, leading to *Titanic*-tinged visions.

Deck Areas

- **SWIMMING POOLS** on some ships may be mistaken for footbaths or ornamental fountains. Fancy pool areas with swim-up bars, waterfalls and other pool novelties tend to get clogged up with passengers under 16.

- **JOGGING TRACKS** can be found on many of the newer ships on a sports deck high atop the ship. Some of these are so short that it takes 13 (on *Radisson Diamond*) or 14 (on Seabourn) laps to make a mile. Never, under any circumstances, book a cabin under the jogging track.

- **CHILDREN'S WADING POOLS** can be found on some ships and can be identified by their singular lack of children; most prefer to spend their time belly-whopping into the adult pool.

Shuffleboard can reach fever pitch on a classic liner such as the **Rotterdam**.

- **SHUFFLEBOARD** is a popular deck game that can reach fever pitch on a classic liner such as the *Rotterdam*. On other ships, some passengers mistake it for hopscotch.

- **PROMENADE** is the deck that goes all the way around the ship, giving passengers a chance for a brisk, breezy walk. Six or seven times around usually equals a mile. Do not attempt to exchange pleasantries with a grim-faced walker counting laps.

Lounges and Public Rooms

- **SHOW LOUNGES** in the daytime are the setting for line dancing lessons, bingo games and port information lectures, but in the evening become Broadway and Las Vegas with musical extravaganzas or, all too often, the last refuge of magicians, jugglers, puppeteers and ventriloquists last seen on the "Ed Sullivan Show."

- **CINEMAS** are where recent movies are screened; on some ships they are also considered an ideal spot to nap after lunch. On the Big Red Boats, passengers under 12 vie with each other for the record number of times they can come and go opening the entry doors wide enough to wipe out the image on the screen.

The disco is the place to dance the night away or people-watch. Some feature live bands.

- **DISCOS** are the place to meet junior officers in white uniforms late at night. On older ships like the *Dolphin IV*, *OceanBreeze* and *SeaBreeze* they're located deep in the bowels of the vessel and in the daytime look like a place where Dracula would sleep. On Carnival ships the discos flash with neon and rock videos and throb with amplified sound. Never book a cabin over, under or beside the disco.

- **PHOTO GALLERIES** are where the ship's photographers mount the pictures of passengers they've snapped at odd moments throughout the cruise. They're always crowded with people buying photos they want to keep and others buying photos they don't want anyone else to see.

- **TEEN CENTER** is a euphemism for a video games arcade that is frequently filled with males far past their teens. A modern refinement introduced by Carnival's *Holiday* lets the kids use their own ship ID card to access the games in lieu of dogging dad for more quarters; the charge goes right into the billing computers along with Dad's bar bills and Mom's shipboard shopping.

- **DUTY-FREE SHOPS** are the places to buy Lladro porcelain, Rolex watches, sequinned garments and other useless items. Essentials such as toothpaste, aspirin and sunblock are harder to find since the profit margin is considerably smaller.

- **CASINOS** are a philosophical proving ground where optimists arrive and pessimists depart. A real gambler heads for the roulette table, taking a chance on whether the sea motion is in his favor or against it.

- **LIBRARIES** on most ships are the places to find books to read. They are also populated by competitive trivia quiz aficionados looking up answers in order to win still another bookmark or key chain. You can tell how much your cruise line trusts you by noting whether the glass cases are locked or unlocked.

- **CARD ROOMS** are the refuge of avid bridge players whose conversation beyond bids is limited to port of call observations such as, "It's only Hong Kong, shut up and deal." Only a masochist should let himself be roped into being a fourth for bridge after lunch.

Fielding
WORLDWIDE

CRUISE
SHIPS

AREA SHOWN | NEXT PAGE

1. **Jogging Track,** Sunrise Deck
2. **Bar,** Sports Deck
3. **Suites,** Sports Deck
4. **Restaurant,** Resort Deck
5. **Cafe,** Resort Deck
6. **Restaurant,** Entertainment Deck
7. **Gambling,** Entertainment Deck
8. **Lounge,** Promenade Deck
9. **Restaurant,** Plaza and Promenade Decks

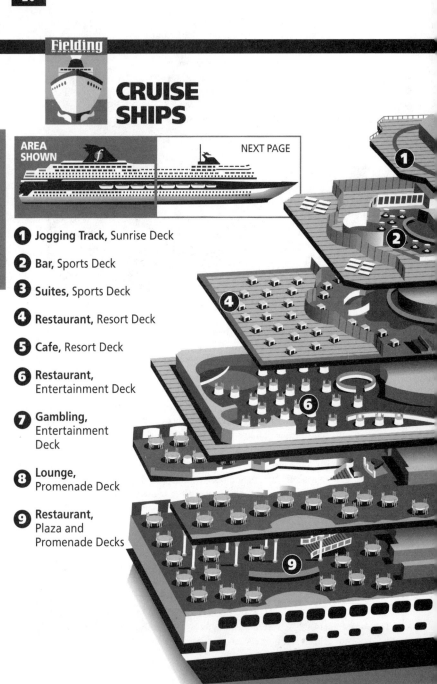

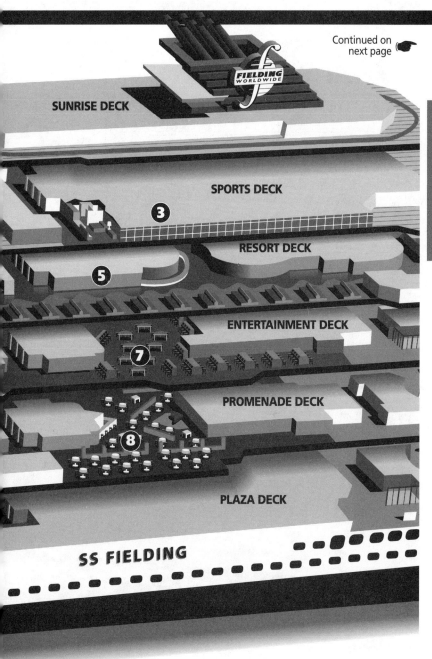

Continued on next page 👉

SUNRISE DECK

SPORTS DECK

RESORT DECK

ENTERTAINMENT DECK

PROMENADE DECK

PLAZA DECK

SS FIELDING

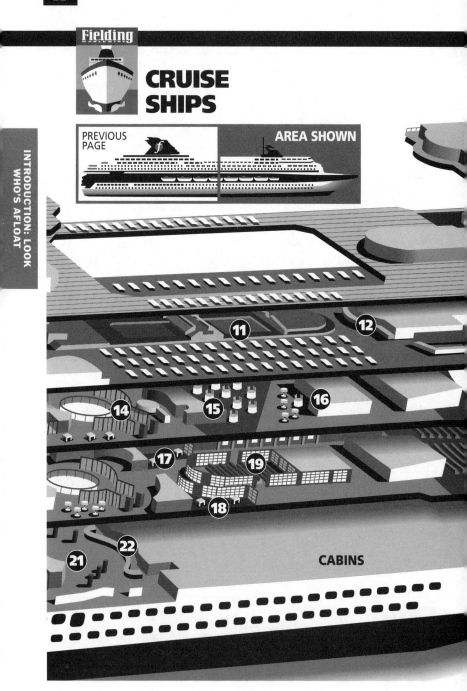

10 **Lounge**, Sports Deck

11 **Swimming Pools**, Resort Deck

12 **Bar**, Resort Deck

13 **Spa**, Resort Deck

14 **Lounge**, Entertainment and Promenade Decks

15 **Cafe**, Entertainment Deck

16 **Lounge**, Entertainment Deck

17 **Card Room**, Promenade Deck

18 **Library**, Promenade Deck

19 **The Cinema and Conference Center**, Promenade Deck

20 **Theatre**, Entertainment and Promenade Decks

21 **The Grand Foyer**, Plaza Deck

22 **Guest Relations and Lobby**, Plaza Deck

SS FIELDING

Elevators come in all shapes and sizes, including this neon-lit glass elevator on Carnival's Fantasy.

- **ELEVATORS** on ships should be avoided at all costs, since the exercise of going up and down stairs is a major defense against weight gain. Elevators should only be used in an emergency except, of course, they do not operate during emergencies.

- **BEAUTY SALONS** are where all the women on board gather between 5 and 7 p.m. on formal nights. Naughty hairdressers direct them back to their cabins via the deck, where the wind destroys the comb-out and everything has to be done all over again.

All About Cabins

- **CABINS** come in all shapes and sizes, mostly small. As a rule, the higher the deck location, the higher the price, but the smoothest ride is amidships (in the middle) on a lower deck.

- **OUTSIDE CABIN** with a window has a square or rectangular panel of glass with light coming through. If the glass is round, it is a **PORTHOLE**. If you fling the curtains open and find yourself facing a blank wall, you have an **INSIDE CABIN**.

- **OUTSIDE CABINS ON PROMENADE DECK** (premium-priced) are always admired by passers-by who look into the windows as they stroll by. On some ships the glass is covered with a special tinted film so outsiders see their own reflections during the daytime. But after dark, the situation is reversed, with the cabin occupants starring in their own X-rated TV shows for the passersby outside. Windows and portholes in the cabin cannot be opened, except on very ancient vessels such as the Mayflower.

- **VACUUM MARINE TOILETS**, which flush with a loud "whoooosh," along with a tub or shower and wash basin are found in each cabin's private bathroom. The best-designed toilets have the flushing device situated where it cannot be activated until the toilet lid is closed, an essential safety feature for absent-minded passengers.

- **ELECTRICAL APPLIANCES**—Before plugging a hair dryer or other appliance into a wall socket, check whether the ship's electrical system is 110 volts and AC (alternating current) or 220 volts and DC (direct current). Plugging one of the former into one of the latter may blow more than the hairdo. Many ships carry voltage converters that will solve the problem; check with the purser's desk.

- **TEMPERATURE CONTROL KNOBS** can be found in each cabin. When your choices are limited from cold to colder or hot to hotter, call Housekeeping to send up a repairman.

- **CABIN WALLS** on all but the newest ships can be very thin, and an entertaining alternative to a TV set or radio. The disembodied voice that gives greetings or commands from the cabin walls is usually the cruise director on the public address system, unless he's droning on about sea temperatures and windspeeds and nautical miles, in which case it's the captain. A panel of knobs located near the bed can tune in shipboard music programmed by overworked staffers at the reception desk who play "The Sound of Music" for three days in a row.

- **CLOSETS** on board are designed to remind passengers that they should have left behind half the clothes they brought.

- **LIFE JACKETS**, somewhere within the closet or under the beds, appear humorous at first glance but are extremely important should there be a problem at sea. Always attend the lifeboat drill and never leave without learning to don the jacket properly, check for the whistle and light, and find which lifeboat is yours.

- **PAPERS** which arrive under the cabin door are not junk mail. Each has some message to impart, whether it is the full schedule of activities for the next day with the suggested dress code for the evening or a 20 percent discount on perfume or gold chains in the gift shop. Read all papers shoved under the door, no matter how boring they appear. One might be an invitation to dine at the captain's table.

Service Areas

- **PURSER'S DESK**—usually located in the lobby. It's the desk with the long line of people waiting to register a complaint, break a $100 bill into singles or buy postage stamps.

- **SHORE EXCURSIONS DESK**—where you go to buy overpriced bus tours of minor cities which always stop at a local landmark and then an hour-long shopping opportunity at the gift shop of the guide's cousin.

- **RADIO ROOM**—where you arrange to pay $15 a minute to send a fax to your office or make a call home to your answering machine and find out bad news that ruins your vacation.

The dining room—this one is aboard RCCL's Viking Serenade—*is a favorite shipboard gathering spot.*

The Dining Room

- **TABLES** rarely come with only two chairs but most often in fours, sixes, eights or even tens. Couples who worry about being bored (or boring) are safer at tables of six or more. After dining together throughout the cruise, passengers always wind up sending Christmas cards to each other.

- **MEAL SEATINGS** are the arbitrary times the cruise line has decided its passengers will eat. **MAIN** or **FIRST SEATING** offers lunch at noon and dinner at 6 or 6:30, but breakfast is at 7 a.m. **SECOND** or **LATE SEATING** passengers dine fashionably at 8 or 8:30, breakfast at a comfortable 8:30 or 9 in the morning, but can't have lunch until 1:30. This is why three-hour deck buffet breakfasts and lunches were invented.

- **SECOND SEATING** is preferred by really dedicated gourmands, who can fit in early riser's coffee and a few samples from the buffet breakfast before reporting for the regular dining room breakfast. Then morning bouillon at 11 settles any remaining hunger pangs until time for a hot dog or hamburger from the deck grill as an appetizer for the buffet lunch. Lingering over the 1:30 lunch fills the empty moments until teatime, with cocktail hour, dinner and midnight buffet left to round out the day—and the figure.

- **SPECIAL DIET MENUS**—low in fats, calories or salt—demanded by passengers at the beginning of a seven-day cruise but most passengers throw abandon to the winds midweek, then wonder why their shipboard diet plan didn't work.

- **MIDNIGHT BUFFETS** served at 10:30 p.m. rank high on the senior circuit. Swinging singles should seek vessels such as Carnival's with midnight buffet at midnight, followed by the night owl buffet at 2 a.m.

The Only Ten Nautical Terms You Ever Need to Know

1. **Port**: the left side of the ship when you're facing the pointy end.

2. **Starboard**: the right side of the ship when you're facing the pointy end.

3. **Forward**: toward the front, or pointy end.

4. **Aft**: toward the back, or blunt end.

5. **Bow**: the pointy end.

6. **Stern**: the blunt end.

7. **Tender**: a boat carried aboard the ship that can ferry you ashore if the ship is not tied up at the dock; to use the boat to ferry passengers ashore.

8. **Gangway**: the detachable outside stairway from the ship's deck down to the dock or tender.

9. **Embark**: to get on a ship.

10. **Disembark**: to get off a ship.

Ten Questions to Ask Yourself Before Calling a Travel Agent

Before you sail away into the sunset, you need to know what you want and be able to communicate that information to a travel agent, since virtually all cruise lines prefer or require bookings to be made through agents. Read these questions and know the answers to them before you call the travel agent. It will make her job much easier and ensure that you'll get the right cruise for you.

1. What are you looking for—adventurous explorations of Alaskan waters, duty-free shopping, a stress-free, do-nothing getaway, a razzle-dazzle good time with plenty of entertainment?

You can get them all on a cruise, but not necessarily on the same ship. Try to be specific as to what you want. A working couple with young children might opt for a family cruise, giving them quality time with the kids and still the chance to be alone together while the youngsters join in special shipboard youth programs. With more young people cruising Alaska, lines are offering kayak tours, river rafting, horseback rides and flightseeing.

2. How long can you be away?

Alaska sailings can be seven-day cruises, 14-day sailings, even 30-day Northwest Passage itineraries. First-timers usually opt for three to seven days, frequent cruisers for a longer period of time.

3. Where do you want to go?

Seven-day cruises with air/sea packages let you sail Alaska's Inside Passage or Gulf of Alaska. Some ports of call may be included on both.

4. Are you traveling as a single, one of a pair, or part of a group of family and friends?

Others may have different needs or desires, so confer with them before making any decisions. A ship good for singles may not work so well with family groups.

5. What do you want in the way of shipboard lifestyle?

Decide what you think are the most important elements of a good vacation, jot them down and have them handy when you make your initial call to a travel agent. While many stressed-out travelers picture a cruise ship as a place to lounge quietly by the pool with a good book, they may be ready after a couple of days for livelier activities. Virtually all cruise ships today offer gym equipment, aerobics, lectures, shoreside golf and tennis, dancing, bridge or crafts classes and even shopping.

6. Do you want a large, medium-sized or small ship?

Big ships have more entertainment, bigger casinos and spas and longer lines; medium-sized ships have scaled-down versions of the same. Small ships are more apt to be free of regimentation and rigid dress codes, but you may be on your own for entertainment. Small to mid-sized vessels usually provide a more relaxed ambiance, while glittering megaliners throb with music and bright lights most of the night. But there's not a vessel afloat that doesn't have a sunny, secluded corner for reading or a lively spot around the bar for socializing.

7. Do you want a classic (read older) or contemporary (read newer) ship?

Most new ships will remind you of a chain resort hotel like Hyatt or Marriott, complete with atrium, glass elevators and identical modular cabins, while ships built 20 or more years ago have ocean liner looks, odd-sized cabins and nostalgic promenade decks.

8. Do you want frequent opportunities to wear your nicest party clothes, or would you prefer to stay casual day and night?

Super-deluxe small ships are quite dressy, expedition and sailing ships casual, and big ships usually have two dress-up evenings a week. Sometimes people who work in an office that requires business attire every day welcome the indulgence of casual sailing or adventure cruising.

9. Do you want to go island-hopping on a ship that stops at a lot of ports or spend your time relaxing aboard ship?

If relaxing is more important, look for itineraries that designate one or two days at sea during a seven-day cruise. You'll still have ports to visit but can get some rest in between.

10. What do you want to learn about the places you'll visit?

If the history, culture, flora and fauna is important, look to expedition ships that emphasize natural history lectures and birdwatching boatrides. Adventure and expedition cruises always seem to attract a lot of doctors, lawyers, teachers and other professionals who diligently attend all the lectures, then happily splash ashore in rubber landing craft to go on nature hikes. If you prefer to know where to shop for souvenirs, any big mainstream cruise ship will fill the bill.

INSIDER TIP

Don't let price be the major factor when you choose your first cruise, especially if you assume all ships and cruises are alike. They're not, and the difference of $20 a day could mean a huge improvement in the quality of your shipboard experience. Once you've taken a couple of cruises, then you can afford to experiment, but a first-time cruise experience that doesn't meet your expectations could turn you away from cruising for good. A smart travel agent will try to steer you toward the most positive cruise experience for you and your family; that means future repeat business for the agent.

How to Read a Brochure

Whenever a new flock of brightly plumaged cruise brochures arrive, we find ourselves leafing through them and visualizing, not the romantic days at sea they portray, but an overworked copywriter in a tiny cubicle high atop a metropolitan office building.

Our fantasy copywriter, thesaurus at the ready, stares through a dirt-streaked window at a rainy sky between bouts of turning out hyperbolic sentences about "hibiscus-scented nights" and "elegant lounges where the decor is luxurious and plush."

Sometimes we wish cruise lines would spend a little less on the four-color pages and take the poor copywriter out on a cruise someday. It would certainly help clear up the vague and overblown prose.

In the meantime, however, the safest path for a potential cruise passenger is to skim the prose lightly and **CONCENTRATE ON THE PICTURES AND CHARTS**—you'd be surprised how much information you can glean from them—and then turn immediately to **READ THE "FINE PRINT"** on the inside back pages for the real nitty-gritty.

First, take a careful look at all the color photos. Don't get lost in reverie, imagining yourself standing on the deck photographing a glacier—that's the intention of most successful advertising photography.

Instead, first **STUDY THE MODELS**, those beaming, bronzed beauties in each shot, then notice the slightly out-of-focus "real people" in some, but not all, of the backgrounds. The models represent the line's idealized version of their perfect prototype passengers, while the people in the background are real passengers on board during the photo shoot. If the ship seems suspiciously empty, the real passengers were all chased away so they could photograph the models alone. If the background people and the foreground people look as if they would be invited to the same party, you have a cruise line that is marketing realistically.

Next, flip quickly through the entire brochure to **GET AN OVERVIEW**. Where is the emphasis? If you see lots of nightlife and casino shots, the company is trying to tell you they're proud of the ship's after-dark entertainment. Where you see smiling waiters and cabin attendants, the line is telling you you'll get special treatment from their staff. If you see smiling children and their happy parents, the line is tipping you off that they welcome families on board. And if you see lots of food pictures, they're telling you, Miss Scarlett, you'll never be hungry again!

The **ITINERARY TABLES** are also valuable sources of information. If the copywriter extols a particular Alaskan port famous for sea kayaking, and the itinerary says you dock at 9 a.m. and sail at noon, there's no way you'll have time for it.

Watch out for the little **ASTERISKS THAT DENOTE "CRUISE BY"** for some ports or islands. While you may get a look at them through binoculars or telephoto lenses, you won't set foot ashore.

Be sure, too, to note the **DAY OF THE WEEK** you're scheduled to arrive in each port. If there's a special museum you want to visit, check to be sure it's open on the day you're there.

DECK PLANS are helpful in spotting extra niceties on board that aren't always promoted—the library, card room, sauna and spa, beauty and barber shop, hospital, covered decks and enclosed galleries.

DINING ROOM DIAGRAMS can tip you off as to how close together the tables are and if there are many tables for two available. Note that on older ships the dining room is usually on a lower deck, where your only view is of closed draperies backlit with fluorescent tubing to give the illusion of daylight.

What **ABOUT THE FOOD** on board? A discerning gourmet can usually tell from the photographs. Don't waste too much time studying the overwrought, gelatin-encased gala buffet; it's as standard on mass market seven-day ships as the deck chairs and about as tasty.

In today's more health-conscious world, salmon has supplanted beef as the food photo of choice in cruise brochures, and more space is given to appetizers and small plate dishes than main courses or gala buffets, suggesting to the nervous first-timer that he won't necessarily gain weight on this ship. In fact, Alaska passengers can count on plenty of fresh Alaska salmon on the menu.

You can usually tell from the pictures whether the cruise line will go out of its way to offer an interesting excursion ashore or simply sell you a three-hour bus tour.

CABIN SIZE is better determined from deck plans than photographs. In the latter, the photographer is usually shooting with a wide-angle lens while braced in the doorway or crouching in the shower. These lenses can distort a standard-sized berth into a bed fit for Magic Johnson.

And watch out for the brochure that shows **ONLY PICTURES OF DESTINATIONS AND CLOSE-UPS OF ATTRACTIVE MODELS DRINKING CHAMPAGNE**. Unless the ship was still under construction or undergoing extensive refitting when the photos were made, you suspect, maybe rightly, that they're trying to hide something from you.

After practicing a while with the pictures and diagrams, you should be in fine shape to tackle the prose and read between the lines. For additional assistance, check out **The Brochure Says** and **Translation** segments for each ship in the ship review section.

EAVESDROPPING

"I expected something Noel Cowardish on my first cruise, but instead there were all these people in polyester acting like every night was New Year's Eve, the deck chairs were all jammed up together and the man next to me was listening to rock-and-roll on his radio. Later I learned ways of finding quiet, remote hiding places for reading, and some of the people turned out to be very nice." A female passenger who chose the wrong cruise line for her first cruise.

CHOOSING A CRUISE

Sometimes equating a ship with a hotel can help a first-time cruiser visualize it better; this soaring atrium lobby from Royal Caribbean's Nordic Empress *may remind you of your favorite Marriott.*

Pick a Ship, Any Ship

OK, you say, a cruise sounds great. Where do I sign up?

That's like saying a hotel is a hotel, book me a room. If you're a Ritz-Carlton regular, you might not be happy at the Motel 6. We feel a lot of otherwise experienced travelers might be more comfortable with cruising if they could equate a cruise line with a hotel company, so we've taken a bit of poetic license to give you a chance to relate your favorite type of land accommodations to the possibilities at sea. Bear in mind, however, that although ships are looking more and more like land hotels, the cruise ship experience is often superior, especially in service and entertainment, to its shoreside equivalent.

Bed-and-breakfasts	**Alaska Sightseeing**	*page 189*
	Clipper Cruises	*page 255*

Hyatt Regency	**Princess Cruises**	*page 337*
Inter-Continental	**Celebrity Cruises**	*page 239*
Marriott	**Norwegian Cruise Line**	*page 325*
	Royal Caribbean Cruise Ltd.	*page 375*
MGM Grand	**Carnival Cruises**	*page 219*
Relais & Chateaux	**Radisson Seven Seas**	*page 367*
Ritz-Carlton	**Crystal Cruises**	*page 263*
	Seabourn	*page 387*
Westin	**Holland America Line**	*page 291*
Summer camp	**World Explorer**	*page 417*

Choosing a Cabin

Prices for the cruise are determined by the **cabin category**, which in turn is based on **deck location**, **amenities**, whether the cabin is **outside** (with a porthole or windows) or **inside** (with no daylight), and sometimes, but not always, on cabin **size**.

Don't expect to snap up the bottom-priced loss leader (the one advertised in big print in the ads) because some cruise ships may have only four or six of these, long since allotted or sometimes assigned to cruise staff or entertainers.

Standard cabin amenities always include a **bed** or berth for each passenger, closet and **storage** space, some sort of table or **dresser, private bathroom facilities** (except on P&O's *Canberra* and some sailing ships) with toilet, sink, tub or shower. Most have **individual temperature controls, telephone and radio and/or TV**.

Grand suites have many pleasurable extras such as separate living and sleeping areas and entertainment centers.

Pleasurable extras in upper price categories may include **private verandas**, suites with **separate living room** and bedroom, **mini-refrigerators**, **sitting areas** and **picture windows**.

Families with children or several people traveling together will save money by booking cabins with third and fourth upper berths, pull-down bunks that go for much less money (sometimes free) than the first two beds in a cabin.

Disabled travelers will find most vessels have one or more cabins that are specially configured to take care of wheelchairs with **wider doors, turning space, low or flat sills and grab rails in the bathroom**.

Dining Room Know-How

Your cruise ship dining room will operate in one of three ways:

1. **Totally open seatings**, usually on small or ultra-luxury vessels, in which the passenger arrives within a given time frame and sits where and with whom he pleases.

2. **Single meal seatings**, in which the passenger arrives within a given time frame and occupies an assigned table for the duration of the cruise.

3. **Two meal seatings**, in which passengers are assigned to dine at a particular table at a specified time, usually 6 p.m. or 8:30 p.m. for dinner, with breakfast and lunch comparably early or late as well.

The two-seating arrangement is the most common. You'll probably be asked at the time of booking which you prefer, but there's no guarantee you'll get it. If you don't get **a card with a specified dining time and table number** in advance or find it in your cabin when you arrive on board, go immediately to the maitre d'hotel in the dining room or another designated area and arrange your seating.

First seating times are the most in demand in Alaska. Don't be upset if you don't get your first choice on a cruise, particularly if the ship is full, but if it means a lot, **chat quietly with the maitre d'hotel, expressing your desire while tactfully holding a $20 bill** and you may be able to negotiate a change.

You can request first or second seating, a smoking (on those ships that still allow smoking in the dining room) or nonsmoking table and the table size you wish. Most first-time cruisers request tables for two, which are relatively rare, but find they enjoy being seated at a larger table for six or eight. The most potentially problematic table size is for four. If you can't stand your tablemates and want to move, be decisive—**make your move at the end of the very first dinner**. Don't wait a couple of days to see if they get more charming. They won't.

Some ships offer alternative restaurant dining by reservation; there is no charge except sometimes a request to tip at point of service. This enables passengers seated at a large table in the regular dining room to have a private dinner for two or an opportunity to dine with new acquaintances.

Some ships offer in addition to the regular dining room an alternative restaurant available at no extra charge but by reservation only, such as Crystal Cruises' Prego Italian restaurants.

Cruise Line Cuisine

It seems to us that TV's "The Love Boat" was on the wrong track. Episode after episode, the passengers seemed to spend an inordinate amount of time falling in and out of love. You hardly ever saw anybody agonizing about what to order for dinner.

But if you took a poll of real-life cruise passengers, you'd find more of them looking forward to encountering a lobster thermidor than a shipboard romance, and to lighting into a dish of cherries jubilee instead of starting a flame in someone's heart.

Dessert buffet displays are shipboard favorites.

Cruise ship brochures entice us with full-color photographs of voluptuous midnight buffets, centerfolds of sensuous bananas flambé, lush melons and wicked croissants on a bedside tray. Is it any wonder we bound up the gangway anticipating a tryst with a tournedos of tenderloin Rossini?

But all too often our hopes are cruelly dashed, like the heartsick swain on a recent trans-Pacific cruise who spent six fruitless days and nights searching for the grand buffet of his dreams. "It was right there on page eight in the brochure," he sighed, "but I couldn't find it anywhere on the ship."

In the fantasy world of cruise-ship advertising, every meal is a gourmet feast fit for a king, or even a restaurant critic. But in the real world onboard, that's not always the case.

Think for a minute about your favorite little gourmet restaurant, the place you go once or twice a year to celebrate a special occasion. Does it serve two full dinner seatings an evening to between 500 and 2000 people, plus offering breakfast and lunch?

Does it operate a cafeteria on the side, along with a tearoom, half-a-dozen bars with snacks and hot hors d'oeuvres, a specialty pizzeria or ice cream parlor, and a catering service that produces beach picnics, deck barbecues and delivers meals to your door?

Is it atop a remote mountain peak or on an island in the middle of the ocean, hundreds of miles from a reliable source of food supplies?

No? Then don't try to compare most cruise ship cooking to a three-star *Michelin Guide* restaurant. Of course, there are a few exceptions.

Small ships, on the other hand, usually turn out tastier food because they don't have to deal with as much volume, but on the down side, their menus are usually more restrictive.

Five Food Fanatic Tips About Ships

1. Most large ships serve high-quality **hotel banquet food**, most often capably prepared and attractively served. You'll encounter a few truly memorable dishes, some

mediocre ones and, at least once during your cruise, will be served something unidentifiable that you're sure you didn't order until the waiter affirms that it is indeed the chef's version of gazpacho or pecan pie.

2. Before you sign on the dotted line with your friendly neighborhood travel agent, ask to **see some menus** from the ship you're considering—not prototype menus like some publish in their brochures, but actual menus that have the date printed on them from a recent cruise, preferably one the agent picked up during her cruise. (Because you fussy eaters are not going to accept an agent's recommendation unless she's been aboard that ship, at least for lunch, are you?)

3. Most mass-market, mini-cruise and seven-day cruise lines have **rotation menu plans** that are not repeated during a single cruise but rather follow each other every seven or 14 or 21 days. This allows more control over food costs and supplies, especially in Alaskan waters.

4. Once on board, **shop around early in the cruise** for the location of the breakfasts, lunches and snacks that really sing out to you, and once you've found a winner, stick with it. Menus are usually posted ahead of time, so you can do your window-shopping in advance.

5. **Talk to your waiter**, and if he's good, learn to trust him. He's there to make you happy; his tip depends on it. Let him know what you like and dislike early in the cruise, and he'll always lead you through the menu. We treasure a memory of one of our first cruises, a Sitmar waiter named Tony who delivered the luncheon dish we'd ordered but materialized a few minutes later with another dish we hadn't ordered, murmuring, "I thought you might like to taste this one, too." Our choice was wrong; his was right.

DID YOU KNOW?

Cruise line food has improved tremendously in the 15 years we've been covering the scene. We remember a Dutch chef on the Rotterdam world cruise in 1985 who was going to retire at the end of that 100-day journey, and went to bizarre extremes not to repeat a single dish during the entire cruise. By the time we got on for the last leg, he was down to truly terrible combinations.

Five Tips on Reading a Shipboard Menu

1. See if it gives you **a variety of lunch options** from brunch-type dishes if you missed breakfast (omelets, for instance) to lighter fare (sandwiches and main-dish salads) to something hearty if you're hungry.

2. Check the **light or low-calorie recommendation**. We saw a ship once listing the day's diet special as Cobb Salad, that high-fat, high-calorie concoction of chopped bacon, blue cheese, avocado, and eggs with a gloppy-thick dressing. You'd never lose weight on that diet.

3. See how much **fresh food versus canned** or preprepared dishes they offer. Fresh catch of the day may be prefrozen, but that's to be expected unless you're cruising in Alaska. Watch out for that long list of seven appetizers, most of them tinned juices.

4. See if they're pulling out all their stops on the dessert menu. A lot of lines cut food costs by **stuffing passengers with sugary sweets** and stodgy starches—you'll note the macaroni salads and jello on the buffets—spending about $1.98 a day per passenger on raw materials.

5. Eye the dish descriptions carefully to make sure the line isn't **blanding out all the dishes** with cream-based sauces instead of fresh herbs, garlic or imaginative seasoning.

INSIDER TIP

Check the nationality of the ship's officers, chef or dining room staff. Princess ships have British and Italian officers but an Italian dining room and galley staff, so you can expect continental cuisine with a definite Italian accent. Greek ships are going to serve continental dishes plus Greek salads and appetizers and at least one Greek menu a cruise. The Norwegians like to put out lavish seafood smorgasbords somewhere along the way.

How to Avoid Pigging Out at Sea

Take advantage of the exercise classes and spa aboard the ship; you've paid for them just as you have all that food you feel compelled to eat. Here, wanna-be Antarctic explorers work out aboard the **World Discoverer.**

1. Shop around, reading posted menus in advance and **checking out the entire buffet display** before plowing in.

2. **Don't stuff yourself.** Help save the whales by not being one; let the fishes finish your food.

3. Unless your metabolism is fantastic, **skip a meal every now and then**, substituting teatime for lunch or scheduling an hour in the disco before judiciously checking out the late buffet.

4. **Beware of Greeks** (or Italians or Jamaicans or Austrians) **bearing dishes**; a soulful-eyed waiter usually has his tip rather than your figure in mind when he coaxes you into ordering an appetizer, soup, salad, fish, meat and two desserts.

5. **Steer clear of piña coladas** and any other drink you can't see through or that has an umbrella in it. Opt instead for mineral water or diet soda, a glass of wine or light beer.

6. Take advantage of **the exercise classes and spa**; you've paid for them just as much as you have all that food you feel compelled to eat.

7. You'll find **vegetarian and low-fat** or low-calorie dishes on practically every menu these days, as well as a wider range of fish and poultry and less red meat.

8. If we want a vegetarian dinner, we sometimes order a plate of all the **side vegetable dishes** on the menu rather than the same old boring steamed cauliflower, broccoli and carrots.

9. Try ordering **dishes without the sauce**. Contrary to the famous Jack Nicholson "whole wheat toast" scene from *Five Easy Pieces*, most waiters will be happy to bring you sauce on the side or lemon wedges instead of salad dressing.

10. When you lunch on deck, plan to wear your tightest jeans or shorts, and **check out the slender young sylphs and Adonises** (or for that matter, the not-so-slender ones) for positive reinforcement before you fill your plate.

Ship Sanitation Inspections

The way food is handled from its very arrival aboard the ship to its storage, as here in the food storage lockers on Cunard's Vistafjord, *and its final holding and preparation can affect the ship sanitation score.*

A great deal of attention is being paid these days to the "green sheet" ship sanitation inspection scores from U.S. Public Health's Center for Disease Control that are issued every two weeks.

It's laudable that the Center for Disease Control is carrying out the program because it keeps the cruise lines on their toes, making them train and carefully observe the galley employees, who may speak a dozen languages.

But by **the time the score has been published, it's history**, and the infraction has been corrected long ago. As a rule, ships are inspected every six months, but may go a year or even longer without a reinspection unless the cruise line requests one. Many cruise lines employ a trained sanitation expert to establish and monitor their own sanitation practices.

The only real value of the scores for a potential passenger is as a longtime study of a specific ship over a couple of years. If the vessel is a consistent failure, then chances are its galley and sanitation practices are sloppy.

CHOOSING A CRUISE

A single 30-point infraction causes the ship to fail automatically, since 86 out of a possible 100 is the passing grade. Improper methods of handling food are responsible for most major point losses, with temperature violations in food holding, preparation and serving areas the most critical.

Unannounced inspections are carried out at regular intervals on foreign-flag ships that call even occasionally in U.S. ports. When a ship fails, it can (and almost always does) request a reinspection as soon as possible to show the problem has been cleared up.

We went through all the "green sheets" for a one-year period and found an interesting pattern. Some of the cleanest and most highly regarded ships were occasionally among the failures. The super-deluxe *Seabourn Pride,* which scored a 74 on Feb. 19, 1995, but was retested March 21 and scored a 94; the spic-and-span *Rotterdam,* which scored a 78 on April 18, 1995, but bounced back with a 93 on May 24; and the stately *Sagafjord* (now the *Gripsholm* for Saga Holidays), which failed with an 81 on April 23, 1995, but rescored a 96 on June 12. On the other hand, some vintage budget ships—notably the *Regal Empress* from Regal Cruises—held a score of a 95 during most of the time period, dropped to an 86, still passing, during a later period, and scored a 97 on the June 24, 1995, inspection. This despite the fact that before its first scheduled sailing from New York, officials went down to the dock and handed out flyers pointing out sanitation levels so low passengers might not wish to sail with her. In the first quarter of 1996, the *Crystal Symphony* and Celebrity's *Century* both scored a rare 100.

Ships most commonly fail on the last inspection before they're sold or transferred, probably because the crew is less motivated. Brand-new ships or new cruise lines (the latter the case with Regal Cruises) are usually given a couple of preliminary inspections with notes before getting a published score. "It's not unusual for a new ship to fail, because generally you have a lot of new people with new equipment," one of the inspectors told us.

The CDC inspectors have improved the quality of ship sanitation tremendously over the years, as well as carrying on an education program for kitchen workers who may come from a culture with different sanitation standards. Very few land-based restaurants could score an 86 or better under the CDC standards, according to former program head Tom Hunt, who had previously been a restaurant inspector. Unless a ship consistently fails over a period of time, there's no real way of determining whether a passenger might suffer a gastrointestinal illness aboard.

In fact, we were inadvertently once the cause of a ship sanitation rating failure when photographing the dining room for a food magazine. The chef had stuck a bouquet of fresh flowers in the walk-in refrigerator to keep them fresh until the shoot, and the CDC inspectors on the surprise inspection seized them as a major infraction—non-food items stored with food items.

Six Questions About Ship Sanitation Scores

1. **Does anyone ever score a perfect score?**
   Yes, the first ship to make 100 on the numerical listings, which were initiated in 1989, was Carnival's *Fantasy* on April 30, 1990, followed by Windstar's *Wind Spirit* which scored 100 on Aug. 27, 1990. More recently, *Crown Dynasty,* now *Crown*

Majesty, scored 100 on Feb. 8, 1994, and the *Crystal Symphony* and Celebrity's *Century* made it in early 1996.

2. What's the lowest score ever recorded?

The lowest one we've found was a 23 for Epirotiki's *Oceanos* back in 1989; that ship sank off the coast of South Africa in 1991.

3. Can the CDC keep a ship from sailing because of poor sanitation?

Cooperation is voluntary on the part of the ship being inspected. The vessel sanitation program cannot forbid a ship with extreme sanitation problems to sail until its problems are corrected; it can only recommend that it not sail.

4. Who pays for these inspections?

The cruise lines themselves.

5. Are all cruise ships inspected?

The CDC's jurisdiction covers all ships carrying 13 or more passengers that sail in international waters. It does not include U.S.-flag vessels sailing in U.S. waters such as those of American Hawaii, Delta Queen Steamboat, Alaska Sightseeing/Cruise West, or American Queen. Those ships are the responsibility of the Food and Drug Administration and the state health departments within their cruising areas.

6. How can I get a copy of the latest scores?

Via Internet, ftp.cdc.gov//pub/ship_inspections/shipscore.txt, or by calling ☎ *(404) 332-4565* and requesting Document No. 510051.

Safety of Life at Sea

Commonly called SOLAS, Safety of Life at Sea regulations govern cruise ships that call at U.S. ports. Whenever a new ship comes into service, or enters a U.S. port for its first call, it must undergo a rigorous set of inspections by the U.S. Coast Guard covering fire safety drills, use of emergency equipment, crew drills and detailed examinations of the condition and safety of the vessel's hull and its machinery. After the initial series of inspections, the ships are reinspected quarterly. Unlike the CDC inspectors described above, the Coast Guard has the power to detain a ship from sailing if it is deemed unsafe for its passengers.

The Coast Guard's Traveling Inspectors team boards ships with emergencies to investigate causes, such as numerous ships running aground, engine room fires, main engines down, or passengers suffering gastrointestinal outbreaks.

Still, stringent new SOLAS regulations being implemented beginning in 1997 seriously affect the cruise industry, because they require detailed (and costly) amendments and additions to older vessels, from sprinkler systems to freon-free air conditioning systems and low-level lighting systems.

INSIDER TIP

Many of the older ships are being sold to operators abroad to sail exclusively from non-U.S. ports, and so do not come under U.S. Coast Guard inspections and SOLAS regulations. Be cautious about buying a bargain cruise on a ship that sails only from foreign ports if you're concerned about ship safety.

Five Hints for a Hassle-Free Cruise

1. The shorter the cruise, the younger and more casual the group on board is likely to be. For most first-time cruisers, a **good Alaska introduction is aboard the seven-day** Inside Passage cruise.

2. If you want a smooth, trouble-free sailing, **avoid any shakedown, inaugural, maiden voyage or first sailing on the heels of major renovations**. Although some ships have sailed through these with flying colors, this is when the vessel is most vulnerable to plumbing, heating, air conditioning and water pressure problems.

3. If you are considering booking a ship that never sails from a U.S. port and your travel agent has no firsthand knowledge of it, take some time to **check it out before putting down a deposit no matter how tempting the price**. Some lesser-known vessels or very low-priced sailings may feature discounted cabins left over from a group or charter, or a cruise marketed primarily in another country, and you could find yourself odd man out. Also, these vessels are no longer inspected regularly by the U.S. Coast Guard and could represent a safety hazard.

4. When dealing **with waiters and stewards** to whom English is a second or third language, speak slowly and distinctly and **be ready with an alternative word** when they don't understand your initial request. That way you'll be spared the problem one infuriated passenger had with her Scandinavian stewardess who did not know what a "cantaloupe" was; if the passenger had switched to the word "melon," she would have gotten a serving of breakfast fruit instead of the envelope that was delivered by the bewildered Norwegian.

With waiters and stewards to whom English is a second language, like this Greek bartender, speak slowly and distinctly when ordering something.

5. **Read the fine print** at the end of the company brochure and on the back of your ticket/contract, and you'll find **the line is not responsible for missed ports of call**, changed itineraries or liabilities in connection with independent contractors such as airlines and ground tour operators.

Seven Ways to Protect Yourself from Travel Scams

1. **Be skeptical**. If an offer seems too good to be true, it probably is. Unsolicited "prizes" you get through the mail or over the phone promising a free cruise usually involve your calling in and giving someone your credit card number or paying a "service fee" for a trip that never materializes.

2. **Follow up**. If you book through a discount agency's toll-free 800 number, don't send them checks or money orders. Use a credit card, but only after ascertaining that the cruise line rather than the agency will process the charge. Verify the reservation by demanding the vendor's confirmation number.

3. **Never give out your credit card number on the phone to someone who called you**.

4. **Don't buy a cruise from a toll-free 800 telephone number if you haven't checked them out**; it's better to visit the office in person and **talk face-to-face with a travel agent**. Several major cruise travel agencies with 800 numbers, some of them in business for years and regarded as reliable, went bankrupt suddenly in the past year or two, leaving clients high and dry and cruise-less.

5. Check any agency you're dealing with to see if they're **members of professional travel organizations** such as ASTA (American Society of Travel Agents), ARTA (Association of Retail Travel Agents), CLIA (Cruise Line International Association) or NACOA (North American Cruise-Only Agencies).

6. **Double-check with the cruise line** itself to confirm bookings and all payments.

7. When in doubt, **call the National Consumer's League Hotline**, ☎ *(800) 876-7060*.

SPECIAL CASES

Many ships sail with a number of gentlemen hosts aboard to dance with unattached ladies; here a dance class is in progress.

Singles

Anyone browsing through a cruise brochure notices sooner or later that ubiquitous term "per person, double occupancy" in conjunction with prices.

But what happens to passengers, as many as 25 percent of all potential travelers, who travel alone?

Generally, when one person occupies a double cabin, a surcharge that runs from 125 to 200 percent of the per person double occupancy rate is charged.

There are only two sure-fire ways to avoid the singles surcharge:

Opt for a **guaranteed share** from lines that offer it, which means the line will attempt to find another passenger of the same sex, general age range and smoking preference to match up with you or let you have the double cabin to yourself at the per person double occupancy rate.

Find a ship, usually an older vessel, that has **designated single cabins** and pay the listed fare, which often works out to be nearly as much as a double cabin surcharge. Single cabins are available aboard Cunard's *Vistafjord* and *QE2*, World Explorer, Holland America's *Rotterdam* and Ivaran's *Americana*, which often prices single cabins at the same or lower price as the per person double occupancy rates.

Over-50 single women with social dancing and bridge-playing on their minds will find ships that carry social hosts (see below) have a definite appeal.

Everything You Ever Wanted to Know About Social Hosts

1. What lines carry them?

Cunard Line, World Explorer, Crystal Cruises and Holland America are among the lines that carry hosts in Alaska.

2. Who are they?

Usually retired businessmen or military men, single, divorced or widowed, and upwards of 50 years old.

3. Can I count on romance?

No, just socializing, dancing, bridge playing and companionship at mealtimes and on shore excursions. Anything else, including spending too much time with one passenger, is forbidden. However, some social hosts have met ladies aboard and continued to see them on land without having to follow the cruise line's rules. Several marriages are said to have come out of meetings between social hosts and passengers.

4. How many hosts are usually on board?

Anywhere from two to 10 or more, depending on the size of the ship and how many single female passengers are booked for that sailing.

5. How can someone get a job as a social host?

The leading (and perhaps only) agent for social hosts is Lauretta Blake of **The Working Vacation**, *4277 Lake Santa Clara Drive, Santa Clara, CA 95054*, ☎ *(408) 727-9665*. She screens and books hosts for several cruise lines for $150 fee per week at sea, paid by the host.

The cruise lines themselves do not charge a fee for placing hosts; you could send a letter, picture and resume directly to the cruise line's personnel department or director of entertainment. Most hold regular "auditions."

The hosts usually receive no payment beyond the free cruise, economy class airfare to and from the ship, and a modest allowance for onboard expenditures such as wine and bar bills. Cruise lines usually require their hosts take two or three cruises back to back, and sleep two to a cabin.

Five Tips for Cruising with Kids

1. Book a ship that is likely to have other young children aboard. Whether a kid is six or 16, he's happy if he can find someone near his own age. Otherwise he can get bored and fidgety. (See "Five Best Ships for Families," page 4).

2. Don't expect free 24-hour baby-sitting. The youth counselors are there to enrich your child's vacation, not take him off your hands. A few lines offer baby-sitting in the evenings in the youth center, usually with a surcharge.

Children love diving into the plastic balls aboard the playrooms on many ships.

3. Don't take the kids on a cruise line that doesn't offer a children's program, discounts on their fare and counselors on staff—that's a tipoff the ship and its regular passengers would be happier without children on board.

4. Check with the cruise line if your child is under two; many lines have minimum age limits.

5. Look for the lines that offer families special shore programs in Alaska, such as Holland America.

Ten Cruise Tips for Seniors

1. A ship's size and itinerary have a direct relationship with how quickly sophisticated medical care can be obtained in an emergency; large ships have more medical staff and facilities onboard, and more importantly, some have a landing pad for a helicopter to land and evacuate a seriously ill passenger.

2. Have your doctor write the details of any ongoing medical condition, as well as any prescription drugs or serious allergies, on an index card and give it to the ship's doctor when you board.

3. Study the deck plan of the vessel you're considering for elevators if you use a wheelchair or tire easily climbing stairs.

4. Check to make sure the cabin category you're booking provides two lower beds rather than an upper and a lower, which can make getting in and out of bed more difficult.

5. Check itineraries to determine where the ship will dock as opposed to where it anchors and tenders; going down a gangway on the side of the ship and transferring to a bobbing launch calls for steady footing.

6. Exercise care and moderation in food and drink; avoid any major changes in your normal eating pattern.

7. Pick and choose; sample the six or eight meals a day a few at a time, skipping lunch, perhaps, in favor of a big breakfast and afternoon tea, or have a light dinner to save room for the midnight buffet.

Pick and choose among the many meals and snacks offered every day, perhaps enjoying teatime treats in lieu of lunch.

8. Don't overtax yourself in every port of call; take a half-day tour instead of a full-day tour, or take an early morning stroll around the port town, come back to the ship for a midday break and then go back in late afternoon for a second look if you wish.

9. Remember that comfort is more important than fashion in Alaskan ports of call; wear broken-in walking shoes and loose-fitting clothing.

10. Mix and mingle; don't seclude yourself or limit your choice of companions to others your own age.

Getting Married Aboard

While the popularity of honeymoons at sea has been increasing steadily for the past five years, some cruise lines now offer the additional option of getting married aboard ship. Then the bride and groom can sail away on their honeymoon cruise with—or without—other members of the wedding party.

Couples on a budget like the convenience and romance of a shipboard wedding, where they can have a smaller ceremony with only a few guests. By marrying on a ship instead of celebrating a big wedding ashore, they might even save enough to pay for the honeymoon cruise.

Contrary to popular belief, a ship's captain is not empowered to conduct a wedding ceremony, "at least not one that will last longer than the cruise," one captain jokes.

But couples booked on the sailing may get married in port, using either an officiate provided by the cruise line, or a minister, rabbi or priest they bring themselves.

Packages vary from basic (under $300 for a notary and witnesses, cake and champagne for the newlyweds) to elaborate (a two-hour reception with open bar, hot and cold buffet and champagne toasts for around $75 a person). Many are coordinated for the cruise line by private wedding consultant companies.

Ports where weddings can be arranged on Alaska sailings include Vancouver, B.C., and Juneau, Alaska.

Cruise lines that offer wedding packages include Carnival, Celebrity, Holland America, Norwegian Cruise Line, Princess and Royal Caribbean.

EAVESDROPPING

"Twenty-five years ago if you took a honeymoon cruise, your name was Rockefeller. Now it's Smith or Jones," says Bob Dickinson, president of Carnival Cruise Lines.

Five Tips for Honeymooners at Sea

1. Check when booking if you want a double or king-sized bed; some vintage vessels have twin beds that cannot be pushed together.

2. Tables for two are not always guaranteed; some cruise lines put couples at tables of six or eight. Your travel agent can request a table for two or arrange for you to be seated with other honeymooners at a large table.

3. If you want to be singled out for congratulations, special onboard parties for newlyweds and the like, let your agent know. But if you want anonymity, say so in advance or you may be serenaded by the waiters in the dining room when you'd rather be left alone.

4. Check to see which lines offer complimentary champagne, souvenir photos or special receptions with other honeymooners. Others can provide extra goodies with add-on packages adoring friends or relatives might like to donate.

5. Since most cruise lines limit the number of onboard weddings per sailing, it's a good idea to make plans and reservations as far in advance as possible.

Cruising for the Physically Challenged

More and more of the estimated 36 million physically challenged Americans are booking cruise vacations, either with groups or as independent travelers. Most experience the same pleasurable holiday other cruise passengers do, but a few report everything from minor inconveniences to major problems.

The problem for some independent physically challenged passengers is the requirement or request from virtually every cruise line that they be accompanied by an "able-bodied" companion. One way around this would be to book a special group tour that would have its own escorts and personnel aboard to take the extra responsibility away from the ship's staff for alerting deaf or sightless travelers in case of an emergency.

Cruising is one of the very best vacations for wheelchair travelers so long as the ship has elevators, wide corridors and cabins specially configured to take care of wheelchairs with wider doors, turning space, an absence of high sills, and grab rails and a pulldown shower seat in the bathroom. Often, but not always, these cabins may also have a lower hanging rack and storage shelves placed conveniently low. But sometimes cabins are designated accessible and their bathrooms don't comply. Even if there is no sill to negotiate and the door is 25 inches rather than the standard 22 inches wide—both adequate for wheelchairs—should the door open in and to the right, for instance, and the toilet is behind it, there's no way a wheelchair occupant can use it.

While going ashore by tender is normally difficult or impossible for wheelchair travelers, the large tender from NCL's Norway *handles them with ease. Unfortunately, it does not sail in Alaska.*

While some wheelchair travelers will improvise with portable toilet and basin facilities in order to be able to sail on an otherwise inaccessible ship, others are rightly indignant if a line promises accessibility and they don't get it. Unfortunately, many cruise line employees don't have access to the specific cabin measurements for all their ships. You're better off booking through a travel agency that specializes in trips for the disabled.

Going ashore by tender in some cases is difficult or impossible for wheelchair passengers. An exception is the broad-decked *Little Norway* from NCL's *Norway,* which can be loaded level with the gangway doors, allowing wheelchairs to be rolled on and off the tender. Sometimes cruise lines can offload mobility-impaired passengers through the lower deck crew gangway, which is level with the dock, rather than the passenger gangway, which can be steep in many ports. Check with your travel agent or the line ahead of booking.

Under the cruise lines and ship reviews beginning on page 179, we have tried to point out ships that have accessible cabins that we have personally inspected.

AGENCIES SPECIALIZING IN TOURS AND CRUISES FOR THE DISABLED

Flying Wheels Travel
PO Box 382
143 West Bridge Street
Owatonna, MN 55060
☎ *(800) 535-6790*

Marilyn Ryback
Dahl's Good Neighbor Travel
7383 Pyramid Place
Los Angeles, CA 90046
☎ *(213) 969-0660*

AGENCIES SPECIALIZING IN TOURS AND CRUISES FOR THE DISABLED

Mada Edmonds
Cobb Travel Agency
905 Montgomery Highway
Birmingham, AL 35216
☎ *(205) 822-5137*

Joe Regan
Able to Travel
247 N. Main Street
Suite 308
Randolph, MA 02368
☎ *(800) 557-2047*

Joan Diamond & Jill Bellows
Nautilus Tours & Cruises Ltd.
17277 Ventura Blvd. Suite 207
Encino, CA 91316
☎ *(818) 788-60004*
Outside CA (800) 797 6004

Murray Vidocklor
SATH Handicapped Travel
347 Fifth Ave. Suite 610
New York, NY 10016
☎ *(212) 447-2784*

Judi Smaldino
Tri Venture Travel
1280 Court Street
Redding, CA 96001
☎ *(916) 243-3101*

Five Tips for Physically Challenged Travelers

1. Be honest with yourself about what you can and cannot do and pass that information on to the travel agent.

2. Be sure your doctor says your condition will allow you to travel.

3. Take it easy; don't try to do everything that's offered just to prove you can.

4. Do take along an aide or companion. Some agents have a list of retired nurses who'll accompany disabled travelers and share a cabin in exchange for the trip.

5. Seeing-eye dogs are accepted on some ships, but each case has to be individually arranged with the cruise line.

Cruises for Gays

RSVP Cruises, *2800 University Avenue Southeast, Minneapolis, MN 55414,* ☎ *(612) 379-4697.*

Our Family Abroad, *40 W. 57th Street, Suite 430, New York, NY 10019* ☎ *(800) 999-5500.*

Advance Damron Vacations, *Houston, TX* ☎ *(800) 695-0880.*

Cruises with College Classes

Semester At Sea sailings conducted by the **Institute for Seaboard Education** and the University of Pittsburgh gives a student academic credit for some 50 courses from Global Ecology to Caribbean Literature. Classes meet daily when the ship is at sea, and go on field trips when the ship is in port.

Some 500 students sail on each Semester at Sea program, which also operates a cruise ship in Alaska during the summer. The ship serves as the student dormitory, with sailing students sharing two- and three-berth cabins. All meals are provided on board. Adults who also would like to participate in a "voyage of discovery" may enroll either for academic credit or may audit classes or sit in on lectures that interest them. A 100-day around-the-world voyage is offered twice a year for $14,880 per person, double occupancy, or $17,880 for singles.

For details, call **World Explorer Cruises** at ☎ *(800) 854-3835.*

Christian/Church-Oriented Cruises

Vacations-in-the-Son, *PO Box 91591, Longwood, FL 32791*, markets religion-oriented cruises for groups and charters with born-again Christians. Contact them at ☎ *(407) 862-6568.*

Alcohol-Free Cruises

Serenity Trips, a company that specializes in alcohol-free vacations, schedules family cruises. For details, call ☎ *(800) 615-4665.*

Friends of Bill W meetings are scheduled frequently on many cruise ships.

WHO GOES TO ALASKA

Cruise Line	Ship	Page
Princess Cruises	Crown Princess	page 344
	Dawn Princess	page 361
	Regal Princess	page 344
	Sky Princess	page 350
	Star Princess	page 356
	Sun Princess	page 361
Radisson Seven Seas Cruise	Hanseatic	page 370
Royal Caribbean Cruises, Ltd.	Legend of the Seas	page 380
	Rhapsody of the Seas	page 380
Seabourn Cruise Line	Seabourn Legend	page 393
Society Expeditions	World Discoverer	page 403
Special Expeditions	Sea Bird	page 412
	Sea Lion	page 412
World Explorer Cruises	Universe Explorer	page 420

AN ALASKA/ CANADA HANDBOOK

Alaska's native people call them **children of the snow**, those craggy icebergs born from the snowfalls of an ancient time. From the ship's rail, passengers watching gasp and shriek as a sharp, rifle-shot sound from the glacier announces a "calving," or birth, of another iceberg ripped from the mother glacier and tumbling into the icy seas.

From a smaller ice floe, **a harbor seal** observes us, his head lifted in curiosity. We can hear peeps from **colonies of black-winged kittiwake**, and watch **cormorants diving for fish**. **A bald eagle** sits calmly on another iceberg surveying his domain. Sometimes whales indulge in a flirtatious game with the ship, coming in closer and closer, rolling and glistening in the sea, as if posing for the countless snapping cameras.

But **cruising among the glaciers**, while perhaps the most spectacular and eagerly anticipated activity, is only part of an Alaskan cruise. Contrary to what you may think before your first visit, it's a journey you can make over and over with a different experience every time.

INSIDER TIP

Jokes you'll hear more than once:

A sourdough is "sour on Alaska but without enough dough to get out."

A cheechako (tenderfoot) can become a real Alaskan after wrestling with a grizzly, urinating in the Yukon and surviving an amorous bear encounter.

Five Essential Items to Take On an Alaska Cruise

1. A **camera** with telephoto or zoom lens for wildlife shots.

2. A lightweight **down vest** or jacket for cool mornings on deck.

3. **Binoculars**.

4. Sturdy **walking shoes** or hiking boots.

5. **Lightweight silk long underwear** for glacier-watching days.

53

Dramatic totem poles are seen throughout southeastern Alaska; this particular one is in Haines.

DID YOU KNOW

Conversations about Alaskan wildlife can sometimes jolt an environmentalist from the lower 48; we were listening to an avid outdoorsman in Fairbanks talking about the indigenous wild animals. "And Dall sheep," he said, eyes glowing, "makes about the best eating there is."

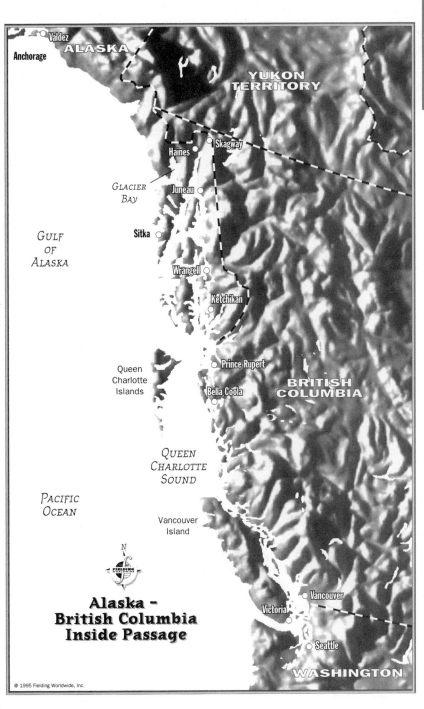

ALASKA

Valdez

Anchorage

YUKON TERRITORY

Haines

Skagway

GLACIER BAY

Juneau

GULF OF ALASKA

Sitka

Wrangell

Ketchikan

Queen Charlotte Islands

Prince Rupert

BRITISH COLUMBIA

Bella Coola

QUEEN CHARLOTTE SOUND

PACIFIC OCEAN

Vancouver Island

N

FIELDING WORLDWIDE

Alaska – British Columbia Inside Passage

Vancouver

Victoria

Seattle

WASHINGTON

@ 1995 Fielding Worldwide, Inc.

Classic and Alternative Alaska Cruises

There are two basic Alaska itineraries. **The classic Inside Passage,** the original and still highly popular, usually sets out from Vancouver for a seven-day round-trip cruise up the Inside Passage, with most, but not all, vessels spending a day cruising around famous Glacier Bay. The **Gulf of Alaska cruise**, a newer itinerary, has gotten tremendously popular in the past few years, both for its cruise past the mighty Columbia Glacier and for repeat Alaska cruisers who have already done the classic Inside Passage.

Most of the Alaska ships are large cruise vessels that offer a traditional shipboard experience and all the luxury and comfort passengers associate with cruises. You can enjoy standing or sitting on deck (or on your own private veranda on some ships) all day watching glaciers and wildlife, then dress up and dance the night away or watch an evening of professional entertainment.

Don't make the assumption, as many do, that if you're on a large ship you miss out on a real Alaska experience. **Alaska residents and park rangers are aboard all the ships, large and small**, to give first-hand commentary, answer your questions and share with you their feelings about their home state. The shore excursions, too, are run by the same few tour operators in every town, so whether you're on a big elegant Princess or Holland America liner or the smaller World Explorer sailings, you're all seeing virtually the same shoreside sights with the same guides.

The small ships in Alaska can cruise into areas some of the larger vessels have to miss and may be able to get you a little closer to the glaciers. But some of the large ships have their own excursion boats that can take you still closer than the small cruise vessels, so it's all a tossup.

On the small ships, the dress code is normally casual and the atmosphere relaxed, with very little in the way of formal entertainment. The emphasis is on an educational experience and a personal discovery.

DID YOU KNOW?

"People from the lower 48 are used to seeing Alaska and Hawaii reduced to the same size in identical little boxes at the side of the maps," Alaskans like to remind us. "They don't know how big Alaska really is."

Ten Best of the Best in Alaska/British Columbia

1. **Alaska Highway Cruises**, a one-two combination punch for someone doing that once-in-a-lifetime Alaska trip, lets you buy a combination land/cruise trip with your own easy-to-drive rental RV. We tried this and loved it; you fly to Seattle (or Anchorage), pick up the vehicle and drive the Alaska Highway (or whatever other combination of drives and cruises you want) in one direction, turn in the rig and cruise the other way to your starting point to fly home. Call them at ☎ *(800) 323-5757* for a free brochure.

2. The **luxury glass-domed rail cars** of Princess Tours and Westours that are hooked on the Alaska Railroad engines to chug between Fairbanks and Anchorage through

some of the most dramatic scenery in Alaska; you can easily add one of these unforgettable journeys onto your Alaska cruise.

3. The **White Pass & Yukon railway's** day tour out of Skagway (OK, so we love trains) past Dead Horse Gulch up to White Pass Summit, giving a dizzying look down at the trails the miners of '98 had to traverse.

4. The **Klondike Gold Rush National Park Service Visitors Center** (free) for films, exhibits and brochures, plus free guided walking tours, of the historic gold rush town of Skagway.

5. **Dawson City**, an optional overland excursion offered on many Alaska cruises that will give a wonderful and authentic look at the past.

6. **Denali National Park**, another once-in-a-lifetime opportunity for game-spotting on the park-led tours into the wilderness aboard school buses operated by the park (moderate but require a waiting list for boarding) or safari buses (more expensive but will take an advance reservation) from ARA Tundra Wildlife Tours, $45, ☎ *(907) 683-2215* in summer, ☎ *(907) 276-7234* in winter.

7. **Glacier Bay**, the icing on the cake for many first-time Alaska visitors who cruise the Inside Passage. This protected national park has 15 active glaciers, numerous seabirds and humpback whales, and the National Park Service until recently limited the number of large ships that could visit during the season because they feared too much traffic might disturb the whales. A weakening of this policy has been implemented with more vessel permits issued for the 1997 season.

8. **The Columbia Glacier**, at 400 square miles as big as the sprawling city of Los Angeles, a highlight of the Gulf of Alaska itineraries.

9. Crystal Cruises and Seabourn are two of the most **deluxe cruise lines**. If you like your glacier-gaping gala, check out itineraries for *Seabourn Legend* and the *Crystal Symphony* or *Crystal Harmony*.

10. The scenery along **Turnagain Arm south of Anchorage** on the road to Seward, named when Captain James Cook told his first mate to turn around again when it turned out not to be the Northwest Passage he was seeking; the interesting footnote here is the first mate was William Bligh, later to command the ill-fated *Bounty*.

Most-asked Questions About the Alaska Cruise

Most Alaska cruise ships embark passengers at Vancouver's Canada Place pier.

1. Why do most Alaska cruise ships set out from Vancouver, Canada, instead of a city in Alaska?

A. Because of an American legislation popularly called the Jones Act, which forbids foreign-flag ships from cruising between two American ports. The law was designed a century ago to protect American cabotage, which refers to shipping and navigation along the United States coast. Technically it is supposed to protect American passenger shipping, which is all but defunct these days, but every time legislation is introduced to repeal it, as has been attempted several times lately by lawmakers representing Alaska and Washington state ports, it is fought by American cargo shipping interests who fear that any weakening of the age-old rules could harm their business. The only U.S.-flag cruise lines in Alaska these days are small-ship companies—Alaska Sightseeing/Cruise West, Clipper Cruise Line and Glacier Bay Tours & Cruises. *Sea Lion* and *Sea Bird* from Special Expeditions are also U.S.-flag vessels.

2. How cold is it in Alaska? Will I need my long johns?

A. While it can be very chilly standing on deck watching glaciers, it can also be sunny and 80 degrees, so plan on a variable wardrobe of thin layers that can be added or eliminated as the weather changes. We usually carry silk long underwear for cool, windy days, since it's warm, lightweight and takes up almost no space in the baggage. You can order it from a number of sources, including L.L. Bean, *(800) 221-4221*, and WinterSilks, *(800) 831-0909*.

3. Is it true that almost all Alaska cruisers are older people and retirees?

A. That used to be true a decade ago, but with the tremendous growth of cruising among younger passengers, you'll see nearly as many honeymooners as retirees these days, plus lots of families with children.

4. Weather-wise, are July and August the best months to go?

A. Not necessarily. We've had some of our finest cruise weather in late May, early June and September. There's no predicting Alaska's always-changing climate, and you could have a great day in Ketchikan and overcast and clouds in Sitka—or vice versa. Do take along raingear and an umbrella.

5. I've heard some of the popular flightseeing excursions sell out quickly. Is it possible to book one ahead of time?

A. Some cruise lines will let passengers book shore excursions prior to boarding the ship. Seabourn even requires that certain flightseeing excursions must be booked 30 days ahead of time. Others prefer that passengers board the ship, attend the shore excursion lectures and then make up their minds. Ask your travel agent or the cruise line if early booking on a shore excursion is possible aboard the ship you're taking.

6. What happened to the ban on cruise ship gambling in Alaskan waters?

A. The ban, in effect for several years, was lifted when President Clinton signed legislation in the fall of 1996 permitting gambling on cruise ships sailing between two American ports, but not when ships are in port or on a "cruise to nowhere."

7. I've noticed that some cruise ship Inside Passage itineraries don't include Glacier Bay. Why?

A. Until recently, the National Park Service strictly limited the number of cruise vessels that could enter in a given season by requisite permits that were issued in limited numbers, with priority going to those lines who had been sailing longer in Alaska, such as Princess and Holland America. That in effect limited new lines entering Alaska cruising, forcing them to find other attractive natural areas instead. Interestingly, the limit led to the development and promotion of the so-called Glacier or Gulf of Alaska route, which ultimately became as popular as the Inside Passage/Glacier Bay route. In 1996, restrictions on ship visits were eased somewhat, allowing more vessels to get entry permits. The restrictions were introduced because environmentalists believe large cruise ships coming into Glacier Bay disturb the traditional mating patterns of the humpback whale.

How to Pick the Right Alaska Cruise

The sights and sounds of Alaska by sea—the sharp pistol crack of a calving glacier as tons of blue ice fracture and crash into the sea, the peeps from rocky cliffs teeming with bird life—are like nothing else on earth. What was once considered a once-in-a-lifetime, ends-of-the-earth destination has gone mainstream. And the best way to see this watery state with so few roads is over the rail of a ship.

Some of the best views of Alaska are over the rail of a ship.

Today's passengers are apt to be younger and more active than their counterparts of a decade ago, and the cruise lines are recognizing this by adding more active shore programs, from sea kayaking to mountain biking. Since **more families with children** are booking summer sailings to Alaska, lines are promoting cabins with a third and fourth upper berth at greatly reduced rates for the kids, as well as organizing special onboard and shore activities tailored for different age groups from toddlers to teens.

You'll need to consider several aspects of the Alaska cruise scene in order to decide which is best for you.

First, itinerary—If you have a week or longer and it's your first visit, you'll probably choose either **an Inside Passage sailing or a Glacier Route cruise**. If you've done one of the basic itineraries before, you may want to check out the other route or take a third option for a smaller vessel sailing offbeat itineraries.

Second, think about whether you want **a big ship or a small one**, a lavish luxury vessel or a simpler, family-style "soft adventure" ship, or even an expedition sailing aboard a Russian icebreaker or a sturdy ice-hardened veteran of the Antarctic.

Among the ships, choices range from big, luxurious seagoing resorts with dress-up evenings and lavish entertainment to small boats that cruise into the fjords by day and send passengers ashore to sleep in hotels at night.

One of the famous Chilkat dancers of Haines poses in front of the tribal clan house.

Cruising the Inside Passage

On the classic, seven-day Inside Passage itinerary, ships typically depart Vancouver and visit two or three ports that may include Juneau, Skagway, Ketchikan, Sitka, Haines or Victoria. On this route **the seas are generally calm and protected and the shoreline is never out of sight**. Scenery includes evergreen-clad slopes, soaring bald eagles, costumed Native dance troupes and colorful old gold rush towns.

And just as St. Thomas is on everybody's wish list on a Caribbean cruise, Glacier Bay National Monument—with its 15 active glaciers and wildlife that includes sea birds and humpback whales—has come to encapsulate **the splendor of Alaskan scenery**. To protect that environment, large ships are restricted during June, July and August to a certain number of cruising days there. If Glacier Bay is a must-see for you, make sure the ship you're considering will visit there during the dates you're planning to go.

Shore excursions, available at extra cost, include helicopter flights that can set you down on a glacier, streamside salmon bakes at old gold mines, salmon, halibut or fly fishing excursions, float trips and a narrow-gauge train that took the Stampeders of '98 uphill the same way a century ago.

Cruising the Glacier Route

Juneau is a popular port of call on both Inside Passage and Glacier Route itineraries.

The newer seven-day itinerary, almost outstripping the Inside Passage in popularity, is called the Glacier or Gulf of Alaska Route. **Ships sail across the Gulf of Alaska between Vancouver and Seward** (or sometimes Whittier) with more open water than the Inside Passage. But you'll still get plenty of Inside Passage scenery as you sail from Vancouver.

Calls at Sitka, Juneau, Skagway and Ketchikan may be on the agenda, as well as the magnificent Columbia Glacier and College Fjord with its 16 glaciers.

In addition, dozens of **add-on programs from Anchorage** take you deep in the heart of Alaska—by luxury dome car train to Fairbanks and Denali National Park, home of Mount McKinley and wildlife that includes moose, caribou and Dall sheep. Motorcoach tours may take you across to Dawson City, site of the Klondike Gold Rush, or flights can whisk you to the Eskimo village of Kotzebue above the Arctic Circle or Prudhoe Bay on the shores of the Arctic Ocean.

Whichever route you choose, you can still opt for the add-on excursions.

Selecting the Ship Size and Type

Large ships in Alaska, like the 960-passenger **Crystal Harmony,** *anchored here in Sitka, offer more activities and facilities than small ships.*

Big ships offer lots of action, the widest variety of shipboard experiences and entertainment. Activities from aerobics and dance classes to bridge lessons and slide lectures on Alaskan history are scheduled virtually every waking moment, along with first-run feature films, art auctions, napkin folding demonstrations and cooking lessons.

You can expect a couple of dress-up evenings during the week and after-dinner entertainment ranging from variety shows and casinos to Big Band music for dancing or production show extravaganzas. Fully equipped fitness centers, spas and beauty centers are staffed with hairdressers, masseuses, exercise instructors and manicurists.

Meals are usually served at two seatings, with dinner around 6 or 6:30 on first seating and 8:30 or so on second seating. The first seating is always more in demand in Alaska.

The giants of Alaska cruising are Princess Cruises and Holland America Line, and each has half-a-dozen ships or more on the Alaska circuit each summer, along with its own land tour company, luxury rail cars and posh lodges and hotels.

But more and more familiar cruise lines from the Caribbean have entered the Alaska market, including Carnival, Celebrity, Cunard, Norwegian Cruise Line and Royal Caribbean, all offering big-ship experiences similar to those described above.

Mid-sized ships carry fewer passengers but offer scaled-down versions of the activities of the large ships. The *Crown Majesty* with 800 passengers and the *Universe Explorer* with 726 are good examples of mid-sized vessels in Alaska. The *Crown Majesty* is a bit newer and more mainstream than the *Universe Explorer*, which specializes in 14-day sailings that cover almost all the ports in Alaska, plus showcasing lectures, slides and educational films about Alaska along with some traditional cruise ship fun and games.

Small ships are more intimate and generally offer a more close-up look at the scenery. They range from the super-deluxe 200-passenger *Seabourn Legend* to the simpler, more adventure-minded *Wilderness Explorer* from Glacier Bay Tours and Cruises, with a fleet of two-person sea kayaks on board, or Alaska Sightseeing's *Spirit of Discovery*, carrying only 54 passengers.

Small ships like the Spirit of '98 *can take passengers into narrow fjords.*

Vessels under 100 gross registry tons have been considered tour boats rather than cruise ships by the National Park Service, and so have been permitted into Glacier Bay without the special permits.

Generally, the smaller the ship the closer it can get to glaciers, waterfalls and coastlines where wildlife hangs out. There's **less regimentation on board**, with passengers usually sitting where and with whom they please at mealtime, which is at a single seating rather than two. On many of the small vessels, meals are served family-style.

Don't expect bingo, casinos, formal evenings or after-dinner entertainment (except on the *Seabourn Legend*, which has a small, discreet casino, some sophisticated, low-key entertainment and plenty of opportunities to dress up). Plan instead to take along jeans and windbreakers, sturdy footwear and binoculars.

Adventure vessels such as Clipper Cruises' *Yorktown Clipper* or Special Expeditions' *Sea Lion* and *Sea Bird* carry inflatable rubber landing craft to enable passengers to venture into secluded fjords, get close to glaciers and go ashore in wilderness areas.

Passengers board inflatable rubber landing craft to go exploring in the Pribilof Islands.

History

It was derided as "Seward's Folly" or "Seward's Icebox" when Secretary of State William H. Seward bought the 586,400 square miles that is Alaska from Russia in 1867 for $7 million, plus another $200,000 to clear the title and tie up all the loose ends. Seward had been tipped off to the area's potential riches by William Dall, who had crossed the interior of Alaska in 1865 to study the feasibility of laying telegraph cable to Europe across the Bering Strait and through Siberia.

The press and politicians alike thundered about "a dark deed done in the night," and described the new territory as "a dreary waste of glaciers, icebergs, white bears and walruses."

The transaction was so reviled that the House of Representatives balked and refused to pass the appropriations for it, and the embarrassed officials had to participate in the formal takeover ceremony in Sitka with the funds not yet paid. It was another year before the Russians got their money.

Russia claimed the territory in the early 18th century when the Danish explorer Vitus Bering, in the employ of Czar Peter the Great, discovered in 1741 the strait between Siberia and Alaska that bears his name. As things went in those days, he also got credit for "discovering" Alaska, although it was already inhabited, however sparsely, by Aleuts, Inuits and Athabascans who had crossed the land bridge from Siberia thousands of years before.

Most of its exploiters considered it a "cash cow" and wasted no time harvesting whatever riches they could take from it, enslaving and misusing the native people to harvest the spoils. The 18th century Russians depleted the Aleutian Islands of furs and almost killed off the Aleutian Indians as well, then moved south and started in on the Tlingits. Under Alexander Baranof, the Russians got as far south as northern California (Fort Ross was originally a Russian fur station) before they were stopped.

Fishermen and whalers came in from everywhere and starting decimating the whale population, then the salmon. But the disgruntled new American owners weren't really sure they'd made a good bargain until gold was discovered near present-day Juneau in 1880. The discovery of gold and the rush to claim it settled and shaped Alaska, particularly its Panhandle, as well as Canada's Yukon Territory, in the last two decades of the 19th century.

Costumed guides at Gold Creek help today's visitors pan gold in the "salted" stream.

The Juneau Gold Rush

They didn't build a city here; they found gold. That's the whole story of Alaska.

Ruth Allman, Alaska pioneer

After some gold had been found in British Columbia's Cariboo goldfields in 1858, prospectors continued to work the area, spreading north to the Yukon and Alaska. Richard Harris and Joe Juneau had come by canoe from Sitka, climbed up Snow Slide Gulch and were camped by the mouth of Gold Creek at Silver Bow Basin when they found gold and staked their claim.

The town grew up as a ramshackle collection of waterfront buildings on piers and wooden cabins straggling randomly up and down hillsides. Later, when the Klondike rush started, Juneau considered itself a notch or two above Johnny-come-lately Skagway.

Today's Juneau remembers yesterday's gold miners, who put Alaska on the map.

DID YOU KNOW?

The law prohibited importing liquor into Juneau in the 1880s, so steamships tied up at the dock, then tossed their illegal barrels of beer and whiskey overboard. Saloon keepers were waiting in a rowboat under the dock, "found" the barrels and towed them ashore. The rightful owners then paid the steamship operators.

The Gold Rush of '98

Canadian author and historian Pierre Berton called the Klondike "the last great gold rush." His own father had crossed the Chilkoot Trail in 1898, and the author spent his boyhood in Dawson.

The incredibly rich watershed of the Yukon River contained gold in dust, flakes and nuggets that had been ground up by the ceaseless erosion of the rocks and rivers, spread out across 330,000 miles of near-virgin land from British Columbia to the Bering Sea.

The lode along Bonanza Creek, south of present-day Dawson, had actually been discovered on Aug. 17, 1896, by George Carmack and his two Tagish Indian brothers-in-law, Skookum Jim and Tagish Charley. When word got around in the Yukon and Alaska, experienced miners flooded in from places such as Fortymile and Sixtymile, Circle City and Juneau.

By the time the winter ice melted and the first two ships from the Klondike, loaded with more than two million dollars in gold, brought the news to Seattle and San Francisco in the summer of 1897, all the best diggings had been spoken for. But the Stampeders didn't know this, and the people who stood ready to profit from their migration—outfitters, grubstakers, ship owners, uninformed "guidebook" writers and the like—were not about to tell them.

DID YOU KNOW?

The newly wealthy George Carmack ran away with a bawdy-house operator from Seattle and his Tagish wife Kate returned to Caribou Crossing with her brothers. Tagish Charley built the Caribou Hotel, where it was said he was his own best customer, particularly in the bar. He drowned when he fell off a bridge late one night.

The little town of Carcross (formerly Caribou Crossing) in the Yukon has a population of 183; this is St. Saviour's Church.

Getting There

GOLD! GOLD! GOLD! The steamer Portland passed up the (Puget) Sound with more than a ton of solid gold aboard.

Seattle Post-Intelligencer July 17, 1897

The hills were alive with the sound of tenderfoots during the Klondike Gold Rush of 1898. The Stampeders came from everywhere with their dreams and their supplies and their "sled dogs," often pet poodles and terriers dognapped from Seattle back yards.

A shipful of Norwegians sailed around the Horn, a boatload of Australians came across the Pacific, and a luxury yacht carrying British aristocrats, their valets, an orchestra and a French chef set out from England bound for adventure in the frozen north.

Even more unlikely, a dozen would-be prospectors sailed up the Klondike River from the icy Bering Sea, and a pair of Boston women announced a campaign to enlist a thousand women to cycle with them to Dawson.

The Klondike was in Canada's Yukon Territory, but the major access to the goldfields took travelers across the northern end of Alaska's Panhandle on their way into Canada.

It was, in the words of Pierre Berton, "just far enough away to be romantic and just close enough to be 'accessible.'" Footloose writers such as Jack London and Joaquin Miller went to chronicle the day-to-day life. Salesmen brought their inventories, gamblers their card skills, women their bodies for sale or their scrubboards and sadirons. And everyone intended to get rich.

DID YOU KNOW?

Even the eccentric and renowned inventor Nikola Tesla got into the Klondike action, attempting to market an X-ray machine that could detect gold in stream beds.

Scenery was regarded sourly by many of Alaska's early visitors. It was one more obstacle separating them from the gold they had come to gather. The Stampeders had set out from Seattle crowded into any vessel that would float—and some that didn't—sleeping 10 to a cabin and lashing their requisite ton of supplies to decks already teeming with nervous horses, oxen and dogs. Gold fever ran high.

They were in no mood to appreciate the voyage past the rugged evergreen slopes lining the thousand-mile Inside Passage to Skagway, or to marvel at the pistol-crack of a calving glacier tumbling tons of blue icebergs into the sea. All they wanted was to get to the Klondike, pick up enough nuggets to fill a burlap bag and go home as millionaires before Christmas.

The infamous Five Finger Rapids on the Yukon River scared many of the Stampeders.

...By Sea from San Francisco

It looked like a pile of yellow shelled corn.

Eyewitness account of the first Klondike gold to arrive in San Francisco aboard the Excelsior, July 15, 1897

The news of the Klondike gold strike electrified a nation in the throes of an economic recession, a country that seemed to be running out of the frontier adventure that had been its diet and salvation for a hundred years.

San Francisco had already weathered one gold rush in the 19th century, but that in no way diminished the excitement of the second, and every vessel the Stampeders could find was immediately pressed into service. Enough ships left San Francisco headed for points north to carry 100,000 people and six million pounds of freight.

...By Train to Seattle

Seattle has gone stark, staring mad on gold.

New York Herald, July 1897

A canny journalist named Erastus Brainerd cashed in quickly on the Klondike Gold Rush, publicizing Seattle as "the only place" Stampeders could adequately supply themselves for the north, and the city, which had been suffering a depression along with the rest of the Northwest, found a bonanza in Alaska outfitting.

DID YOU KNOW?

The veteran American prospector Ed Shieffelin, who made more than a million dollars from silver he discovered in Tombstone, Arizona, came up the Yukon from the Bering Sea in 1882 and found some gold. But fall was coming on, and the grizzled old man gave up and headed back to Arizona's sun without following up.

...By Ship from Vancouver

Hurrah for the Klondike!

Standard greeting exchanged on departures to the goldfields

Aboard one Canadian steamer which sailed from Vancouver carrying 500 would-be miners, the dining room could handle only 26 people at a time and so meals lasted seven hours. Hungry passengers took to lying in wait near the galley for the stewards and snatching handfuls of food from the trays.

...Skagway: Gateway to the North

An historic photo of Skagway around the turn of the century.

> Skagway was about the roughest place in the world. . . little better than a hell on earth.

Superintendent Samuel B. Steele
Northwest Mounted Police

The popular newspapers and periodicals of the day published trail maps to the Klondike that made the trip seem as easy as a stroll through Central Park. Stockbrokers and dentists, schoolteachers and poets, farmers and shoe clerks set out with high hopes, lugging huge burlap bags to carry home their bounty. A *cheechako* (tenderfoot) was an easy mark in those days, and any sheep ready to be fleeced was swiftly and smoothly accommodated in Skagway.

The grave of con man Soapy Smith outside Skagway was dug six feet away from the town's Pioneer Cemetery so as "not to desecrate the hallowed ground."

One Jefferson Randall "Soapy" Smith and his gang of 200 men ran con and shell games out on the trail and in the streets and saloons of Skagway, while in rows of cribs and the upstairs cubicles of the Red Onion Saloon (still standing today) ladies of the evening—Peahull Annie, Klondike Kate, the Belle of Skagway and Miss Kitty Faith—plied their trade at fees that ranged from $1 to $5.

For two rowdy and frantic boom years, thousands of eager gold-seekers crowded into the tent-and-board town, many of them unable to go on to Dawson and unwilling to turn around and go home.

Many Stampeders never made it to Dawson, stopping in Skagway instead.

Each person headed into the Klondike from Skagway over the infamous Chilkoot Trail was required by the Canadian government to carry a ton of supplies, and often the only way was on his own back a painful 100 pounds at a time, caching the first lot at the top of the 1200 icy steps of the "Golden Staircase," then going back for the second lot, and so on. One miner said he walked 1500 miles from Skagway to Bennett Lake, a distance of only 45 miles. The wealthier hired the Tlingit and Chilkoot Indians to carry their gear for the fixed price of one dollar a pound. The photographs from the period immortalize the endless chain of men, like an army of black ants, struggling up the "Golden Staircase" through the snow.

A simple hiking trail marker designates the infamous Chilkoot Trail.

DID YOU KNOW?

Outfits for one man and one year in the Klondike as advertised in the Chicago Daily Tribune included 70 pounds of clothing, 1200 pounds of groceries, 200 pounds of hardware and camping equipment, 20 pounds of armament and two pounds of medicines. The total weighed 1492 pounds and cost $264.

...Whitehorse

A bunch of the boys were whooping it up in the Malamute Saloon . . .

**Robert W. Service
"The Shooting of Dan McGrew"**

Robert W. Service, long remembered as the bard of the Klondike, wasn't actually there during the gold rush years but arrived in 1904. He was working as a bank teller in Whitehorse in 1905 when he was asked to recite something at a church concert, preferably something he wrote himself.

"It was a Saturday night," he recalled later, "and from the various bars I heard the sound of revelry."

The first line popped into his mind, and he headed into the quiet of his teller's cage to work. The startled night guard drew his revolver and shot at the mysterious figure but fortunately missed. And "with the sensation of a bullet whizzing past my head, and a detonation ringing in my ears, the ballad was achieved."

At a replica of Robert W. Service's cabin in Dawson City, an actor presents readings of his poems.

Today in Whitehorse you can often hear Service's poems recited between energetic dance-hall numbers at the popular "Frantic Follies," a vaudevillian re-creation of the gold rush days replete with ricky-tick piano, banjos, fiddles and hoary old jokes that verge on double-entendre.

The sternwheeler *Klondike* is tied up on the banks of the Yukon, serving as a museum, and not far away are several whimsical log cabin "skyscrapers." At the MacBride Museum is the original Lake LeBarge cabin of Whitehorse freighter and prospector Sam McGee, who gave Service permission to use his name in a poem.

...Dawson

The Parks Canada historical recreation of Dawson during its days of glory is ongoing.

This isn't the end of the world, but you can see it from here.

Popular saying around Dawson

Here, where the Klondike River meets the Yukon, on a muddy meadow where moose browsed, a tent city turned into a mining camp, a mining camp became "the Paris of the North," where 30,000 residents could do or buy anything they could afford. And less than 10 years after the first tents were erected, the town sank quietly into oblivion. A few people stayed on; today perhaps a thousand live there, most of them only in summer.

In 1960, Parks Canada began a painstaking restoration of Dawson's buildings; that work continues as funds and properties become available. But Dawson is not a museum, dusting off its exhibits for guided tours. It remains a tough and stubborn town that refused to die.

Two weary buildings in Dawson City await restoration.

The Winter of '97–'98

By the time the first sizable contingent arrived in the autumn of 1897, Lake Bennett, which lay on the route from Skagway to Dawson, was already frozen over. Before the winter was out, some 30,000 people had set up the largest tent city the world had ever known. All winter long, they built clumsy boats and rafts, ready to head down the Yukon River to Dawson as soon as the ice broke up. The migration began on May 29, and within 48 hours all 7124 boats, loaded with 30 million pounds of food, had set out for Dawson.

DID YOU KNOW?

Greek-born theater tycoon Alexander Pantages, who arrived in the Yukon unable to speak a word of English, worked as a waiter until he began his $15 million empire with the Orpheum Theatre in Dawson.

The restored Palace Grand Theatre in Dawson presents musical revues about the Klondike in summer.

...And On to Fairbanks

O God, please show me the way out.

> **Gambler-banker Silent Sam Bonnifeld,
> kneeling on the snow in front of his failed bank.**

In 1902, when the Klondike excitement had quieted down a little, a prospector named Felix Pedro discovered gold in the Tanana Valley near present-day Fairbanks, and a new rush was on. The prospectors and gamblers from Dawson hurried west to the new boomtown, rose the crest of the newest wave, then crashed in the depression that followed.

A typical Alaska cabin with raised food cache in the rear is on display in Fairbanks at Alaskaland.

POSTSCRIPT

While 100,000 people set out for the gold fields of the Klondike, only some 30,000 to 40,000 actually reached Dawson. Of that number, just 15,000 to 20,000 even bothered to look for gold. Some 4,000 found gold, 300 of them enough to be considered rich, but only 50 of those managed to hold on to their wealth. By 1901, the combined goldfields of the Yukon Territory had yielded $50 million.

Klondike Gold Rush Historical Park

EAVESDROPPING

"There's still plenty of gold down there—they haven't even scratched the minerals yet. But everybody wants a nine-to-five job. Mining is hard work."

Ruth Allman, Alaska pioneer

Alaska Today

Historic Kirmse's Jewelry and Curios in Skagway first opened in 1897 in a tent; this store dates from the turn of the century.

While modern-day prospectors can still find places in Alaska to pan for gold (most often tourist attractions "salted" with a few flecks of color), today's travelers are more intent on riches of a different sort—the gold of a midnight sunset off a ship's rail in Juneau; the jangling echoes of tinny pianos, laughing dancehall girls and miners' hobnailed boots clomping along the wooden sidewalks of Skagway; the silver icons of old Russia in Sitka's onion-domed church; the silken fur and lustrous eyes of a baby seal on an ice floe; the flash of a silver salmon struggling upstream to spawn.

Today's luxurious cruise ships bear no resemblance to the spartan, over-crowded vessels the Stampeders boarded, but the land itself, with its rocky islands rich with wildlife and pristine wilderness, its gigantic fields of ice grinding inexorably against the mountains, remains much as they first saw it. In such a stupendous vastness, modern man has scarcely left a mark.

"People from the Lower 48 are used to seeing Alaska and Hawaii reduced to the same size in identical little boxes on the side of the U.S. map," Alaskans like to point out. "They don't know how big Alaska really is."

DID YOU KNOW?

Although only five per cent of Alaska–28,000 square miles–is encased in ice, the state contains more than half the world's glaciers.

A Glacier Glossary

Hanging glacier	*a glacier set high on a mountain wall in a U-shaped valley.*
Calving	*when enormous pieces of ice fall off a glacier into the sea.*
Icefall	*a mass of rapidly moving glacier ice hanging over a cliff or mountainside.*
Moraines	*dirt and rock picked up by the glacier as it moves downhill; a terminal moraine is the debris pushed downhill and found at the foot of the glacier.*
Ogives	*wave patterns formed at the base of a glacier when it moves over steep declinations in its bed.*
Crevasse	*a fracture in the glacier surface, indicating stress from below on the moving ice.*
Glacier flour	*finely ground rock.*
Glacier milk	*glacier flour suspended in water, turning it milky.*
Firn	*hardening grains of snow turning into ice.*
Ice sizzle	*the loud popping of bubbles when glaciers or icebergs melt.*
Iceworms	*worms which lay their eggs in freezing temperatures between snow and glacier ice and burrow more deeply into the ice the colder it gets.*

Great Galloping Glaciers!

These mighty rivers of living ice surge through the coastal mountains toward the sea at a rate that alternately accelerates and slows to some mysterious rhythm. As they move, they carve and sculpt the landscape, sometimes gouging it dramatically. One early naturalist, Louis Agassiz, called them "God's Great Plough."

If you gave awards to the finest in Alaska and Canada, the following might be the Grammys of glaciers:

The Athabasca Glacier on Alberta's Icefields Highway has receded during the last decade.

Athabasca

A "drive-in glacier" along the roadside on Alberta's Icefields Highway between Banff and Jasper, part of the Columbia Icefield.

Black Rapids

Famous for having advanced four miles in only three months back in 1936, the Black Rapids, nicknamed "The Galloping Glacier," came close to engulfing the Richardson Highway in central Alaska.

Columbia

The largest glacier in Prince William Sound, more than 40 miles long and 440 square miles in size, is predicted to retreat 20 miles in the next 50 years.

Grand Pacific

One of 15 active tidewater glaciers in Glacier Bay, at the north central part of the bay, and notable for willy-nilly receding back into Canada, then advancing into Alaska again.

Hubbard

The longest tidewater glacier in North America, 76 feet long with a six-mile-wide ice cliff face, is located near the head of Yakutat Bay.

Johns Hopkins

One of nine glaciers on Johns Hopkins Inlet, it has an awesome icefront 200 feet high.

LaPerouse

Located in the Gulf of Alaska's Fairweather Range, this is the only tide-water glacier in Alaska whose calving drops directly into the Pacific.

Le Conte

Much admired by John Muir, this glacier starred in the 1960 Richard Burton film *Ice Palace* and frequently contributes ice to the fish packing industry in nearby Petersburg.

Malaspina

Heard about a diamond as big as the Ritz? This is a glacier as big as Rhode Island.

Margerie

This glacier in Glacier Bay's Tarr Inlet calves frequently, to the delight of camera-carrying cruise passengers and the kittiwakes who nest nearby, waiting for the splashing ice to stir up some fish for their lunch.

Mendenhall

The star of the Juneau Icefield, Mendenhall is often called the "drive-in glacier" for its accessibility.

Muir

This highly active glacier at the northeastern end of Glacier Bay was named for renowned writer John Muir, who lived in a cabin at its base in 1899 before it receded more than 18 miles.

Portage, an easy-to-reach "drive-in glacier," is Alaska's most-visited attraction.

Portage

Another roadside "drive-in glacier," the Portage is the most-visited attraction in Alaska, located by Portage Lake a short drive from Anchorage.

Victoria

The elegant glacier at Chateau Lake Louise is still the subject of debate about whether it was named for the daughter of Queen Victoria or the wife of the governor of Alberta.

The Icefields Highway

Several cruise companies offer optional journeys into Alberta and the Canadian Rockies, including one self-drive version by RV from Alaska Highway Cruises.

The monumental, rambling Banff Springs Hotel, even amid the awesome mountains, still takes your breath away.

Chateau Lake Louise wraps itself around the most exquisite view in the world. A cold turquoise lake, its edges still touched with snow, is cupped in a semicircle of rocky mountains, with a long tongue of glacier in the center upstage area and a trim of dark evergreens delineating the sides.

The Canadian Rockies and the Banff/Lake Louise area is especially glorious during the spring and fall, when roads are less clogged with tour buses and you have the best chances of spotting wildlife.

Rocky Mountain sheep are often spotted beside the Icefields Highway.

Not long ago, we drove the Icefields Highway between Banff and Jasper in early June, and by 9 a.m. had seen a small black bear standing by the roadside near Rampart Creek. Not 10 minutes later, we photographed a grizzly (brown) bear in a roadside meadow, eating the new green grass with a hearty appetite. Between mouthfuls, he would gaze at us with a puzzled look, then lower his head again to tear out mouthfuls of the grass.

Four big-horned sheep were next, again standing by the roadway, munching from leafy low green bushes and looking shaggy and motheaten after the long winter. Glossy black ravens as big as small dogs swooped overhead, and deer crossed the road in front of us.

DID YOU KNOW?

The term "hooch" to apply to distilled alcohol came from the Hootchinoo Indians of British Columbia's Admiralty Island, who were taught by an army deserter how to make it from molasses and sugar, and threw themselves wholeheartedly into its production.

*A rare close-up sighting of a brown (grizzly) bear, hungry from the winter's
hibernation, by the road in early June.*

Talking Alaskan

Sourdough — *anyone who's been in Alaska longer than one season, as in "sour on Alaska without enough dough to get out."*

Outside — *anywhere that isn't Alaska; generally, the lower 48 states.*

Native — *not just anyone born in Alaska, but only those with Eskimo, Aleut or Indian blood.*

Cheechako — *tenderfoot or newcomer.*

Musher — *a dog team driver.*

The Bush — *any place reached by plane instead of road or Alaska ferry.*

Permafrost — *the permanently frozen subsoil that covers much of the state.*

Frost heave — *a buckled section of roadway broken and thrown up or sunk during the winter freeze.*

The Big Break-up — *the exact moment each spring when the frozen Nenana River begins its annual thaw; the time is recorded by a tripod set in the river with a line attached to a clock—when the tripod tips over, the line stops the clock.*

The Ice Pool — *the big cash prize awarded to the winner who guesses the exact minute; only Alaskans can enter.*

Black Ice — *the thin, hard-to-see slick coating on highways in cold weather.*

Ice Fog — *a mix of ice crystals and auto exhausts that creates a thick, white fog.*

Ann-wahr (ANWR)   *Arctic National Wildlife Refuge, a previously protected area that some*
politicians want to see opened to oil development.

Lodge   *any establishment with beds and/or food available for sale, most often*
a rudimentary roadside cafe with a straggle of cabins in back and gas
tanks out front, and a cashier/waitress who also sells fishing licenses,
pumps gas, makes bed and does the "home cooking" in her spare
time.

CRUISING TO ALASKA'S AND BRITISH COLUMBIAS'S TOP PORTS PLUS THEIR RATINGS

The following are the most popular ports in Alaska and British Columbia and are rated based on the **port's appeal to the day visitor from a cruise ship**. We take into consideration the following factors:

Access to town from the port.

Courtesy or attitude of locals.

Interesting shore excursions.

Access to local attractions.

Shopping.

Cultural opportunities.

Photo opportunities.

Each port is rated from one to five stars. Our port star ratings are based on the needs of a day visitor rather than a vacationer who may spend several days in this area, and ratings are affected by visitor security and local politics as well as safety on the streets and accessibility of attractions.

★★★★★ A great port of call for a day, with plenty to do on tour or on your own.

★★★★ An appealing port that offers well-planned shore excursions and has some attractive shopping and independent sightseeing options.

★★★ A port that offers a variety of traditional shore excursions and some on-your-own things to do ashore.

★★   Perhaps not as polished and scenic as you
                    would like, but you can find something in-
                    teresting to do.

★   You may want to stay on the ship.

In addition to the rating, the major attractions of each port will be depicted in Fielding Rating Icons (see front of book). Also given at the head of each port listing is the local language and currency, whether English is generally spoken and U.S. dollars accepted, and the best way to get to town from the pier. Shore excursion price estimates are reflected in $signs.

$ Under $20

$$ $20–$50

$$$ Over $50

On inland "ports" reached by optional overland excursions or remote and exotic areas visited by expeditions, we omit the ratings and icons in favor of a general description of the place.

RATING THE PORTS OF ALASKA AND BRITISH COLUMBIA

The city of Anchorage, for all its northern exposure, has surprisingly classic restaurants; here, Simon & Seafort's.

Anchorage, Alaska ★★★★

Language:	**English**	*English Spoken?:*	**Yes**
Currency:	**US$**	*US$ok?:*	**Yes**
To town:	**Walk; shuttle from Seward**		

Only a few ships actually sail into the city of Anchorage. Most Gulf of Alaska cruises disembark passengers in the **port of Seward** (or occasionally Whit-

tier) for an overland transfer to Anchorage. For all its northern exposure, Anchorage is a surprisingly urbane city. In fact, Alaskans call it "Los Anchorage" and quip that it's only 40 miles from Alaska. **Shore excursions** include a bus tour down Turnagain Arm to Portage Glacier, one of the state's most accessible ice-choked lakes ($$) or a city tour ($$) that includes the landscape of Earthquake Park, tilted and broken in the disastrous 1964 quake. But the top option is a two- or three-day cruise extension to Fairbanks ($$$) aboard a **luxury dome railway car** (both Westours and Princess Tours operate them daily) and an **overnight stopover at Denali National Park** and a bus ride into the wilderness to glimpse moose, mountain goats, Dall sheep, perhaps even brown bears. (Private vehicles are not allowed on the road into the park in summer.) Getting a glimpse of majestic Mt. McKinley itself is a bit rarer; park rangers estimate one clear day out of three as a rule. On your own in Anchorage, check out the art museum and the Imaginarium science museum with its polar bear den and Northern Lights exhibit. If you want to eat out, try the Marx Brothers Cafe, Simon & Seafort's for seafood or the Double Musky Inn at Girdwood.

Haines, Alaska ★★★

Language:	**English**	*English Spoken?:*	**Yes**
Currency:	**US$**	*US$ ok?:*	**Yes**
To town:	**Walk**		

Chilkat dancers at Fort Seward in Haines present a program of tribal dances.

Haines is **a sleeper as Alaskan cruise ports go** because few ships call here, but this charming little town, the former Fort William H. Seward from 1904,

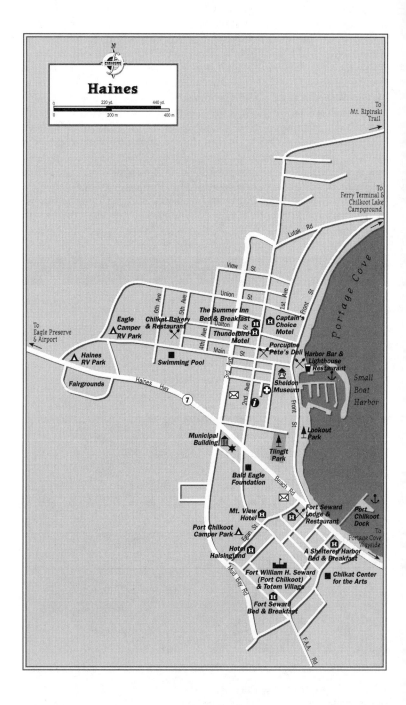

gives a great insight on the real Alaska. It's also one of the few towns in southeastern Alaska that can be reached by road from the Alaska Highway via British Columbia Route 3 and Alaska's Route 4 over Chilkat Pass. If you're lucky, **a person costumed as an eagle will meet your cruise ship** at the pier, tipping you off that this is **one of the best places in Alaska to see eagles**. Long a stronghold of the Chilkat Tlingit Indians, Haines is still the place to see **the best of Chilkat culture**, especially on the evenings when the local dance troupe performs ($$–$$$) inside a replica tribal house. Often the dancing is preceded by an outdoor salmon bake, with red salmon grilled over an open alderwood fire and served, along with a salad bar and barbecue ribs, in the late-evening sunshine. The Southeast Alaska State Fair also takes place here in mid-August. Other Haines shore excursions include a city and cultural tour that includes the Sheldon Museum and the Alaska Indian Arts Center ($$), a **Haines glacier flightseeing tour** ($$$) that includes a view of Mt. Fairweather, the highest peak in Southeast Alaska and a three-hour **float trip or jet boat tour to the Bald Eagle Preserve** ($$$). Do-it-yourselfers will enjoy a bicycle tour that covers six miles in a mild to moderately strenuous fashion ($$) or a canoe journey along the Chilkat River with a good chance for eagle-spotting ($$$).

Homer, Alaska   ★ ★ ★

Language:	**English**	*English Spoken?:*	**Yes**
Currency:	**US$**	*US$ok?:*	**Yes**
To town:	**Shuttle bus, taxi**		

Homer's Salty Dawg is one of Alaska's funkiest famous bars.

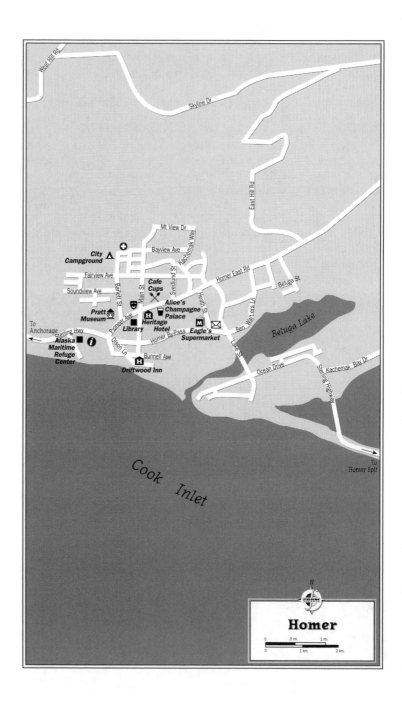

Homer

Familiar to many Americans as the town where humorist Tom Bodett settled to broadcast his radio show and Motel 6 commercials, Homer is also **an artists' community**. Cruise ships dock at a new port facility off Homer Spit, a five-mile sandbar in Kachemak Bay, and transfer passengers into town by tour bus. The city tour ($$) is the basic **shore excursion** here, generally **a bus ride from one art gallery or homemade jam shop to another**. Sometimes buses go to the top of Baycrest Hill for the vista of Kachemak Bay or stop at Pratt Museum to see Aleut, Russian and Indian artifacts. Helicopter tours ($$$) take a limited number of passengers aloft, four at a time, to see the "river of ice" snowfields and perhaps, conditions permitting, land on Droshin Glacier. The most colorful spot in town, and far too crowded on cruise ship days with crew members and passengers, is the famous **Salty Dawg Saloon**, a log cabin on the spit with a lighthouse tower above it. Scarcely big enough for dozen drinkers at a time, the landmark is notable for surviving both the town's big fire of 1907 and the earthquake of 1964. **Best buys** include jars of Alaska Wild Berry Products' jams and jellies, watercolors or oil paintings, canned or smoked Alaskan salmon and lighter-than-air scarves, stoles or caps made from **qiviut, the soft, feathery underwool of the musk ox**, expensive but worth it for its light weight and warmth.

Juneau, Alaska ★★★

Language:	**English**	English Spoken?:	**Yes**
Currency:	**US$**	US$ok?:	**Yes**
To town:	**Walk**		

The Gold Creek Mine gold-panning shore excursion sets out from Juneau.

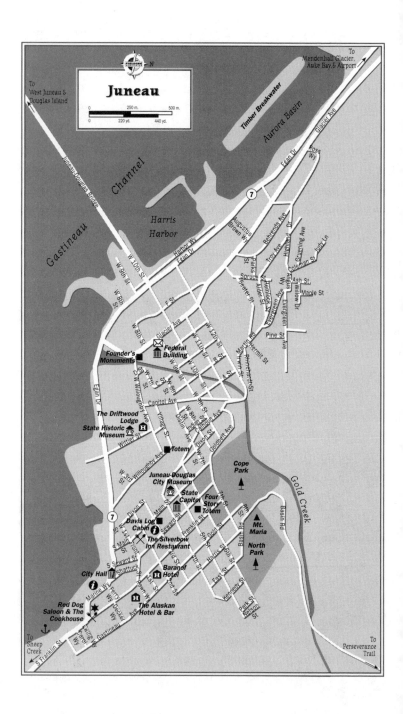

Juneau remains **Alaska's capital city**, even though it has no roads leading into it. The setting is striking with the featureless cement high-rise government buildings clumped klutzily against a solid backdrop of green-covered mountains. Ships dock at the edge of town, where it's an easy stroll to **the famous Red Dog Saloon** with its sawdust-strewn floor. You could spend a bundle on the **shore excursions** here, with six of the options topping the $100 mark. Options include a Mendenhall Glacier and city tour by motorcoach ($$) or van ($$$), an all-you-can eat salmon bake ($$), a Mendenhall Glacier float trip ($$$), a very popular flight to remote Taku Lodge ($$$), a float-plane flight "back to the ice age" ($$$), a glacier helicopter flight with a walk on the glacier ($$$), gold-panning ($$), sportfishing ($$$), the musical Lady Lou Revue ($), Taku Glacier and Scenic Wilderness cruise ($$$), kayaking ($$$) and the old duffer's ultimate tour, nine holes of **golf with a Mendenhall Glacier view** from every hole ($$$). The bottom line is, Mendenhall is called **the "drive-in glacier"** because it's an easy 10-minute cab ride from town if you don't want to bother with a tour. On your own in town, walk over to the fine Alaska Historical Museum, take a carriage ride or tour the historic Wickersham House. Get free maps at the Davis Log Cabin on Third Street.

Ketchikan, Alaska   ★ ★ ★ ★

Language:	**English**	*English Spoken?:*	**Yes**
Currency:	**US$**	*US$ok?:*	**Yes**
To town:	**Walk or tender**		

Ketchikan brags about its cloudy weather, but the sun is always shining when we're there; this is the famous Dolly's bordello on Creek Street.

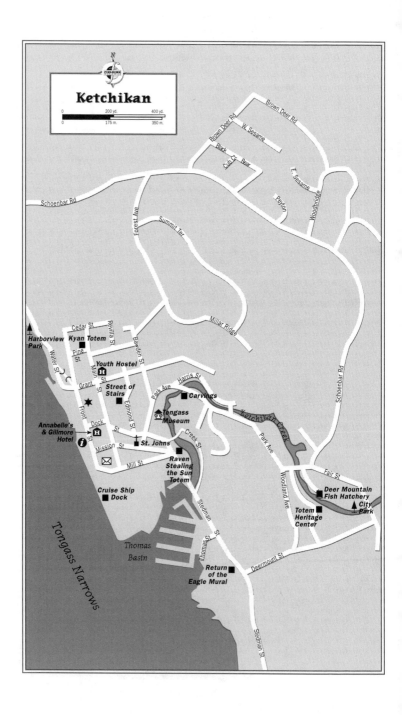

Ships either dock right in town in Ketchikan's pretty harbor, filled with fishing boats and framed by snow-capped mountains, or anchor and tender into the dock. While the town has a reputation for being rainy and overcast, we've found it bright and sunny on almost all our visits. **Totem poles** are the big attractions here—it claims to be the totem pole capital of the world—and shore excursions offered include a town and totem tour ($$), a visit to a **traditional Tsimshian village** ($$), a very popular flight to Misty Fjords ($$$), an historical waterfront cruise ($$), mountain lake canoeing ($$$), kayaking ($$$), sportfishing ($$$), jetboat excursion to Salmon Falls with lunch ($$$) and a **mountain bike tour** ($$$). The small ships of Alaska Sightseeing/ Cruise West also offer a **delightful walking tour** of Ketchikan ($) with Native American Joe Williams, who'll tell you a lot about Tlingit culture. You could also take a cab on your own to **Totem Bight State Historical Park**, 11 miles north of town, to go inside a hand-carved ceremonial house. Walking around on your own in town, you can visit the Totem Heritage Center and Nature Path, then cut across to the Deer Mountain Hatchery and Salmon Falls fish ladder at Ketchikan Creek, where you'll learn **more than you ever wanted to know about spawning salmon**. Visitors always go to Dolly's House ($) on Creek Street, which operated as a brothel until the 1950s, and a sign points out it's "the only place in the world where both the fish and the fishermen went upstream to spawn." Tourist shopping is centered around **Creek Street** and **Saxman Village**, the latter a good place to find **Native American crafts** and the world's largest collection of standing totem poles. On our last visit here, we took the outdoor elevator up the hill from town to the handsome **Westmark Cape Fox Lodge** and had a delicious lunch, as well as a great overview of the harbor. The new **Southeast Alaska Visitor Center**, just across from the pier, has some excellent exhibits of Northwest Indian life (free, optional film screening $1).

Nome, Alaska ★ ★ ★

Language:	**English**	*English Spoken?:*	**Yes**
Currency:	**US$**	*US$ok?:*	**Yes**
To town:	**Shuttle bus**		

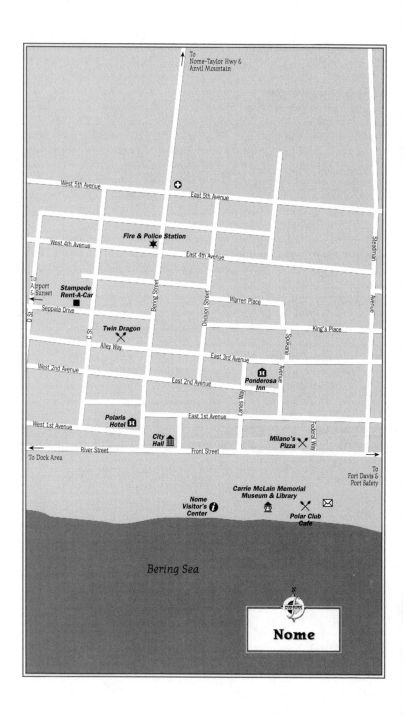

Nome

Expeditioners milling about in front of Nome's Nugget Inn.

Nome is one of Alaska's legendary towns, notable as the end of **the classic Iditarod Trail Dog Sled Race** held every March over 1100 miles of icy track from Anchorage. The course follows a dogsled mail carrier route from 1910, and it commemorates the mushers who carried anti-diptheria serum to the remote town in 1925 after an outbreak of the deadly disease. Passengers don't visit Nome on any of the usual large ship Alaska cruises, but only aboard small expedition vessels that are usually heading into or out of the Northwest Passage or to the Russian Far East or the islands of the Bering Strait. Famously funky, Nome is the kind of place you wouldn't be surprised to run into Jimmy Hoffa, Judge Crater or Amelia Earhart, maybe even Elvis if you sit around the Nugget Inn bar long enough. If you stay awhile, you can **catch a summer dogsled demonstration run on the beach (yes, Nome has a beach!) or try your hand at gold panning**. If you're offered a city or area tour here, you'll probably be boarding a yellow school bus.

Petersburg, Alaska ★★

Language:	**English**	*English Spoken?:*	**Yes**
Currency:	**US$**	*US$ok?:*	**Yes**
To town:	**Walk, shuttle**		

By all means try to be out on deck when your vessel maneuvers its way through the Wrangell Narrows as you enter or leave Petersburg. A Norwegian fishing town founded at the turn of the century, the quiet town has stuck to its workaday ways despite its **beautiful setting against glacier-covered mountains**. A steady business of fish canning and fish packing thrives instead

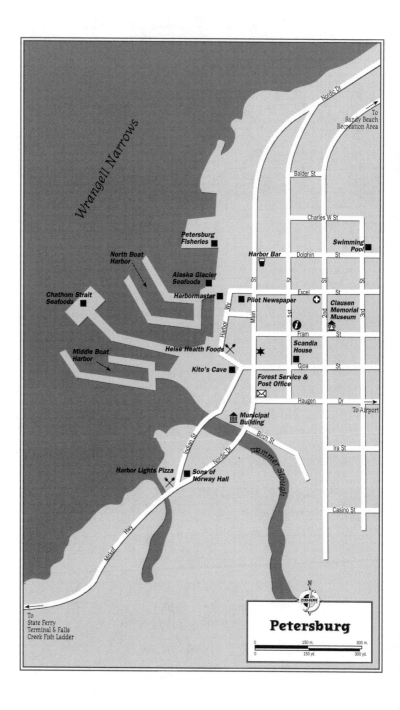

Wrangell Narrows

To
Sandy Beach
Recreation Area

Nordic Dr

Balder St

Charles W St

Petersburg
Fisheries

Harbor Bar

Swimming
Pool

North Boat
Harbor

Dolphin   St

Alaska Glacier
Seafoods

Excel   St

Chathom Strait
Seafoods

Harbormaster

Pilot Newspaper

Clausen
Memorial
Museum

Harbor Hwy

Main St

1st St

2nd St

3rd St

Fram   St

Helse Health Foods

Scandia
House

Middle Boat
Harbor

Kito's Cave

Gjoa   St

Forest Service &
Post Office

Haugen   Dr

To Airport

Municipal
Building

Birch St

Ira St

Indian St

Nordic Dr

Hammer Slough

Harbor Lights Pizza

Sons of
Norway Hall

Casino St

Mitkof Hwy

To
State Ferry
Terminal & Falls
Creek Fish Ladder

N

FIELDING

Petersburg

| 0 | 150 m. | 300 m. |
| 0 | 150 yd. | 300 yd. |

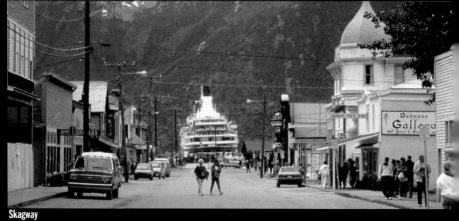

Skagway

Flightseeing Alaska view

Ft. Seward, Haines, Alaska

of gold mining or oil. The availability of ice from nearby glaciers, including LeConte, was instrumental in the choice of the town site back in 1897 by Peter Buschmann, town founder. The Sons of Norway Hall is the center of the town's social life, and a Little Norway festival is celebrated in mid-May every year. It's also **a great place to spot eagles** or buy Scandinavian souvenirs, and you can usually see some Stellar's sea lions hanging out around the harbor. Sing Lee Alley in Hammer Slough is a particularly colorful spot for photographers who like weathered houses, fishing boats, nets and crab pots. It's named for a Chinese businessman who was murdered in the 1930s. Local marshals were implicated in the killing, and the town marshal himself was murdered. The federal marshal fled town and soon was found dead in Seattle—which is much worse than sleepless in Seattle.

Seward, Alaska   ★ ★

Language:	**English**	*English Spoken?:*	**Yes**
Currency:	**US$**	*US$ok?:*	**Yes**
To town:	**Shuttle bus, longish walk**		

Colorful Seward barely survived the 1964 earthquake, which destroyed 90 percent of the town.

Seward is the most frequently used port for Anchorage on seven-day itineraries to and from Vancouver, so if you're signed up for a Gulf of Alaska itinerary, you're sure to see Seward. It's a fairly nondescript town surrounded by spectacular scenery that includes **Kenai Fjords National Park** with its fjords, sea lion colonies and bird rookeries at Resurrection Bay. Shore excursions here include **flightseeing trips over the Kenai Peninsula** ($$$), a float trip

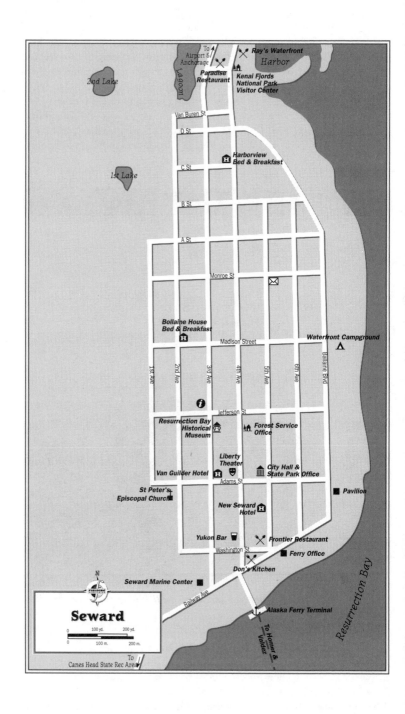

Seward

and salmon bake on the Kenai River ($$$), a sled-dog demonstration and visit to Exit Glacier ($–$$), and a bus tour to Chugach National Forest and Moose Pass ($$). If you want to walk around on your own, drop by the public library to catch a showing of *Seward Is Burning*, **shots of the 1964 Good Friday earthquake** that destroyed 90 percent of the town. The Resurrection Bay Historical Museum also includes earthquake artifacts. The misnamed Millionaires' Row designates bungalows and cottages built just after the turn of the century by railway officials and bankers. The hill behind the town, Mt. Marathon, is the scene of a famous Fourth of July footrace. August brings the even more renowned Silver Salmon Derby; the winner gets **$10,000 for the biggest salmon caught**.

Sitka, Alaska ★ ★ ★

Language:	**English**	*English Spoken?:*	**Yes**
Currency:	**US$**	*US$ok?:*	**Yes**
To town:	**Tender from ship**		

Sitka was once the capital of Russian America; here a statue of a gold miner at the Pioneer's Home.

Sitka's big story is that it was once **the capital of Russian America**, and the town still retains more than a little of its exotic accent, notably the pretty onion-domed **St. Michael Russian Orthodox Cathedral**, rebuilt in 1966 after a fire, and the **New Archangel Russian Dancers**, a group of local women who perform folk dances. Shore excursions include a town tour and dance performance ($$), a motor launch cruise to Silver Bay with a chance of spotting eagles and old gold mines ($$), a visit to the eagle center and historic tour

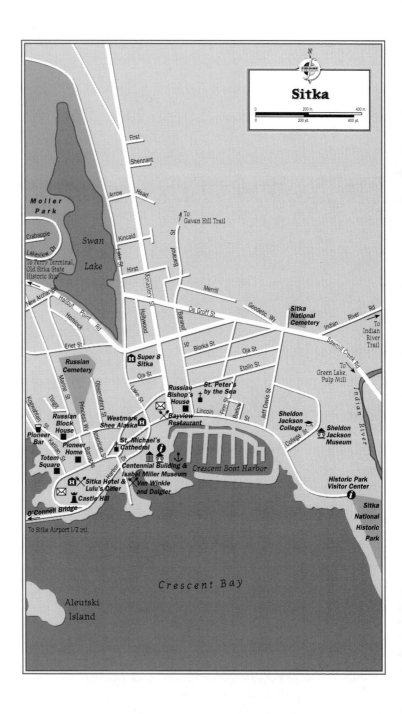

($$), a sea otter and wildlife quest ($$), kayaking ($$), sportfishing ($$$) and a catamaran wildlife-spotting cruise ($$$). But if none of these excursion ideas thrill you, Sitka is a very easy town to stroll around on your own, looking inside the cathedral at the **original icons**, an 18th-century jeweled chalice, a 19th-century silverbound Bible and tablecloths hand-embroidered by the wife of the last Russian governor of Alaska. There's an old Russian cemetery, the restored Bishop's House, a replica of the blockhouse and, most beguiling of all, **Sitka National Historic Park**, where you can wander through an evergreen forest on cushiony brown pine needles past some splendid standing totem poles. In the visitor center, craftsmen demonstrate the making of Haida button-ornament red capes and Tlingit totems. The Sheldon Jackson Museum is between the park and town.

Skagway, Alaska ★★★★

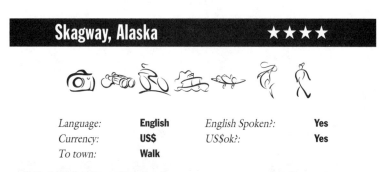

Language:	**English**	*English Spoken?:*	**Yes**
Currency:	**US$**	*US$ok?:*	**Yes**
To town:	**Walk**		

The White Pass & Yukon Railway is a turn-of-the-century narrow-gauge train that takes you up to the White Pass the same way the miners went to the Klondike in '98.

Our favorite shore excursion here is the **White Pass & Yukon Railway** ($$$), a journey by vintage narrow-gauge train up the Dead Horse Pass, but big spenders also have a shot at historical Skagway by motorcoach ($$)—**this is really a waste of money unless you have trouble walking, because the park rangers give free historic walking tours of town**—a bus tour to White Pass summit

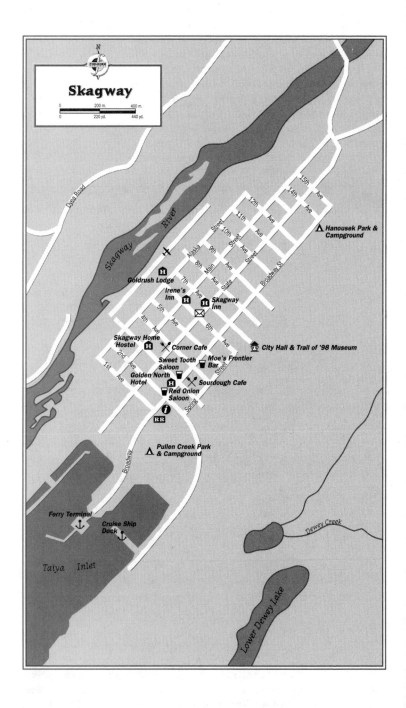

and a gold rush trail camp ($$), a streetcar tour of Skagway ($$), a van tour to White Pass Summit ($$), a helicopter lift to the Chilkoot Trail and a glacier walk ($$$), an overflight of Glacier Bay ($$$), a bus and walking flora and fauna tour ($$$), a glacier flightseeing and bald eagle float trip ($$$), sportfishing ($$$), a mountain bike tour ($$$), a glacier hike and train tour in Tongass Forest ($$$) and a deluxe helicopter tour ($$$). We have to confess we liked Skagway better in the old days before the main street was paved and helicopter tours roared off every few minutes from the field between town and the cruise ship dock, but it's still a terrific port of call. Gold rush historians fall in love with this colorful town where 100,000 would-be miners paused on their way to the Klondike to be fleeced by con man Soapy Smith and his gang. Today most of the town is included in the **Klondike Gold Rush National Historic Park**, and park rangers show **free films and slide shows and conduct free historic walking tours** for interested visitors. Impeccably restored buildings make Skagway look today very much the way it did at the turn of the century.

Valdez, Alaska

Language:	**English**	*English Spoken?:*	**Yes**
Currency:	**US$**	*US$ok?:*	**Yes**
To town:	**Shuttle or taxi**		

Valdez calls itself the "Switzerland of America."

Valdez is synonymous with oil for many people, first its connection as **terminus of the 800-mile Trans-Alaska pipeline** and then, from 1989, as the center of cleanup activities for the **11-million gallon *Exxon Valdez* oil spill**. Unless you would find the pipeline tour riveting—and some people do—**you might want**

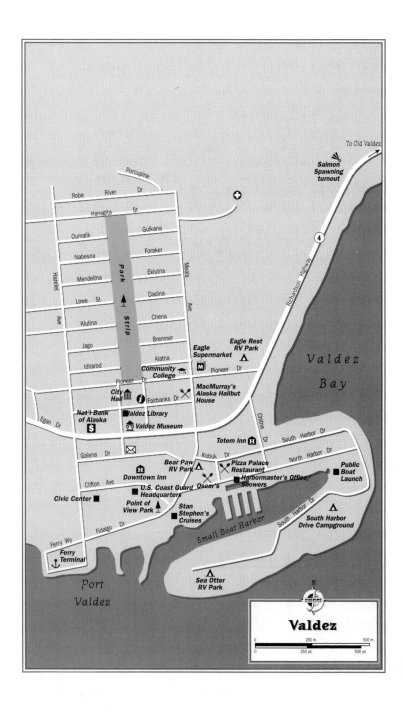

to stay onboard. Today's Valdez, despite its beautiful setting against the Chugach mountains, is singularly lacking in charm. The town itself was rebuilt in a different location after the devastating earthquake of 1964 destroyed virtually every building. The major shore excursion here is a bus trip to the pipeline terminus ($$), which usually includes a look at the terminal complex, oil storage tank farm, ballast treatment facility and perhaps the sight of a tanker taking on oil. Participants may not leave the bus except at one viewpoint and smoking is not permitted. Other options here are a tour to Thompson Pass and the Worthington Glacier ($$), rafting in Keystone Canyon ($$) and a helicopter tour of Prince William Sound ($$$). On your own in town, you might want to wander into the Valdez Museum to see pipeline models, earthquake and mining exhibits, or take a look from the **Salmon Spawning Viewpoint** on Crooked Creek, where you can observe the fish spawning in July and August.

Wrangell, Alaska ★

Language:	**English**	*English Spoken?:*	**Yes**
Currency:	**US$**	*US$ok?:*	**Yes**
To town:	**Walk**		

If you're on one of the few cruises that calls at Wrangell, the local citizenry will get themselves up in period costume and come down to meet your ship.

Costumed greeters sometimes meet the few cruise ships that call regularly at Wrangell. The area's Stikine River is one of the **fastest-moving rivers in North America**, so a day-visitor highlight here is the shore excursion on the Stikine River Jet Boat ($$$). Other options here are a botanical walking tour ($) and a city tour ($$). **Take your umbrella**, because Wrangell is often cool

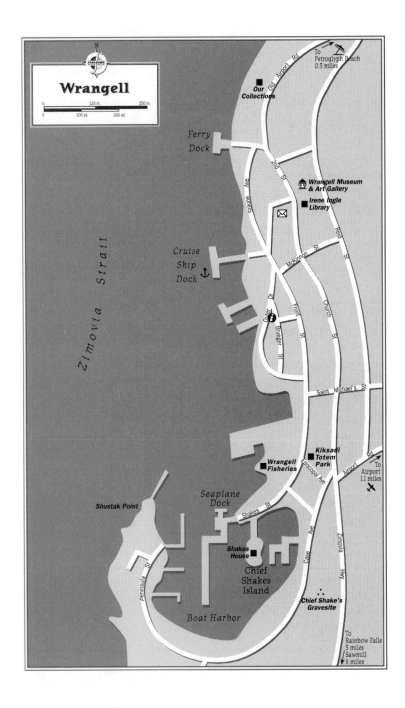

and misty. On your own, you can strike out for the visitor's center (beside the tall totem pole) where you can also pick up maps and brochures. Some petroglyphs—ancient, carved stones—on a rocky beach, the **eagles who live in the trees nearby** and a building full of local memorabilia and junk called Our Collections are the highlights of the city tour. The town's biggest employer is a Japanese lumber mill.

Alert Bay, British Columbia　　★ ★ ★

Language:	**English**	English Spoken?:	**Yes**
Currency:	**Can. $**	US$ok?:	**Canadian preferred**
To town:	**Walk**		

Small ships sometimes call in Alert Bay, home of the Nimpkish River tribes.

A very few small ships—Clipper's *Yorktown Clipper* is one—visit this tiny island off the northeastern tip of Vancouver Island, an ancient Kwakiutl settlement and present-day home of the Nimpkish River Indians. Not least among its attractions is what is said to be **the world's tallest totem pole**, 170 feet high and dating from 1972. The Nimpkish Indian Cemetery is home to many dramatic totem poles, some carved by the late Mungo Martin, a major Kwakiutl artist. A local **cultural center houses many potlatch artifacts**—the lavish gifts chiefs gave at big ceremonial parties. The government, at its most paternal, confiscated them in 1922 and didn't give them back until 1979. Don't expect shopping or any fancy tours here, but you will find it a friendly and fascinating port to see local Indian culture.

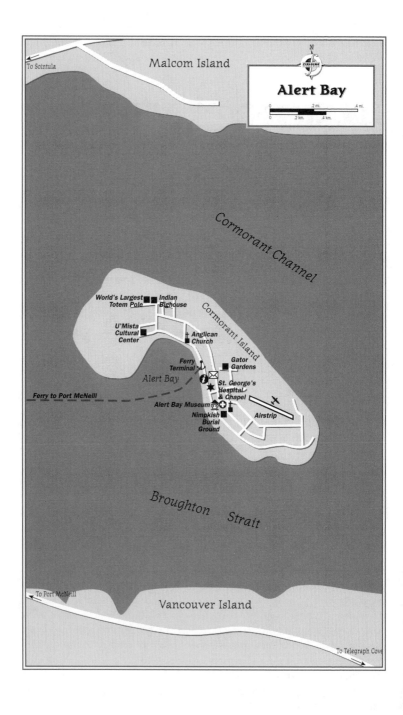

Prince Rupert, British Columbia ★★

Language:	**English**	*English Spoken?:*	**Yes**
Currency:	**Can. $**	*US$ok?:*	**Canadian preferred**
To town:	**Shuttle bus**		

Prince Rupert welcomes occasional cruise ship visitors.

Large cruise lines like Royal Viking used to call here in the early 1980s, but it's fallen out of favor lately except for visits aboard Clipper's *Yorktown Clipper* on an itinerary they call "Hidden Islands and Fjords" and a port of disembarkation for Society Expeditions' *World Discoverer*. Although we haven't been there for many years, we've always treasured Prince Rupert as the setting for the funniest **bus tour** we've ever taken on the Alaska cruise run, treasured in the same way we would love a truly tacky souvenir. It started when our cheerful driver turned to us with an incredulous look on her face and said, "I don't know what all you people are doing in Prince Rupert—there's nothing to see here! All we send away is fish, and everything else has to be brought up here to us." Then she showed us, in fairly rapid succession, the salmon cannery ("You don't want to go in there because there's all kinds of guys with long sharp knives and they don't know and don't care who you are!"), the shelter for abused wives ("People get really depressed here in the winter") and the sparsely-inhabited retirement home ("Anybody who can afford it moves down to Seattle or Vancouver to retire"). The town was founded, she said, by a man named Charles Hays, who visualized it as a rival to Seattle and Vancouver. He set out for Europe to raise some investment money for the area but unfortunately booked his return passage on the *Ti-*

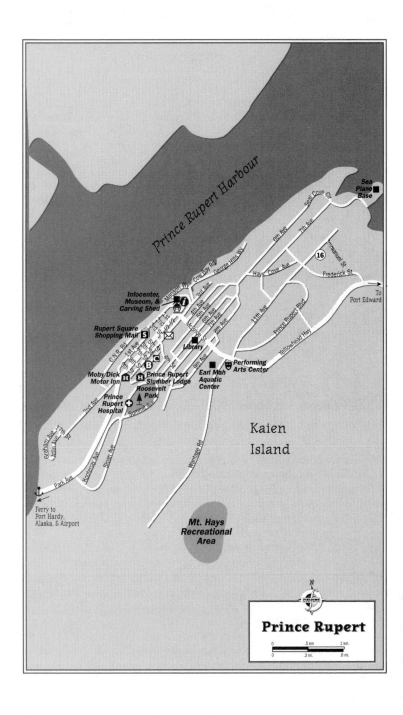

Prince Rupert

tanic. "When that sank, all Prince Rupert's fortunes sank with him," she said. We hear the town has been gentrified lately into a charming ferry port with **good fish and chips (local fresh halibut)** available from Smiles Seafood Cafe on the waterfront.

Vancouver, British Columbia ★ ★ ★ ★ ★

Language:	**English**	*English Spoken?:*	**Yes**
Currency:	**Can. $**	*US$ok?:*	**Sometimes**
To town:	**Walk from Canada Place, taxi or shuttle from Ballentyne Pier**		

Vancouver's Canada Place cruise terminal and the city skyline.

The bustling home port for most Alaska cruises, Vancouver uses both the handsome, **sail-shaped Canada Place pier** downtown, built for the 1986 Expo, and the edge-of-town Ballentyne Pier, a bus or taxi ride away from downtown. Surrounded by mountains and water and set like a jewel amid the coastal mountains on a peninsula thrust into the Georgia Strait, Vancouver is **one of the most beautiful cities in the world**. The colorful bars and shops of Gastown are a short walk away from Canada Place, as are the elegant shops and European cafe ambience of Robson Street. Stanley Park is great for jogging or walking, and Vanier Park has the Maritime Museum with the Royal Canadian Mounted Police patrol ship *St. Roch*, and Vancouver Museum's planetarium, Indian galleries and historic exhibits, including a Hudson Bay Company trading post. Shore excursions offered here (if you're taking a pre- or post-cruise package) include a city tour ($$) that usually takes a look at Stanley Park, Granville Island Public Market, the Lions' Gate Bridge, col-

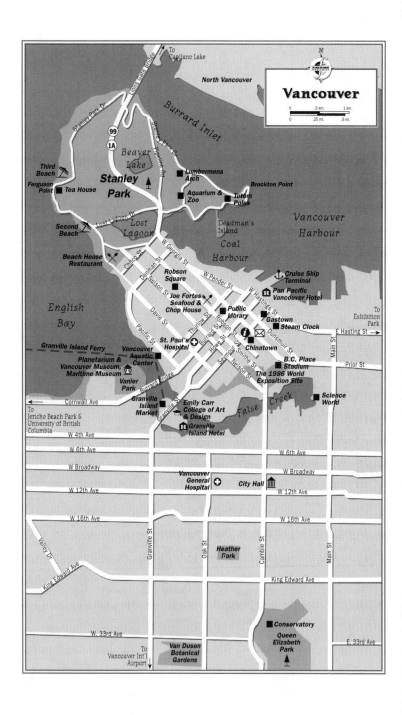

orful Gastown with its unique steam clock, Chinatown and downtown's handsome art deco buildings.

Victoria, British Columbia ★★★★★

Language:	**English**	English Spoken?:	**Yes**
Currency:	**Can. $**	US$ok?:	**Sometimes**
To town:	**Taxi shuttle**		

The stately Empress Hotel in Victoria is famous for an afternoon tea that is so in demand these days it goes on from 11 a.m. to 5 p.m.

The two must-do things here are the **famous afternoon teas and a stroll through beautiful Butchart Gardens**. And surprise! Your cruise ship will have a shore excursion offering both—but not on the same tour. You get a city tour and Butchart Gardens visit ($$) or a city tour and tea ($$) at a seaside hotel—not at the famous Empress Hotel—but not tea and Butchart Gardens. You could also visit Butchart Gardens on your own by cab (it's 13 miles from town, and be warned that tour groups often get entry priority over individual tourists) or pick up a local bus tour at the Empress Hotel just to the gardens that may be cheaper than the one sold on board the ship. If you want to do tea at the Empress on your own, reserve well ahead of time; in summer it's served at regular intervals between 11 a.m. and 5 p.m. **If you don't like gardens and don't want tea**, a third shore excursion option is a city tour and Craigdarroch Castle ($$), a 39-room mansion built by a local coal baron. But **you're gonna get that city tour** no matter what excursion you book! And hey, it's a lovely city, almost **more English than England** these days, with its cream teas, red double-decker buses, shops selling tweeds and English

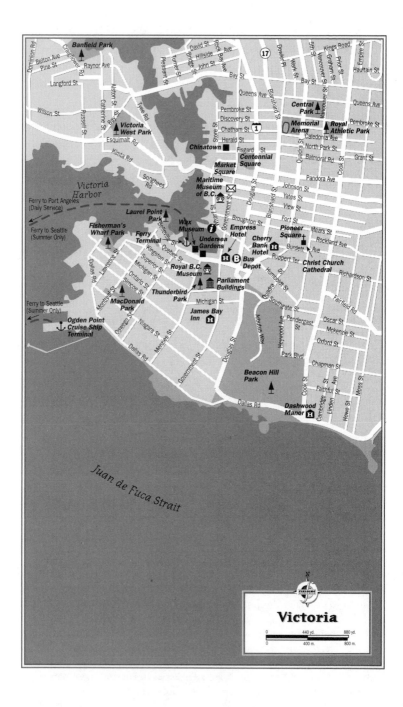

Victoria

bone china, and the Olde English Inn replica of Anne Hathaway's cottage in Stratford-upon-Avon. On your own, head first for the splendid **Royal British Columbia Museum** ($) with its reconstructions of a turn-of-the-century street and a section of George Vancouver's ship *Discovery.* The handsome Parliament Buildings and Empress Hotel are also in the same vicinity.

THE INLAND "PORTS" OF ALASKA AND WESTERN CANADA, THE RUSSIAN FAR EAST AND GREENLAND

Denali, Alaska ★★★★★

Language:	**English**	*English Spoken?:*	**Yes**
Currency:	**US$**	*US$ ok?:*	**Yes**
To town:	**Walk, shuttle bus**		

Mt. McKinley from the Alaska Railroad south of Denali on a clear day.

119

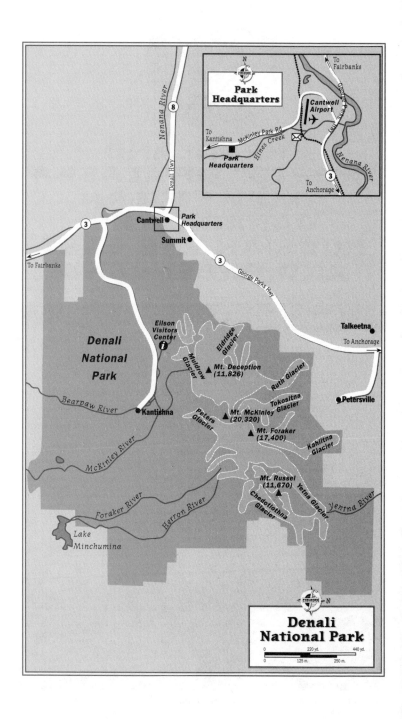

This area, formerly known as Mt. McKinley National Park for the 25th president of the United States, who was assassinated in 1901, has been re-named Denali, the Athabascan term for "high one." At 20,320 feet, the name is appropriate. The park has six million acres, but even so can seem aw-fully crowded on a midsummer day around the entrance and visitor center. The annual visitor count is nearing one million. To get away, **book a shuttle bus into the park's interior** ($–$$) or take a hike on one of the trails. Private cars and RVs are not permitted to drive into the park's interior. Take along cameras, binoculars, a strong mosquito repellant and some rain gear. Many visitors on a cruise/tour package will take the train or a motorcoach between Fairbanks and Anchorage with a two-day stop at Denali, about midway be-tween the two cities. **Don't count on seeing Mt. McKinley**—it's obscured by clouds as often as it's "out" in summer.

Fairbanks, Alaska   ★ ★ ★ ★

Language:	**English**	*English Spoken?:*	**Yes**
Currency:	**US$**	*US$ ok?:*	**Yes**
To town:	**Walk, bus tour**		

The Pump House is not only one of Fairbanks's best restaurants but also on the National Register of Historic Places.

Up around Fairbanks, you can still find a few vestiges of the old days if you look behind the strip malls and fast-food joints. **Alaskaland**, not as commer-cial as its name sounds, recreates the history of the gold mining days with many of Fairbanks's original cabins, a replica Indian village, the Crooked Creek & Whiskey Railroad and the old sternwheeler *Nenana*. A newer rep-

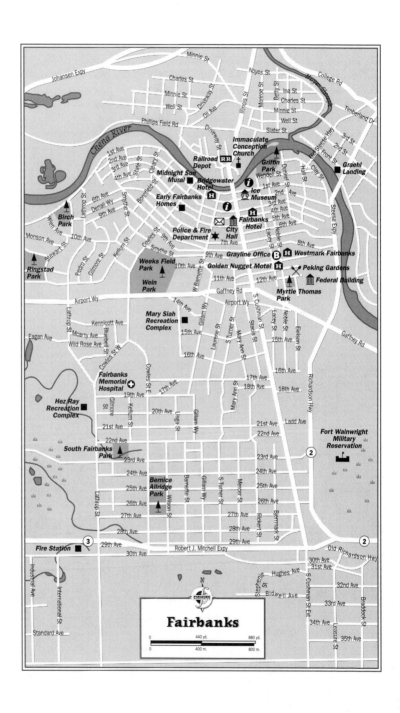

Fairbanks

lica sternwheeler takes you along the Chena and Nenana rivers, stopping sometimes to visit an Athabascan fishing village, and the **still-working El Dorado Gold Mine** is a popular tour bus halt. Both are usually included as part of the cruise/tour package. The colorful **Pump House** (a restaurant created from an historic pump house) makes a good meal stop, or, if that's not your style, you can eat at the northernmost Denny's in the world. **The Northern Lights (Aurora Borealis) is the best free show in town** on one of the 240 or so nights it plays. But the show is dark (that is to say, not visible) during summer's midnight sun. The University of Alaska Fairbanks has an excellent University Museum, including a 36,000-year-old bison found in the permafrost by some miners.

Kenai, Alaska ★★★

Language:	**English**	English Spoken?:	**Yes**
Currency:	**US$**	US$ ok?:	**Yes**
To town:	**Tour bus**		

The frequently foggy Kenai Peninsula offers some of the best wildlife spotting in Alaska.

The town of Kenai is the larger of a pair of twin cities with Soldotna (below). If you didn't check a map, **you'd expect Kenai to be the nearest gateway to Kenai Fjords National Park, but such is not the case.** Seward is the closest, with Homer second-closest (by air; there are no roads between) and both are frequent or occasional cruise ship ports of call. Only if you're doing an overland excursion will you also be offered Kenai or Soldotna. If you want to visit from Anchorage, **do not set out on a Friday afternoon or head back on a Sunday**

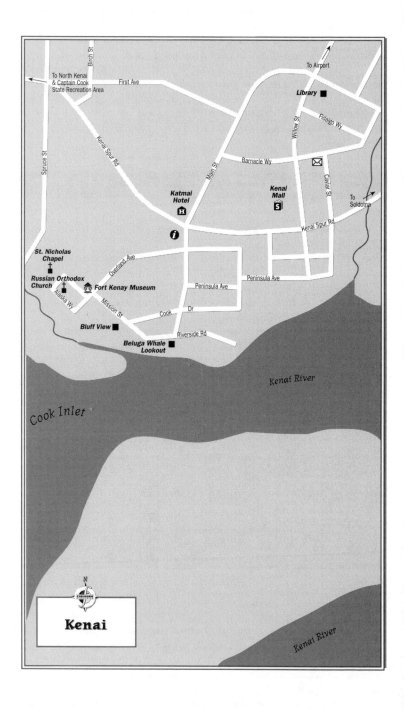

evening or Monday morning; the Kenai is the primary weekend destination for residents of Anchorage. Among the offbeat annual celebrations is the Kenai Lions Rubber Ducky Race in mid-September.

Kotzebue, Alaska ★★★

Language:	**English**	*English Spoken?:*	**Yes**
Currency:	**US$**	*US$ ok?:*	**Yes**
To town:	**Walk, bus tour**		

Probably the most prosperous of the Alaskan Eskimo towns, Kotzebue lies 26 miles north of the Arctic Circle, and is a popular fly-in destination for travelers interested in Eskimo culture. Visitors are usually entertained with some drum dances and a blanket toss. The latter, which resembles an Arctic version of a trampoline, was used to bounce a lookout high enough to spot offshore whales. There's a fine **Living Museum of the Arctic** with dioramas of Inupiat history and culture. There's also a museum called the **Ootukahkuktuvik** (meaning "Place Having Old Things") which requires that you pronounce the name before you can come in. In the local cemetery you'll see **spirit houses atop many of the graves**. One reason for the town's prosperity is the Red Dog Mine, **the world's biggest zinc mine**, a scant 100 miles to the north. There's no alcohol permitted in Kotzebue, but you'll find some familiar fast food names like Dairy Queen.

Soldotna, Alaska ★★★

Language:	**English**	*English Spoken?:*	**Yes**
Currency:	**US$**	*US$ ok?:*	**Yes**
To town:	**Tour bus**		

At the hub of the Kenai Peninsula, Soldotna offers wildlife spotting, **fantastic salmon fishing**, Kenai Canyon raft trips and 33 other activities from berry picking to mountain biking. The largest king salmon ever caught by a sports fisherman was here in 1985, when a local resident named Les Anderson hooked a 97-pound four-ounce fish in the Kenai River. The annual Soldotna Silver Salmon Derby takes place in late August with a $5000 top prize. The local library shows a free Alaska video screening at 2 p.m. every Saturday in summer. A homesteaders' village of historic log buildings is sometimes open for visitors during the summer months on Centennial Park Road. If you're homesick for the lower 48 states, you'll find plenty of mini-malls and fast

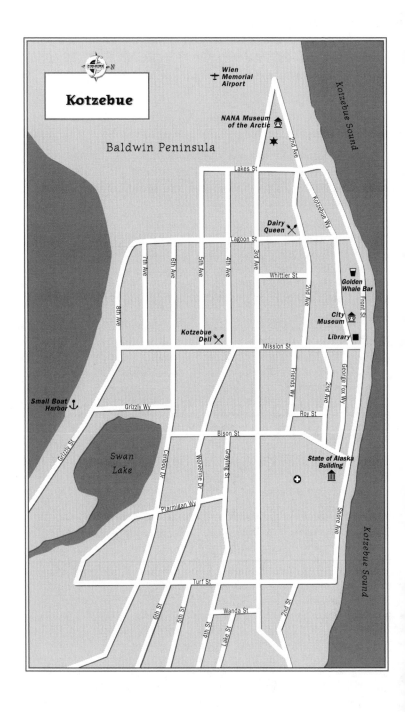

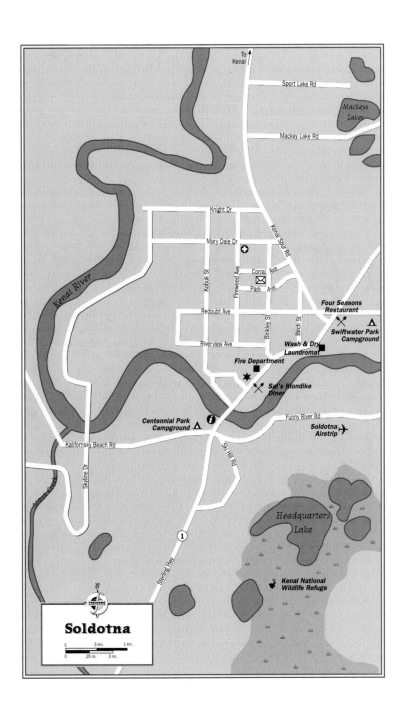

Soldotna

food outlets, including a Dairy Queen. The wildlife watching is excellent in the area.

Tok, Alaska   ★ ★ ★

Language:	**English**	*English Spoken?:*	**Yes**
Currency:	**US$**	*US$ ok?:*	**Yes**
To town:	**On bus tour**		

Rika's Roadhouse, a historic lodging and restaurant with gift shop, not far from Tok.

While not particularly distinguished on its own, Tok (pronounced "toke") is in the center of some scenic and historic sightseeing, from Kluane National Park and Kluane Lake to the historic Rika's Roadhouse, near where the Alaska Pipeline crosses the Tanana River. **Native American crafts** you can buy include moccasins, birch baskets, boots and jewelry, and the Burnt Paw gift shop does dog-team demonstrations and displays its sled dogs, including awwwww-fully cute puppies. The town is also noted for **moderately priced Tok Gateway Salmon Bakes** that offer salmon or buffalo burgers, salmon or halibut steaks or reindeer sausage, along with baked beans, sourdough rolls, salad bar and lemonade. Tok has a **Public Lands Information Center** in the middle of town with exhibits and stuffed wild animals.

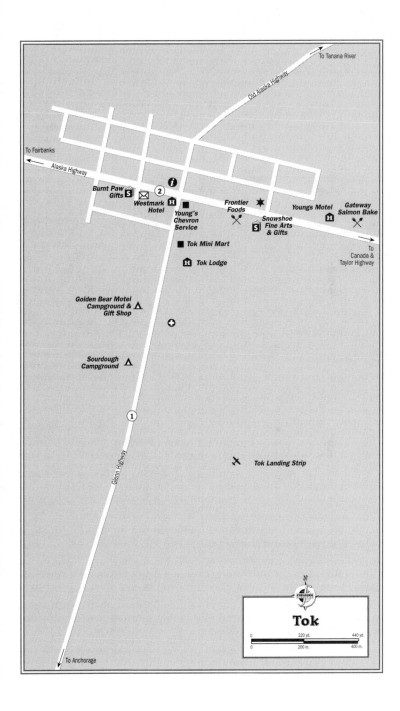

To Tanana River

Old Alaska Highway

To Fairbanks

Alaska Highway

Burnt Paw
Gifts

Westmark
Hotel

Young's
Chevron
Service

Frontier
Foods

Snowshoe
Fine Arts
& Gifts

Youngs Motel

Gateway
Salmon Bake

Tok Mini Mart

Tok Lodge

To
Canada &
Taylor Highway

Golden Bear Motel
Campground &
Gift Shop

Sourdough
Campground

Glenn Highway

Tok Landing Strip

N

Tok

| 0 | 220 yd. | 440 yd. |
| 0 | 200 m. | 400 m. |

To Anchorage

Banff Springs, Alberta   ★ ★ ★ ★ ★

Language:	**English**	*English Spoken?:*	**Yes**
Currency:	**Can. $**	*US$ ok?:*	**Canadian preferred**
To town:	**Tour bus**		

A couple of elk take a casual stroll through a park in downtown Banff Springs.

The jewel in the town is spectacular Banff Springs Hotel, built in 1888 and looking like **a rugged Scottish stone castle set amid mountain forests of evergreens**. Banff Springs itself is charming and tempts visitors—they are chockablock in summer—to explore it on foot for its many shops, restaurants and cafes. As a year-round resort, Banff Springs proffers plenty of summer and winter activities, along with handsome foliage displays and nearby wildlife in autumn and spring. Cruise/tour excursions may include an optional **gondola ride for great photo ops of bighorn sheep**, as well as a visit to Moraine Lake in Valley of Ten Peaks. In town, we especially like the restaurant Le Beaujolais ($$$) with prix fixe and tasting menus as well as an excellent wine cellar, and Coyote's ($$) with Calgary/California cuisine. There are **three museums** in town, one filled with models of taxidermy from the pre-1930s, when "predator-control" hunting was permitted; the Whyte Museum of the Canadian Rockies with the tourism history of the area; and the Natural History Museum with geology, flora and fauna, as well as a popular film on volcanos, despite the fact that none are in the vicinity.

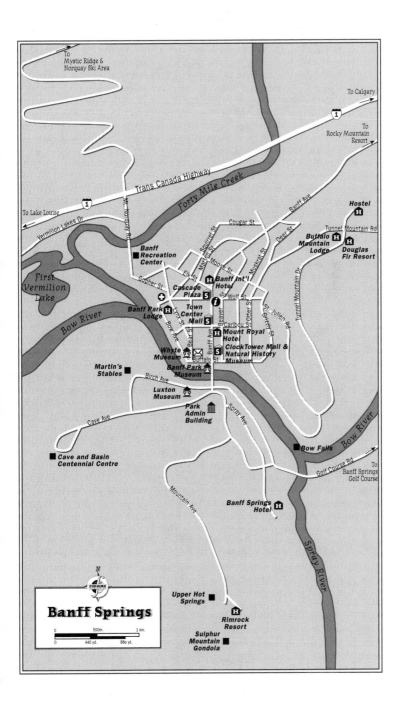

Calgary, Alberta ★ ★ ★ ★

Language:	**English**	*English Spoken?:*	**Yes**
Currency:	**Can. $**	*US$ ok?:*	**Canadian preferred**
To town:	**Shuttle bus**		

Calgary's Prehistoric Park on St. George's Island displays life-sized dinosaurs against a background setting of the city's skyline.

Calgary is the most American of Canada's cities, **brash and energetic as Texas** with a wild west/cowboy/oil drilling attitude. It made a splashy debut on the world's consciousness with the Winter Olympic Games in 1988. Gateway to the magnificent Canadian Rockies, the city offers frequent international airlift, good roads and easy car rental access. In town, the splendid **Glenbow Museum is worth a special visit** for its displays about the history and culture of the Canadian West. **Devonian Gardens**, a protected indoor garden complex on the fourth floor of a skyscraper, lets you head into an outdoor environment any time of year. The 60-acre **Heritage Park** has more than a hundred restored historic buildings, working craftsmen, a steam train, streetcar, horse-drawn bus and paddlewheeler. And there's a dinosaur park by the zoo on **St. George Island**. To the south, near Fort Macleod on route 785, make a beeline for the **Head-Smashed-In Buffalo Jump**. Although the name is odd, the recently-built $10 million museum is extraordinary, set on the cliffs over which Blackfoot hunters used to drive buffalo to their deaths to harvest a season's worth of meat and fur.

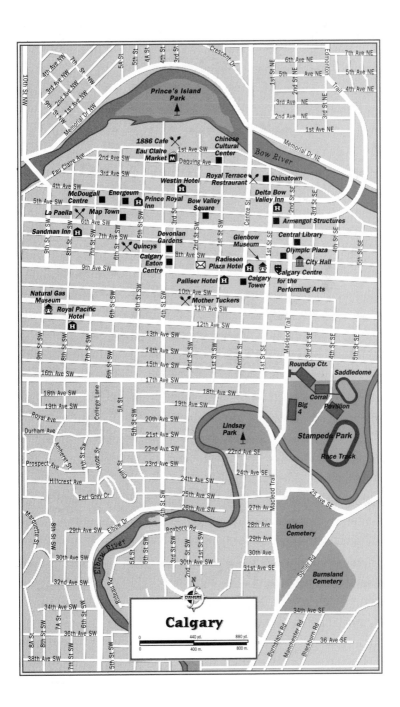

One of the dramatic displays at Head-Smashed-In Buffalo Jump in Fort Macleod, Alberta.

Jasper, Alberta   ★★★★

Language:	**English**	*English Spoken?:*	**Yes**
Currency:	**Can. $**	*US$ ok?:*	**Canadian preferred**
To town:	**Tour bus or VIA Rail**		

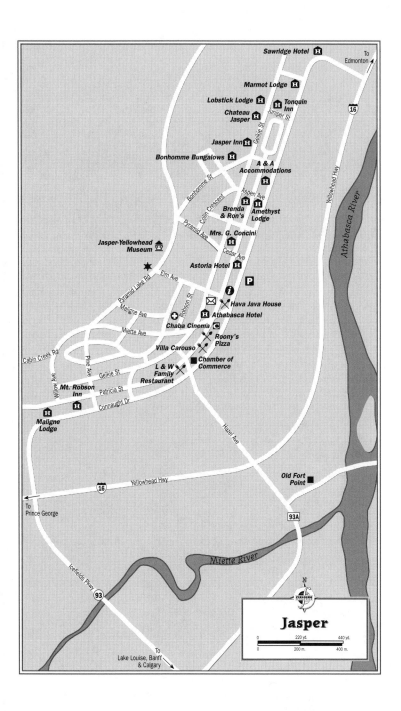

Jasper

Canada's luxury VIA Rail outside Jasper.

On cruise/tour programs, Jasper is **often visited by train** aboard Canada's luxury VIA Rail in restored Pullman cars from the 1950s or on the special Rocky Mountaineer excursion train. The **Jasper Park Lodge in Jasper National Park** provides a handsome array of individual or duplex cabins as well as traditional hotel rooms in a sprawling, lushly landscaped complex. If you visit, don't miss **the elegant Edith Cavell Restaurant** ($$$) in the lodge, serving arguably the best Canadian cuisine you'll ever taste. Sample delicious wild salmon, Alberta rack of lamb glazed with Vancouver Island fireweed honey or a delicate, rich soup made from fresh mushrooms gathered in the park. You can head for the **Athabasca Glacier** for a special snowcoach ride or cruise around the lake at the lodge in a paddle boat.

A dessert of chocolate shortcake with fresh Canadian berries, as served in the Edith Cavell Restaurant at Jasper Park Lodge.

Lake Louise, Alberta ★★★★★

Language:	**English**	*English Spoken?:*	**Yes**
Currency:	**Can. $**	*US$ ok?:*	**Canadian preferred**
To town:	**Tour bus**		

Chateau Lake Louise enjoys an incomparable setting by a turquoise lake and a glacier-capped mountain.

One of the grande dame stars of the world resort circuit is the Chateau Lake Louise, built in 1924, **a romantic, year-round attraction for scenery lovers as well as just plain lovers**. Skiers and ice skaters adore Lake Louise in winter, while summer visitors love a stroll around the circular lake, rising early for the sunrise and lingering over cocktails for the summer sunsets. The newly restored railway station in the village of Lake Louise, a couple of miles downhill from the chateau, is a fitting spot to visit, as is the charming little Post Hotel, a member of the prestigious French Relais & Chateaux group. Don't be surprised to run across countless busloads of honeymooning Japanese (who, the hotel manager tells us, demand twin rather than double beds) all summer long at the chateau.

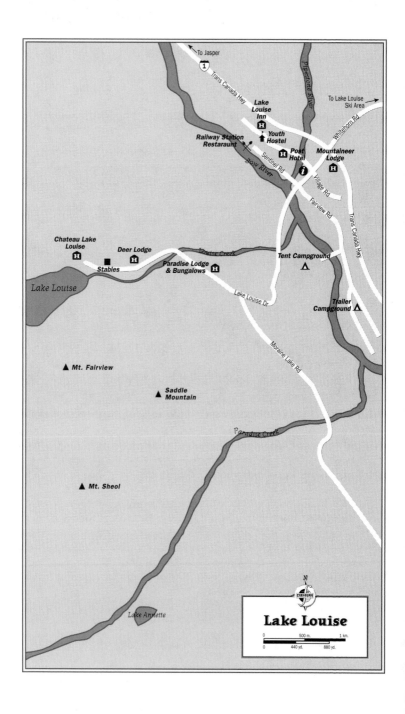

Lake Louise

Kamloops, British Columbia ★★★

Language:	**English**	*English Spoken?:*	**Yes**
Currency:	**Can. $**	*US$ ok?:*	**Canadian preferred**
To town:	**Shuttle bus**		

Rocky Mountaineer excursion trains take cruise/tour passengers between Jasper and Kamloops through all-daylight tours of the Canadian Rockies.

A terrific cruise/tour option is an excursion train journey between Jasper and Kamloops, offered by Princess Tours. The **Rocky Mountaineer excursion train travels through the Canadian Rockies entirely by daylight** so you don't miss a bit of the scenery, much of it accessible only by rail, such as dramatic Hell's Gate, where the Fraser River forces itself through a narrow gorge. The train follows the Thompson River, but if you're driving your own vehicle, such as an RV from Alaska Highway Cruises, you can take the fast and scenic Coquihalla Highway, where you'll also have **a good chance of spotting a roadside moose or two**.

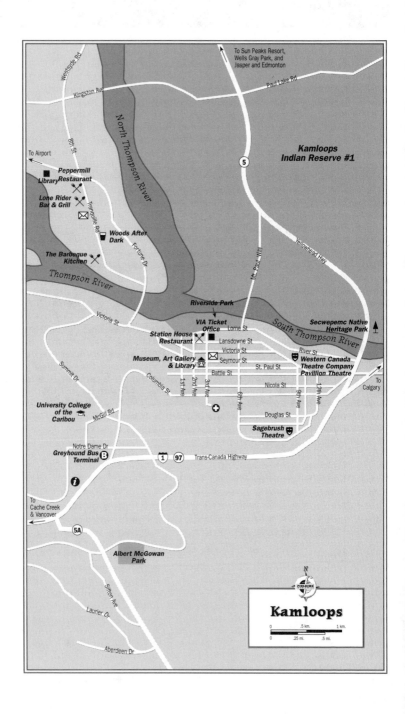

Dawson City, Yukon ★ ★ ★ ★ ★

Language:	**English**	*English Spoken?:*	**Yes**
Currency:	**Can. $**	*US$ ok?:*	**Canadian preferred**
To town:	**Shuttle bus**		

Klondike Kate's is one of Dawson's most enduring restaurants.

Coming to Dawson City for the first time is like meeting a childhood idol or your favorite movie star three or four decades later and finding, to your surprise, that not only is the old dear alive but **lively enough to dance a fandango, pull a slot machine lever and tell a couple of salty tales**. Far from being a recreation of a prototypical historic village or a saccharine gold rush amusement park, Dawson is a very real town, occupied by real people year-round in many of the buildings that date back to the Klondike days. The biggest gold mine today is **Diamond Tooth Gertie's Casino, the only legal gambling parlor in the Yukon**. The most interesting time to go is late in the season, after the termination dust (first snow of fall) has fallen and the seasonal workers are hitting the tables trying to win enough money to go to Hawaii for the winter. Parks Canada has done an exemplary job with the ongoing restoration. Don't miss the **Gaslight Follies at the Palace Grand Theatre**, the energetic (and corny) show at Diamond Tooth Gertie's, the hamburgers at Klondike Kate's or the Jack London look-alike who reads adventure tales in the afternoons outside London's cabin.

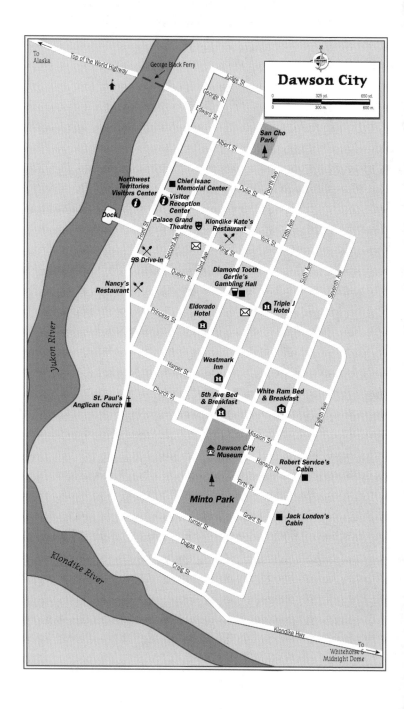

Whitehorse, Yukon   ★ ★ ★ ★

Language:	**English**	*English Spoken?:*	**Yes**
Currency:	**Can. $**	*US$ ok?:*	**Canadian preferred**
To town:	**Shuttle bus**		

The narrow-gauge White Pass & Yukon Railway still travels the same railroad between Whitehorse and Skagway the Stampeders took in 1898.

Whitehorse is the metropolis of Canada's far north and regional headquarters for the Royal Canadian Mounted Police, formerly the Northwest Mounted Police. The narrow-gauge **White Pass & Yukon Railway makes roundtrip journeys between Skagway and Whitehorse** with a midway stop at Fraser. The historic *SS Klondike* is tied up on the Yukon River and can be toured with a guide every half hour during summer days. The Yukon Transportation Museum, the Yukon Visitor Reception Center and the Yukon Gardens are all worth a bit of time during your visit. **Raft float trips through Miles Canyon** ($$) set out frequently from a dock out at the edge of town, but real adventurers should look into the new **Nahanni River Adventures, whitewater rafting on the Yukon**. "Frantic Follies" is the live gold rush musical, staged in the **Westmark Whitehorse Hotel**, with a plethora of corny jokes and enthusiastic if unpolished performance. Try the Talisman Cafe ($) for tasty, healthful dishes, including some vegetarian options. Good shopping for local Yukon Indian crafts is available at Northern Images, owned by a Native cooperative.

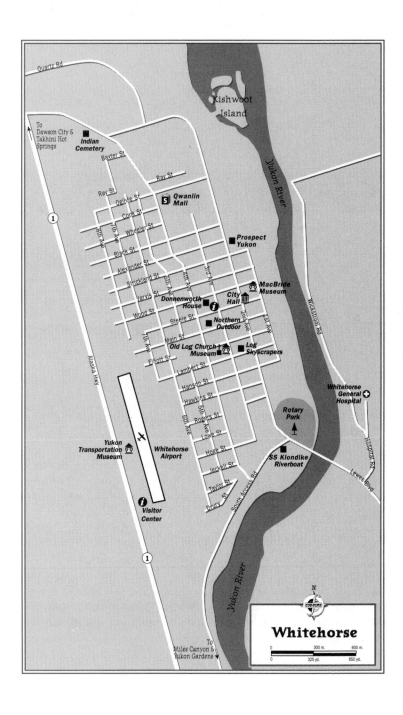

Whitehorse

ALTERNATIVE CRUISES: THE RUSSIAN FAR EAST AND BERING SEA

Expeditioners, like those aboard World Discoverer, *have different expectations from a cruise.*

To anyone accustomed to the uniform howls of outrage when a mass market cruise ship changes or cancels an announced port of call, the calm and understanding response of the *World Discoverer* expeditioners arriving in Nome several years ago to find no ship to board was astonishing. The ground staff met the arriving passengers—114 altogether, including the two of us—at the airport and explained that because of heavy seas the ship had not been able to come into Nome to make its turnaround. Instead, the embarking passengers would be taken on a two-hour school bus ride across the tundra to the community of Teller, where the ship was anchored offshore.

The passengers, all but a few of them over 55, took the news in stride, although some of the European passengers had originated in London or Frankfurt and been in transit for more than 24 hours. When told to don par-

145

kas and rubber boots for their ongoing journey, they obediently opened up their bags on the airport floor and pulled out the necessary gear. We heard no complaints from these well-traveled veterans, only good-humored joking among themselves.

After being taken to a local restaurant for free drinks and food, the expeditioners boarded Nome school buses in the 10 p.m. Alaska twilight and arrived in the midnight darkness on a rocky beach, where they put on life jackets and loaded into Zodiacs, inflatable rubber landing craft, for a trip across the cold, dark sea to the ship. The baggage followed later, in a series of 2 a.m. Zodiac shuttles and passengers found their suitcases outside their cabin doors the next morning.

Not every expedition cruise starts this way. Usually plans go as arranged, but any experienced expeditioner knows patience and fortitude is as necessary as a hefty bank account when travels take you to the ends of the earth.

Expeditioners have very different priorities from the usual cruise passenger. Instead of bingo, casino or song-and-dance shows, they prefer nature-oriented videos. Dressing for dinner means putting on a clean shirt, and shopping takes a back seat to birdwatching.

On this Russian Far East journey, the latter was particularly important, since that area, along with the Aleutians and Pribilof Islands are among the richest areas in the world to see nesting seabirds during the summer season.

In addition, our expeditioners got good looks at rare Stellar sea lions, fur seals, walruses and Alaskan brown bears (also called grizzly bears), the latter catching spawning salmon in streams on the Katmai Peninsula to fatten up before winter hibernation.

Port lectures don't deal with where to shop and what to buy, but rather tell passengers how to relate to the local tribal groups—Chukchi in the Russian Far East, Siberian Yupiks on St. Lawrence Island, Aleuts in the Pribilofs—encountered on the island ports of call.

Shore excursions may be a trudge through the tundra in rubber boots.

Shore excursions may be Zodiac "wet landings"—disembarking in the water on beach landings—and a trudge through the tundra in rubber boots to see rare plants or a splashy ride to craggy cliffs to look at nesting murres lined up like a row of penguins on their narrow rock ledges.

After a restful first day at sea spent filling out Russian customs forms and trying on or swapping rubber boots to find a pair that fit, passengers spend a second day with three different calls. The first stop is at Arakamchechen Island, uninhabited except for some officers of the Russian fish and game service, who gather local wild mushrooms as a dietary staple. Passengers choose between tundra walks—the botanist can find an entire world of plants in a square foot of tundra—or hiking gingerly to the edge of a cliff in groups of ten to see the walrus "haul-out." This is the beach where the huge mammals drag themselves from the water, often piling up in heaps atop each other. Unfortunately, on this day, we saw only one dead walrus washed up on the beach, bereft of his ivory tusks. The others were swimming in jovial groups of six or eight, best seen through high-powered binoculars.

The second call was the Chukchi village of Yanrakynnot, where we interacted with some of the villagers and visited a state-owned fox farm where Arctic foxes are bred to be sent to Provideniya to become silver fox coats.

This statue of Lenin facing the grim Siberian city of Provideniya may be the only one left standing in Russia.

After dinner, in the foggy twilight, we went ashore by Zodiac to Whale Bone Alley, Yttygran Island, where some unknown ancient tribe has set out skulls and jawbones of bowhead whales in a ritualistic design.

A Zodiac ride around the cliffs of Sireneki gave dedicated birders a good look at nesting fulmars, puffins, murres and glaucous gulls, and an afternoon in Provideniya provided a village museum and a cultural program heavy on teen-aged accordion players.

In the Bering Sea, we re-entered Alaska at remote St. Lawrence Island, where the citizens of Gambell, most of them Siberian Yupiks who crossed the land bridge 2000 years ago, showed us how they dry and stretch walrus skin to make their boats.

The Pribilof Islands, rich in fur seals and nesting puffins, usually get a day of exploration apiece, with good possibilities for photographing birds and fur seals.

In the Aleutians, Zodiac excursions to some of the Semidi and Shumagin Islands, part of the Alaska Maritime National Wildlife Refuge System, turn up still more seabirds and sea lions, as well as a petrified forest on the beach. With binoculars, we see Alaskan brown bears fishing for spawning salmon in the scenic Katmai National Park, but so far away the bear is but a dot in the center of the camera frame if you try to photograph him.

For anyone taking this cruise, we'd recommend several changes of practical clothing that can be layered; you're going to get wet. Rubber boots, rain pants and warm waterproof parkas are essential.

ALTERNATIVE CRUISES: THE RUSSIAN
FAR EAST AND BERING SEA

Wet landings like this one on a rocky beach in the Russian Far East call for rubber boots; in the foreground, a dead walrus.

Ports of the Bering Sea

Little Diomede Island

Little Diomede Island, Alaska, is only three miles from the Siberian island of Big Diomede.

The closest U.S. territory to the Russian Far East is the tiny island of **Little Diomede**, Alaska, three miles across the Bering Sea from the Siberian island of Big Diomede.

There was a time when the inhabitants of the two islands, most of them related to each other, visited back and forth, especially during winter when they could meet on the ice and chew the fat, so to speak. But then came the Cold War, and on the Russian side, the residents of Big Diomede were moved somewhere inland and replaced by a surveillance post. In those years, one resident told us, anyone who went over to Big Diomede never came back.

While we had not expected a replay of "Nanook of the North" on our first trip above the Arctic Circle in 1985, it was a little disconcerting to have a six-year-old Eskimo boy taking pictures of our Zodiac landing with his brand-new Polaroid camera.

From our notes: A dozen grinning little boys are standing in the surf to help beach our rubber boats. Nearby, the decaying empty-eyed head of a walrus is lying against some seaweed, and almost every house on the steep, rocky hillside has wooden racks of blackened walrus and seal meat hanging out to dry.

We have been invited to the new $5 million school, which teaches children from kindergarten through eighth grade, as well as serving as the town's cultural center and most popular gathering spot, especially in winter. The residents can roller skate or play basketball inside in the gymnasium in winter, as

ALTERNATIVE CRUISES: THE RUSSIAN
FAR EAST AND BERING SEA

well as rehearse the traditional tribal dances they perform for visitors. Someone said they also play baseball and football inside the gym, since nowhere else on the island is flat enough.

During the dancing, the men play flat tambourine-like drums of split walrus belly skin stretched between wooden hoops similar to embroidery hoops, beaten from underneath rather than on the top. Women and a few young men performed the dancing. The women, eyes downcast, never lift their feet from the floor but instead bend and bob at the knees and wave their arms rhythmically while chanting. The young male dancers, most of them wearing Adidas and jeans, were more animated, looking and pointing in what was probably a hunting ritual dance.

St. Lawrence Island

A walrus skin stretched for drying is used for making boats on remote St. Lawrence Island.

Gambell, the major settlement on Alaska's St. Lawrence Island, is inhabited by Siberian Yupiks who migrated here during the late 19th century after the earlier Native population, who had come from Siberia 2000 years before, were virtually wiped out by epidemic diseases introduced by whalers.

The land mass is one of the few remaining remnants of the land bridge that once connected Siberia and Alaska. The island belongs to the United States despite its proximity—40 miles—to the coast of Siberia.

The female mayor greeted us with a brief speech, then the villagers took us for a walk around and showed us how they dry and stretch walrus skin to make their boats. They still hunt walrus and whales in traditional fashion with *umiak* (walrus-skin boats) and a harpoon, and speak a Siberian dialect as well as English. Generally, they are considered the most culturally autonomous of all Native Alaskans.

They are also more entrepreneurial than their cousins on the Siberian side, charging $5 each way for a all-terrain vehicle ride across the rough rocky terrain between town and the site of the concert, which for some mysterious reason is a couple of miles away on the other side of the island.

The mayor of Gambell, Alaska, descended from Siberian Yupiks who migrated here across the Bering Strait.

The heart of town life is the general store, filled with most of the usual conveniences from the Lower 48 states, including disposable diapers and ice cream. While the Natives in the Canadian Arctic have their supplies arrive by annual barge, the Alaskan islanders have goods flown in. There doesn't seem to be a shortage of anything.

Outside the store, dozens of all-terrain vehicles are parked at random angles. They toodle around on the gravel and rock terrain, striking out cross-country as often as on the so-called roads. No one seems to walk anywhere except for the expeditioners, who maneuver their slick rubber boots carefully across the rocky terrain. What little earth there is in Gambell has been torn up by the roaring ATVs.

All-terrain vehicles in Gambell are common as bicycles in China.

The village elders have arranged a concert of Yupik music and dance for us on the far side of town beside the sea, despite an icy breeze that flows in off the water. Many dances were solo story-telling episodes, including one young village man who danced the story of how he had gone into the Airborne and wounded his knee during a parachute jump.

Some 550 people live in Gambell. When we photographed one smiling family aboard their ATV, we couldn't help remembering a quip from one of the lecturers on board—"A typical Eskimo family consists of a mother, a father, two children and an anthropologist."

The Pribilof Islands

Young male fur seals, left out of the breeding process, gather on a "bachelor beach" in the Pribilofs.

This group of five small islands in the south central Bering Sea was discovered by 18th century Russians looking for fur seal colonies. To harvest the furs from the uninhabited islands, the Russians took Aleut slaves from the nearby Aleutians and forced them to resettle in St. Paul and St. George. For almost a century, the fur hunting continued, and when the United States purchased Alaska in 1867, the federal government took over the administration of the islands, the people and the wildlife. Only in 1983 were the residents given autonomy over their lands.

Today, **St. Paul** and **St. George** combined have the largest Aleut settlement in the world, its residents descendents of those fur trade slaves. Some 650 of St. Paul's 950 year-round residents are Aleuts. In the winter crab season, the population swells to 1200. King crab fishing has become a big moneymaker for the islands, and the formerly quiet communities are suddenly booming with fishermen and fish processing plants.

When we went ashore, we spotted what we first thought were a number of small black dogs, which turned out to be Arctic foxes, who only turn white in winter. There are no trees on St. Paul but also no permafrost, and the temperature is a steady 25 to 50 degrees Fahrenheit, with 66 the highest ever recorded.

The island is lined with seal rookeries, where mother and baby seals and the beach master (the large male seal who dominates the harem) lounge about on the rocks, the pups playing in the surf or tussling over a rope of kelp. Not far away is the bachelors' beach, where the unsuccessful males have spent the summer lying around glumly like lumps in the sand. The beach master may have a harem of from one to a hundred female seals, with 20 to 25 the average. The official fur seal count for St. Paul and St. George is roughly one million. Many of the pups will die in the first year of life, perhaps from sea lion or orca kills or even being stepped on by the beach master, who is apparently not very paternal.

Buildings in town are simple but attractive, painted in pastels. The King Eider Hotel, the school and other public buildings are painted the same shade of blue.

St. George, undisturbed by humans for centuries, has incredibly rich bird life, with 211 species reported here. It is the largest seabird rookery in the Northern Hemisphere. In addition, some 250,000 fur seals gather here each summer to breed.

The bird cliffs at **Zapadni Bay** are a sort of bird apartment house, with each one knowing his own niche. The puffins are usually at the edges or above the murres, and interact charmingly with each other, often flying off or back in pairs.

The murres, looking more and more like penguins to us, are lined up on ledges in crowds; they don't seem to want to be alone. One of the naturalists describes their behavior as waiting around wondering if it is time to go feed again. Finally one murre will say, I think I'll go feed, and set out with a swoop, and the others will say, That sounds like a good idea, and take off after him.

Down on the beach we spot red-legged kittiwakes, one red-faced cormorant, and a group of tiny winter wrens are hopping around the rocks and sand amidst lots of fresh Arctic fox tracks. The foxes pad along the clifftops stealing murre eggs. The local Aleuts also gather the murre eggs in June for eating.

A moldering Russian Orthodox church on St. George Island retains memories of the days when Russia ruled here.

The little town of **St. George** has a picturesquely peeling Russian Orthodox church that was decorated inside with every artificial flower in the Arctic for a special religious holiday. The caretaker is an old Aleut who remembers the wartime days, the bombings by the Japanese and the relocations to mainland Alaska.

"The young people don't go to church any more," he told us sadly.

Monkshood grows amidst the tundra on St. Matthew Island in the Pribilofs.

St. Matthew, still uninhabited, is covered with animals and wildflowers such as purple monks hood. But offshore, at Pinnacle Rock, a huge colony of now-rare Stellar sea lions were sunning themselves on the rocks, while puffins, kittiwakes and fulmars floated on the water or flew just above it.

The Aleutians

Reminders of World War II such as this pillbox are everywhere in the Aleutians.

At **Dutch Harbor** and **Unalaska** in the Aleutians, relics of World War II from pillboxes to an occasional unexploded grenade recall the days when the Japanese attacked the island. The hills surrounding the area are honeycombed with bunkers and pillboxes, tunnels and trenches from the war. With the dearth of housing and Japanese fish factories working full-blast, a few people have converted pillboxes into basic habitations.

The Japanese attacked Dutch Harbor on June 3, 1942, when an aircraft carrier launched 20 planes that bombed the army base at Amaknak Island; the same planes attacked again the same day.

Today, the monolithic Japanese-financed fish factories work around the clock to produce fish products for Japan, as much as $90 million worth in every container ship that sails from here. Giants such as UniSea began here in 1975 processing crab, but that subsided in the early 1980s, replaced with cod and pollock, the latter the main ingredient in sirimi, artificial crabmeat.

If you want to go eagle-spotting, head for what the locals call "the eagle sanctuary," which is the town dump. Sad to say, our national bird is a bit of a scavenger. Eagles like to hang out in Unalaska and Dutch Harbor because of all the fish processing plants.

A grave behind the Russian Orthodox Church of the Holy Ascension of Christ in the Aleutians, the oldest one in America, dating from 1824.

A postscript for shoppers—Carl's Store is the only supermarket we've ever seen that sells fur coats. And the rugged Elbowroom in Unalaska was once named "the roughest bar in the world" by Playboy magazine.

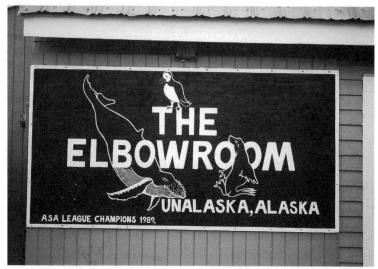

The Elbowroom in Unalaska, The Aleutians, was once named by Playboy magazine as "the roughest bar in the world."

Zodiac excursions to some of the Semidi and Shumagin Islands, part of the Alaska Maritime National Wildlife Refuge System, turned up still more seabirds and sea lions, plus a petrified forest on the beach.

The Katmai Peninsula

Rainy, foggy Katmai Peninsula is a good place to go bear-spotting, but you'd better take binoculars to see him.

In the scenic **Katmai National Park**, we watched brown bears fishing for spawning salmon from our Zodiacs "a safe distance away," which is say unless a photographer had a 500 millimeter lens, a bear closeup was not possible. Katmai is across from Kodiak, which is home to the famous Kodiak brown bear, but most experts say the Kodiak brown bear, the Katmai brown bear and the grizzly bear are all the same and all the same size.

Anyhow, the bear sort of lumbered around in the stream that ran down into the bay, caught some salmon—we could see the flash of silver skin— nibbled on it as if snacking, but didn't finish it. Then he caught another fish and did the same thing. There were plenty of gulls around to get the bear's leftovers.

Ports of the Russian Far East

Arakamchechen Island

Author Harry Basch uses a scope to look for walrus at the "haul-out" sign on Arakamchechen Island.

Arakamchechen Island, just off the coast near Provideniya, uninhabited except for some officers of the Russian fish and game service, is part of a planned **Beringia International Park** under development as a joint project between the United States and Russia. The park will preserve the historic and natural sites around the Bering Sea in both Alaska and the Russian Far East.

The site under consideration here is the Pacific walrus "haul-out" where these huge 2500-pound mammals, we are told, literally pull themselves onto the beach here and lie about in heaps. Only 10 of us at a time are permitted to approach the cliff edge that overlooks the "haul-out," and when our turn comes, we do see distant walrus, sort of. They are swimming, not lying on the beach, and with a scope we are able to see a group of six bobbing around out in the water in an odd rhythmic pattern like a chubby chorus of Floradora girls. One dead walrus, sans tusks, has washed up on the beach. The Siberian native tribes of Chukchi can legally hunt the walrus for subsistence, but taking the tusks and leaving the meat means the animal was killed by poachers.

Provideniya

Author Shirley Slater being welcomed to Provideniya by a costumed Russian with the traditional bread and salt.

The town of **Provideniya**, Russia's main Arctic port, leaves a lot to be desired in the scenery department. Huge heaps of coal are dumped along the dock area for distribution to the subsistence villages like Yanrakynnot, and behind it are the buildings of the town terraced up a bare rocky hill.

Our guide here is Sasha, a Ukrainian from Odessa who is working here in order to send money home to his family "who are having hardships these days." He leads us around the town for a tour of the brewery, a look at the museum and then a walk uphill to the cemetery. From the gravestones, we note few of the residents ever reach the age of 50; alcoholism and the brutal climate have taken their toll. Every year as many as 5000 Russians who were posted here under the Soviets pack up and go back home, Sasha says.

But the people who remain turn out in their finest dress for a party and folkloric show at the town cultural center for the passengers. We are treated to a series of accordion solos by several very serious teenagers, their proud mothers beaming from the audience, as well as a gypsy dance and a very modest "exotic dance," along with a buffet of local reindeer sausage and soft drinks from the state-owned brewery.

Two children in Provideniya in a field of wild daisies.

Sireneki

Nesting murres along a cliff edge leave their eggs on the bare rock.

Sireneki is for the birds, thousands and thousands of nesting seabirds who come back every summer to these fish-rich waters in the Russian Far East. The craggy, mossy cliffs outside the rather ordinary-looking village are alive with the sounds.

Expedition ship passengers have a birds-eye view of nesting murres that line up like a row of penguins on their narrow, rocky ledges, their eggs balanced on the bare rock crevice; kittiwakes, their graceful white wings dipped in black at the tips; long-necked black cormorants; big, raucous gray-and-white glaucous gulls who lord it over the others by perching atop the highest rocks; stiff-winged fulmars who seem to soar about for the sheer exuberance of flying; and tiny least auklets who float on the swells of the iron-gray sea.

The sky is filled with clouds and swarms of birds hurrying out to feed on fish and then bring the food back to the nest. They are pelagic birds, which means they come ashore only to breed and nest, then return to roam the restless seas again.

The puffins are the most enchanting birds in the Arctic with their bright cartoon faces.

But most enchanting of all are the puffins, veritable cartoons of birds, plump-bellied, their white faces tucked into a black monk's cap and outlined with clown-like black eyeliner, fat red or yellow beaks and wide, duck-like red webbed feet.

We expeditioners are equally bright, bundled up against the weather in shiny red parkas, yellow rain slickers and blue waterproof pants.

This gray, chill, often rainy outing, while it wouldn't thrill a sunseeker, is a birdwatcher's fantasy. Most of the passengers are Americans, but there is a sturdy contingent of birders from Britain, as well as a number of Germans, Swiss and Dutch, all out bouncing around in the Bering Sea, binoculars and cameras at the ready.

Yanrakynnot

A worker at the fox farm in Yanrakynnot displays one of the animals destined to become part of a coat.

One of our guest lecturers aboard the cruise is Nikolai Drozdov, the Moscow equivalent of Marlin Perkins or George Page, who for 23 years hosted "The World of Animals" for 200 million viewers across Russia. When Nikolia escorts us ashore to the village of **Yanrakynnot**, he is a celebrity. Forget the tourists, Nikolai is here.

We are met by an effusive Russian woman in a fur coat who looks like an Intourist guide in a minor Russian city.

"Nikolai Nikolaivich," she burbles, and clutches his hand to her breast.

She turns out to be the wife of the manager of the state-run fox farm, the town's biggest industry, and, so far as we could see, the only one.

The farm is a dismal collection of half-a-dozen rotting wooden buildings like chicken houses on stilts, each holding several hundred fox cubs and adults. There are six to eight nervous arctic foxes crowded into each small wire-floored cage about pet-shop size. The stilts, we are told, are to protect the foxes from the town's motley collection of sled dogs. The foxes are fed on ground walrus meat shaped into patties like hamburgers. When sufficiently fattened, they are shipped off to Provideniya to be turned into silver fox coats.

We learn later that while we were watching the poor captive foxes running in panicky circles in their wire cages, a group of Siberian Chukchi and American Eskimo (a team that would have been unthinkable only a few years ago) have joined for the annual two-day reindeer kill and skinning that is happening just over the ridge from town.

This Chukchi girl in Yanrakynnot was wary of a stranger with a camera.

The Chukchi children follow us with their bright eyes. One little girl has dressed up her baby brother and propped him in his carriage like a doll on display. We ask to photograph them, as well as another girl in a distinctive grimy cap that once was white; she nods assent, then carefully wipes her nose on her sleeve before posing warily for the camera.

Yttygran, Whale Bone Alley

Whalebones stuck into the earth like these vertabrae at Whalebone Alley may be a mysterious message from the past.

We went ashore by Zodiac in the twilight to the island of **Yttygran**, better known as **Whale Bone Alley**. At some time in the past, unknown people lined up the skulls and long slender jawbones of bow whales in a series of patterns along a shingle beach, something like the giant statues of Easter Island. Carbon testing of bone samples date them to the late 17th century, but none of the present indigenous tribes claim any knowledge of them.

While we were ashore, squeaking about in the tundra in our tall rubber boots, necessary for our wet landings on the beach, a thick fog came in and enveloped our ship so we could no longer see it, even though it was less than a half-mile away, adding still more mystery to the spooky site.

Whale Bone Alley is part of the new **Beringia International Park** under development as a joint project between the United States and Russia to preserve the historic and natural sites around the Bering Sea in both Alaska and the Russian Far East.

Sailing the Northwest Passage

Author Shirley Slater in the icy Arctic waters of Franklin Bay.

Nothing in the Arctic is predictable, especially the ice. It has a way of moving and changing, splitting and melding, with each shift of wind or temperature. It is a living force, quite capable of taking a small ship prisoner and carrying it for months, or crushing it suddenly, like a cold iron fist closing against an eggshell.

For passengers aboard a small ship here, the clunks and growls of restless ice floes scraping against the steel hull are so noisy some think the ship is dropping anchor. From the deck the rising sun at 4 a.m. turns the sky red and orange, and the chunks of ice glow like coals in the dark water. It is a world of fire and ice in a vast, flat sea.

There is no guarantee of getting through and no definite itinerary along the way. For many of the passengers aboard, there is the tug of the unknown, the "because it's there" spirit. Some, if pressed, admit they want to be part of what may well be the last great adventure for well-heeled travelers who have been everywhere else. The frozen Arctic is still as mysterious and hostile as it was when it reduced doughty explorers and expeditioners to starvation, murder and cannibalism, and wiped whole ships off the face of the earth.

But with today's modern communications and the assistance of patrolling Canadian icebreakers, shiploads of passengers have made it through the passage on most, but not all, the scheduled sailings since the first successful passenger transit by the *Explorer* (then the *Lindblad Explorer*) in 1984.

The typical transit crosses between Nome and Greenland, sailing across the Arctic archipelago, the world's largest island group. The total coastline exceeds the circumference of the earth. Most of the journey is spent in Canada's vast Northwest Territories, 1,304,903 square miles of territory inhabited by some 44,000 people, or .03 persons per square mile.

The icepack varies from year to year during the brief late August/early September window when ships can pass. It thickens in some areas to nine-tenths, or 90 percent ice to open water. Negotiating the Beaufort Sea may mean a zigzag route through water so shallow there may be only four feet below the hull. The ice floes are eerily beautiful, turquoise and aquamarine on the bottom, and they flop over suddenly, as if top-heavy, in the wake of the slow-moving ship.

The cautious progress continues day after day. Passengers who request it are awakened at 2 or 3 a.m. to see, in the pre-dawn skies, the Aurora Borealis cavorting capriciously, swirling and streaking in sulfurous shades of yellow-green.

From time to time, the ship anchors off a village like Cambridge Bay, where there is a thin layer of fresh snow on the ground, and the wind-driven sleet feels like little nails being hammered into the skin. In the Queen Maud Gulf south of the island of Jenny Lind, a storm came up with gale force winds of 45 knots, reading eight to nine on the Beaufort Scale, and the captain orders cabin portholes covered on all the lower decks. At midday in the Requisite Channel, passengers are forbidden to go on deck as the ship rolls and pitches in a turbulent sea.

The Canadian Coast Guard icebreaker *Camsell* relays by radio the information that the storm has destroyed many of the buoys in the narrow, shallow Simpson Strait, and offers to lead the *World Discoverer* through, after which the Canadians are welcomed on board the cruise ship for a festive evening.

Relics, graves and skeletons from the ill-fated Sir John Franklin expedition from Britain in 1845 have been found on King William Island. The British had been endeavoring to find a shortcut to the Orient since 1576, and the 59-year-old Franklin, stubborn, duty-bound and accident-prone, had apparently chosen on his third Arctic expedition to sail south down the west side of King William Island, through the heavy ice pack of Victoria Strait, because his map did not show the Rae Strait on the eastern side. Franklin's body was never recovered, and his two ships, *Erebus* and *Terror*, were most likely crushed to bits in the grinding ice.

Numerous expeditions set out to search for evidence of the Franklin party during the next decade, spurred on in part by a reward of 10,000 pounds offered by the British government for conclusive evidence about the party's fate. Many of the searchers died of starvation and exposure. Ironically, even as the "civilized" explorers starved or fell ill with scurvy, or suffered frostbite in their inadequate clothing, generations of Eskimo families whom they considered ignorant savages lived out their normal lives only a few miles away, building snow houses, dressing in skins and furs and waterproof walrus hide, and chewing raw meat rich in vitamins.

The fog-shrouded Bellott Strait that divides the Boothia Peninsula from Somerset Island is narrow and confined, with steep rock walls rising on each side, making it quite clear why early explorers usually missed it entirely.

A rare bowhead whale, one of the estimated two to four thousand left in the world, plays tag with the ship for half an hour in Prince Regent Inlet, teasing with arches and arcs, tumbles and rolls and spouts, its elephant-gray skin gleaming in the water.

The graves of three men from the 19th century Franklin Expedition (and a fourth from a later expedition) are on the shores of barren Beechey Island.

At Beechey Island, ships stop to let passengers visit the graves of three sailors from the Franklin Expedition, as well as a fourth sailor from a later expedition. One, John Torrington, was disinterred, examined and photographed in 1984 in a remarkable state of preservation. Across the rocky little island from the gravestones is a food cache and "post office," a hollow post early visitors used for leaving notes and letters for those who would come after them.

After Beechey Island, the ship encounters the first large icebergs from Greenland's glaciers and makes some calls at ports on Baffin Island. The official end of the Northwest Passage on a west-to-east sailing comes as the ship crosses into Baffin Bay and the waters of the Atlantic Ocean.

Ports of the High Arctic and Northwest Passage

The Arctic Archipelago is the largest island group in the world; its total coastline exceeds the circumference of the earth. But it doesn't look quite the way one would expect.

In fact, we're tempted to subtitle this section "No, No, Nanook," because the old cliché of the Arctic is no longer true—if it ever was. Give up the notion of polar bears floating by on ice floes (possible but not probable), cuddly baby seals, Eskimos families in snow-block igloos, dog teams mushing along the trail.

The short August window that allows ship travel through the high Arctic is not always the best time for wildlife, and the scenery—much of it vast tracts of tundra—is not as magnificent as the Antarctic. The reason you go is because it's there, because you grew up on stories of stalwart explorers suffering terrible deprivations to discover new places, because you're interested in man's adaptation to the Arctic environment, or because you've been everywhere else and want to check off these places on your Century Club roster.

Barrow and Prudhoe Bay, Alaska

Monument to Will Rogers and Wiley Post, who died in a Barrow plane crash in 1935.

Barrow first hit the world press in 1935 when humorist Will Rogers and his daredevil pilot friend Wiley Post died in a place crash there. Today there's a monument dedicated to them.

The only road in Barrow goes 11 miles out to Gas Line Road where the natural gas installation is, but we met one Barrow woman whose car has

20,000 miles on it. She says, "It's amazing how much mileage you can put on just driving around town."

Barrow is the county seat or capital of the 88,000 square mile borough, so everyone from the small North Slope villages has to come here for permits, court hearings and legal matters. The only place in town to stay is the Top of the World Hotel, owned by a Native corporation, with single or double rooms starting at around $165 a night. If you want to eat out, Pepe's North of the Border is the best place in town. The owner claims it's the northern-most Mexican restaurant in the world, but it's probably the highest as well, with combination plates going for around $25 apiece. Arctic Pizza is not much cheaper. If you want to go shopping, the Alaska Commercial Company sells everything from refrigerators to potato chips.

Resident in typical attire on an icy August morning in Barrow.

Off **Prudhoe Bay** we got our first glimpse of the phenomenon of "loom-ing," with the skyscraper buildings reflecting upside down and rightside up in several layers, as if suspended in gray aspic between sea and sky. The city is home to the Prudhoe Bay Oilfield and starting point for the Trans-Alaska Pipeline, as well as home to several thousand oil workers.

Herschel Island, Yukon

A Zodiac landing on Herschel Island.

The northernmost point in the Yukon Territory can be reached by charter outfitter plane as well as ship. The island was a major whaling station in the late 19th century, when the bowhead was hunted almost to extinction. Today the island with its ramshackle buildings serves as an open-air museum.

Two vessels from Pacific Steam Whaling Company spent the winter of 1890 here. By the winter of 1894-95, there were as many as 2000 whalers and Inuits here, and by 1896 one Reverend I.O. Stringer, "alarmed by the demoralization of the natives," set up a mission. By 1903, the Royal North West Mounted Police established an outpost, primarily to police the American whalers who were whooping it up with the same abandon they were noted for all over the world. Whaling died out around 1910, and today the island is usually deserted.

On the beach we saw several recent kills, a caribou, torn into pieces with one leg away from the rest of the body, a seal that had been ripped open at the belly and licked clean inside. A young snow goose and a pectoral sandpiper seemed unruffled when we came near them with our cameras.

In summer the tundra is a thick mat that looks monochromatic from a distance, but if you get down on your knees and take a closer look, you'll see dozens of wildflowers competing for that tiny window of sunlight in the short Arctic season—Arctic lupines, yellow poppies, tiny wild roses, vetches, forget-me-nots, parnassus grass, saxifrage and false asphodels, all perfect miniatures.

The tundra is fascinating, a close mat of astonishing variety, lichens and moss and tiny bright wildflowers that blend into the overall beige from a distance. It's spongy, almost springy, to walk on. Around the island are all sorts of man's leftovers—weathered boats, rusted animal traps, a big rusted steam boiler, coffee pots, pans, a broom. In another area were several graves where the permafrost had pushed up the coffins and broken them.

Greenland

The interior of Greenland, the world's largest and iciest island.

If Greenland and Iceland had been discovered by real estate developers instead of Vikings, the geyser-puffing, steam-heated, lush emerald landscapes of Iceland would be "Greenland" and the perpetually frozen, snow-encrusted land of Greenland would be "Iceland."

Maps of Greenland show the ice-cap island (the world's largest island) as a huge, bare white center fringed with narrow pink or green borders delineating the tiny extent of human penetration. In some parts of the interior, the ice is more than 11,000 feet thick and if it ever melted, according to National Geographic's cartographic division, the level of the world's oceans would rise about 20 feet.

Expedition cruise ships visit ports around the edges of Greenland, and some offer helicopter flights into the interior to land and let passengers set foot on it. Each town has both a European name and an Inuit name. The Inuit spoken in Greenland, interestingly enough, is very similar to that spoken in Northern Canada and Alaska.

Jacobshavn (now called **Ilulissat**, which means "icebergs") is framed by ice fjords 25 miles long and three miles wide. The population consists of some 4000 people and 6000 dogs. The latter, limited by law to Greenlander sled dogs but no pets or any other species, survive on a diet of dried fish. When they set up their evening howl about 5 p.m., one after another, the din is deafening.

The Greenland city of Jacobshavn is now called Ilulissat, which means "icebergs" in the Inuit language.

As in most Greenland cities, housing is provided in high-rise blocks of modern apartment houses, each one with a balcony where fish, walrus and seal are hung out to dry.

A Greenland couple in traditional dress at their Sunday morning wedding in Sisimut (Holsteinborg).

In the little town of **Sisimut (Holsteinborg)**, we saw a traditional wedding on a Sunday morning. Men and boys wore a simple but elegant white parka with dark trousers, while the girls and women were attired in sealskin knickers tucked into high red or white boots trimmed with lace and embroidery, and blouses of shiny royal blue or scarlet, topped with short hand-beaded capes.

Nuuk (Godthab) is the capital and largest city with a population of about 15,000. Outside the Greenland Museum was an open-air market, where a fisherman was offering freshly killed gulls for sale, and hunters were unloading chunks of caribou and tossing them down on a folding table.

The remarkably preserved mummies of Qilakitsoq were found in 1972 in a hillside cliff.

Inside the museum are the famous mummies of Qilakitsoq, the remarkably well-preserved remains of three Inuit women and the infant child of one of them. ("It looks just like a doll!" one woman marveled.) All of them are bundled into sealskin trousers, fur anoraks and boots stuffed with insulating layers of grass.

The mummies, carbon-dated back to around 1450, were found in two shallow rock-covered graves in an overhang on a cliff back in 1972 by two brothers out hunting ptarmigan. Because the sun rarely hit the hillside and a constant cold, frigid wind blew through, the mummies were for all practical purposes freeze-dried.

In this part of town, traditional wooden houses perched on the mossy rocks are painted red, mustard, light blue, bright blue, forest green, teal blue and pumpkin, a colorful touch to the monochromatic landscape.

From the museum we drove past a new cemetery, where every grave was jauntily decorated with clusters of vivid pink, red and blue plastic flowers. "Our people like plastic flowers on graves so the dead can hear it raining," the guide said.

The Hotel Greenland is a good place to sample a typical Greenlander buffet lunch. Check it out—eight varieties of herring with onions and capers, smoked salmon with cucumber slices, baby shrimp with lemon, gravlax (marinated raw salmon), deep-fried scallops, crab casserole, marinated halibut slices, halibut with mussels and mashed potatoes, and fried halibut with canned corn. That was the seafood. On the meat table were dishes of lamb, pork with mushrooms, beefsteak, reindeer steak, smoked reindeer, a local bird called razorbill with a gamey taste, liver paste with pickles and ham with onions, along with canned white asparagus, red cabbage, rye bread and Danish cheeses.

Coastal Greenland towns are reminiscent of Scandinavia.

Northwest Territories/Nunavut

In the vast, wild expanses of the Northwest Territories, the population is estimated at about one person per 60 square miles. Along the northern Arctic Coast, in the newly designated Nunavut Territory (effective in 1999) the Inuit make up 85 per cent of the population.

A cruise through the Northwest Passage will usually call at some of the following communities; on the first-ever west-to-east cruise ship transit in 1985, the *World Discoverer* called at all of them.

Tuktoyaktuk, which means "something like a caribou," is also the pingo capital of the world. A pingo looks like a little hill or mountain, but is actually frozen lake water upthrust and frozen into a solid core, then covered and surrounded by tundra. The pingos here date from more than 1300 years ago. From a ship anchorage, it takes 90 minutes by tender to get into town, so very few cruise vessels call here.

Our Lady of Lourdes, *a Roman Catholic mission ship for 37 years in the Beaufort Sea area, ended up in Tuktoyaktuk after a storm.*

Pre-cut houses are shipped here in pieces by barge, then assembled on lots to provide housing for the town's 900 or so residents. Also here: the Igloo Cafe, a large Bay (formerly Hudson Bay Company) store, some oil company camps, lots of dogs, and no beer for sale. Bleached caribou racks are set atop buildings, reputedly to keep away evil spirits. As at Barrow, there is a conspicuous destruction and replacement of the gadgets of civilization in a pattern of buy and break down, buy and break down, but never repair.

The remote Yukon town of Tuktoyaktuk is typical of the Canadian Arctic.

The traditional Northern Games also take place in Tuktoyaktuk. A printed program outlined some of the events for women: Seal Skinning, Goose Plucking, Caribou Leg Skinning, Tea Boiling. Other competitive events, presumably for anyone, include One Foot High Kick, Musk-Ox Wrestle, Knuckle Hop and Airplane.

The Arctic village of Holman on Victoria Island provides some excellent crafts shopping.

The hamlet of **Holman** on Victoria Island offers some surprisingly sophisticated crafts shopping for a population of under 400, with fine quality Inuit prints, parkas with fur collars, stencilled greeting cards and note papers with Arctic themes, copper-bladed *ulus* (the curved chopping blade with handle), soapstone carvings, appliqued wall hangings and pompom yo-yos. Printmaking was brought here by a mission teacher before World War II. Previously the Holman Inuit were nomadic people who went from camp to camp gathering meat and fish. Now they stay settled in the village but go out to hunt and fish. We saw a number of freshly killed seals on the beach, covered with wood to keep the meat from spoiling. One fisherman came in with a boatload of 30-pound Arctic char.

The altar cloth in the Holman church depicts the Last supper in pieces of seal fur.

Inside the town's small Anglican church is an altar cloth depicting The Last Supper in various seal furs, with kneeling cushions of the same fur.

Women here, particularly the older ones, wear traditional floral Mother Hubbards under fur parkas. Generally the women are very shy but the children are not.

A June Midnight Sun festival called Kingalik Jamboree attracts tourists who fly in from Yellowknife for the dancing, games and feasts.

This Inuit family resides in Cambridge Bay, population 1106, one of the major towns of the high Arctic.

Cambridge Bay is a center of Arctic tourism, with companies that offer excursions for hunting, fishing, hiking or wilderness photography. Plants here process more than 100,000 pounds of Arctic char a year, with fishing going on year-round, including open-water sports fishing in July and August and ice-fishing in winter.

Three mission churches—Anglican, Roman Catholic and Glad Tidings Memorial Pentecostal—serve the 1100 residents. The local co-op store has its own crafts shop with fur parkas, Inuit carvings, appliques and fur dolls.

"It's not too bad in the summer," one worker transplanted from southern Canada told us. "It's the dark period that gets you down. It'll go down to minus 60 at times. Now that's not so cold, it's the wind that's so bad. You get a chill factor of 120 below. It sure keeps you alert when you go outside."

Residents of Gjoa Haven have welcomed visitors since the days of Roald Amundsen.

Gjoa Haven (pronounced Joe Haven) on King William Island is called Ursuktuk in the local Netsilik dialect. Roald Amundsen and his ship *Gjoa* wintered here twice during his search for the North Pole. He termed it "the best little harbor in the world," an understandable opinion under the circumstances.

The town is fairly tidy, with rows of brightly painted wooden houses, half-a-dozen broken snowcats, barking dogs tied to posts, several three-wheelers and a bright red double-cab pickup. One back yard clothesline sports a drying musk-ox hide, another a polar bear skin. Craft work here, as in the other villages, is quite attractive, including tiny figures carved from caribou horn, hand-carved fish spears, and knit caps with tassels.

Beechey Island, its landscape barren as the moon, is one of the most fascinating stops in the Arctic, because it was here that three sailors from the Franklin Expedition of 1845–46 were buried. One of the bodies was exhumed in 1984, still remarkably preserved.

Foggy mists rise from the sheer cliffs of the island, spare, sparse, empty as the badlands with towering gray buttes, gray stones, gray shingled beach, and no sign of life except a few lichens and mosses.

On the barren beach, rusted tin cans are everywhere, along with rusty barrel hoops and staves and wooden pieces of a ship's mast. We are fascinated by the thick lead soldering on the cans, remembering that the Franklin Expedition was the first to carry new-fangled canned foods, and wonder if the men of the expedition died gradually from lead poisoning. Some earlier visitor has erected a cross made from the cans.

A stone cairn and small house structure are monuments to the Franklin Expedition. Everyone who has come by over the years has felt the need to leave a cairn or marker. The "post office" monument has a cache in the back of the post to hold messages left by visitors.

The modern world has entered Arctic Bay and changed many lives.

Nanisivik and Arctic Bay are a pair of adjacent communities on the Borden Peninsula, memorable on our journey because of a speech the mayor, Philip Qamaniq, made aboard the ship. He remembered one of our lecturers coming to Arctic Bay when he himself was a child of four or five, and spoke movingly of the many improvements in the quality of life in the Arctic. "Even finding materials like wood to make a few sleds was impossible. There was not much here. Finding material to make arrowheads out of was almost impossible then." That same day we noted arrowheads are no longer necessary; the seals laid out along the beach ready for skinning had been shot with rifles. The tundra around the village was cluttered with broken snowmobiles and ski-doos, and the teens in town had pierced ears, punk hairdos and chewing gum. One little boy wore a knit cap that said "Miami Vice."

Resolute Bay, on the southern end of Cornwallis Island facing Barrow Strait, is the metropolis of the Canadian High Arctic, with scheduled air service, satellite television, rental vehicles and fine dining in its Narwhal Inn.

UP-FRONT AND PERSONAL

Your Guide to Our Guide

The main body of this book is a thorough compilation of those cruise lines, ships and cruises in Alaska and Western Canada, plus details on other smaller and alternative vessels.

The cruise companies—most are cruise lines but a few are marketing companies who represent various foreign cruise lines—are described first, in alphabetical order, and following each company's description the ships are then described individually or, in the case of identical sister vessels, in a group, but rated individually. In some cases a line's ships may alternate seasons in Alaska.

You may note in the book and even within certain segments of it information repeated several times, because we feel many readers will dip into the book at random rather than read it in sequence.

Eight Terms You May Meet for the First Time in This Guide

1. **Repositioning**—When a vessel moves seasonally from one cruising area of the world to another, it makes a "positioning" or "repositioning" cruise; because the ship has to make the journey whether passengers are aboard or not, the cruises may be discounted, offer an eclectic and unusual itinerary or a lot of leisurely days at sea.

2. **Refit**—The redecoration or remodeling of a vessel, which can be in drydock (the ship above the waterlevel so hulls can be repainted) or wetdock (the ship in the water). "Soft furnishings" are all the upholstery, draperies, sheets, towels, tablecloths and so on. "Cosmetic" refits are sort of like face-lifts—they don't make the ship's life longer, just help her look a little fresher.

3. **The Jones Act**—The term commonly applied to the 1886 Passenger Service Act, an obscure turn-of-the-century passenger cabotage act designed to protect American shipping by not permitting any foreign-flag vessel to transport people between two points in the United States without calling at one or two foreign ports in between. Since there is very little American passenger shipping left, movement has been underway to strike out the antiquated law, but cargo shipping interests zealously

protect it because they feel if it were struck down it would threaten their cargo shipping as well.

4. **U.S.-flag ship**—For a ship to qualify as a U.S.-flag vessel, it must have been built and registered in the United States, be staffed by a primarily or totally American crew and never have been re-flagged to another country. The only exception to this rule was made in 1979 by Congress for American Hawaii's *Independence*, which lost its U.S. flag when it was sold to a Hong Kong shipping company.

5. **Flags of convenience**—A euphemism for ship registrations made in Panama, Liberia, the Bahamas, Cyprus and other nations with low ship taxes and non-hindering union requirements by ship owners who want to save money.

6. **Cruise-only**—The fare quoted is for the cruise itself and does not provide an air transfer from your home town to the port where you board the ship. You're responsible for getting yourself to the port on time, and getting yourself back home afterwards.

7. **Air add-ons**—Usually extra fees added on top of a cruise fare that may (or sometimes may not) already include some airfares. The usual routine is to book an air/sea package through the cruise line whenever it's available since the airfare will usually be lower than you could negotiate on your own. But some travelers want to use frequent flyer awards or fly a specific airline or upgrade to business or first class. While upscale lines may offer this option in their air add-ons, the normal cruise line is going to fly you in the cheapest seats on the most inconvenient schedule that can be blocked out. They don't like it; you don't like it. They're at the mercy of the air carriers, and that's why you don't get your air tickets until a few days before you leave on your cruise.

8. **Meet-and-greets**—These are land-based employees of the cruise line who do all the gathering up and shuttling of passengers between the airport and the ship. They are usually in a uniform of some sort and always carry a sign or clipboard with the name of your cruise line or ship on it. When you see them, check to make sure they have your name on their clipboard list or you may not get a seat on the bus that will take you to the ship.

Eight Things to Remember

1. **Report Card**—The ratings for ship cabins, food and entertainment based on the way your high school English teacher used to grade your book reports.

2. **Average Price PPPD**—The average per-person per-day price, based on double occupancy, for the cruise ship cabin under review.

3. **The Bottom Line**—Personal observations and ruminations about the vessel or cruise line under review.

4. **GRT**—Gross Registered Tonnage, not a ship's weight, but rather a measurement of a ship's enclosed cubic space which tallies all revenue-producing areas aboard for the purpose of harbor dues.

5. **Passengers—Cabins Full**—The maximum number of passengers aboard if all the beds, including upper berths, are filled.

6. **Passengers—2/Cabin**—The normal complement of passengers with two passengers to each cabin.

7. **PSR**—Passenger Space Ratio, a figure reached by dividing the number of passengers carried into the Gross Registered Tonnage, which gives a general idea of how much total enclosed space is available for each passenger; a sort of seagoing comfort index.

8. **Seating**—The number of meal seatings per evening; most ships have two seatings, a first, early or main seating, and a second or late seating. When there is a single seating, passengers often have some latitude in arrival time, unlike two seatings, which require on-time arrival.

The Ratings

When the *Fielding Worldwide Guide to Cruises* first began in 1981, the late Antoinette DeLand initiated the rating system of stars that has always been associated with this guide. We have decided to simplify the system somewhat by eliminating all the pluses but adding an extra star.

The present authors have been aboard all the ships rated with black stars and anchors in the following pages, and the **black star ratings** reflect our personal opinion of the ship and the cruise experience it offers.

White stars represent ships that are in transition from one company to another, which we have been aboard in the vessel's earlier life, or new vessels that are sister ships to existing, already inspected vessels due to come on line in the near future.

Anchor ratings were created by the publishers to reflect a cruise experience that was enriching and rewarding aboard an adventure, expedition, river or coastal vessel where the pleasure of the journey far exceeds the physical quality of the cruise vessel. A few ocean-going ships that offer expedition and educational sailings will carry both star and anchor ratings.

Unrated ships are those the authors have not been aboard in the ship's present incarnation.

★★★★★★   The ultimate cruise experience
★★★★★   A very special cruise experience
★★★★   A high quality cruise experience
★★★   An average cruise experience
★★   If you're on a budget and not fussy
★   A sinking ship

ALASKA HIGHWAY CRUISES

3805 108th Avenue N.E., Suite 204, Bellevue, WA 98004
☎ *(206) 828-0989, (800) 323-5757*

The famous Mile 0 sign at the beginning of the Alaska Highway in Dawson Creek.

History . . . .

Holland America Line veterans Gary L. Odle and Brent Hobday came up with the idea of offering a combination cruise ship and recreation vehicle tour of Alaska, booked in one easy package. The company's first year of operation was 1994, and in early May that year, the first three RVs (one of them driven by the authors) set out along the legendary Alaska Highway. Since that first season, Alaska Highway Cruises' motorhome fleet has grown to 45 vehicles and a choice of 10 different itineraries plus a drive-your-own-RV program and an RV rental program.

Concept . . . .

Many people making a first visit to Alaska consider it a once-in-a-lifetime trip, and want to see as much of the vast 49th state as possible. So the highway cruises idea is simple and convenient: See Alaska by land and by sea. Passengers can choose between taking a Holland America Line cruise along the Inside Passage and into Glacier Bay first and then picking up one of the company's motorhomes in Alaska, or driving the overland portion from Seattle or Edmonton, Canada, to Alaska and ending the vacation with a cruise.

Seeing Alaska with an RV lets you choose your photo stops, like this lake in British Columbia's Stone Mountain Provincial Park.

Signature . . . .

A thorough, step-by-step introduction to the RV, easy even for people who have never driven one before, plus a toll-free Roadside Assistance Line for any questions along the route. A book of campground vouchers for prepaid reservations at designated stops along the route means the passenger can take a leisurely drive, stopping as often as he wishes, and still have a guaranteed campground hookup for the night.

Gimmicks . . . .

A new wrinkle adds the possibility of RV owners driving their own vehicles along the Alaska to Anchorage, then turning them over to Alaska Highway Cruises to be shipped back to Tacoma in a covered transport vessel while the RVers board a cruise ship to sail back.

Who's the Competition? . . . .

No one, really, because the program itself is unique. While it's possible for travelers to bring along their own RV or rent one independently, no one else provides prepaid reservations at campgrounds along the Alaska Highway in places that normally fill up by noon in high season.

Who's Aboard . . . .

More than half the Alaska Highway Cruises passengers have never driven RVs before. They make up all age groups from honeymooners to families with children to grandparents, with or without the grandkids along.

Who Should Go . . . .

Anyone who prefers an independent driving tour to a conducted motorcoach tour around Alaska and Canada's Yukon, British Columbia and Alberta. The opportunities for glimpsing wildlife along the roadways, stopping at a promising fishing lake or taking a serendipitous and photogenic detour down a side road give a sense of freedom and independence. This is a particularly good program for families with children. The Holland America ships have an excellent program for kids, and traveling through Alaska in an RV will provide them a camping-type adventure they'll never forget.

Who Should Not Go . . . .

Anyone who wants to be part of a large group led by guides along well-worn tourist pathways. Anyone who adamantly refuses to cook or wash dishes, even occasionally, while on vacation. (There are not a great many restaurants along the Alaska Highway.) And pets, with the exception of qualified service animals for disabled passengers, are not permitted.

A pair of Stone sheep licking the roadway for residual salt.

The Lifestyle . . . .

For too many years, the RV industry has extolled the virtues of a so-called "RV lifestyle," leading novices to believe anyone behind the wheel of a recreation vehicle is a member of the same club with all the same interests. We disagree. The wonderful thing about traveling by recreation vehicle is the way it adapts totally to one's own lifestyle and becomes an extension of it. On the Canadian stretch of the Alaska Highway, expect to drive with your headlights on all day (required by law), and don't expect to "make time" on the road. Since it's daylight almost around the clock, you'll need to draw your blinds when you go to bed at night, but you can also expect to get early morning starts with good opportunities for wildlife spotting.

The interior of a typical Alaska Highway Cruises motorhome that sleeps two to four, looking across the kitchen sink past the dinette and sofa to the cabover bed at top right.

The Vehicles.................................

The Type C-type motorhomes used by Alaska Highway Cruises range from 18 to 29 feet long and sleep from two to six people. The smaller units have a cabover double bed plus a sofa that makes into a bed, while larger units for families provide a double bed in back and the cabover double bed, plus sofa or dinette unit that makes into a bed. They have full bathroom with toilet and shower, a wardrobe hanging unit, kitchen with stove, microwave and refrigerator, water heater, roof air conditioning and a furnace for chilly nights. The gamut of kitchen furnishings includes an electric toaster and coffeemaker. All towels, pillows, sheets and blankets are also included. You can expect to get from eight to 12 miles a gallon, using regular unleaded fuel. It's a good idea to top off your tank wherever you find gas stations open along the route. You'll also have a portable CB radio in the vehicle.

Wardrobe.................................

You won't need dress-up clothes for the driving portion of the journey, just comfortable casual clothing you can layer, with a pair of good walking shoes. Take along a raincoat or plastic slicker and a warm jacket or sweater in case the weather turns wet or cool. You will want a couple of dress-up outfits for the ship for the captain's welcome aboard and farewell dinners; you may wish to pack them in a separate suitcase from your casual clothing and store them during the RV portion of your trip.

Bill of Fare.................................

See Holland America Line (page 291) for your shipboard cuisine information. On the RV portion of your journey, you'll be able to prepare your own meals if you wish, picking up groceries along the way. Be warned, however, that in the far north, there's not a lot of choice and prices are high. Shop where you pick up the RV, either in Seattle, Edmonton or Anchorage, for the best variety. Remember you'll have a freezer. While there are various lodges and restaurants along the Alaska Highway, most local food is memorable more for quantity than quality.

Discounts . . . .

Alaska Highway Cruises does offer early booking discounts, just as other cruise companies do.

Itineraries . . . .

In 1997, Alaska Highway Cruises offers RV/cruise packages aboard Holland America's *Rotterdam*, *Ryndam*, *Statendam*, *Noordam* and *Nieuw Amsterdam* that can be combined with any of nine driving tours for a total vacation of from 10 to 21 nights. (There's also a seven-night fly/drive program through the Canadian Rockies that does not include a cruise, priced from $956 per person double occupancy.)

A 10-night program takes you on a cruise along the Inside Passage from Vancouver to Skagway, where you pick up an RV to drive the Yukon Highway to Whitehorse and Dawson, then along the Top of the World Highway to pick up the Alaska Highway in Tok. The itinerary also includes Fairbanks, Denali National Park and Anchorage, where you turn in your RV and fly back to Seattle. Prices begin at $2026 per person, double occupancy, with early booking savings, but vary depending on the shipboard accommodations and departure dates you choose.

A 14-night program begins with a seven-night cruise between Vancouver and Seward (for Anchorage), where you pick up your RV for an Alaska driving loop. The driving itinerary covers Palmer and the Matanuska Valley, Denali National Park, Fairbanks and Glenallen, before you return to Anchorage. Prices start at $2,096 per person, double occupancy, with early booking discounts.

A 21-night program lets you drive the Alaska Highway and Yukon Highway, starting from Seattle and ending up in Anchorage two weeks later, where you turn in the RV and board the ship to cruise back to Vancouver. Fares begin at $7,676 per person, double occupancy, with early booking discounts.

Another 14-night package flies you from Seattle to Edmonton to pick up the RV, then you drive along Alberta's Icefield Highway through Jasper National Park, Banff and Lake Louise, then into Seattle to turn in the vehicle and transfer to Vancouver for a seven-night cruise along the Inside Passage and into Glacier Bay. The prices begin at $1,816 per person, double occupancy, including early booking savings. Various other itineraries and special options let you mix and match various routes for the land portion of your trip. Note: You will be required to make a refundable $500 RV damage deposit with your credit card when picking up the RV.

Chicken, Alaska, is a colorful stop en route from Canada's Yukon to Fairbanks.

The Bottom Line

This is our favorite way of traveling in Alaska, combining the restful pampering aboard a luxury cruise ship through the breathtaking scenery of a sea journey along the Inside Passage or through the Gulf of Alaska on the glacier route with a self-drive, semi-camping trip into the interior in a snug and comfortable motorhome. The itineraries average less than 200 miles a day, allowing plenty of extra time for photos, fishing or hiking stops or side-road exploring. Alaska Highway Cruises provides a full individualized itinerary printout, a book of prepaid campground vouchers and additional maps and guidebooks to enrich your sightseeing.

For detailed information about the cruise portion of your trip, see Holland America Line, below, page 291.

Alaska Sightseeing CruiseWest

Fourth and Battery Bldg., Suite 700, Seattle, WA 98121
☎ *(206) 441-8687, (800) 426-7702*

History

The near-legendary World War II pilot Charles B. "Chuck" West came back from the China-Burma-India theater to start an Alaska bush pilot service in 1946, which he turned into world-famous Westours, Inc. After selling Westours to Holland America Line in 1973, he went on to found Alaska Sightseeing/Cruise West (AS/CW), at first offering day cruises on Prince William Sound and along the Inside Passage, and in 1990, adding overnight cruises in Alaska on the 58-passenger *Spirit of Glacier Bay*, now sailing as *Spirit of Discovery.*

In May 1991, West, by now also known as "Mr. Alaska," reintroduced U.S.-flag sailings between Seattle and Alaska for the first time since Alaska Steamship Company suspended its passenger operations in 1954. He used one 82-passenger ship the first year, adding a second 84-passenger vessel in 1992, then a 101-passenger ship in 1993.

Today, with West's son Richard as president and CEO, the family-owned company's vessels cruise in Alaska, British Columbia, Puget Sound, the Columbia and Snake Rivers and the San Francisco Bay/Sacramento Delta.

—AS/CW is the biggest little-ship cruise company in North America, with six overnight vessels and two day-cruise vessels, each carrying fewer than 101 passengers.

—All the line's vessels are under 100 tons, which allows the company full access to Glacier Bay without having to qualify for the limited number of permits issued annually for entrance.

—The company runs a longer sailing season in Alaska than its rivals, beginning in early April and continuing until October.

—Captain Leigh Reinecke and Captain Becky Crosby, two of the very few female captains at sea, command AS/CW vessels.

Concept

This Alaska-savvy company feels that putting passengers in small vessels is the best way to get a close look at and a feel for the true Alaska experience. Eco-tourism and the environment are primary concerns at AS/CW, and schedules are deliberately styled to be flexible so the captain can take a different course to show passengers a mother bear and her cubs feeding in a rich patch of grass, or spend an hour watching a chorus line of 15 orcas lined up across British Columbia's narrow Grenville Channel, so close to the ship that one frustrated passenger complained she couldn't get them all in one shot with her 50-millimeter lens.

Signatures . . . .

A unique bow-landing capability on four of the line's vessels allows passengers to troop down a front gangway and right onto shore without using a tender or inflatable landing craft. This device was originally designed and built by Luther Blount of American Canadian Caribbean Line, whose company also promotes its own bow-landing vessels. Blount's Warren, Rhode Island, shipyard constructed the former *New Shoreham I* and *New Shoreham II*, which now sail as the *Spirit of Discovery* and the *Spirit of Columbia*.

An open bridge policy gives passengers daytime access to the navigation bridge except in severe weather, letting wanna-be skippers chat with the captain, stare at the radar or study the charts. It's also a good place to watch for wildlife without getting wet when it's raining.

There is an emphasis on the foods, wines and boutique beers of the Pacific Northwest. Several regional wines are usually available by the glass as well as by the bottle.

A new repeat passenger club called Quyana ("thank you" in Yupik Eskimo dialect) has been introduced with its own newsletter.

Seamless Service is the line's new trademarked program, providing "a high degree of personalized service, and linking that service from ship to shore."

CHAMPAGNE TOAST

Bartenders aboard these small vessels will let passengers who want a glass of wine at cocktail time in the bar, then another with dinner in the dining room, save money by buying a full bottle at the bottle price and keeping it in the bar refrigerator with the cabin number written on the label.

Gimmicks . . . .

"Our Bear...Their Bear" ad campaign has a closeup photo of bears on a rocky shore taken by an amateur photographer from the deck of the *Spirit of Alaska*. Beside it is a long view photo of an Alaska shoreline with a circle pointing out a distant speck on the shore..."Their Bear."

DID YOU KNOW?

In addition to its overnight cruise ships, AS/CW also operates two highly successful day-cruise vessels that are not rated in this guide—the Glacier Seas, which makes daily eight-hour crossings of the Prince William Sound, and the Sheltered Seas, which takes passengers on five- or six-day cruises of the Inside Passage with overnights spent at land hotels.

Who's the Competition ....

AS/CW competes head-on with two similar vessels operated in Alaska by New York-based Special Expeditions, the *Sea Bird* and *Sea Lion*, which offer a somewhat more rugged version of Alaska and Pacific Northwest cruises with excursions in inflatable rubber landing craft and a permanent rather than transitory company of naturalists. Clipper Cruises *Yorktown Clipper* carries 140 passengers on similar sailings into hidden fjords and glaciers from Juneau and Ketchikan.

The AS/CW flagship *Spirit of '98*, a replica riverboat built in 1984, has a competitor for its Columbia/Snake River itineraries in the *Queen of the West*, a replica paddlewheeler built by Seattle-based Bob Giersdorf, who operated now-defunct Exploration Cruise Lines with some of the vessels now in AS/CW's fleet, and who is a longtime rival of the West family in Alaska tourism services.

Who's Aboard ....

American and Canadian couples and a few singles, most past retirement age, with a sprinkling of younger (read late 40s-early 50s) people and some parents with adult offspring. On each sailing there's usually a handful of foreigners—British, Germans, Australians and New Zealanders—who have come to experience Alaska for themselves after hearing about it from friends or relatives back home. For many aboard, it is their first cruise and they have deliberately chosen what they anticipate is an untraditional, non-fancy cruise experience.

ALASKA SIGHTSEEING/
CRUISE WEST

These homey, unpretentious vessels are ideal for people who want to see Alaska close-up and personal.

Who Should Go ....

These vessels are ideal for people who want to see Alaska up close and personal with a friendly and energetic staff of young Americans (most of whom are here because they love Alaska). While most of the passengers on the cruises we've taken are seniors, we feel younger couples interested in the environment and wildlife would also enjoy the bed-and-breakfast ambience of the vessels for a casual, low-key holiday. There are plenty of options for active rather than passive shore excursions, things like kayaking, river rafting, salmon fishing or bicycling down a mountain. As the company's brochure says, it's "for people who'd rather cruise in the wilderness than shop-till-you-drop."

Who Should Not Go

Families with young children, because there's nowhere on these small vessels for children to play or run about.

Night owls who like a lot of slick entertainment, casinos and discos.

People who want to dress up and show off their jewelry.

Anyone who decided to take a cruise after watching a Carnival commercial.

NO NOs

Smoking is not permitted anywhere indoors on this line's ships; passengers are requested to smoke only on the open decks.

The Lifestyle

Casual, very nature-oriented, friendly and unpretentious. Passengers dine at one seating, arriving soon after the meal call is broadcast and sitting where they please at tables for six. Most choose to wear their name tags that give first name and home state or country, to make casual conversation that much easier with fellow passengers.

All the ships have deck areas for brisk walking, as well as a couple of exercise machines tucked away in a corner somewhere, which is as close as they come to a fitness center.

Entertainment is provided by energetic young crew members who perform improvisational comedy and re-enact corny melodrama scenes so badly they break themselves up as passengers look on with paternal pride. Lectures are ad hoc, provided perhaps by a pair of wilderness rangers paddling in by kayak to show off their territory from an inside point of view (as in, "Right over there last week we found a mountain goat that had slipped and fallen a couple of thousand feet and drowned.") Daytime activity at sea consists of watching the scenery from indoors or out, chatting with each other, reading, playing cards and writing postcards. It's very relaxed and family-like, and passengers share many interests and common backgrounds.

Wardrobe

There is no dress code and no dressing up for dinner. You may show up in whatever you happen to be wearing, so long as it's decent. Casual clothing prevails, with sweaters and slacks or jeans with jogging shoes the Alaska uniform. An in-cabin booklet says it best: "Dress is always casual...(you can) save on dry-cleaning bills once you have returned home...(and) there is no time wasted changing clothes."

Bill of Fare . . . . .B

Young chefs prepare American-style food that is quite tasty compared to the sometimes bland banquet cuisine aboard the big ships, even veering giddily close to the cutting edge for some passengers. One day when the breakfast special was described as lox and bagels, a woman at our table from California's Central Valley asked in sweet confusion, "And what exactly is that?"

Meals are served family-style; you sit where and with whom you please.

There is a set menu for each meal with one or two or, sometimes at dinner, three choices, perhaps fresh Alaska salmon, Cornish game hen or a vegetarian eggplant or lentil dish, but a limited range of alternatives can be ordered ahead of time by people who want something different. At the end of dinner each evening, the chef appears and describes what he's preparing for the next day. Passengers turn in their orders on a slip of paper, somewhat as one does in a railway dining car.

Hot hors d'oeuvres are served in the lounge before dinner, perhaps baked brie in a pastry crust with a garnish of grapes, a pâté, pizza or hot sausages with mustard.

The first course is often already on the table when passengers arrive, so that "yes" or "no" is more appropriate than "this" or "that." Desserts are usually familiar and tempting (a rich pecan tart and a Klondike pound cake were memorable).

Breakfast may be a choice of almond seven-grain pancakes or eggs, bacon and hash brown potatoes, enhanced by a self-service buffet at the room entrance with oatmeal, fresh fruit, juices and muffins. In addition, there's a self-service early riser breakfast of coffee, tea, juice and breakfast pastries.

At lunch, there's usually a substantial salad and/or sandwich, along with a hot soup, or you can request a hamburger or hot dog on special order.

Special dietary requirements—i.e., vegetarian, low salt, low-fat or Kosher—can be requested at time of booking.

There is no cabin food service (except in the Owners Suite on the *Spirit of '98*), but if you're feeling under the weather, one of the cheerful and caring Passenger Service Representatives (a euphemism for cabin and dining room stewardesses) would probably bring you something anyhow.

A modest selection of wines, most of them from California and the Pacific Northwest, are available by the glass or bottle at reasonable prices.

Discounts. . . . .

No special fares or discounts are offered, but low-cost air add-ons from 75 gateway cities are available. Early booking is essential on these ships, which frequently sell out by spring for the entire season.

The Bottom Line

This is a particularly beguiling cruise experience for novices and veterans alike. Quintessentially American in style and cuisine, it should be a must for non-North Americans who want to get a sense of typical American hospitality, humor and food. The staff is young, dedicated and genuinely enthusiastic about what they're showing you, and there's never a discouraging word on board. This is due in equal measure to the passengers, who are the kind of people who travel cheerfully without a litigious attitude or complaint-driven monologue. While not pretending to claim they're perfect for everyone, AS/CW has a way of winning over even a dyed-in-the-wool curmudgeon, should one ever clomp aboard.

Interestingly, the company, like Carnival, has apparently chosen to compete with land-based vacations rather than other cruise products, and they structure their brochures and marketing efforts toward audiences who might book a Tauck Tour or Grand Circle Travel trip, spelling out the itinerary in coach tour terms. "Breakfast, lunch, dinner" is listed as included on each day's itinerary aboard ship, as if other cruise lines did not also provide them gratis. Photos of destination highlights far outnumber depictions of life on board in the land-oriented brochures.

On the down side, there is nowhere to get away from your fellow passengers except in the cabin or ashore. Most of the ships have a single lounge that doubles as bar, lecture room, card room, reading room and gift shop.

Going Ashore

The company's shore excursions during your cruise are generally included in the overall fare and may vary from ship to ship. Additional overland add-ons are available. You can even book these tours if you're cruising aboard another line's ship or flying to Anchorage independently.

Thunderbird Park, Victoria, B.C.

Parliament, Victoria, B.C.

Empress Hotel, Victoria, B.C.

Gastown, Vancouver, B.C.

Six land tours are available, in addition to a clutch of one- and two-night Denali extensions.

Most Exotic
Nome-Kotzebue Arctic Tour
$469 per person, double occupancy.
A two-day itinerary with a jet flight from Anchorage to Kotzebue, the second-largest Eskimo village in Alaska, where you can watch the ever-popular blanket toss, skin sewing and ivory carving, along with story dances. Overnight in Kotzebue, then fly to Nome the next day for some dog sled demonstrations and a visit to a reindeer corral. This extension cannot be purchased by itself but must be added on to a tour beginning or ending in Anchorage.

Best Game-spotting Opportunity
Denali Backcountry Lodges
$388 per person, double occupancy.
Offers a substitute lodging package that lets you trade in the standard hotel and bus wildlife tour in the main park area for three days, two nights, at the end of the road in Kantishna Gold Mining District. Choose between rustic cabins or hotel-type rooms at Kantishna Roadhouse or North Face Lodge, with all meals and lodge activities included, as well as transportation from the park entrance.

Good Glacier-Gazing
Glacier Seas Daylight Yacht Tour
$289-$345 per person, double occupancy, depending on the season.
Takes you from Anchorage to Valdez by motorcoach, through Matanuska, Sheep Mountain, Copper River Valley, across the Thompson Pass and along the Keystone Canyon through the Switzerland of America. Overnight in Valdez and then cruise the return trip aboard a comfortable 65-foot yacht that takes you through Prince William Sound, by the Columbia Glacier, through narrow Esther Passage and into Barry Arm.

Spirit of Alaska
Spirit of Columbia

⚓⚓⚓⚓

⚓⚓⚓⚓

Our first cruise aboard the Spirit of Alaska *was sailing through Washington's San Juan Islands, something like bopping along a scenic maritime road, watching the scenery and looking for wildlife, then pulling into sleepy little port towns. We found a whaling museum staffed by volunteers dedicated to the three pods of 89 or so orcas who inhabit the San Juans, a hotel where Teddy Roosevelt once slept (he'd still recognize it today) and evening concerts on an Aeolian pipe organ in a turn-of-the-century mansion turned resort hotel.*

A forward seat in the lounge gives a good vantage point for seeing glaciers.

Seeing the gradual transformation on these two vessels from basic boats to attractive cruise options has been inspiring. The *Spirit of Columbia*, which we first sailed when it was ACCL's *New Shoreham II*, is dramatically changed after being stripped down to the bare bones and rebuilt in a somewhat more luxurious mode. The *Spirit of Alaska*, built in 1980 as the former *Pacific Northwest Explorer* from Exploration Cruise Lines, has also been considerably spiffed up recently.

These sister ships are clean and comfortable without a lot of big-cruise-ship extras like a beauty parlor, casino or buffet restaurant. But then there's little need to have your hair groomed, since a few minutes in the fresh breeze (or fog and rain) can make it a mess again; gambling is not of interest to most of the passengers aboard; and having an alternative place in which to eat is superfluous when you have a menu of very tasty food at every meal and all-day self-service coffee and tea available. A bow-landing ramp on the front of the vessels allows passengers to disembark quickly and easily at remote island beaches.

The Brochure Says

"The sleek *Spirit of Alaska* is equipped for bow landings, with ample outside viewing areas and an open wheelhouse."

Translation

You can sometimes get off the ship by queueing up behind the rest of the passengers and trooping down a steep, narrow gangway onto land. There's a lot of open deck with railings and various items of nautical hardware underfoot where you can lounge about if you don't mind sharing space with the handful of smokers that are usually aboard, and you can drop by the bridge any time to share your navigational observations with the patient captain.

Cabins & Costs

Fantasy Suites: . . . . .B
Average Price PPPD: $485 plus airfare in Columbia/Snake River.
The brand-new Owner's Suite added to the *Spirit of Columbia* forward on the Upper Deck, with its queen-sized bed, view windows, TV/VCR, mini-refrigerator, bathtub with shower and stocked bar, has generous storage space in both drawers and hanging closets.

Small Splurges: . . . . *C-*
Average Price PPPD: $517–$546 plus air add-ons.
While not strictly suites since the sitting area and the sleeping area are awfully close together, these accommodations will meet the requirements of most non-fussy passengers who don't like big cruise ships. What you get is a window or two, a sink that's in the cabin rather than in the bathroom and a shower.

The San Juan suite aboard Spirit of Alaska is a "small splurge."

Suitable Standards: . . . . D

Average Price PPPD: $395 plus air add-ons.
You get two lower beds, a nightstand, closet, in-cabin lavatory and bathroom with toilet and shower in an area that measures roughly nine feet by 11 feet.

Bottom Bunks: . . . . D-

Average Price PPPD: $275–$303 plus air add-ons.
Take the same facilities as above, push them into a somewhat smaller space, and eliminate the window in favor of a portlight, a hole high up on the cabin wall that you can't see through but that lets a little daylight in, and you have the bottom category C cabin. The good news is, there's only one of these on each ship.

Where She Goes

The *Spirit of Alaska* offers two 10-day "adventure" (read "repositioning") cruises from Seattle to Juneau at the beginning and end of each season (late April and early September), with extra time in the Inside Passage to go exploring in rarely visited areas such as Sea Otter Sound and Prince of Wales Island, as well as the more familiar ports and cruising areas that make up the regular season itineraries. Season-long, seven-night all-Alaska itineraries follow, exploring Alaska's Inside Passage in detail on two alternate itineraries. In the fall, the ship makes seven-night cruises roundtrip from Seattle along Canada's Inside Passage, cruising Powell River and Desolation Sound, Knight Inlet, Princess Louisa Inlet, Canada's Gulf Islands and Washington's San Juan Islands, and calling at Victoria, Chemainus, Vancouver, Friday Harbor and Orcas Island.

Spirit of Columbia spends the whole season from late March through mid-November sailing from Portland roundtrip on seven-night cruises along the Columbia and Snake Rivers.

The Bottom Line

The shallow-draft *Spirit of Alaska* was refurbished extensively in 1995, which got rid of most of her former ugly duckling features. The *Spirit of Columbia* was extensively rebuilt from the hull up in a style intended to suggest a national-park lodge, with a generous use of wood. Since there's no elevator on either vessel, mobility-impaired travelers should consider booking the line's *Spirit of '98* instead, which has an elevator (although no cabins designated for the disabled) and cruises some of the areas these ships do. While the per diem prices may seem high for these simple vessels, the product is so successful that the company does not need to discount or make any special two-for-one offers.

Fielding's Five

Five Good Spots to Stake Out

1. A seat on the sheltered amidships covered area on Bridge Deck on the Spirit of Alaska or on the warm Sun Deck on the Spirit of Columbia that gives a view to both port and starboard.

2. A dining room seat by the windows so you can see wildlife sightings on either side of the vessel; the best whale sightings almost always seems to happen at mealtimes.

3. A forward seat in the Glacier View/Riverview Lounge in order to view glaciers, rivers and other points of interest.

4. A vantage point on the Bow Viewing Area to chat with a visiting ranger or photograph a whale.

5. An Upper or Bridge Deck cabin with doors that open directly onto the Great Outdoors when a wildlife-spotting opportunity arises (or a nicotine addict has to have a cigarette).

Five Good Reasons to Book These Ships

1. The tireless and enthusiastic young American crew.

2. You never have to put on a tie.

3. You can sit anywhere you wish at mealtime.

4. You can walk or jog around the Upper Deck area as many times as you wish with no obstructions to slow you down.

5. You can go places in the Inside Passage or along the Columbia River that few if any other ships visit.

Five Things You Won't Find On Board

1. Breakfast in bed.

2. A blackjack table that takes real money.

3. A self-service laundry.

4. An intimate little hideaway lounge away from the other passengers.

5. Anywhere for children to stay or play.

Spirit of Alaska
Spirit of Columbia

Registry	U.S.
Officers	American
Crew	American
Complement	21
GRT	97
Length (ft.)	143
Beam (ft.)	28
Draft (ft.)	7.5
Passengers-Cabins Full	82
Passengers-2/Cabin	78
Passenger Space Ratio	NA
Stability Rating	Fair
Seatings	1
Cuisine	American
Dress Code	Casual
Room Service	No
Tip	$10 PPPD pooled among staff incl. bar

Ship Amenities

Outdoor Pool	0
Indoor Pool	0
Jacuzzi	0
Fitness Center	Yes
Spa	No
Beauty Shop	No
Showroom	No
Bars/Lounges	1
Casino	No
Shops	1
Library	Yes
Child Program	No
Self-Service Laundry	No
Elevators	0

Cabin Statistics

Suites	3
Outside Doubles	24
Inside Doubles	12
Wheelchair Cabins	0
Singles	0
Single Surcharge	Yes
Verandas	0
110 Volt	Yes

Spirit of Discovery ⚓⚓⚓

NOTE: The former *Spirit of Glacier Bay* was renamed *Spirit of Discovery* at the beginning of 1997.

> *The littlest and plainest vessel in the overnight fleet, the Spirit of Discovery has a tougher style than the other "soft adventure" vessels and the capability of cruising into remote inlets and out-of-the-way places. We could imagine it dedicated to more rugged adventure and expedition sailing, and, since it offers the least expensive of AS/CW's cruises, it might attract younger people who want to experience Alaska in a more active fashion.*

Small-ship fans who gravitate toward the *Spirit of Discovery*, the smallest overnight vessel in this small-ship fleet, should know it's also the slowest, cruising at only 10 to 11 knots. But its size gives it unique access to wilderness inlets in Admiralty Bay, home of numerous black and brown (a.k.a. grizzly) bears. The top category cabins usually sell out first on this ship because they have windows. The lounge is forward, with banquette seating and view windows, and the dining room is aft on the same deck, with four cabins in between. Since it has only three passenger decks, space is at a premium. A recent refurbishment has improved the decor.

INSIDER TIP

Claustrophobes should avoid all cabins on the Lower Deck on this ship because they have portlights (small portholes high up in the cabin that offer no view and only a minimum amount of light) instead of windows. Because they're over the engine room, they're also noisy.

Fantasy Suites: .... NA

None

Suitable Standards: C

Average Price PPPD: $430 plus air add-on.

With a double bed or two lower beds (that crowd it a bit in this 8 x 9 foot space), these basic category A cabins offer a lavatory actually in the bathroom instead of the sleeping area, but a shower that sprays over the entire bathroom.

Bottom Bunks: .... D

Average Price PPPD: $300 plus air add-on.

The largest number of cabins on this ship are 13 category B cabins with two lower berths and a portlight (see "Insider Tip," above) wedged into a seven x 10 foot space. These are so small you have to go out in the hall to change your mind, so we'll call them Unsuitable Standards.

INSIDER TIP

One of the writers, a card-carrying claustrophobe, once had the misfortune of bunking in a cabin like this with a rival cruise line; if you're stuck with one, try turning on the bathroom light and pulling the shower curtain across the doorway so you can pretend it's a window.

Where She Goes

The *Spirit of Discovery* makes two- and three-night cruises from Whittier (for Anchorage) that sail Prince William Sound and call at Valdez on the three-night itinerary. They can also be combined with overland tours for a seven- or eight-night package.

The Bottom Line

As the smallest, plainest and oldest overnight ship in the fleet, the *Spirit of Discovery* doesn't always get the proper respect. Built in 1971 as the *New Shoreham I*, it was one of Luther Blount's first no-frills vessels for American Canadian Caribbean Line. But there are two appealing upscale cabins, 309 and 310, plus two much-in-demand single cabins, 301 and 302. The doughty little vessel can go almost anywhere, including not only lots of places the big ships can't go, but even a few nooks and crannies the other AS/CW vessels can't visit. Even after remodeling, the ship is still not up to the modest glamour of her bigger sisters.

Fielding's Five

Five Things You Won't Find On Board

1. An indoor ashtray.
2. An elevator.
3. A majority of cabins with windows.
4. An afternoon teatime.
5. Wash basins in the cabins; they're in the bathrooms in Category B.

Five Good Reasons to Book This Ship

1. To cruise where nobody else can.
2. It's a little less expensive than the other overnight vessels in the fleet.

3. To sleep in one of "The Condominiums," a pair of freestanding cabins on the aft end of the upper deck, with one picture window facing aft and one facing the side.

4. The prime rib of Angus beef roasted on a bed of rock salt.

5. The flexible itinerary.

Spirit of Discovery   ⚓⚓⚓

Registry	**U.S.**
Officers	**American**
Crew	**American**
Complement	**21**
GRT	**97**
Length (ft.)	**125**
Beam (ft.)	**28**
Draft (ft.)	**6.5**
Passengers-Cabins Full	**57**
Passengers-2/Cabin	**54**
Passenger Space Ratio	**NA**
Stability Rating	**Fair**
Seatings	**1**
Cuisine	**American**
Dress Code	**Casual**
Room Service	**No**
Tip	**$10 PPPD pooled among staff incl. bar**

Ship Amenities

Outdoor Pool	**0**
Indoor Pool	**0**
Jacuzzi	**0**
Fitness Center	**Yes**
Spa	**No**
Beauty Shop	**No**
Showroom	**No**
Bars/Lounges	**1**
Casino	**No**
Shops	**1**
Library	**Yes**
Child Program	**No**
Self-Service Laundry	**No**
Elevators	**0**

Cabin Statistics

Suites	**0**
Outside Doubles	**12**
Inside Doubles	**13**
Wheelchair Cabins	**0**
Singles	**2**
Single Surcharge	**Yes**
Verandas	**0**
110 Volt	**Yes**

Spirit of Endeavour ⚓⚓⚓⚓⚓

We remember this ship as Clipper Cruise Line's Newport Clipper, first of the trio of small, U.S.-flag ships that brought a warm, fresh American style to cruising in the 1980s. Since then, it's served through a couple of incarnations (including one company that painted it with lots of pink) but AS/CW spent most of a year refurbishing it, and it looks great again.

The low, sleek, yachtlike lines of the new *Spirit of Endeavour* mark a different shape and profile from the line's other taller, boxier vessels. Cabins, more luxurious than on the other ships, are fairly similar, with three slightly larger ones in the top category, and all of them contain TV/VCRs. Most cabins boast large view windows, especially nice in Alaska; only the four forward cabins on Main Deck have portholes instead. The bathrooms are identical throughout the ship, quite compact with shower but no tub. All the cabins on the Upper Deck and the four aft cabins on the Lounge Deck open directly to the outside—nice when it's sunny but a little annoying if it's raining. The dining room has wide windows so you won't miss the scenery during mealtimes, and both it and the lounge have been lushly refurbished with plenty of oak, teak and marble, as well as all new fabrics. There is no elevator aboard.

The Brochure Says

"Our newest ship...features a variety of comfortable staterooms, all with windows or portholes."

Translation

Cabins are slightly larger than on some of the other vessels in the line, and you can see the scenery from them.

Cabins & Costs

Note: Prices quoted are the published brochure rates per passenger, double occupancy, per day.

Fantasy Suites: .... NA
None.

Small Splurges: .... B+
Average Price PPPD: $496-$607, depending on sailing date, plus air add-ons.
There are three deluxe cabins, each with a pair of twin beds inside converting to a queen-sized bed on request. There is a long counter on the desk/dresser with chair, a mini-refrigerator and a pullman upper berth for an optional third occupant. Wardrobes are the same size as in the other cabins. Deluxe cabins measure roughly 10 x 15 feet.

Suitable Standards: .... B+
Average Price PPPD: $385 to $532 depending on season and category, plus air add-ons.
All the remaining cabins on the ship are 13 feet x 8 feet four inches, but prices and categories vary. Basically, they contain twin beds (some but not all convert to queen-sized so check when booking), a standard size desk/dresser with chair and adequate double-door wardrobe.

Bottom Bunks: .... B+
Average Price PPPD: $360 to $470, depending on sailing date, plus air add-ons.
These four bottom-priced cabins have portholes instead of view windows, and a slight narrowing toward the bow of the vessel with a small desk/dresser and shelves along the window wall. The twin beds cannot be put together to make a queen-sized bed.

Where She Goes

Spirit of Endeavour cruises Alaska's Inside Passage between mid-April and mid-September, with add-on overland options that can extend your holiday to eight-, 13- or 17-night packages. The ship cruises between Seattle and Juneau, sailing Desolation Sound, the Inside Passage, Misty Fjords and Glacier Bay, and calling in Ketchikan, Petersburg and Sitka.

The Bottom Line

The newest vessel in this rapidly-growing fleet offers the same warm, friendly service, tasty meals and environmentally-oriented cruising, with the added plus of a sleeker, more elegant interior and silhouette.

Fielding's Five

Five Good Reasons to Book This Ship

1.   To call at rarely visited Petersburg, a town that's more like the real Alaska than tourist-filled Skagway or Sitka.

2.   To visit your captain (he or she will welcome you) on the bridge.

3.   To sample the line's cornmeal pistachio cookies.

4.   To lounge about in the elegant lounge.

5.   To get near enough to Admiralty Island to watch for bears through your binoculars.

Spirit of Endeavour ♨♨♨♨♨

Registry	**US**
Officers	**American**
Crew	**American**
Complement	**32**
GRT	**99**
Length (ft.)	**207**
Beam (ft.)	**37**
Draft (ft.)	**8**
Passengers-Cabins Full	**107**
Passengers-2/Cabin	**102**
Passenger Space Ratio	**NA**
Stability Rating	**NA**
Seatings	**1**
Cuisine	**American**
Dress Code	**Casual**
Room Service	**No**
Tip	**$10 PPPD pooled among staff incl. bar**

Ship Amenities

Outdoor Pool	**0**
Indoor Pool	**0**
Jacuzzi	**0**
Fitness Center	**No**
Spa	**No**
Beauty Shop	**No**
Showroom	**No**
Bars/Lounges	**1**
Casino	**No**
Shops	**1**
Library	**Yes**
Child Program	**No**
Self-Service Laundry	**No**
Elevators	**0**

Cabin Statistics

Suites	**0**
Outside Doubles	**51**
Inside Doubles	**0**
Wheelchair Cabins	**0**
Singles	**0**
Single Surcharge	**175%**
Verandas	**0**
110 Volt	**Yes**

Spirit of Glacier Bay   ⚓⚓⚓⚓

NOTE: The *Spirit of Glacier Bay* is the former *Spirit of Discovery*. The ships exchanged names in 1997.

> *On Miner's Night, the bartenders and dining room servers get down and dirty with raunchy red long johns, toy revolvers and popguns, and painted-on whiskers, which are especially funny on the females. While all the vessels in this line have a high degree of bonding among the passengers, Spirit of Glacier Bay seems particularly sociable.*

Miner's Night aboard **Spirit of Glacier Bay** *leads to crew highjinks.*

Built in 1976 for now-defunct American Cruise Line and named the *Independence*, perhaps because of the bicentennial spirit we all had that year, this shallow draft coastal vessel went through a stint as the *Columbia* before being renovated and renamed *Spirit of Discovery*. But in 1997, the ship was renamed *Spirit of Glacier Bay* when it was assigned to cruise that body of water. A favored spot on the ship whether at sea or in port is the trim, open Bow Viewing Area, the place to be to sip late afternoon cocktail in Ketchikan sunshine or watch for humpback whales in Glacier Bay. A colorful information bulletin board with pictures and details about the cruising area is changed daily. Cabins are compact but attractively furnished, and there is a gift shop with books, maps and logo sweatshirts and windbreakers.

Cabins & Costs

Fantasy Suites: . . . . **NA**
None

Small Splurges: . . . . **C**
Average Price PPPD: $346–$420 plus air add-ons.
Each of the four 10 x 12-foot deluxe rooms on Sun Deck has a queen-sized bed, writing desk and chair, TV/VCR, mini-refrigerator and bar, and big windows.

Suitable Standards: . . . . **C**
Average Price PPPD: $309–$383 plus air add-ons.
The 10 Category Two cabins on Lounge Deck open directly to the outside deck, with two lower beds, a full-length hanging closet, vanity with desk and chair and in-room lavatory. Baths have showers only.

Bottom Bunks: . . . . **D**
Average Price PPPD: $279–$353 plus air add-ons.
The two Category Four cabins with upper and lower berths, because they are forward on the Main Deck, are curved from the contours of the hull, eight-and-a-half feet at the widest point and narrowing toward the bathroom, which has a shower only. There is a view window, but no chair, and the lavatory is located in the cabin rather than in the bath.

Where She Goes

In spring, *Spirit of Glacier Bay* cruises Canada's Inside Passage on seven-night roundtrips from Seattle, cruising Powell River and Desolation Sound, Knight Inlet, Princess Louisa Inlet, Canada's Gulf Islands and Washington's San Juan Islands, and calling in Victoria, Chemainus, Vancouver, Friday Harbor and Orcas Island.

In summer, the ship sails between Seattle and Juneau on seven-night itineraries, calling in Sitka, Petersburg and Ketchikan, and cruising Glacier Bay, LeConte Glacier, Misty Fjords and Desolation Sound. On shoulder seasons, the vessel sails Canada's Inside Passage roundtrip from Seattle on seven-night itineraries, calling in Campbell River, Chemainus, Victoria, Vancouver, Friday Harbor, La Conner and Port Townsend, and cruising Desolation Sound, Princess Louisa Inlet, Howe Sound and the San Juan Islands.

Tlingit teenagers from Ketchikan come aboard Spirit of Glacier Bay *to talk about local culture and crafts.*

The Bottom Line

These cruises, while fascinating, are fairly pricey, and optional shore excursions carry an additional cost. But the food and camaraderie on board are excellent, and it's pleasant to stand on the Bow Viewing Area with no nautical machinery to stumble over. If you want to make new friends and see some wildlife, this may be the ship for you.

Fielding's Five

Five Special Things About This Ship

1. The two single cabins, which may be booked at a flat rate rather than a singles' surcharge.
2. The food, especially the peanut butter pie and the fresh Dungeness crab.
3. On some cruises, the riveting evening talk about Tlingit culture by Native American Joe Williams, along with songs and dances by teenagers from his extended family in Ketchikan.
4. The wall of floor-to-ceiling windows in the Glacier View Lounge.
5. The sign-up sheet for passengers who wish to be awakened for wildlife sightings or the Northern Lights.

Spirit of Glacier Bay   ⚓⚓⚓

Registry	**U.S.**
Officers	**American**
Crew	**American**
Complement	**21**
GRT	**94**
Length (ft.)	**166**
Beam (ft.)	**37**
Draft (ft.)	**7.5**
Passengers-Cabins Full	**84**
Passengers-2/Cabin	**82**
Passenger Space Ratio	**NA**
Stability Rating	**Fair**
Seatings	**1**
Cuisine	**American**
Dress Code	**Casual**
Room Service	**No**
Tip	**$10 PPPD pooled among staff incl. bar**

Ship Amenities

Outdoor Pool	**0**
Indoor Pool	**0**
Jacuzzi	**0**
Fitness Center	**Yes**
Spa	**No**
Beauty Shop	**No**
Showroom	**No**
Bars/Lounges	**1**
Casino	**No**
Shops	**1**
Library	**Yes**
Child Program	**No**
Self-Service Laundry	**No**
Elevators	**0**

Cabin Statistics

Suites	**0**
Outside Doubles	**43**
Inside Doubles	**0**
Wheelchair Cabins	**0**
Singles	**2**
Single Surcharge	**Yes**
Verandas	**0**
110 Volt	**Yes**

Spirit of '98 ⚓⚓⚓⚓⚓

We watched her sail into Ketchikan looking tiny and top-heavy, even a little ungainly, compared to a big cruise ship, which was approaching the dock from the south, but as she got closer, she whizzed around the end of the pier and into her little inside spot while the other ship seemed to be standing still.

Passengers on the bow of **Spirit of '98** *get close in to shore.*

We first saw this ship, now the flagship of Alaska Sightseeing/Cruise West, back in 1984 in St. Thomas, when it was the newly built *Pilgrim Belle* for now-defunct American Cruise Line. As the *Colonial Explorer*, it sailed for also-defunct Exploration Cruise Line, then was briefly the *Victorian Empress* for Canadian-flag St. Lawrence Cruises.

A replica of a Victorian riverboat, the *Spirit of '98* is much more appealing than you might expect, with fairly spacious cabins furnished in reproduction

Victorian antiques, good dresser and closet hanging space and large, if rudimentary, bathrooms with shower. Only the lavish owner's suite (see "Fantasy Suites," below) has a bathtub. Like the other vessels of the line, the *Spirit of '98* has only one major lounge where the passengers gather, although there is a smaller, quieter area called Soapy's Parlour aft off the dining room, where the bar is rarely if ever manned.

EAVESDROPPING

"I hate to go home," sighed an Arizona woman on the last morning of her cruise. "This has been the most wonderful trip of my life—beyond my wildest expectations."

INSIDER TIP

This is usually the most popular ship in the fleet, so if you want to sail aboard, book as early as possible or put yourself on a wait-list in case there's a cancellation.

Cabins & Costs

The Small Splurge cabin nomination for the Spirit of '98—the category one cabins on Main Deck forward.

Fantasy Suites: ....A

Average Price PPPD: $747 plus air add-on.

The Owner's Suite is a lavish 552-square-foot apartment set all by itself on the topmost Sun Deck behind the navigation bridge, with big windows on three sides for optimum viewing. The living room has a sofabed, loveseat, two chairs, end tables and coffee table, as well as a full built-in entertainment center, wet bar stocked with complimentary drinks and a game and dining table with four chairs. A separate bedroom has a king-sized bed, and the green marble bath contains a tub/shower combination. This cabin is the only one on the ship that has full room-service privileges, even at dinner, as well as complimentary beverages, including bar drinks, and cabin hors d'oeuvres service nightly.

Small Splurges: ....B
Average Price PPPD: $518 plus airfare add-on.
We particularly like the category one cabins all the way forward on Main Deck, because they're spacious with very little foot traffic passing by. You do hear the engines, but not with a deafening roar, just a quiet, steady throb. Bigger than most of the other cabins, this pair narrows with the curvature of the ship's hull. There's a queen-sized bed, covered with a handsome dark-green-and-black-striped quilted spread and a clutch of lush pillows, including bolsters, in case you want to lie down and read in bed.

A three-drawer nightstand on either side, along with two drawers built in under the bed and a large wooden armoire, provides generous hanging and wardrobe space for anything you'd carry on a weeklong cruise. A desk, reading lamp, mini-refrigerator, TV/VCR and two chairs round out the furnishings, and the bath, large but basic, has a big shower, lavatory and toilet. A small basket of toiletries is also presented.

Suitable Standards: ....B
Average Price PPPD: $471, plus airfare.
Category two and category three cabins open onto outer decks, and have big windows, twin or queen-sized beds, chairs, closet and spacious bathroom. Furnishings are virtually identical to those described above.

Bottom Bunks: ....B
Average Price PPPD: $364 plus airfare add-on.
A pair of category five cabins on the Upper Deck have upper and lower berths, along with a built-in deck and chair, closets and bath with shower, not bad at all for minimum accommodations. They open directly onto the outdoor deck.

DID YOU KNOW?

Kevin Costner as Wyatt Earp was aboard to film the final scene of the Western of the same name; you can see his autograph, along with those of other cast and crew members, on the life ring displayed near the dining room entrance (look at the area where eight o'clock would be on a clock face).

Where She Goes

The *Spirit of '98* spends the summer—from May through September—cruising on seven-night itineraries between Seattle and Juneau, with calls in Ketchikan, Sitka, Skagway and Haines, plus cruising through Desolation Sound, Misty Fjords and Tracy Arm.

Waitresses serenade passengers aboard the **Spirit of '98.**

CHAMPAGNE TOAST

When the time comes to disembark, all the officers and crew line up at the end of the gangway to say a personal goodbye, and only the most reserved passengers settle for a 'thank you' and handshake. Most of them exchange hugs and addresses, and take photos of each other.

The Bottom Line

This is a classy "soft adventure" with a roster of affluent and intelligent passengers, many of them taking a first cruise, who selected the vessel for its historic character and up-close-and-personal looks at Alaska. The American crew is young, energetic and enthusiastic, the food and service are quite good, and there's really nothing to complain about except the utilitarian, less-than-lavish bathroom facilities—and they're not THAT bad. *Spirit of '98* is a real winner for anyone who wants to travel through southeast Alaska in comfort and style.

Fielding's Five

Five Special Spots On Board

1. The forward viewing area on lounge deck, great for spotting orcas and bald eagles.

2. The giant checkerboard aft on Bridge Deck, good for a group game of checkers or chess.

3. Soapy's Parlour, a quiet hideaway for reading aft of the dining room where nothing ever happens in the daytime unless someone comes in to swap a video cassette.

4. The Klondike Dining Room, with big windows and tables for six, and open seating that allows you to sit where and with whom you please.

Comfortable booths by big view windows in the dining room mean passengers don't miss any scenery at meal times.

5. The Grand Salon with its small, appealing bar, Continental breakfast and cocktail hour hors d'oeuvres buffet, cozy and crowded with small tables, chairs and sofas for chatting, reading, card-playing or catching up on correspondence.

Five Good Reasons to Book These Ships

1. You can open the cabin windows.

2. The cruises begin and end in Seattle.

3. It's the only vessel in the line that has an elevator.

4. You can lounge in the sun or shade on the Sun Deck, feet propped against the rail, watching the gorgeous scenery along the Inside Passage.

5. Settle into the Owner's Suite in luxurious comfort (see "Fantasy Suites,").

Five Things You Won't Find On Board

1. Kevin Costner—at least not this year. (See earlier "Footnote.")

2. A library with hardback best-sellers.

3. A stuffy attitude.

4. A key to lock up your cabin.

5. A high crew-to-passenger ratio.

Spirit of '98   ⚓⚓⚓⚓

Registry	U.S.
Officers	American
Crew	American
Complement	26
GRT	96
Length (ft.)	192
Beam (ft.)	40
Draft (ft.)	9.3
Passengers-Cabins Full	101
Passengers-2/Cabin	98
Passenger Space Ratio	NA
Stability Rating	Fair
Seatings	1
Cuisine	American
Dress Code	Casual
Room Service	No
Tip	$10 PPPD pooled among staff incl. bar

Ship Amenities

Outdoor Pool	0
Indoor Pool	0
Jacuzzi	0
Fitness Center	Yes
Spa	No
Beauty Shop	No
Showroom	No
Bars/Lounges	1
Casino	No
Shops	1
Library	Yes
Child Program	No
Self-Service Laundry	No
Elevators	1

Cabin Statistics

Suites	1
Outside Doubles	48
Inside Doubles	0
Wheelchair Cabins	0
Singles	0
Single Surcharge	Yes
Verandas	0
110 Volt	Yes

)] Carnival.®

3655 NW 87 Avenue, Miami, FL 33178
☎ *(305) 599-2600, (800) 327-9501*

Carnival designer Joe Farcus stands amid the flash and dazzle of his signature atrium lobby.

History . . . .

"The most popular cruise line in the world," as the slogan goes, was founded by Ted Arison, who had sold an air-freight business in New York in 1966 and headed back to his native Tel Aviv to retire. According to Arison's son Micky, now chairman and CEO of Carnival, his father never intended to go into cruising, but once he was back in Israel, he took over the management of a struggling charter cruise operation and turned it into a success.

When that vessel, a ship called *Nili*, was returned to the Mediterranean because of the owner's continuing financial difficulties, Arison had several cruises booked but no ship. As Micky tells it, "Ted heard the *Sunward* was laid up in Gibraltar, so he called (Norwegian shipping executive) Knut Kloster and said, "You've got a ship, I've got the passengers, we could put them together, and we'd have a cruise line.' So in effect, they started NCL (Norwegian Cruise Line) that way."

When that partnership dissolved in 1972 after some disagreement between the principals, Arison went out and bought the *Empress of Canada*, renamed it *Mardi Gras* and started Carnival Cruise Lines. The line's first sailing with 300 travel agents aboard ran aground. There was nowhere to go but up.

Today Carnival Cruise Lines operates a fleet of 11 ships with four more scheduled to arrive by 1998. Parent company Carnival Corporation also owns all or part of three other cruise lines: Holland America, Windstar and Seabourn. Founder Arison, an intensely private billionaire and philanthropist, has retired to Israel but still keeps an active eye on the company. *Mardi Gras, Festivale* and *Carnivale* have also retired from the fleet; two were sold to Greek-owned Epirotiki Lines, and the *Festivale* became Dolphin's *IslandBreeze*.

Carnival went public in 1987 and is traded on the New York Stock Exchange.

—The largest cruise line in the world, based on the number of passengers carried.

—Claims the largest staff of trained and qualified youth counselors in the industry (80 full-time employees) to handle some 100,000 kid cruisers a year.

—First cruise line to build a dedicated performance stage in the show lounge (*Carnivale*, 1975).

—First cruise line to use TV commercials on a saturation schedule during the network news hour around the country (1984).

—Pays off a $1,065,428.22 "MegaCash" jackpot to two cruisers from Alaska (aboard the *Jubilee*, March 1994).

—Introduced the world's largest passenger ship, the 101,000-ton, $400 million *Carnival Destiny*, in November 1996.

—Made an agreement with Korea's Hyundai Group for a 1998 joint venture project using the *Tropicale* to develop the Asia cruise market out of Inchon (September 1996).

Concept . . . .

The fledgling company took off when Arison and a young vice president of sales and marketing named Bob Dickinson created a new concept. They cut prices and added casinos and discos to attract more passengers. By loosening the traditional structure of the cruise market with its formality and class distinctions, they created the "Fun Ships" concept for a vast new cruise audience, a segment of the population that had never cruised before. The company calls itself a "contemporary product" aimed at a mass market, and the cruises are meant to tap the fantasy element to stimulate passengers rather than soothe them, turning the ship into a theme park for adults. Carnival's architect, Joe Farcus, the Michael Graves of the cruise industry, says, "The ships give people a chance to see something they don't in their ordinary lives...Instead of sitting in a theater watching, they're in the movie."

Signatures . . . .

Carnival's distinctive winged funnel painted in bright red, white and blue is instantly recognizable in warm water ports all over the Caribbean and Mexico, as well as in Alaska. Chosen originally as a design statement, the funnel, which vents the smoke off to each side, surprised everyone when it actually worked.

Almost as recognizable is the bright blue corkscrew slide into the amidships pool on every "Fun Ship."

Splashy, fog-and-laser shows with contemporary pop music and spectacular dancing are a regular feature aboard Carnival ships; the bigger the ship, the bigger the show.

DID YOU KNOW?

Carnival's ship designer Joe Farcus, famous for his splashy "entertainment architecture," got his start with the line when a Miami architectural firm he worked for was contracted to go to Greece in 1975 to turn the Empress of Britain into the Carnivale. When Farcus' boss got sick and no one else in the office was free to go, the young architect got the job, and the rest, as they say, is history.

Gimmicks . . . .

Smiling waiters in tropical colors circulate around the decks on embarkation day with trays of Technicolor drinks in souvenir glasses, which first-time cruisers sometimes accept without realizing they have to pay for them.

Who's the Competition . . . .

In Alaska, the Carnival product vies with Royal Caribbean and Norwegian Cruise Line for under-40 couples and singles. The line still perceives land-based resorts as its primary competition, and exerts a lot of effort to entice first-time cruisers. Dickinson himself says the former competitors are all "moving upscale" and leaving the field to Carnival and what he flippantly calls "the bottom feeders," low-budget cruise lines with old ships.

Who's Aboard . . . .

Despite the line's early reputation for swinging singles' party ships, Carnival attracts a broad spectrum of passengers from newlyweds to families with small children to middle-aged couples to retirees. About 60 percent are first-time cruisers, down from 80 percent in the 1980s, and some 23 per cent have taken a Carnival cruise previously, up from nine percent in the 1980s.

Families compose a large part of the line's mini-cruise business.

CARNIVAL CRUISE LINES

Who Should Go.............................

Families with children and teenagers will find plenty of diversions for the kids aboard including a well-thought-out Camp Carnival program with youth counselors. They'll find playrooms stocked with games and toys, a full program of daily activities at sea including special aerobics classes and karaoke parties, a kiddies' pool tucked away on its own deck area and the trademark slide at the adult pool (see "Signatures"). Baby-sitting is usually available as well.

Who Should Not Go ....

People whose favorite cruise line was Royal Viking; early-to-bed types; or anyone allergic to twinkle lights and neon.

The Lifestyle ....

About what you'd expect if you've seen the Kathy Lee Gifford commercials—you know, "If they could see me now..." (Gifford says that when she auditioned for the job she almost didn't get it; she was sixth down on the list of performers they wanted to see.)

While the ships are glitzy, they are also very glamorous if you like bright lights and shiny surfaces, and the humor and whimsy Joe Farcus brings to the designs comes closer to *gee-whiz*! than *omigod*! The casinos and the spas are among the biggest at sea, the disco stays open very late, there's often an X-rated midnight cabaret comedy show, singles get-togethers, honeymooner parties, around-the-clock movies on the in-cabin TV set, plenty of fitness classes, trapshooting, shuffleboard, knobby knees contests, ice-carving demonstrations, bridge and galley tours and all the other usual shipboard folderol.

> ### INSIDER TIP
>
> *No passengers under 21 years of age are permitted to travel without a parent or adult guardian, unless they're a young married couple, and new I.D. cards issued to every passenger, including youths, flags a bar computer to report an underage wanna-be drinker.*

Wardrobe...............................

While Carnival ships are a bit less dressy than more traditional lines, many of the passengers look forward to dressing up on the one to two formal nights a week, when formal dress or a dark suit is suggested. You will see more sequins and tuxedos those nights than sport coats without a tie. The pattern is usually two formal nights, two informal nights (the line suggests sport coat and tie for men) and three casual nights that call for resort wear. For daytime, almost anything goes (or almost nothing, if you opt to sunbathe in the secluded upper-deck topless sunbathing area). To go ashore in Alaska, casual, comfortable clothing and good walking shoes are best. Don't forget to take a sun hat and sunblock.

Bill of Fare............................ B+

From a predictable mainstream seven-day menu rotation on its ships featuring Beef Wellington and Surf 'n Turf several years ago, the line has made some changes in its menus after finding a 300 percent increase in the number of vegetarian entrées ordered and a 20 percent rise in chicken and fish. Fewer than half the passengers order red meat these days, says Carnival's food and beverage director; a popular fresh fish "catch of the day" is now offered on every dinner menu. Alaska menus feature a different version of salmon each evening.

That's not to say Beef Wellington and Surf 'n Turf have disappeared—they haven't—but rather that menus have moved a little closer to the cutting edge without scaring diners with huitlacoche mushrooms or fermented soybean paste; "Fun Ship" fans will still encounter those ubiquitous theme nights (French, Italian, Alaskan and Oriental) and flaming desserts parade, and children can order from their own special menus of familiar favorites.

Three-quarters of all the passengers opt for buffet breakfast and lunches rather than going to the dining room to their assigned seating, so a much wider range of casual, self-service options has been added.

All the shipboard dining rooms are smoke-free on Carnival. You can breakfast in bed and order simple menu items such as sandwiches and fruit and cheese 24 hours a day from room service. Big midnight buffets are followed by a second mini-buffet at 1:30 a.m. on these late-night ships.

NO NOs

The brochure warns that Carnival passengers are not permitted to bring alcoholic beverages of any kind aboard the ship or to consume any beverages purchased in a foreign port in the public rooms or on deck.

Showtime. . . . . .A+

Lavishly costumed, fully professional entertainment is one of the line's hallmarks. The company produces its own musical shows in-house with high-tech lighting, sound and special effects. Different shows are featured on different ships (much as the Broadway shows on Norwegian Cruise Line ships vary from one vessel to another) so if you're a fan of big production shows, you'll want to cruise them all sooner or later.

Three live bands and a piano bar are usually playing around the ship in the evening.

The Alaska sailings carry a naturalist, as well as lecturers who tell you where to shop.

Discounts . . . .

Deduct up to $1200 per cabin from the listed brochure rates if you book early. Savings amounts are reduced over time based on demand, so earliest bookings get the lowest rates. Some restrictions apply.

The Bottom Line

Carnival is not just for party-time singles any more. The new generation of sleek megaliners that began with the *Fantasy* in 1990 and continues through the *Ecstasy, Sensation, Fascination, Imagination, Inspiration* and, in 1998, the *Elation* and *Paradise,* are real crowd-pleasers.

While the public areas pulse with their abstract sensory stimulation, fiber optics, neon, Tivoli lights, state-of-the-art stagecraft and virtual reality machines, there are a few quiet areas to get away from it all—in the massage rooms, the indoor whirlpool spas, the top deck jogging track or the outdoor deck wings aft behind the indoor Lido Deck bar. Cabins are adequate in size and comfortably free of glitz, with all-day movies and room service, although not so cushy you'll spend your whole cruise there rather than hitting the bars and casino.

On the other hand, if you want a quiet, relaxing cruise, better book another cruise line, because these are the "Fun Ships." While they're not to our own particular cruising taste—we find it hard to spend more than three or four days aboard before the color, lights and pinging slot machines get to us—most Carnival passengers think they've died and gone to heaven. For flat-out fun-and-games cruising, nobody does it better.

Note: The *Tropicale,* which cruises Alaska in 1997, is more subdued than the *Fantasy*-class vessel which will probably cruise there in 1998.

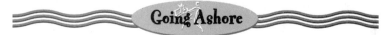

Going Ashore

Carnival CruiseTours extends your seven-night cruise to a 10- or 11-night vacation that lets you see more of mainstream Alaska from your Anchorage base by flying to Fairbanks one-way and traveling in the other direction by luxury rail car.

Northbound travelers can book a 10-night program ($850 per person, double occupancy) that follows the Glacier Route cruise with a flight to Fairbanks, a gold mining tour and overnight stay, then a luxury rail transfer to Denali National Park aboard the McKinley Explorer luxury train. Overnight in Denali, then reboard the train to continue along the scenic route to Anchorage. The 11-night program ($990 per person, double occupancy) begins with a city tour and overnight in Anchorage, then the rail trip to Denali aboard the McKinley Explorer with an overnight and a natural history tour of the park, followed by an afternoon McKinley Explorer journey to Fairbanks. Overnight in Fairbanks, take a gold mining tour and a riverboat cruise, spend a second night in Fairbanks and fly back to Anchorage the next day.

Southbound CruiseTours follow the same land itineraries with the cruise added on at the end of the program.

Carnival offers some 61 shore excursion opportunities that range from a $16 Mendenhall Glacier transfer to a $269 flyfishing adventure by floatplane out of Juneau.

The luxurious McKinley Explorer with its dining and dome cars carries you in comfort through Alaska's most breathtaking scenery.

Best Fun Ship Buys On a Budget

1. Gold Creek Salmon Bake, Juneau

$24 adults, $16 child, 1.5 hours.

The original Alaskan salmon bake is held at the remains of an old gold camp, and features salmon grilled over an open alderwood fire, ribs, rice pilaf, baked beans, salad, cornbread, soda, beer and wine, with marshmallows to roast later while you listen to the live music from local entertainers.

2. Totem Heritage and Ketchikan City Tour

$29 adults, $14.50 children 12 and younger, 2.5 hours.

Cheaper than the same tour from some other cruise lines, this excursion takes you 10 miles out of town to the Totem Bight State Park and ceremonial clan house, to the world's largest pulp mill, and to Ketchikan's lively Creek Street, former redlight district, "where both the fish and the fishermen went upstream to spawn."

Don't Bother to Book

The Historical Sitka Tour

$29.50 adult, $14.75 child.

Covers very little you couldn't do on foot with a guidebook or notes from the shore excursion lecture. The Sitka National Historical Park is the only area that isn't in town, and it's a level 1/3-mile walk away.

Note: At press time Carnival had not announced which of the following *Fantasy*-class vessels will be assigned to Alaska in 1998.

Ecstasy	★★★★★
Fantasy	★★★★★
Fascination	★★★★★
Imagination	★★★★★
Inspiration	★★★★★
Sensation	★★★★★

"All I can say is, Wow!" sings spokeswoman Kathy Lee Gifford in the Carnival commercials, and passengers walking for the first time into these ships with their soaring seven-deck atriums, glass elevators and moving sculptures are saying the same thing—except for an occasional, "Oh my God!" from those who pretend to more refined tastes.

On the Fantasy, the huge clear-glass skylight in the dome ceiling seven decks above drenches the atrium with natural light during the daytime, but as dusk approaches, the room is suffused with color from miles of neon tubing that circle every level of the space. The effect is strangely impressive, but disorienting, something like walking into a giant jukebox. If you don't like the color, hang around for a while and it will change.

This is no place like home.

Toto, I don't think we're in Kansas any more.

Are you listening, Elvis? Las Vegas is alive and floating.

The *Fantasy*-class ships are all virtually identical in superstructure and deck plan, but each is dramatically different inside. We find ourselves doing a lot of standing by the rail looking down, both inside from the upper atrium levels down into the lobby, watching the glass elevators glide up and down, and outside from the upper decks down into the amidships pool deck with its bright blue water slide, at the impromptu dancers in bathing suits who always begin to gyrate on deck when the band comes out on the raised stage.

The 12,000-square-foot Nautica spas with their large whirlpool spas and well-equipped gyms are among the best at sea.

On the topmost deck is a rubberized jogging track, then down one deck on Veranda Deck is the huge Nautica spa with one of every exercise machine known to man, 26 suites with private verandas and on the aft deck, a sunbathing area and pool with two Jacuzzis.

One deck down on Lido is a large glass-walled self-service cafe with indoor and outdoor dining and the amidships pool area with its stage.

The Promenade Deck and Atlantic Deck contain most of the bars, lounges, showrooms and dining rooms, along with a galley on Atlantic Deck that makes the aft dining room a you-can't-get-there-from-here proposition. Directly behind that dining room is the teen club and children's playroom, and on the deck just above, the wading pool, all completely removed from the adult areas of the ship. Forward on the same deck is a second dining room, a small lounge and library, the atrium, shops and the main level of the showroom. One deck up on Promenade is the showroom balcony, the atrium, a vast casino on port side and an enclosed "avenue" on starboard side with sidewalk cafes and bars, another lounge and a disco, then still another lounge and a cabaret showroom aft.

The remainder of the cabins are on four decks below Atlantic; the base of the atrium with the ship lobby and information desk is one deck down on Empress. Three banks of elevators and three sets of stairs access the cabins.

These are "get up and get out and have fun" ships; the cabin TV runs the same daily feature over and over in any 24-hour period, and with only a minimal library of books, you mustn't expect to snuggle down and read.

The Brochure Says

"The best vacation on land or sea! Children have plenty to do on a "Fun Ship" cruise. Relax on acres of sun splashed decks. Kick up your heels to one of our many live bands. Pamper yourself with our Nautica Spa program. Our attentive staff will wait on you 24 hours a day. Savor a fabulous array of food from around the world. We bet you'll have a great time in the largest casinos at sea. Enjoy lavish Las Vegas-style entertainment."

Translation

Every sentence is accompanied by a picture making the intent very clear—"Children" are eating pizza with a youth counselor serving them and no hovering parents in the background. "Relax" shows rows of sunbathing bodies holding flower-garnished drinks. "Kick up" depicts a pair of sedate middle-aged couples doing what kids today call close-dancing, meaning they're dancing while holding each other in their arms, like people over 50 do sometimes. "Pamper" shows shapely young bodies, mostly female, on gym machines with smiling male instructors. "Our attentive staff" is a waiter serving breakfast in bed to a happy couple. "Savor" shows a table of six-plus passengers (the table edge is cropped, but a six-top is the smallest table you can usually find on these vessels). "We'll bet" is a croupier at the roulette wheel with a lot of happy couples, all of whom seem to think they're winning. "Enjoy lavish Las Vegas-style entertainment" depicts a bevy of chorines in pink feathers and towering headdresses. Altogether, it's Cruising 101 Illustrated for first-timers.

INSIDER TIP

Sometimes passengers are so hypnotized by the dazzle that they just stand there staring indecisively at the elevator buttons, the buffet selections, the ice cream dispensing machine, the coffee dispensing machine, lost in space or reverie. You may have to nudge them to move them along.

DID YOU KNOW?

There are 226 slot machines, 23 blackjack tables, three craps tables, two roulette wheels and a giant wheel in the Crystal Palace Casino on the Ecstasy.

EAVESDROPPING

Designer Joe Farcus says passengers should feel romance, excitement and the anticipation of boarding a new ship, "and when they come on board, I don't want them to be disappointed; when they leave, I want them to feel they got more than they expected."

Cabins & Costs

Fantasy Suites: . . . . A
Average Price PPPD: NA for Alaska.

CARNIVAL CRUISE LINES

The *Fantasy*-class ships have some of the best veranda suite buys at sea, with 28 Upper Deck veranda suites and 26 Veranda Deck demi-suites. But opt for the top— one of the Upper Deck suites with separate sitting area is big enough for entertaining and furnished with an L-shaped sofa, two chairs, coffee table, cocktail table, built-in wood cabinetry that includes a mini-refrigerator, glassware and TV with VCR, and a teak-floored private veranda with lounger, two chairs and a small table. The bedroom area has twin beds that can convert to queen-sized bed and marble counter desk/dresser with five drawers. The bath is fairly large with a marbleized counter, inset porcelain sink, Jacuzzi tub and tile walls and floor. There's an entry with walk-in closet, one full-length and two half-length hanging spaces, shelves and a large safe.

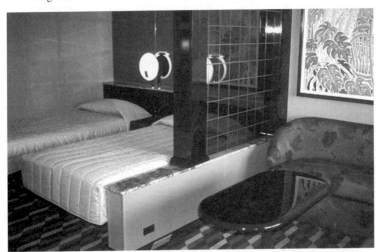

Fantasy-class suites like this veranda suite on the **Imagination** *are good buys.*

Small Splurges: . . . . A
Average Price PPPD: NA for Alaska.
The demi-suites on Veranda Deck have twin or queen-sized beds, big windows, private veranda with two chairs and a table, sitting area with sofa, table and chair and a bath with tile shower. Some have partially obstructed views due to hanging lifeboats.

Suitable Standards: . . . . B
Average Price PPPD: NA for Alaska.
Carnival's standard cabins are consistent throughout this class, 190 square feet with twin beds that convert to queen-sized, dark gray carpeting thinly striped in bright colors, an armchair and matching stool, a built-in corner table, wall-mounted TV set and desk/dresser with four drawers. The closets have one enclosed and one open full-length hanging space plus shelves. The tile bath has a big shower, a counter around the sink and a glass-doored medicine cabinet.

Bottom Bunks: . . . . D
Average Price PPPD: NA for Alaska.
The lowest category cabins are insides with upper and lower berths placed perpendicular to each other, considerably smaller than the standards (the brochure calls them "cozy"), similar closet space and a tile bath with shower. There are only nine

of these on each ship, plus 28 more with upper and lower berths in higher price categories that are slightly roomier.

The Bottom Line

These ships come to life at night when the dramatic colors and lighting are highlighted against the many glass surfaces. They are tactile (touch the surfaces of the chairs, tables, walls and floors on *Imagination*), aural (changing sounds of nature—the surf, rain, wind and chirping birds—wash by on *Sensation's* Sensation Boulevard) and intensely visual (fiber optics and neon panels "jump off" the walls as passengers walk by on the *Sensation*).

Elsewhere, we call the *Fantasy* a lava lamp for the 1990s, but we mean it in a fond sense. This series of ships is constantly amazing and amusing, thanks to the ingenuousness and genius of Joe Farcus, whose own innocence and clarity of image keep them from being vulgar.

Are they gaudy? Sometimes. Do they tread dangerously close to maxing out? Perhaps. But they can match the much-praised pair of Crystal ships in marble, crystal and glove leather, dollar for dollar, ton for ton. Whether they strike you as glitzy or glamorous depends on your own individual taste, but they're never boring. Carnival delivers precisely what it promises, and if you've seen its advertising, you should already know whether it's the right cruise line for you.

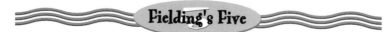

Fielding's Five

Five Fabulous Spaces

1. The Old Curiosity Library aboard the *Imagination* boasts replicas of Bernini's altar columns from St. Peter's in Rome along with genuine and reproduction antiques to give the atmosphere of an antique shop.

2. Also on the *Imagination*, the classy Horizon Bar & Grill with its 24-hour pizzeria (also serving calzone, Caesar salad with or without grilled chicken and garlic bread), jukebox, elegant cast aluminum chairs, granite and aggregate floors, Matisse-like hand-painted fabric tabletops under resin, fresh flowers, cloth napkins and silverware already on the tables and lots of drinkable wines by the glass.

3. Diamonds Are Forever on the *Fascination* is a James Bond take on a disco, with fiber optic diamonds on the walls and ceilings, tabletops that glitter with handset "diamonds", and carpets woven with diamond shapes; the black granite floor and banquette bases emit smoke/fog at night when the disco is going full blast. It's hot, hot, hot!

4. The Universe show lounge aboard the *Fantasy*, which in the words of one passenger "looks like it's ready to blast off" with its carpet covered with comets and swirling ringed planets, its black upholstery flocked with tiny, intensely bright metallic microchips in red, blue, silver and gold, and its ability to turn from a gigantic stage with a 33-foot turntable in the center to a ballroom closed off by a wall of beveled gold mirrors with a sunken orchestra pit that rises to eye level.

5. The 12,000-square-foot Nautica spas on every ship with Steiner of London beauty services from facials to aromatherapy and massage, an abundance of state-of-the-art exercise machines facing a glass wall overlooking the sea, sauna and steam rooms, fully mirrored aerobics room and big twin Jacuzzis lit by the sun through an overhead skylight.

Five Off-the-Wall Places

1. Cleopatra's Bar on the *Fantasy*, patterned after an ancient Egyptian tomb, with stone floor, hieroglyphics on the walls, gilded sarcophagi and full-sized seated and standing Egyptian gods and goddesses. In the center of the room is a glossy black piano bar, and as random laser lights spotlight details around the room, you half expect to hear a chorus of "My Mummy Done Ptolemy."

2. Cats Lounge on the *Fantasy*, inspired by the set for the musical of the same name, with oversized tin cans and rubber tires, bottle cap and jar lid tabletops, and walls lined with soap and cereal boxes; you enter through a giant Pet milk can and the band plays atop a giant rubber tire laid on its side.

3. Touch of Class piano bar on the *Sensation*, entered through a doorway framed by hands with long red fingernails; the same supporting hands cup the barstool seats (making for some funny images from the back when the stools are filled) and support cocktail tables, while the walls are covered with ceramic tile handprints.

4. The movie star mannequins spotted all around the *Fascination*, from Vivien Leigh and Clark Gable standing by the faux fireplace in the Tara Library to Bette Davis sitting in a corner booth of the Stars Bar with her ubiquitous cigarette, amid delightful Al Hirschfeld drawings under glass on the tops of the small white cafe tables. Passengers stand in line to photograph each other hugging a movie star; it's a big hit.

5. The Rhapsody in Blue bar aboard the *Inspiration* with its rippling blue fabric ceiling and Manhattan-deco upholstery.

Five Good Reasons to Book These Ships

1. To have fun in an unintimidating, relaxed atmosphere without worrying about picking up the wrong fork or wearing the wrong clothes.

2. To try to win a million dollars.

3. To eat, drink, gamble, dance and watch movies all night long if you want to; it's your vacation.

4. To show the snapshots of the ships to your neighbors back home "so they can see you now..."

5. To get married on board (the line can arrange it) and spend your honeymoon at sea, all for less than a formal church wedding at home would probably cost; call Carnival's Bon Voyage Department at ☎ *800-WED-4-YOU* for details.

Five Things You Won't Find On Board

1. Lavish gift toiletries, even in the suites; all you get is a sliver of soap.

2. A table for two in the dining room.

3. A lot of books in the library.

4. A cruise director who spells Knobby Knees (as in the contest) with a "k"; every program we've seen calls it "Nobby Knees."

5. An atrium sculpture that doesn't move; some of them are inadvertently hilarious.

Ecstasy	★ ★ ★ ★ ★
Fantasy	★ ★ ★ ★ ★
Fascination	★ ★ ★ ★ ★
Imagination	★ ★ ★ ★ ★
Inspiration	★ ★ ★ ★ ★
Sensation	★ ★ ★ ★ ★

Registry	**Panama**
Officers	**Italian**
Crew	**International**
Complement	**920**
GRT	**70,367**
Length (ft.)	**855**
Beam (ft.)	**104**
Draft (ft.)	**25' 9"**
Passengers-Cabins Full	**2594**
Passengers-2/Cabin	**2040**
Passenger Space Ratio	**34.49**
Stability Rating	**Good**
Seatings	**2**
Cuisine	**International**
Dress Code	**Traditional**
Room Service	**Yes**
Tip	**$7.50 PPPD, 15% automatically added to bar checks**

Ship Amenities

Outdoor Pool	**3**
Indoor Pool	**0**
Jacuzzi	**6**
Fitness Center	**Yes**
Spa	**Yes**
Beauty Shop	**Yes**
Showroom	**Yes**
Bars/Lounges	**5**
Casino	**Yes**
Shops	**3**
Library	**Yes**
Child Program	**Yes**
Self-Service Laundry	**Yes**
Elevators	**14**

Cabin Statistics

Suites	**28**
Outside Doubles	**590**
Inside Doubles	**402**
Wheelchair Cabins	**20**
Singles	**0**
Single Surcharge	**150-200%**
Verandas	**54**
110 Volt	**Yes**

CARNIVAL CRUISE LINES

Note: The *Tropicale* cruises Alaska in 1997 only, after which it repositions to Asia.

Tropicale ★★★

When Ted Arison announced in 1978 that he was ordering his line's first new ship, the 36,674-ton Tropicale, 20,000 tons was considered large for a cruise ship. The wisdom of the day was that he'd never fill it. (Today the Tropicale is the smallest ship in the fleet.)

When it was delivered in 1982, he further confounded industry insiders by taking it out of the Caribbean and positioning in on the west coast for Mexican Riviera cruises out of Los Angeles. It wasn't very long until the vessel was operating at 100 percent-plus capacity.

The smallest ship in Carnival's fleet, the *Tropicale* might appeal particularly to people who like the "Fun Ship" cruise style but don't want to sail on megaships. With 1022 passengers and a single dining room with two seatings, it's a little easier to get to know fellow passengers, at least by sight.

Some of the details on the *Tropicale* reflect design styles of older vessels, and again may have been influenced by the former *Festivale*. The dining room, for instance, is on a lower deck with no windows, making it an awkward three-deck climb up to the show lounge, which is forward on Empress Deck.

At the same time, it modestly forecasts some of the bells and whistles that would distinguish the later new ships—the Exta-Z disco with its glass dance floor lit from below, the swimming pool with a slide leading down into it, the distinctive split T-shaped funnel that vents the smoke off to each side.

Cabins are modular, virtually the same size in all categories except for the slightly larger top deck veranda suites.

The Brochure Says

"You'll see more of Alaska's magical landscape when you cruise with Carnival. And because you're on a 'Fun Ship,' you can count on having Your Kind of Fun!"

Translation

We're a little bit nervous at Carnival about how many of our younger, with-it, sun-bathe-and-piña-colada crowd will go for glaciers, let alone putting more clothes on to go on deck. Maybe we can distract them with the Midnight Sun or something.

Cabins & Costs

Fantasy Suites: . . . . B

Average Price PPPD: $393 without airfare.

The veranda suites with private balconies are best, especially if there's a glacier or Northern Lights sighting on your side of the ship. The suites contain twin beds that convert to king-sized in a separate sleeping area, with a comfortable sitting area as well. There is a pulldown upper berth and a sofa that makes into a bed, in case you want to take two additional family members along. The private veranda has a couple of chairs, the bath has a tub, and a low room divider separates sleeping and sitting areas. It could work as a family suite, especially since the kids (or adult occupants) would pay only $599 apiece for the cruise.

Small Splurges: . . . . NA

There's nothing that really qualifies; all the rest of the cabins are standards, and prices change only according to the deck and whether the cabin is inside or outside (Carnival calls the latter Ocean View cabins).

Suitable Standards: C

Average Price PPPD: $293 plus airfare.

Upper Deck outsides in category Eight offer windows and twin beds that convert to king-sized beds. A corner table, wall-mounted TV set, chair and desk/dresser with drawers, closet and bath with shower are what you get. Eleven cabins have been modified for the physically challenged and provide 32.5 inch-wide doors.

Bottom Bunks: C

Average Price PPPD: $243 plus airfare.

A few bottom-price insides with upper and lower berths are on the *Tropicale* with furnishings similar to all the other ships in the fleet. The good news is they're larger than on most other vessels, the bad news is there are only nine of them.

Where She Goes

Between May and September, the ship offers Wednesday departures on Gulf of Alaska sailings between Vancouver and Seward (for Anchorage), calling in Skagway, Juneau, Ketchikan and Sitka (northbound) or Valdez (southbound), and cruising College Fjord, Columbia Glacier, Lynn Canal and Endicott Arm, Tracy Arm or Yakutat Bay. Cruise tours for 10 or 11 days add optional land programs to Fairbanks, Denali and Anchorage.

The Bottom Line

The ship is in very good condition except for some worn natural teak decking that appears to be gradually being replaced.

Since the *Tropicale* is the line's smallest ship and has cruised in Alaska before, it was a logical choice to sail the territory. The downside, of course, is the lack of a retractable glass roof over the pool and sunbathing area for sometimes inclement Alaska weather, but there are wind baffles that shelter the central area.

The enclosed promenades on each side of the casino make a comfortable and attractive place to sit between whale-watching and glacier-spotting. It's certainly cheerful enough with its school bus yellow and black chairs and floor squares, inset with a Mondrian-pattern carpet in primary colors on the floor and walls, along with plastic-topped tables in red, yellow, blue and purple.

One advantage Carnival's affiliation with Holland America Westours offers is a seasoned and well-tested program of CruiseTour options.

The awesome Columbia Glacier is on view from Carnival's Alaska ships.

Fielding's Five

Five Fun Spots

1. Chopstix, a dazzling piano bar that was added to the ship in a remodeling, has tabletops bordered with piano keys, a carpet sprinkled with musical notes, arches that are neon-lit piano keys, and a black piano covered with piano keys and encircled with black barstools.

2. The Boiler Room Bar & Grill, with its deliberately exposed pipes painted in rainbow colors and industrial-looking tables of brushed chrome with a bottle of catsup sitting on each; this is where the buffet breakfasts and lunches are served.

3. The Tropicana Lounge with its sofas and long curved banquettes in a dark batik print shot through with gold threads and a Picasso-print carpet; the stage doubles as a raised dance floor.

4. The Paradise Club Casino, where the most comfortable barstools on the ship are—where else?—in front of the slot machines.

5. The Exta-Z Disco, with a glass floor lit from underneath with bright bands of neon plastic high-backed banquettes piped in shocking pink, chrome chairs and tables and Tivoli lights.

Five Good Reasons to Book This Ship

1. It offers two very good itineraries—northbound and southbound between Vancouver and Seward (for Anchorage) with an afternoon of cruising Prince William Sound and views of Columbia Glacier and College Fjord. (See Where She Goes, above, for full itineraries.)

2. If you book ahead of time, you can deduct as much as $1200 a cabin from the cruise price, perhaps enough to cover your airfare add-ons; contrary to the other sailings, Carnival's Alaska cruise prices do not include air.

3. To hear special programs from an onboard naturalist.

4. To join (Carnival hopes) a younger and livelier crowd on this traditionally senior destination; actually, we see more and more younger couples and families in Alaska every year.

5. To sample the low-fat, low-cal Nautica Spa cuisine.

Five Things You Won't Find On Board

1. A 24-hour pizzeria; that's unique to the megaliners.

2. An outdoor Jacuzzi.

3. Ash trays in the dining room; Carnival has a no-smoking policy in all its dining rooms.

4. A view from the dining room.

5. A kosher meal.

Tropicale   ★ ★ ★

Registry	Liberia
Officers	Italian
Crew	International
Complement	550
GRT	36,674
Length (ft.)	660
Beam (ft.)	85
Draft (ft.)	23' 1"
Passengers-Cabins Full	1400
Passengers-2/Cabin	1022
Passenger Space Ratio	35.88
Stability Rating	Fair to Good
Seatings	2
Cuisine	International
Dress Code	Traditional
Room Service	Yes
Tip	$7.50 PPPD, 15% automatically added to bar checks

Ship Amenities

Outdoor Pool	3
Indoor Pool	0
Jacuzzi	0
Fitness Center	Yes
Spa	No
Beauty Shop	Yes
Showroom	Yes
Bars/Lounges	5
Casino	Yes
Shops	4
Library	No
Child Program	Yes
Self-Service Laundry	Yes
Elevators	8

Cabin Statistics

Suites	12
Outside Doubles	312
Inside Doubles	187
Wheelchair Cabins	11
Singles	0
Single Surcharge	150-200%
Verandas	12
110 Volt	Yes

CARNIVAL CRUISE LINES

Celebrity Cruises, Inc.

5201 Blue Lagoon Drive, Miami, FL 33126
☎ (305) 262-8322, (800) 437-3111

A passenger volunteer assists executive chef Walter Lauer in a cooking demonstration aboard the **Meridian.**

History

The Greek-based Chandris Group, founded in 1915, began passenger service in 1922 with the 300-ton *Chimara*, and by 1939 had grown to a 12-ship family-owned cargo and passenger line. In the post-World War II years, the company acquired a number of famous cruise liners, most of which have been retired.

In April 1989, Chandris formed Celebrity Cruises with the intention of creating an upscale division with a premium cruise product. The *Meridian*, a massive makeover of the classic liner *Galileo Galeilei*, debuted in April 1990, followed the next month by the all-new *Horizon*. In April 1992, sister ship *Zenith* followed.

In October of that same year, Chandris formed a joint venture with Overseas Shipholding Group (OSG), a large, publicly held bulk-shipping company, and entered into the next expansion phase, ordering three 70,000-ton ships to be constructed by Joseph L. Meyer in Papenburg, Germany. The first of these, the innovative *Century*, debuted at

CELEBRITY CRUISES

the end of 1995, followed in the fall of 1996 by sister ship *Galaxy* and the fall of 1997 by sister ship *Mercury*.

—Chandris introduced the fly/cruise concept in the Mediterranean in the early 1960s.

—Pioneered fly/cruise packages in the Caribbean in 1966.

—Celebrity pioneered affiliations with land-based experts from London's three-star Michelin restaurateur Michel Roux to Sony Corporation of America to create innovative onboard products and programs.

Concept . . . .

Celebrity from its beginning has aimed at presenting the highest possible quality for the best price, and offers luxury service and exceptional food with a very solid value for the money spent. These stylish ships illustrate the decade's new values—luxury without ostentation, family vacations that don't just cater to the kids and close-to-home getaways that provide pure pleasure.

Celebrity's celebrity came in part from its exceptionally good food, created and supervised by Guide Michelin three-star chef Michel Roux; here, a whimsical touch adorns a buffet dish at lunchtime.

Signatures . . . .

Perhaps the single best-known feature of this fleet is its excellent cuisine, created and supervised by London master chef Michel Roux, a longtime *Guide Michelin* three-star chef, who takes a hands-on approach, popping in for surprise visits to the ships, training shipboard chefs in his own kitchens and sending key supervisory personnel for regular culinary check-ups.

Gimmicks . . . .

The Mr. and Mrs. icebreaker game. At the beginning of each cruise, a man and a woman on board are chosen to represent Mr. and Mrs. (*Horizon, Zenith, Meridian, Century*). During the cruise, passengers are encouraged to ask individuals if they're the Mr. and Mrs. selected, and the first to find them gets a prize. In the meantime, everyone gets acquainted. Anyone for musical chairs?

Who's the Competition . . . .

In its brief seven years of service, Celebrity has managed to virtually create a class of its own by providing a product priced competitively with Princess and Holland America but with a more serious and consistent level of food. Previously, the line limited its itineraries to Caribbean and Bermuda sailings, but has expanded to include Alaska and Panama Canal sailings, and will enter the Mediterranean in 1998 with the *Horizon*.

Who's Aboard . . . .

Young to middle-aged couples, families with children, and senior citizens. Celebrity attracts some European and French Canadian passengers as well as Americans. Although the line is less than 10 years old, it has many frequent cruisers with double-digit sailings.

Who Should Go . . . .

Anyone looking for a good value for the money; discriminating foodies who will find very little if anything to complain about; families with children; couples of all ages. When the line was first introduced in 1990, Al Wallack, then Celebrity's senior vice president for marketing and passenger services, had several suggestions: "People who are joining country clubs but not necessarily the most expensive or exclusive country club on the block"; passengers of the former Home Lines and Sitmar ships who did not merge into Princess and who like "ships that look like ships, ships that have a European quality."

Who Should Not Go . . . .

Anyone who calls for catsup with everything or after perusing the menu asks the waiter, "But where's the surf and turf?"

The Lifestyle . . . .

Upscale without being pretentious, sleek and fashionable without being glitzy, the Celebrity ships offer a very comfortable seven-day cruise that is very proficient in the areas of food, service and surroundings. Evenings aboard are fairly dressy, with jacket and tie for men requested on both formal and informal nights; only casual nights suggest a sports shirt without jacket. Meals are served at assigned tables in two seatings.

Book a suite and you get all-day butler service; take the kids along during holiday and summer sailings and you'll find well-trained youth counselors on board. Ladies looking for a dancing partner will find social hosts on many sailings.

Evenings the ships present musical production shows and variety shows, recent feature films, and duos or trios playing for dancing or listening in small lounges around the ships. Daytimes bring popular culinary demonstrations by the executive chef, arts and crafts lessons, trapshooting, napkin folding, golf putting, lectures on finance or current affairs, a trivia quiz, basketball, exercise classes and bingo.

Wardrobe................................

A seven-night cruise normally schedules two formal nights, in which the line suggests "both men and women may prefer more dressy attire, such as an evening gown for women and a tuxedo or dress suit for men." In our experience aboard the line's ships, a cocktail dress or dressy pants suit for women and a dark suit or blazer with tie will be acceptable.

Two nights are designated informal, and men are asked to wear a jacket and tie, women a suit or dress, and three casual nights when a sport shirt and slacks are acceptable for men, dresses or pantsuits for women.

Daytime wear is casual, with good walking shoes a must. Passengers should take a jacket or sweater, hat or scarf, for going ashore.

A rolling cart of wines available by the glass serves the buffet restaurants.

Bill of Fare..............................A

Celebrity's executive chef, Vienna-born Walter Lauer, who goes from one ship to another constantly checking quality, describes it as "creating something new, where you can't cook everything in advance. Here there is the chance to do something new, more of the high standards in cuisine." One example: All the stock for soups is made from scratch on board rather than using prepared bases as many cruise kitchens do.

Lauer's mentor, Michel Roux, says, "The most important thing is to have a very good quality product and to rely on cooking skill more than the richness of the product." Fresh ingredients cooked to order figure prominently, and the menus are changed every six months.

Basically, the idea of serving simple but sophisticated dishes prepared from fresh ingredients as close as possible to serving time was revolutionary in the basic banquet/hotel catering kitchens of big cruise ships. But it succeeds splendidly. Usually if we find two or three dishes a meal that tempt us we're happy, but we could cheerfully order one of everything straight down the menu on these ships.

For lunch you might find a vegetable pizza or minestrone to start, then a main-dish salad of romaine with Mediterranean tabouli, hummus and pita bread garnished with garlic chicken; a piperade omelet with ham, tomatoes, peppers and onions; broiled ocean perch; roasted chicken with Provençale potatoes; spaghetti with fresh tomato sauce; grilled calf's liver with bacon and onions.

Dinner could begin with New England clam chowder or a pasta tossed with cilantro, oregano, ancho chile and fresh cream; a low-fat version of coquilles Saint-Jacques on vegetable tagliatelle; a pan-seared darne of salmon; roast lamb with garlic, thyme, fresh mint and olive oil with country roasted potatoes; broiled lobster tail or prime rib of beef. The dessert menu always includes one lean and light suggestion, along with fruit and cheese, pastries, ice creams and sorbets and a plate of showcase sweets presented to each table by the waiter, who describes them in mouth-watering detail. Full vegetarian menus are offered at every lunch and dinner.

A substantial 24-hour room service menu, gala midnight buffets, barbecues on deck, continental breakfast in bed, late morning bouillon and afternoon tea are other meal options during a typical cruise.

Lunchtime buffets are reminiscent of Impressionist paintings, with displays of fresh fruits and vegetables, woven baked baskets holding bread and wonderfully crunchy homemade breadsticks, fresh and crisp salads, a huge display of fresh vegetables, a rolling cart of wines by the glass, cold and hot main dishes and plenty of desserts.

A variety of entertainment from production musicals to, as here, classical string quartets in the **Horizon's** *Centrum.*

Showtime . . . . A

The production musical shows have a lot of verve and are well-performed and well-costumed; they follow the usual musical revue formats with salutes to Broadway and/or Hollywood, but with fresh looks at vintage shows like *Hair* and *Jesus Christ Superstar.* Variety performers, musical soloists and duos and a dance band round out the evening entertainment. Daytimes are chock-a-block with games, movies, lectures and exercise classes. The new *Century* and *Galaxy* introduce still more technological marvels from rooms with "video wallpaper" to a nightly light-and-sound spectacular.

Discounts . . . .

Special advance purchase fares save up to 45 percent for passengers who book well ahead of time; ask a travel agent for details.

The Bottom Line

In today's world with value for the vacation dollar so important, it's comforting to sail with a cruise line that delivers high-quality food and service on a stylish ship at moderate prices. We sense welcome and commitment from every employee, even the cleaning crew who polish the brass and chrome and the deck crew who pick up dirty dishes and wet towels more promptly than on many ships. All the ships in the line, even the not-built-from-scratch *Meridian*, have our highest recommendation for quality for the money.

Going Ashore

Celebrity offers some 60 shore excursions priced from $24 for a three-hour city bus tour of Vancouver to $229 for a "pilot's choice" two-hour helicopter tour and landing from Juneau at the Juneau Icefield or from Skagway over the rugged Gold Rush terrain, including a landing and disembarkation at a secluded spot.

Best Active Adventures

1. Mountain Biking—Chilkoot Lake and Glory Hole, Haines

$92, 11 miles, for experienced mountain bikers in excellent health.
A three-hour adventure into the Bald Eagle Preserve, around Chilkoot Lake and to a remote salmon spawning pool. Good wildlife sightings possible.

2. White Pass Train and Bike Combo, Skagway

$135, must be in excellent health, an experienced bike rider comfortable with hand brakes, and over 4'2" tall.
Three-hour adventure begins with a train ride up to the White Pass aboard an historic narrow gauge train, then a transfer to 3292-foot Klondike Summit and a bike ride down the hill to sea level.

3. Sea Kayaking Adventure, Ketchikan

$69 adults, $45 children, requires moderate strength and endurance.
Paddles both inside the town of Ketchikan and across the Tongass Narrows to Pennock Island and its rainforest, where you may spot eagles.

Best Historical And Cultural Overviews

1. Chilkat Indian Dancers and Salmon Bake, Haines

$52 adults, $32 children, 3 hours.
Sample fresh red salmon fillets cooked over an open alderwood fire, barbecued ribs and a salad bar in a traditional Chilkat tribal house, followed by a colorful program of legends and dances by the famous Chilkat dancers.

2. White Pass and Yukon Rail/Bus Combo, Skagway

$130 adults, $75 children, 3.5 hours.
Ride the historic narrow gauge train uphill to White Pass, the route the Klondike Stampeders followed, then return by motorcoach in order to look across to Dead Horse Gulch and see the rail tracks you traveled on. Then pause at the Gold Rush Camp at the foot of the hill to try a hand at gold panning, hearing some of the tales about Skagway's Soapy Smith, and explore the replica tent city with artifacts from the days of '98.

Don't Bother to Book

City Sightseeing by Vintage Street Car, Skagway

$38 adults, $21 children, 2 hours.
Unless you have trouble walking, skip this tour in favor of the free ranger-led 45-minute historic walking tour of Skagway that sets out twice a day from the National Park Service Visitor Center.

Note: The *Galaxy* will cruise to Alaska in 1998.

Century ★★★★★

Galaxy ☆☆☆☆☆

During the inaugural sailing of the first of these "ships of the future"—a joint venture between Celebrity and Sony Corporation of America—we found ourselves wandering around the decks trying to decipher this brave new world. There were the very appealing intimate game booths for two or more in the Images Lounge, three high-back booths with very expensive built-in game screens on tabletops. While we never quite got the hang of them, a young cou-

ple in the booth next door was bent intently over the screen, playing with great concentration when we first saw them, then later, when we checked in again, they looked up at each other from the game and began kissing passionately. We wanted what they had, but apparently it was a different game.

Celebrity's chairman John Chandris calls his new pair of babies "the ships I've always wanted to build...ships for the next century" and tags them super-premium, saying they are for "discriminating consumers who demand the highest quality experience at the best possible value." There are a lot of exciting new features on board. Take the state-of-the-art spa with its hydro-pool underwater "air beds" to give the body a weightless sensation and jets of water that provide neck massages as well as another spa area with jets of water at different heights that are similar to a stand-up Jacuzzi. Along with the usual hydrotherapy and thalassotherapy is a seagoing first—a mud, steam and herbal treatment called *rasul*. All the AquaSpa programs can be booked in advance with a travel agent.

A lounge called Images utilizes "video wallpaper," hundreds of change-able, custom-designed backgrounds that can be punched up on a wall-sized video display system to change the room's ambiance from tropical palms to low-light jazz club to sports bar or wine cellar, whatever background fits the activity of the moment. Around one end is a series of interactive gaming booths big enough to seat several people at a time. For showtime, there's a Broadway-style theater with row seating, orchestra pit and four-deck fly loft for scenery. A glazed dome in the Grand Foyer changes in a slow transition from dawn to daylight to sunset to night, when astronomically correct "stars" appear in the dome "sky." Sony Corporation of America has created exclusive interactive guest services, touch-screen information kiosks, in-cabin entertainment systems, telephonic video service and special teleconfer-encing equipment for meetings.

The Brochure Says

"Welcome to the new *Century*, a vessel that recaptures the golden age of cruising blended with modern sophistication."

Translation

Perhaps too much emphasis was initially put into the joint venture between Celebrity and Sony. While we think passengers will certainly note the two dozen technological ad-ditions from Sony, they will be even more impressed by the elegant dining room, theater, casino, Michael's Club and the Crystal Room nightclub than by the electronic gadgetry.

Cabins & Costs

Fantasy Suites: .... A

Average PPPD: NA for Alaska.
A pair of lavish penthouse suites measuring 1173 square feet offer a private veranda with its own outdoor hot tub, a living room, dining room, butler's pantry and 24-hour butler service, master bedroom with walk-in closet, living room with wet bar and entertainment center and a guest powder room supplementing the marble bath with spa tub.

Small Splurge: ....A

Average Price PPPD: NA for Alaska.

The eight Royal Suites are spacious inside although the private verandas are fairly narrow. The living rooms have sofa and two chairs, dining table with four chairs and a separate bedroom. Museum "art boxes" in each suite displays themed pieces of art; the suite we saw featured African carvings.

Suitable Standards: ....B+

Average Price PPPD: NA for Alaska.

A typical cabin is furnished with a queen-sized bed under a large window with a striped Roman shade, a marble-topped desk/dresser, two armchairs, a cocktail table, TV set, minibar and big hinged mirror covering shelves and a safe in the wall behind it. The bathroom has a very large white tile shower (chairman John Chandris is very big on spacious shower stalls) with excellent shower head, marble counter and lots of storage.

Bottom Bunks: ....B

Average Price PPPD: NA for Alaska.

All the cabins contain safes, minibars, hair dryers, direct dial telephones and color TV sets, and the smallest is 171 square feet. The bottom units still contain two lower beds which can convert to a queen-sized bed, bath with spacious shower and all the amenities listed above.

The amidships pool on the Resort Deck of Century, Galaxy's sister ship.

The Bottom Line

A lot of the public rooms strive mightily to look like Tomorrowland, especially the lounge called Images that combines elements of both video games and sports bars with a massive video wall and intimate high-backed booths with game screens inset into the tabletops. The overall design also skimps on the deck space, making the pool deck and sun walk above seem crowded when the ship is full. At the same time, only 61 cabins and suites have private balconies, so that means more people are out on deck. The suites aboard are lovely, well worth the splurge—and having your own private veranda means you can skip the deck sunbathing.

Images Lounge features sports bar type video walls plus one-on-one electronic game booths.

Five Good Reasons to Book These Ships

1. The exceptional AquaSpa from Steiners with an elaborate program of beauty and spa appointments that can be booked from home before the cruise via your travel agent.

2. To get a souvenir digital photograph that sets you against an unlikely backdrop of jet skis, yawning alligators, a painter's perch dangling from the bow or on the bridge with the captain.

3. To play video games almost anywhere and use interactive cabin TV service to order food, watch pay-per-view movies or wager on a few hands of video poker.

4. To dine in the elegant two-deck Grand Restaurant that evokes the dining room from the Normandie.

5. To watch a production show in a theater where there are no bad sightlines.

Five Things You Won't Find Aboard

1. Obstructed sightlines in the showroom; the view is perfect from every seat.

2. Visitors.

3. Pets.

4. A golf cart at the simulated golf links.

5. A cigar-smoking ban; aficionados can light up in Michael's Club.

Century / Galaxy

★★★★★
☆☆☆☆☆

Registry	Liberia
Officers	Greek
Crew	International
Complement	843
GRT	70,000
Length (ft.)	807
Beam (ft.)	105
Draft (ft.)	25
Passengers-Cabins Full	2056
Passengers-2/Cabin	1750
Passenger Space Ratio	40
Stability Rating	Excellent
Seatings	2
Cuisine	Contemporary
Dress Code	Traditional
Room Service	Yes
Tip	$9 PPPD, 15% automatically added to bar checks. Suites tip Butler $3 PPPD

Ship Amenities

Outdoor Pool	2
Indoor Pool	0
Jacuzzi	3
Fitness Center	Yes
Spa	Yes
Beauty Shop	Yes
Showroom	Yes
Bars/Lounges	4
Casino	Yes
Shops	0
Library	Yes
Child Program	Yes
Self-Service Laundry	No
Elevators	9

Cabin Statistics

Suites	52
Outside Doubles	517
Inside Doubles	306
Wheelchair Cabins	8
Singles	0
Single Surcharge	150-200%
Verandas	61
110 Volt	Yes

CELEBRITY CRUISES

Horizon
Zenith

Note: The *Horizon* cruises Alaska in 1997 but repositions to Europe in 1998.

Revisiting a ship you've known from its birth is sort of like being a godparent to a child and watching it grow up. The first time we saw the Horizon, at the Joseph L. Meyer shipyard in Papenburg, Germany, she was unprepossessing, a huge brooding structure of dark red steel with bare stairways, dangling wires and cords. Then, at her inaugural sailing, she was an elegant beauty decked out in expensive if understated finery, and when we saw her again not long ago she was prettier than ever, lovingly polished and primped within an inch of her life.

The Horizon's Rendezvous Lounge is a popular before-dinner cocktail spot.

The *Horizon*, which moves its summer cruises from Alaska to the Mediterranean in 1998, has a health club, children's playroom, teen center and plenty of bars and lounges.

Because most of the cabins aboard are modular design, insides and outsides are virtually identical in size (around 176 square feet) and furnishings, with the cabin's deck position determining the price.

INSIDER TIP

In the back of the balcony, tall barstools around a tall table look inviting to latecomers to the shows, but those seats don't swivel and are clumsy to get into and out of; move on down to a regular seat, but avoid the front row of balcony seats where the wooden balcony rail is right at eye level.

The Brochure Says

"Attention to detail...you notice it the minute you come on board."

Translation

The care and attention to detail goes beyond the design and decor into every part of the service. At a second seating luncheon, our waiter was removing the cover plate when he noticed a tiny spot on the tablecloth underneath it and, horrified, immediately began apologizing profusely as he removed all the tableware, tore off the offending linen and snapped on a new cloth, then reset the entire table. When we tried to make a joke about it, he said, "No, this is very serious, and this is my mistake; I'm terribly sorry."

Cabins & Costs

Fantasy Suites: .... A-

Average Price PPPD: $585 plus air add-ons.

The two top suites, called Presidential Suites on the *Horizon*, are 510 square feet with separate sitting room (the one we like has caramel leather sofas and chairs), glass dining table with four chairs, wood and marble counter, TV set and big windows; the bedroom has twin or king-sized beds, walk-in closet with generous storage space and built-in safe, and a second TV set. The marble bathroom is not large but does have a Jacuzzi bathtub. And there's butler service, hot cabin breakfasts if you wish, fresh fruit replenished daily and a welcome bottle of champagne.

Small Splurges: .... A-

Average Price PPPD: $471 plus air add-ons.

Deluxe suites, 18 on the *Horizon*, have two lower beds or a king-sized bed, sitting area with two chairs or loveseat and chair, glass table, large window and small TV, as well as a long marble-topped desk/dresser with chair. The bathroom is very like the one in the bigger suites (see "Fantasy Suites" above). Perks: Butler service, terrycloth robes, hot breakfasts served in-cabin, fresh fruit, a welcome bottle of champagne.

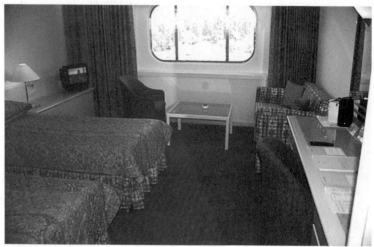

An outside deluxe cabin.

Suitable Standards: ....B

Average Price PPPD: $356 plus air add-ons.

Most standard cabins measure 176 square feet and have two lower beds or a double, two chairs, table, window, large built-in desk/dresser, TV set and bath with shower. Four outside wheelchair-accessible cabins on each ship have generous bedroom and bathroom space for turning, a big shower with fold-down seat, extra-wide doors and ramp access over the low bathroom sill.

Bottom Bunks: ....B

Average Price PPPD: $282 plus air add-ons.

The cheapest insides are also 176 square feet with two lower beds or a double, two chairs, table, TV, wide dresser and bath with tile shower and white Corian self-sink and counter. A vertical strip of mirror on the wall where a window would be lightens and brightens the space. Some have third and fourth fold-down upper bunks.

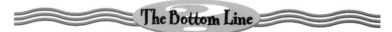

Where She Goes

During the summer of 1997, the *Horizon* offers a series of seven-night sailings between Vancouver and Seward that covers both the Inside Passage and the Glacier Route. The sailings visit Ketchikan, Juneau, Skagway, Hubbard Glacier, Valdez and College Fjord on the northbound itinerary, and Hubbard Glacier, Sitka, Juneau, Tracy Arm, Skagway and Ketchikan on the southbound itinerary.

In May and September the itinerary changes to a seven-night round trip from Vancouver calling at Ketchikan, Juneau, Skagway, Haines and cruising Tracy Arm and Misty Fjords and the Inside Passage.

The Bottom Line

When the line was introduced, executives were careful not to over-hype the new product and bombard the public with extravagant promises. Instead, they let the product speak for itself, and it did—in volumes. Early passengers commented that they had not expected so much for the price, and Celebrity's reputation grew quickly among knowledgeable cruise passengers looking for a good buy.

After sailing aboard all the line's ships, we find very little to criticize, other than the captain's formal parties with their tepid, watery, premixed cocktails; and we often wish, in dining rooms aboard other ships, we had one of Celebrity's menus facing us instead.

Five Great Spaces

1. The shipshape navy-and-white nautical observation lounges high atop the ships and forward, America's Cup on the *Horizon*. Lots of wood and brass trim and snappy blue chairs with white piping around the edges.

2. The self-service cafe, with two indoor and one outdoor buffet line with an inviting array of dishes at breakfast and lunch, waiters on hand to carry passengers' trays to the tables, and a rolling wine cart of vintages available by the glass at lunchtime. The floors are wood and tile, the seats a pretty floral pattern.

3. Harry's Tavern, named for former company president Harry Haralambopoulos, is a small Greek taverna decorated with a mural depicting a Mexican fountain splashing under Greek trees occupied by South American parrots on a Tuscan hillside.

4. The elegant Zodiac Club, with its cabaret/nightclub ambience, wood-toned walls, gently curved bar, and raised seating areas.

5. The show lounge offers optimum sightlines in most areas, with seven seating levels on the two decks facing the large raised stage; multimedia projections and high-tech lighting design enhances the well-costumed shows.

Five Good Reasons to Book These Ships

1. Because the *Horizon* may very well be the best restaurant in Alaska this summer.

2. Because they represent perhaps the best value for the money in the whole world of cruising.

3. Because they take service seriously (see "Translation").

4. Because there's an excellent health center where you can work off the calories.

5. Because the whole family can experience a top-quality cruise experience without mortgaging the farm.

Five Things You Won't Find On Board

1. Hot breakfasts served in standard cabins; you only get it in suites.

2. Private verandas.

3. Permission to bring your own alcoholic beverages aboard for cabin consumption; the brochure spells this out as a No No. You're expected to buy your drinks on board. (Other cruise lines permit passengers to use personal supplies while in the privacy of their cabins.)

4. A hungry passenger.

5. A cinema. Movies are shown daily on the cabin television.

Horizon / Zenith ★★★★★ / ★★★★

Registry	**Bahamas**
Officers	**Greek**
Crew	**International**
Complement	**642**
GRT	**46,811**
Length (ft.)	**682**
Beam (ft.)	**95**
Draft (ft.)	**24**
Passengers-Cabins Full	**1752**
Passengers-2/Cabin	**1354**
Passenger Space Ratio	**34.57**
Stability Rating	**Good**
Seatings	**2**
Cuisine	**Contemporary**
Dress Code	**Traditional**
Room Service	**Yes**
Tip	**$9 PPPD, 15% automatically added bar checks. Suites tip Butler $3 PPPD**

Ship Amenities

Outdoor Pool	**2**
Indoor Pool	**0**
Jacuzzi	**3**
Fitness Center	**Yes**
Spa	**Yes**
Beauty Shop	**Yes**
Showroom	**Yes**
Bars/Lounges	**4**
Casino	**Yes**
Shops	**0**
Library	**Yes**
Child Program	**Yes**
Self-Service Laundry	**No**
Elevators	**7**

Cabin Statistics

Suites	**20**
Outside Doubles	**513**
Inside Doubles	**144**
Wheelchair Cabins	**4**
Singles	**0**
Single Surcharge	**150-200%**
Verandas	**0**
110 Volt	**Yes**

❖ *CLIPPER*

7711 Bonhomme Avenue, St. Louis, MO 63105
☎ *(314) 727-2929, (800) 325-0010*

History . . . .

Founded in 1982 in his native St. Louis by travel entrepreneur Barney A. Ebsworth, who also founded Intrav tour company, Clipper Cruises owns and operates two small ships, the 138-passenger *Yorktown Clipper* and the 100-passenger *Nantucket Clipper*, both U.S. flag vessels built in Jeffersonville, Indiana. The company is privately held by parent company, Windsor, Inc., a real estate and investment company.

The first ship on line was the 104-passenger *Newport Clipper*, which introduced the line's signature Colonial South cruises in 1984. That vessel was subsequently sold and now sails as *Spirit of Endeavour* for Alaska Sightseeing/Cruise West.

The two ships cruise the waterways of North and Central America from Alaska to Costa Rica, the Caribbean to New England, with an emphasis on local culture, art, history, golf and swimming and snorkeling off the side of the ship, depending on the cruising region.

Clipper passengers spot a whale.

255

Concept . . . .

Clipper uses small, shallow-draft vessels to explore America's water-ways, tying up in small, out-of-the-way ports as well as urban areas in walking distance of the sightseeing. The line prides itself on being "a thoughtful alternative to conventional cruising," stressing substance over slickness, naturalist and lecture programs over musical productions and bingo and sneakers over sequins.

Clipper president Paul H. Duynhouwer likes to point out the misconceptions about adventure cruising—"Elitist, expensive, far away and long are common misconceptions," he says. Clipper, on the other hand, makes soft adventure trips that are as short as seven days and more affordable than many of the exotic journeys other lines offer.

Signatures . . . .

Clipper was one of the early providers of golf theme cruises with its southeastern U.S. itineraries offering passengers a chance to play courses such as Kiawah Island, Palmetto Dunes, Wild Dunes, Dataw Island, Osprey Cove and St. Simons Island Club, all during a one-week cruise.

Open-seating meals served by friendly young Americans, many of them just past college-age, are prepared by chefs trained at the famous Culinary Institute of America in Hyde Park.

Gimmicks . . . .

Clipper Chippers—warm chocolate chip cookies served at teatime and other times.

Who's the Competition . . . .

While Clipper offers a fairly unique product because of the scope of its itineraries, it does compete somewhat with Special Expeditions in Alaska, and the all-American style of its food and service, as well as an emphasis on lesser-visited ports and cruising areas, competes with Alaska Sightseeing/Cruise West in Alaska.

Who's Aboard . . . .

Couples and singles past 40, many from the South and Midwest, dominate the passenger list. What the passengers have in common is an interest in history, culture and nature, and a desire to learn more about the world around them. They are destination-oriented rather than pleasure-driven, and would show little interest in a casino or production show, even if Clipper were to offer them. Most represent household incomes of over $70,000 with substantial discretionary income. They're the sort of people who would wear a name badge if issued one.

Who Should Go . . . .

We think more younger couples would enjoy the ship as much as their elders, the same people who would take a bicycling tour through a wine region or stay in bed-and-breakfast establishments. Also, Clipper would appeal to people who have taken package tours or bus tours because they feel safer being escorted around but are tired of all that regimentation, packing and unpacking.

Who Should Not Go . . . .

Families with young or restless children, because there are no places on these ships for them to get away; everyone congregates in one large indoor lounge more suitable to quiet adult activities. Because the ships have no elevators, they are not appropriate for travelers who require wheelchairs or walkers to get around.

The Lifestyle . . . .

Single seating meals with no assigned tables allow passengers to get acquainted more easily than on large ships, and many of the Clipper crowd find they have a great deal in common. Most days the vessels are in port for all or part of the day, with a range of organized excursions and suggestions for on-your-own activities. Naturalists and lecturers are scheduled frequently to talk about special features of the ports of call, and if there is any entertainment, it is apt to be someone from shore performing folk songs or playing jazz.

Wardrobe . . . .

Day dress is casual but in the East Coast preppy or country club style, with topsiders, golf pants, plaid Bermuda shorts and such. Zippered windbreakers, soft hats rather than billed caps and sensible shoes are worn ashore. While there is no specific dress code, passengers usually dress up a bit for dinner, and men will sometimes wear jacket and tie.

Bill of Fare . . . . .B+

As mentioned above, chefs from the Culinary Institute of America are responsible for preparing the excellent contemporary American cuisine on board. We've found the food uniformly good and the menus consistent in their appeal and variety. Half-portions can be ordered for people with small appetites and "light" dishes are offered on every menu. Much of the food is prepared with fresh ingredients from scratch—including homemade crackers served with the day's soups.

DID YOU KNOW?

A free 21-minute video is available for loan from Clipper for any potential passenger who'd like a closer look at the vessels and the life aboard them. Rather than using models as most cruise lines do, the video features actual Clipper passengers. Call ☎ (800) 325-0010 to borrow a copy.

The Bottom Line

These are rewarding and enjoyable cruises, with as many surprises and delights to be discovered in Charleston as in Costa Rica or in Annapolis as in Alaska. The cruises are especially delightful when a passenger is following a subject of particular interest—whether golf, history, museums or Native American legends and lore.

Going Ashore

Clipper Cruises' shore excursion style focuses on less-crowded ports of call and more wilderness and scenic cruising. Highlights during the regular cruise include a call at tiny Wrangell, a cruise through Misty Fjords National Monument, a Zodiac trip ashore at Baranof Warm Springs and a sail up Tracy Arm.

An optional four-night extension ($1080 per person, double occupancy, plus air transportation) before the regular cruise flies you into Anchorage from your home town for an overnight hotel stay before boarding a motor-coach to travel to Denali National Park, stopping to see the starting point for the famous thousand-mile Iditarod dogsled race to Nome. Check into a hotel at the park in early afternoon with plenty of time and daylight for a hike or helicopter tour, then take a guided tour deep into the park the next day. Day four is headlined with a river rafting trip along the Upper Nenana River, followed by a rail trip to Fairbanks aboard the luxurious McKinley Explorer. On the last day, take a cruise from Fairbanks on the sternwheeler *Discovery*, visit an Athabaskan trapping camp with Native American guides and enjoy lunch at The Pumphouse Restaurant, a former working pumphouse that brought water in for the mines, before an afternoon visit to the University of Alaska Museum.

Yorktown Clipper   ⚓⚓⚓⚓⚓

A cruise along the coast of Maine brings back indelible memories of a lunch-time when a humpback whale mother swam by, her nursing calf clinging to her, lazily flapping her white fins in a backstroke wave just outside the dining room windows. On other days, we'd search out the lobster pound in every port, and feast on fresh steamed one-and-a-quarter pounders, promising each other it was in lieu of dinner—and then dinner was always so tempting we'd eat it anyhow.

The *Yorktown Clipper* has four passenger decks reached by stairs; there are no elevators. Topmost is the Sun Deck, with lounge chairs and good observation points; it doubles as an outdoor dining venue from time to time, and, also has four passenger cabins. The Promenade Deck, as its name implies, is wrapped all around by a covered promenade, and cabins on this deck open directly to the outdoors, a boon except when it's raining. Lounge Deck has a forward observation lounge and an outdoor bow area in front of that, along with passenger cabins, some opening into an inside hallway, others at the aft end opening to the outdoors. Main Deck is where the dining room is located, along with additional passenger cabins. All cabins are outsides with windows or portholes.

The Brochure Says

"Lifestyle on board is casual and unregimented. The crowds, commercial atmosphere and hectic activities so often associated with conventional cruise ships are nowhere to be found on Clipper. Your fellow travelers are likely to remind you of the members of your own country club."

Translation
None needed; it's a very precise description of the lifestyle and passengers.

Cabins & Costs

Fantasy Suites: .... NA
Nothing on board really qualifies for this category.

Small Splurges: .... B
Average Price PPPD: $450 plus air add-ons.
The category Six outside double staterooms, eight on *Yorktown Clipper*, are the most expensive digs aboard, primarily because of being slightly larger with more desirable deck locations. Like all the other Clipper cabins, they contain twin beds, bath with shower, desk/dresser with chair plus windows rather than portholes.

Suitable Standards: C
Average Price PPPD: $328 to $421, plus air add-ons.
Same as the above (see "Small Splurges") except slightly smaller, the category Two, Three, Four and Five cabins are very similar but vary slightly in price. Some have twin beds in an L-configuration with a bit more floor space, while the others have the two beds parallel to each other with a small desk/dresser in between. All four categories have bath with shower only and windows instead of portholes.

Bottom Bunks: C
Average Price PPPD: $300 plus air add-ons.
The lowest-priced cabins on board are forward on the lowest passenger deck and have portholes instead of windows. Otherwise, each contains twin beds arranged parallel to each other with a small desk/dresser and chair in between. Baths have shower only.

Where She Goes

Aboard the *Yorktown Clipper*, summer is spent in Alaska, with seven-night sailings from Juneau and/or Ketchikan, plus an 11-night sailing from Juneau to Seattle at the end of the season. Three early May sailings set out from Seattle. Note: Some of the Alaska cruises for 1997 are under charter by Tauck Tours ☎ *(800) 468-2825.*

The Bottom Line

While the prices could be regarded as slightly higher than average—and there's no early booking discount advertised—the value is there. The vessels are comfortable, attractively decorated and always spotlessly clean, although when the ship is full, the lounge sometimes feels crowded. In a few areas they visit, the shallow draft causes more ship motion than some passengers might like. The other downer is getting from the Promenade Deck cabins, which open onto a covered deck, down to the dining room when it's raining. But the food, service, itineraries and overall experience are so delightful that little annoyances about space or rain in the face seem minuscule. We like these ships very much.

Fielding's Five

Five Favorite Places

1. The tasteful Dining Room, just about everyone's favorite hangout three times a day, plus after dinner some evenings when it doubles as a cinema and the crew makes a batch of fresh popcorn.

2. The Observation Lounge, where passengers socialize, listen to lectures, play cards and games, write letters and do needlepoint, is prettily decorated in pastels and subdued pale tones. This is where the chocolate chip cookies are served at teatime.

3. The Promenade Deck, good for getting in a mile walk if you don't mind counting double-digit laps.

4. The bow observation area, a good place to watch for Alaska wildlife, also where you might sip a cup of hot coffee or glass of iced tea.

5. The Sun Deck, where you sit in lounge chairs and observe the scenery, is also the place where a deck barbecue may be dished up.

Five Good Reasons to Book These Ships

1. To get away from glitz and gaming—they don't even offer bingo.

2. To sample Culinary Institute of America cuisine.

3. To enjoy some genuinely warm and friendly American service and delicious American food.

4. To cruise some unusual and interesting waterways.

5. To meet other people around the same age who share the same interests.

Yorktown Clipper ⚓⚓⚓⚓

Registry	US
Officers	American
Crew	American
Complement	40
GRT	97
Length (ft.)	257
Beam (ft.)	43
Draft (ft.)	8.5
Passengers-Cabins Full	138
Passengers-2/Cabin	138
Passenger Space Ratio	NA
Stability Rating	NA
Seatings	1
Cuisine	American, contemporary
Dress Code	Casual
Room Service	No
Tip	$9 PPPD

Ship Amenities

Outdoor Pool	0
Indoor Pool	0
Jacuzzi	0
Fitness Center	No
Spa	No
Beauty Shop	No
Showroom	No
Bars/Lounges	1
Casino	No
Shops	1
Library	Yes
Child Program	No
Self-Service Laundry	No
Elevators	0

Cabin Statistics

Suites	0
Outside Doubles	69
Inside Doubles	0
Wheelchair Cabins	0
Singles	0
Single Surcharge	150%
Verandas	0
110 Volt	Yes

CRYSTAL
C R U I S E S

2121 Avenue of the Stars, Los Angeles, CA 90067
☎ *(310) 785-9300, (800) 446-6620*

History . . . .

Los Angeles-based Crystal Cruises did the cruise line equivalent of coming from 0 to 60 in six seconds. Founded in 1988 by century-old NYK (Nippon Yusen Kaisha), one of the largest transportation companies in the world, the Japanese-financed company set up a long and elaborate program of introducing to the United States a new ship that was still two years away from completion.

The line's first ship, the 960-passenger *Crystal Harmony*, was built in the Mitsubishi shipyard in Nagasaki, Japan, and made its debut in Los Angeles in July 1990, to great critical acclaim. A sister ship, the *Crystal Symphony*, built in Finland's Kvaerner-Masa Yard, made its debut in New York in May 1995.

—First line to offer two alternative dinner restaurants to all passengers at no surcharge (*Crystal Harmony*, 1990).

DID YOU KNOW?

Interestingly, this very upscale line deliberately chose as godmothers for its ships actresses that are better-known for popular television series than for feature films or theater, Mary Tyler Moore for the Crystal Harmony *and Angela Lansbury for the* Crystal Symphony.

Concept . . . .

From its inception, Crystal set out to define "luxury" by trying to provide the best of everything—food, entertainment, service and shipboard accommodation—and to offer "warm and personal service in an elegant setting." They say, "The line provides sophisticated travelers and experienced cruisers with an intimate and luxurious cruise experience."

Signatures . . . .

The turquoise seahorses on the Crystal stacks have become a recognized logo in most of the great ports of the world, and that particular shade is carried through on logo caps and T-shirts and other Crystal souvenir merchandise.

In the lobby of each ship is a "crystal" piano made of lucite, along with bronze-colored statuary, a waltzing couple on the *Harmony* and a pair of ballet dancers on the *Symphony*, and waterfalls with crystal cut-glass cylinders and Tivoli lights.

Gimmicks

Using costly Louis Roederer Cristal Champagne for special occasions such as christenings.

Extension telephones in the bathrooms.

Who's the Competition

In its brief five years of cruising, Crystal has garnered an enviable reputation for service and overall quality, so that it virtually stands alone at the head of its class. It would have rivalled the former Royal Viking Line, and we do note some crossover from Cunard's *Royal Viking Sun*. It also attracts veterans of Princess and Holland America, as well as Seabourn and Sea Goddess.

Who's Aboard

Most of the passengers are successful couples between 40 and 70, with a sprinkling of older singles who enjoy the gentleman host program aboard. Very few of the passengers are Japanese, but those that do sail represent the upper strata of independent travelers rather than group tourism. Some 90 percent of the line's passengers are 45 and up with a median age of 60, and 80 percent are married. Of the line's total passengers, nearly half have traveled with Crystal before. A recent passenger list shows guests from the United States (both East and West coasts), Canada, Saudi Arabia, Japan, Australia, Hong Kong, Mexico, Switzerland, Brazil, Germany and Belgium.

Who Should Go

Younger passengers and upscale first-time cruisers who will enjoy the excellent entertainment, the high quality of food and service and the only pair of Caesars Palace casinos at sea.

Who Should Not Go

Anyone who doesn't like to dress up and socialize.

The Lifestyle

These ships offer one of the finest versions of classic, traditional, luxury ship cruises available, with a fairly formal dress code and assigned dining at two seatings but with two alternative restaurants available most evenings as well by advance reservation. Lavish surroundings, pampering service, excellent housekeeping and superlative dining keep the same passengers coming back again and again. Daytime activities are frequent and fascinating, shore excursions very well handled and evening entertainment top-notch.

Wardrobe

Dressy, dressy, dressy. We're frequently carry-on people with only a little luggage, but we always check a large bag when we're flying to board a Crystal ship. Daytimes and shore excursions can be casual, but the passengers are almost attired in smart casual, or casual elegance (what the Crystal handbook calls "country club attire.") Evenings, women wear cocktail dresses or dressy pantsuits for informal (what some lines now are calling "semi-formal") nights, while men don jacket and tie; on formal nights, women wear evening gowns (we saw as many long gowns as short ones on the inaugural of the *Symphony*) and men don tuxedos or dark business suits.

Bill of Fare . . . . .A

Creative contemporary cuisine, much of it prepared to order, comes out of the Crystal galleys, which are under the direction of executive chef Toni Neumeister, former executive chef for Royal Viking Line. A dinner menu will carry suggestions for a full menu recommended by the chef, a lighter fare menu giving the calorie, fat and sodium counts, a vegetarian menu and cellar master wine suggestions by the glass or by the bottle. Traditionally, you can choose from three or four appetizers (perhaps tempura fried softshell crab with red pepper aioli), two or three soups (maybe a chilled tomato soup with goat cheese quenelles), three salads, a nightly pasta special (such as fusilli with zucchini, garlic, olive oil and onions) and four main dishes (say, seared fresh ahi tuna steak, crisp baby hen, grilled tournedos of beef tenderloin Rossini or roasted Scandinavian venison loin) plus a vegetarian option such as a baby eggplant stuffed with ratatouille. The dessert roster runs to five desserts (maybe a tarte Tatin with vanilla ice cream or a souffle Grand Marnier) plus a cheese trolley and various frozen desserts. A little silver tray of freshly made petits fours always arrives with the coffee service.

But that's only the dining room. There are also two alternative restaurants with special evening menus, one Italian and one Asian (Asian/Pacific Rim on the *Symphony* and Japanese on the *Harmony*) and a wonderful assortment of casual buffet lunch choices from an elegant spread of cold seafoods and meats and hot dishes in the Lido Cafe to our favorite gardenburger, pizza, grilled hot dogs or hamburgers on deck. There's also an ice cream bar.

Showtime. . . . . .A

The entertainment is dazzling, with highly professional productions that are constantly updated, along with prestigious lecturers, concerts, cabarets and game shows. Lecturers include names such as journalist and author Pierre Salinger, ship historian Bill Miller and novelist Judith Krantz. Production shows are gorgeously costumed (some of the hand-beaded wardrobe pieces cost as much as $10,000 each) and beautifully choreographed and performed.

Discounts . . . .

Members of the Crystal Society (previous cruisers with the line) get a five percent discount with no advance booking deadline. If you book a future cruise while you're aboard one of the ships, you get a discount of $250 to $500 per person, and your travel agent gets his or her full commission as well. Pay in full six months ahead of sailing time and you get an additional five percent discount.

The Bottom Line

There are only two possible criticisms demanding luxury cruisers could make—the two-seating dining and the shortage of really generous closet space on very long sailings such as the full world cruise. To the first, we'd point out that you could book the alternative restaurants for 7:30 or order dinner in your cabin for those nights when you didn't want to dine at your assigned table. To the second, we'd suggest if you're taking a really long cruise and you like to dress up, book as high a cabin category as you can, say one of the penthouses or penthouse suites.

The Crystal ships are for those who want—and are willing to pay for—the very best in a traditional big-ship sailing experience.

Going Ashore

Crystal is well-experienced in Alaska, with one of its luxury vessels sailing there every summer. The shore excursions program usually includes some 85 options, including some pre- and post-tours, ranging from a $24 guide-led walk through a rain forest at Wrangell to a $279 Nostalgic Air Cruise.

Three Super Splurges

1. Nostalgic Air Cruise, Valdez

$279, 1 1/4 hours in the air, 3 hours total, offered only if enough people sign up.
Aboard a restored DC-3 with Big Band music and champagne. You'll soar through Wrangell Narrows and fly just above Columbia Glacier, over the Trans-Alaska Pipeline and over the site of the *Exxon Valdez* spill.

2. Glacier Flightseeing and Bald Eagle Preserve Rafting, Haines/Skagway

$201, limited participation; all participants must be in good health and able to swim.
A float trip through the Chilkat Valley's Bald Eagle Preserve and by the Tlingit riverside village of Klukwan is followed by a picnic lunch by the river's edge. Then you board a small plane for a 45-minute flight over the glaciers, ice falls and fjords.

3. Touch A Glacier, Homer

$199, 30 minutes flight, 30 minutes on glacier, limited participation.
Bell helicopters swoop you over a river of ice, then touch down on Grewingk Glacier where you step out on the ice, sip a glass of champagne and learn everything you ever wanted to know about glaciers.

Best Wildlife Spotting

1. Juneau Wildlife Cruise

$95, 3 hours cruising.
The waterjet powered catamaran cruise provides binoculars so you can keep your eyes peeled for humpback whales, Stellar sea lions, harbor seals, Dall's porpoise, Sitka black-tailed deer, bald eagles and marine birds. If you don't see at least three species besides the birds, you get $40 refund.

2. Sea Otter and Wildlife Quest, Sitka

$90, 3 hours.
You'll get a $40 refund on this cruise as well if you fail to see either an otter, a whale or a bear. (You can count on that otter!) You'll probably also see porpoises, cormorants, bald eagles and Sitka black-tailed deer.

3. Puffin Island Marine and Bird Watching Cruise, Sitka

$94, 3 hours, limited to 4–6 guests per departure, take motion sickness medicine before boarding the small boat if you're susceptible.

Saint Lazaria National Wildlife Refuge hosts nesting tufted puffins, murres, auklets and others, as well as bald eagles. The skipper is an experienced naturalist who'll maneuver the 26-foot boat to get as close as possible.

Don't Bother to Book

Valdez's Pipeline Terminal, Valdez

At $24 this vies with the Wrangell rain forest walk for the cheapest excursion aboard, but skip it unless you're absolutely riveted by oil flow, steel pipe and statistics.

Crystal Harmony ★★★★★★
Crystal Symphony ★★★★★★

NOTE: Crystal usually alternates the two ships in Alaska, with the *Crystal Symphony* positioned there in 1997.

The highly successful Crystal ships have had only a few gaffes in their career—and our favorite is the Viennese Mozart Tea, which used to be presented as one of the highlights of the cruise. On the inaugural of the Crystal Harmony in 1990, it was dazzling, with a string trio and all the waiters decked out in white wigs, gold lame frock coats and vests, long white stockings and slippers—visualize Tom Hulce as Mozart in the film Amadeus and you get the picture. On our next outing aboard the Harmony in 1993, the procedure had gotten routine, and the Viennese Mozart tea on that sailing had only three of the waiters (the ones who looked as if they'd drawn the losing straws) garbed in white wigs and partial costumes, but wearing loafers and white tennis socks. The Manila Strings trio were only two, wearing their ordinary daytime garb of white pants and shirts. (The third musician was missing, Harry pointed out, because Mozart didn't write for guitar.) On the inaugural of the Crystal Symphony, there were no white wigs, gold lame vests and knee breeches in sight, just the table of elegant cakes and pastries. The wigs had caused near-revolution in the ranks of waiters, as had the costumes, so the whole fancy-dress thing was written off.

This elegant pair of ships with their sleek, graceful lines offers a lot of sensational cabins with private verandas, a plethora of posh public rooms and an easy-to-get-around layout. The public areas are concentrated on the top two decks and two lower decks with most of the cabins in between. An amidships pool deck is sheltered enough with its sliding glass roof and glass side windows that it provides a cozy sun-trap even on a cool Alaska day. By limiting the major "avenues" to one rather than both sides of a deck, the traffic flows neatly without sacrificing space that could be devoted to a shop or bar. Craftsmanship is meticulous aboard both these ships. Comfortable cruising speed is 16 to 17 knots, but the *Crystal Symphony* on its inaugural was averaging 20 between New York and Bermuda.

An expansive amidships pool and raised whirlpool is surrounded by plenty of sunbathing area.

"From the moment you step aboard the gleaming white jewels known as *Crystal Harmony* and *Crystal Symphony*, you will feel you have arrived at a very special place and have been warmly embraced as part of the Crystal family."

Translation

They're serious about this, folks. There's something called The Crystal Attitude, a service philosophy that is a part of the intensive training each employee goes through, with motivational tapes and videos and classes for upper-echelon employees in notable hotel schools such as L'Ecole Hotelier in Switzerland and Cornell Hotel School. Crystal has the highest crew return factor of any cruise line, with more than 70 percent re-enlisting.

Cabins & Costs

Fantasy Suites: .... A+

Average Price PPPD: $1306 plus air add-ons.
The most lavish quarters aboard are the Crystal Penthouse suites, each measuring 948–982 square feet, with large sitting room, dining area, private veranda, wet bar, big Jacuzzi tub with ocean view, separate master bedroom with king-sized bed, big walk-in closets and a guest bath. There's butler service, of course.

Fantasy suites such as the Crystal Penthouse with veranda aboard the Crystal Symphony are sought after by big spenders.

Small Splurges: .... A+

Average Price PPPD: $790 plus air add-ons.
Eighteen penthouse suites with verandas that measure a total of 491 square feet and 44 penthouses with verandas that measure 367 square feet are spacious and prettily furnished. Butler service is offered in all the penthouses, along with complimentary bar, cocktail hour canapes, and in-room dining with dishes that can be ordered from the dining room or either alternative restaurant.

Suitable Standards: .... A+

Average Price PPPD: $541 plus air add-ons.
The deluxe stateroom with private veranda is the most numerous of the cabin categories on board, with 214 cabins (on the *Symphony*) each measuring 246 square feet, with a private veranda, king-sized bed, loveseat sofa, chair, built-in desk/dresser with plenty of storage space, a safe, mini-refrigerator, TV/VCR, plus a large closet with built-in shoe rack and tie rack, and a marble bathroom with tub/shower combination, double sinks and two hair dryers. Seven staterooms for the disabled are available on the *Symphony*, four on the *Harmony*.

Bottom Bunks: ....A

Average Price PPPD: $430 on the Symphony, *$329 on the* Harmony *plus air add-ons.*

Inside cabins on the *Crystal Harmony* and outside cabins without verandas on the *Crystal Symphony* are the lowest-priced digs aboard. The latter number 202, and some have restricted views due to hanging lifeboats. The insides on the *Harmony* measure 183 square feet and have two lower beds, remote control TV/VCR, full bath with tub and shower, mini-refrigerator, safe, small sofa and chairs with desk/dresser and coffee table. You're not slumming here.

Where She Goes

The *Crystal Symphony* cruises roundtrip from San Francisco on 12-day Alaskan sailings calling in Victoria, Vancouver, Ketchikan, Juneau, Skagway and Sitka, and cruising Glacier Bay, Hubbard Glacier, the Inside Passage and Misty Fjords.

The Bottom Line

While the ship's interior is handsome and dignified, the real sense of the luxury comes not from eye-grabbing architecture but rather fine attention to detail—items such as the Wedgwood teacups in the Palm Court at teatime, Riedel hand-blown wine glasses in the Prego Restaurant, Villeroy & Boch china and Frette linens in the dining room, goose down pillows in each cabin, the designs on the Bistro plates and cups. Passengers are treated like adults rather than children at summer camp. Big-ship cruising doesn't get any better than this.

Fielding's Five

Five Spectacular Spots

1. The Palm Court, a sunny, airy winter garden with wicker chairs and ceiling fans, potted palms and a harpist playing for tea.

2. The Avenue Saloon, the "in" bar on board (you can always tell the "in" bar because that's where the officers and the entertainers hang out) with its wood floors and Oriental rugs, green leather bar rails and movable stools.

3. Caesars Palace At Sea, a truly classy shipboard casino operation that actually (in the Vegas style) gives free drinks to players.

4. The spectacular Crystal Spa and Salon on the top deck with lots of glass windows, aerobics area, gym with lots of machines, sauna, steam and massage.

5. The elegant Prego Restaurant aboard the *Symphony*, the Italian alternative dining option, with its red-and-white-striped pillars and high-backed blue armchairs tied with red tassels and cord, the very essence of a classy Venetian restaurant.

Five Good Reasons to Book These Ships

1. To tell all your friends about your cruise.

2. To show off your wardrobe and jewelry.

3. To be pampered by a happy staff who have the best crew accommodations at sea plus their own gym and Jacuzzi.

4. Cabin telephones with voice mail, and bathroom extension phones.

5. To have a private veranda, which will change your whole picture of luxury cruising.

Five Things You Won't Find On Board

1. Portholes; all the outside cabins have windows.

2. Anyone inappropriately dressed on formal night.

3. A bad attitude or discouraging word.

4. A lot of children, even though there's a youth and teen area provided.

5. A really unhappy passenger.

Crystal Harmony ★ ★ ★ ★ ★ ★

Registry	**Bahamas**
Officers	**Norwegian/Japanese**
Crew	**International**
Complement	**545**
GRT	**49,400**
Length (ft.)	**791**
Beam (ft.)	**104**
Draft (ft.)	**24.6**
Passengers-Cabins Full	**1010**
Passengers-2/Cabin	**960**
Passenger Space Ratio	**51.45**
Stability Rating	**Good to Excellent**
Seatings	**2**
Cuisine	**Contemporary**
Dress Code	**Traditional**
Room Service	**Yes**
Tip	**$10 PPPD, 15% automatically added to bar check**

Ship Amenities

Outdoor Pool	**2**
Indoor Pool	**1**
Jacuzzi	**2**
Fitness Center	**Yes**
Spa	**Yes**
Beauty Shop	**Yes**
Showroom	**Yes**
Bars/Lounges	**7**
Casino	**Yes**
Shops	**4**
Library	**Yes**
Child Program	**Yes**
Self-Service Laundry	**Yes**
Elevators	**8**

Cabin Statistics

Suites	**62**
Outside Doubles	**399**
Inside Doubles	**19**
Wheelchair Cabins	**4**
Singles	**0**
Single Surcharge	**115 - 200%**
Verandas	**260**
110 Volt	**Yes**

Crystal Symphony ★★★★★

Registry	**Bahamas**
Officers	**Norwegian/Japanese**
Crew	**International**
Complement	**530**
GRT	**50,000**
Length (ft.)	**781**
Beam (ft.)	**100**
Draft (ft.)	**24.9**
Passengers-Cabins Full	**1010**
Passengers-2/Cabin	**960**
Passenger Space Ratio	**52,08**
Stability Rating	**Good to Excellent**
Seatings	**2**
Cuisine	**Contemporary**
Dress Code	**Traditional**
Room Service	**Yes**
Tip	**$10 PPPD, 15% automatically added to bar check**

Ship Amenities

Outdoor Pool	**2**
Indoor Pool	**1**
Jacuzzi	**2**
Fitness Center	**Yes**
Spa	**Yes**
Beauty Shop	**Yes**
Showroom	**Yes**
Bars/Lounges	**7**
Casino	**Yes**
Shops	**4**
Library	**Yes**
Child Program	**Yes**
Self-Service Laundry	**Yes**
Elevators	**8**

Cabin Statistics

Suites	**64**
Outside Doubles	**416**
Inside Doubles	**0**
Wheelchair Cabins	**7**
Singles	**0**
Single Surcharge	**115 - 200%**
Verandas	**278**
110 Volt	**Yes**

ALASKA'S Glacier Bay™ TOURS AND CRUISES

520 Pike Street, Suite 1400, Seattle, WA 98101
☎ *(206) 623-7110, (800) 451-5952*

History . . . .

Glacier Bay Tours and Cruises is a spin-off from Seattle entrepreneur Robert Giersdorf's now-defunct Exploration Cruise Lines, which operated eight vessels when it went into bankruptcy in 1988 after a legal dispute with investor Anheuser-Busch. Giersdorf retained his wholly owned, 49-passenger catamaran *Executive Explorer* and Glacier Bay Lodge from the previous company, and added the leased 36-passenger *Wilderness Explorer* in 1992. In 1995, he also founded American West Steamboat Company, introducing the 165-passenger replica paddlewheel steamer *Queen of the West*, cruising the Columbia River out of Portland.

In early 1996, Giersdorf sold Glacier Bay Tours and Cruises and Yachtship Cruise Line to Juneau-based Goldbelt, Inc., an Alaska Native American Corporation, as a turnkey operation, retaining previous staff and crew. At that time, Goldbelt purchased the *Wilderness Explorer.*

A new vessel, the 80-passenger *Wilderness Adventurer*, the former *Caribbean Prince*, was introduced in 1997 for six-night "soft adventure" sailings from Juneau.

Concept . . . .

The company offers a variety of "soft adventure" and "active adventure" sailings in Alaska and British Columbia that emphasize "wholesome meals" and "modest accommodations." Wilderness excursions such as sea kayaking and naturalist walks to see flora and fauna are promoted over shipboard entertainment and cuisine. Because Native Americans own the company, there is a active attempt to serve as "stewards of the environment."

Signatures . . . .

Bow landing access for passengers when the vessel comes ashore.

Some 18 to 20 two-person sea kayaks are carried on board both the *Wilderness Adventurer* and the *Wilderness Explorer*, and use of the kayaks is included in the base fare.

Off-vessel groups are limited to 12, out of sight and sound of each other, when exploring ashore, due to National Park and National Forest regulations.

Gimmicks . . . .

Whale-spotting in Icy Strait, summer home of many humpback whales, is guaranteed or you get your money back from the cruise portion of the trip when you book the one-night Glacier Bay Extravaganza tour.

Glacier Bay Tours and Cruises guarantees you'll spot a whale in Icy Strait or your money back.

CHAMPAGNE TOAST

Port charges are included in the basic fare rather than added on, which is extremely rare among today's cruise companies.

Who's the Competition? . . . .

Quite obviously, Alaska Sightseeing/Cruise West, Special Expeditions, and, to a lesser extent, Clipper Cruises. Much depends on the following of loyal passengers for each line, along with the ability to book charter groups for some soft sailing dates. A major difference here is that, unlike Alaska Sightseeing and Special Expeditions, Glacier Bay's *Executive Explorer* charges for its shore excursions rather than including them in the base fare.

Who's Aboard. . . . .

Older North American couples and singles from 55 to 75 used to predominate the passenger lists, but as they add more active adventures, passengers get younger and younger.

Who Should Go. . . . .

Anyone interested in getting a close-up look at Alaska, going sea kayaking or observing Alaskan wildlife.

Who Should Not Go . . . .

Families with small children, since there's nowhere on these small vessels for them to play; anyone who decided to take a cruise after watching a Carnival commercial.

The Lifestyle

Aboard the *Wilderness Adventurer* and the *Wilderness Explorer*, the lifestyle is simple, family-style and dress-down, in a few words. Accommodations are basic—even the brochure describes them as "modest"—and food is served family-style with sack lunches issued for shore excursions. With no fashion police on board, you can wear anything decent you like, but carry a change of clothes in case you get splashed kayaking.

The more lavish *Executive Explorer* has compact but plush staterooms with picture windows, twin or queen-sized beds, and color TV sets, and Native American artworks displayed throughout the vessel. Mealtimes as well are aimed at fussier passengers who like a little creature comfort, with plate service rather than family-style service.

Meals are served at a single open seating on all three vessels, meaning passengers may sit where and with whom they please rather than at an assigned table.

As for entertainment, don't expect much beyond what you provide yourself, except for an occasional crew show or visiting lecturer or musician from shore.

Gratuities are pooled and divided among the staff.

Wardrobe

Glacier Bay Tours and Cruises recommends that passengers dress in layers, suggesting a combination of shirt, sweater, jacket and raincoat or rain poncho so you can add or subtract items as the weather changes. Wool slacks and medium-weight sweaters are termed "ideal" but you'll also see plenty of jeans and sweatshirts along. For footwear, to supplement the ubiquitous jogging shoes, they suggest you take hiking boots, rubber boots or treated water-resistant shoes for walking on outside decks, hiking in the rainforest or kayaking. (If you forget something, don't worry; they also sell specialty clothing aboard the ships.) If you're booking the *Executive Explorer*, you may want to throw in a dressier outfit for one or two evenings.

Discounts

Early booking nets up to $300 discount per couple, depending on the booking date. If a lower price is offered after you make your booking, they will adjust the price and refund the difference, except on those occasional cruises sold at a special price to Alaska residents.

The Bottom Line

With small vessels, unregimented dining room seating, American officers and crew and a serious approach to Alaska's environmental concerns, Glacier Bay Tours and Cruises offers a good alternative choice to a traditional big-ship cruise for a person who doesn't want to dress up, be entertained by professional performers, gamble or indulge in long, fancy meals or midnight buffets.

Passengers gather on the bow to watch a waterfall.

Going Ashore

As the name suggests, Glacier Bay Tours and Cruises has more than a passing interest in Glacier Bay National Park. The Juneau-based company is owned by Goldbelt, Inc., a Native American corporation, and is an authorized concessionaire of Glacier Bay National Park. One of its non-floating properties is the estimable Glacier Bay Lodge, where passengers can book a stay before or after their cruise for sport fishing programs, sea kayaking, and one-day whale watching, wildlife and glacier cruises.

A two-day Kodiak Adventure Tour ($1168 per person, double occupancy from Juneau, $774 from Anchorage and $944 from Fairbanks) includes roundtrip flight to Kodiak, overnight, a cultural morning tour and visit to the National Wildlife Refuge Center and a flightseeing expedition to look for the famous Kodiak brown bear. If weather permits, the chopper may land so you get an even closer look.

Executive Explorer ⚓⚓⚓⚓

We first boarded this ship in San Diego, far from the glaciers that define her terrain these days, when she was in between an attempt at cruising the Hawaiian Islands and an effort to cruise Baja California in the late 1980s. In both cases, the seas were too rough for her shallow twin hulls, but she's been smooth-riding and happy in the sheltered Inside Passage for years now.

The 49-passenger *Executive Explorer* has twin hulls, a tall profile and squared-off aft, lending her a distinctive if somewhat clumsy profile, but inside everything is prettily arranged and decorated. Cabins, while not large, are very cushy, especially in the two forward Vista Deluxe cabins. All are outsides with view windows. Both forward lounge and aft dining room also have big windows so you don't miss any wildlife while you're eating or socializing. Her small size enables her to get into narrow channels more easily, and an open top deck makes a good vantage point for scenery-watchers and photographers.

The Brochure Says

"The exclusive catamaran design enables the *Executive Explorer* to cruise faster than other small U.S. flag ships. We've designed the cruise itinerary so you visit more ports and attractions, have more time in port, see more glaciers, more stunning scenery, more fascinating communities, and more wildlife."

Translation

At a top cruising speed of 18 knots, this catamaran does move faster than the clumsier, boxier vessels that make up the rest of this line as well as the two main competitors, but speed never guaranteed good wildlife spotting nor a smooth ride on this vessel when it gets out into exposed waters. The itinerary for both ports and cruising areas, however, is top-of-the-line. Take plenty of warm clothing; you'll spend a lot of time on deck.

Cabins & Costs

Fantasy Suites: ....N/A

None.

Small Splurges: ....B+

Average Price PPPD: $487 plus airfare.
Top digs are the two window-walled Vista Deluxe cabins forward on Upper Deck, with built-in windowseat, queen-sized bed, enclosed water closet with shower, lavatory in the cabin and hanging closet. All cabins have color TV sets, VCRs (with free videotapes available for screening) and stocked mini-refrigerator.

Suitable Standards: ....B+

Average Price PPPD: $428 plus airfare.
The category A and AA cabins are fairly similar, with the AAs slightly larger (and slightly more expensive). Both have twin beds that convert to queen-sized, two view windows, desk dresser with mirror, enclosed water closet with shower, lavatory in the cabin and hanging closet. The AAs also have an easy chair. Some cabins in both categories have pull-down berths for third and fourth passengers. All cabins have color TV sets, VCRs (with free videotapes available for screening) and stocked mini-refrigerator.

Bottom Bunks: ....B+

Average Price PPPD: $387 plus airfare.
The sole category B cabin, # 306, has upper and lower berths, two windows, small chest with drawers, water closet with shower, lavatory in the cabin and hanging closet. This cabin is primarily recommended for single passengers, who pay 175 per cent of the per-person double occupancy price. All cabins have color TV sets, VCRs (with free videotapes available for screening) and stocked mini-refrigerator.

The **Executive Explorer** *cruises close to glaciers.*

Where She Goes

The *Executive Explorer* cruises on six-day itineraries between Juneau and Ketchikan, with calls in Petersburg, Sitka, Skagway and Haines, and cruising Tracy Arm Fjord, Glacier Bay, Sergius Narrows, Wrangell Narrows and Misty Fjords. The season runs from mid-May through mid-September.

The Bottom Line

This is one of the most interesting and offbeat ships in Alaska, and the pleasures of cruising with as few as 49 people in relatively plush surroundings cannot be underestimated. An American crew offers friendly, attentive service and the food is tasty. The shore excursions are optional on this vessel, the only one of the line's ships that offers organized in-town tours. However, passengers can strike out on foot or by cab on their own if they prefer. We do feel, even if the fares do include port taxes, that the cabins are overpriced. But so are the competition's, and passengers still seem willing to pay them. We can only suggest early booking for discounts and a tough travel agent to negotiate the real price as compared to brochure price.

Executive Explorer   ♪♪♪♪

Registry	U.S.
Officers	American
Crew	American
Complement	18
GRT	98
Length (ft.)	98.5
Beam (ft.)	36
Draft (ft.)	8
Passengers-Cabins Full	55
Passengers-2/Cabin	49
Passenger Space Ratio	N/A
Stability Rating	Fair
Seatings	1
Cuisine	American
Dress Code	Casual
Room Service	No
Tip	$8–$12 PPPD pooled among staff

Ship Amenities

Outdoor Pool	0
Indoor Pool	0
Jacuzzi	0
Fitness Center	No
Spa	No
Beauty Shop	No
Showroom	No
Bars/Lounges	1
Casino	No
Shops	1 (small)
Library	Yes (small)
Child Program	No
Self-Service Laundry	No
Elevators	0

Cabin Statistics

Suites	0
Outside Doubles	25
Inside Doubles	0
Wheelchair Cabins	0
Singles	1
Single Surcharge	175%
Verandas	0
110 Volt	Yes

GLACIER BAY TOURS AND CRUISES

Wilderness Adventurer ⚓⚓⚓

New to the fleet in 1997, the little *Wilderness Adventurer* is the former *Caribbean Prince* from American Canadian Caribbean Line, carrying 80 passengers. Typical of these small adventure vessels, it has bow landing capacity, meaning passengers can walk down a gangway directly onto the beach or island. Unlike the line's similar *Wilderness Explorer*, all cabins have two lower beds. A small lounge forward and an amidships dining room are the only enclosed public rooms aboard, along with an observation deck in front of the wheelhouse and a covered deck aft of the wheelhouse.

The Brochure Says

"The *Wilderness Adventurer*. . . is being introduced to Alaska 'soft adventure' cruising in 1997."

Translation

"Soft adventure" means a true wilderness trip rather than a port-to-port cruise, with a special circumnavigation and stops ashore at Admiralty Island National Monument, home to the world's largest concentration of brown (or grizzly) bears, as well as a thousand nesting bald eagles. At the same time, it's a gentler, more ship-oriented experience than the "active adventure" cruises aboard the line's *Wilderness Explorer*.

Cabins & Costs

Fantasy Suites: . . . . **N/A**
None.

Small Splurges: . . . . **C**
Average Price PPPD: $382 plus airfare.
The AA cabins on Sun Deck are the top lodgings aboard this fairly simple vessel. At least they're big enough in which to change your mind, with a double bed or two

lower beds (and an occasional third pulldown berth), picture window and compact bath with shower.

Suitable Standards: .... C-

Average Price PPPD: $346 plus airfare.

The dozen A category cabins are located on the same deck with the lounge and dining room, a convenience for passengers who want to be close to the action. We would hesitate to recommend cabin A 201 to anyone but early risers, however, because it's also smack against the galley, where the pots and pans start rattling early in the morning. Each of these cabins has two lower beds that can convert to double, a reasonable amount of turning-around space and a compact bathroom with toilet, shower and lavatory.

Bottom Bunks: .... D-

Average Price PPPD: $313 plus airfare.

Please, please, we beg of you, spring for the extra few bucks to book one of the A or double AA cabins if you're claustrophobic or at all particular about where you sleep. The seven B category cabins (six on the lowest deck, one adjacent to the wheelhouse on the Sun Deck) in the lowest price category are so small the beds almost overlap and cover more than half the total area, leaving very little floor space. These six cabins also have portlights set up high inside instead of windows, which means you may have a little daylight but no views.

Where She Goes

The *Wilderness Adventurer* makes six-night cruises roundtrip from Juneau with an emphasis on "soft adventures" for moderately active, outdoor-oriented passengers. The vessel spends more time cruising and exploring than docked ashore, spending two days cruising Glacier Bay (most cruise ships spend only one day there) as well as sailing around Admiralty Island, cruising in search of humpback whales at Point Adolphus and Icy Strait, sailing along the bays and inlets of Frederick Sound for additional wilderness wildlife spotting and cruising Tracy Arm Fjord. Sea kayaks and other launches are aboard to take passengers in for closer looks, as well as some bow landings that let passengers walk ashore from the ship.

The Bottom Line

As the *Caribbean Prince*, this vessel was been well cared by its owner-builder Luther Blount, so it underwent very few changes in its transition to *Wilderness Adventurer*.

Fielding's Five

Five Good Reasons to Book This Ship

1. If you want to spend more time in Alaska's wilderness than in overcrowded towns.

2. Because your port tax is included rather than added on as a surcharge.

3. To spend two full days in Glacier Bay, twice as long as anybody else cruising Alaska.

4. To go sea kayaking at no extra charge.

5. To take a hike with a maximum of 12 people.

Five Things You Won't Find Aboard

1. A children's program, or any place for small children to play.

2. A self-service laundry.

3. A doctor; the ship is always within 12 miles of land.

4. A beauty salon; if you want to get your hair done, you're on the wrong ship.

5. A bingo game.

Wilderness Adventurer ♒♒♒

Registry	U.S.
Officers	American
Crew	American
Complement	19
GRT	89
Length (ft.)	156.6
Beam (ft.)	38
Draft (ft.)	6.5
Passengers-Cabins Full	80
Passengers-2/Cabin	78
Passenger Space Ratio	N/A
Stability Rating	Fair to Good
Seatings	1
Cuisine	American
Dress Code	Casual
Room Service	No
Tip	$8–$12 PPPD pooled among staff

Ship Amenities

Outdoor Pool	0
Indoor Pool	0
Jacuzzi	0
Fitness Center	No
Spa	No
Beauty Shop	No
Showroom	No
Bars/Lounges	1
Casino	No
Shops	1 (small)
Library	Yes (small)
Child Program	No
Self-Service Laundry	No
Elevators	0

Cabin Statistics

Suites	0
Outside Doubles	32
Inside Doubles	6 (w/port light)
Wheelchair Cabins	0
Singles	0
Single Surcharge	175%
Verandas	0
110 Volt	Yes

Wilderness Explorer ⚓⚓⚓

The *Wilderness Explorer* is Glacier Bay's most basic vessel, aimed at adventurers who want an active, outdoors exploration of Alaska and won't fuss because the cabin has upper and lower berths instead of twin beds or a queen. You can paddle your kayak in pristine waters and still come home to a hot, wholesome meal at the end of the day. Cabins are small and few of them have windows, only portlights high up in the wall that let a bit of light in but don't give you a view. The top deck has an open observation area forward of the pilot house and a covered deck aft, with the ship's only deluxe cabin in between. (We suspect this used to belong to the captain, but now it's sold to paying passengers.) There's a small lounge forward and dining room amidships on the middle deck, with both crew and passenger cabins wedged into the lower deck.

GLACIER BAY TOURS AND CRUISES

Kayaking off the **Wilderness Explorer.**

The Brochure Says

"These *Wilderness Explorer* cruises are geared for the active, outdoor-oriented person who really wants to experience nature in ways that no other Alaska cruise or tour can deliver."

Translation

While everybody talks about offering "a real Alaska wilderness experience," this ship delivers more day-to-day opportunities than most. The line calls the vessel a "Cruising Base Camp," promising that you'll spend all day off the vessel in active adventures, coming back on board mainly to eat and sleep.

Cabins & Costs

Fantasy Suites: C

Average Price PPPD: $264 plus airfare on a five-day cruise.
Don't imagine this as anything approaching a traditional cruise ship suite, but rather as the only fairly large, comfortable space on this ship, even if it does have upper and lower berths. It also has two windows, a pearl beyond price on this vessel. The bathroom, like all the others aboard, has a shower/toilet combination which can leave a lot of residual water around if you don't plan your activities in the right order.

Small Splurges: C

Average Price PPPD: $252 plus airfare on a five-day cruise.
This has to be a record—the only time we've ever used the word "splurge" in conjunction with a cabin with upper and lower berths. But this is an unusual vessel and a special sort of cruise, and the price is much lower than the line's other ships. What you get for your splurge is a AA cabin with a picture window on the main deck with the lounge and dining room. The bad news is, there are only three of them.

Suitable Standards: .... D

Average Price PPPD: $246 plus airfare on a five-day cruise.
Now we're getting basic—these cabins are on the bottom deck with a portlight (a small sort of skylight high up in the wall that you can't see out of) instead of window or porthole. Upper and lower berths, of course, and the same bathroom described above. Spring for the AA category above if you can.

Bottom Bunks: .... D

Average Price PPPD: $232 plus airfare on a five-day cruise.
Don't ask. The three B-category cabins have the aforementioned portlight but are smaller than the A category above—each of them has part of its area donated to stairway adjacent to the wall, so you'll be able to hear footsteps of both passengers and crew bounding up and down.

Where She Goes

The *Wilderness Explorer* offers cruises that last for two, three, four and five nights. The two shorter ones still provide a day and a half in Glacier Bay with a kayaking day and hiking trips. On the three-night cruise, you'll also visit Pt. Adolphus, summer home of the humpback whales, and the Inian Islands. On the four-night itinerary, you'll spend two full days in Glacier Bay National Park, one full day at Pt. Adolphus and the Inian Islands, and have three full days of kayaking, hiking and nature explorations, plus a cruising day in Tracy Arm Fjord. The five-day program adds a full day exploring Tracy Arm by kayak, hiking and other launch vessels. Depending on your cruise, you'll board in Juneau or fly to Glacier Bay Lodge to begin.

The Bottom Line

This is an ideal cruise for the active traveler who has no interest in sitting on deck with binoculars in hand but would rather be out there in the midst of things doing and seeing. The flexibility allows those who are pressed for time to get in a little Alaskan adventuring, or to take several mini-cruises throughout the season instead of one longer one. If you've cruised before, you have to remind yourself that this is a very basic vessel offering a comfortable bunk, a hot shower and a home-cooked meal you don't have prepare yourself. What you get in exchange is a lot of Alaska up-close.

The dramatic ice flow at Margarie Glacier comes from the Fairweather Mountain Range, the highest coastal mountain range in the world.

Wilderness Explorer   ⚓⚓⚓

Registry	U.S.
Officers	American
Crew	American
Complement	13
GRT	98
Length (ft.)	112
Beam (ft.)	22
Draft (ft.)	7.6
Passengers-Cabins Full	36
Passengers-2/Cabin	36
Passenger Space Ratio	N/A
Stability Rating	Fair
Seatings	1
Cuisine	American
Dress Code	Casual
Room Service	No
Tip	$8–$12 PPPD pooled among staff

Ship Amenities

Outdoor Pool	0
Indoor Pool	0
Jacuzzi	0
Fitness Center	No
Spa	No
Beauty Shop	No
Showroom	No
Bars/Lounges	1
Casino	No
Shops	1 (small)
Library	Yes (small)
Child Program	No
Self-Service Laundry	No
Elevators	0

Cabin Statistics

Suites	0
Outside Doubles	4
Inside Doubles	14 (w/ port light)
Wheelchair Cabins	0
Singles	0
Single Surcharge	175%
Verandas	0
110 Volt	Yes

Traditional Chilkat dancers

Ketchikan, Alaska

White Pass and Yukon Railroad, Skagway

HOLLAND AMERICA LINE

300 Elliott Avenue West, Seattle, WA 98119
☎ *(206) 283-2687, (800) 426-0327*

String trios play for teatime and after dinner, as here, aboard the Statendam.

History . . . .

One of the oldest and most distinguished of the cruise lines, Holland America was founded in 1873 as the Netherlands-America Steamship Company, a year after its young co-founders commissioned and introduced the first ship, the original *Rotterdam*, a 1700-ton iron vessel. The new ship left the city it was named for on Oct. 15, 1872, and spent 15 days sailing to New York on its maiden voyage. It carried eight passengers in first class and 380 in steerage. Only a few years later, because all its sailings were to the Americas, it became known as Holland America Line.

—A leading carrier of immigrants to the United States, Holland America transported nearly 700,000 between 1901 and 1914 alone; a steerage fare cost $20.

—After World War II, when middle-class Americans began touring Europe in large numbers, HAL concentrated on offering moderately priced tourist class service with two medium-sized ships that carried 836 tourist class passengers and only 39 first-class passengers.

—The line introduced educational and pleasure cruises to the Holy Land just after the turn of the century, and in 1971, suspended transatlantic sailings in favor of cruise vacations.

—The first line to introduce glass-enclosed promenade decks on its ocean liners.

—First line to introduce a full-service Lido restaurant on all its ships as a casual dining alternative.

—First cruise line to introduce karaoke, a sort of high-tech singalong (on the *Westerdam* in 1990).

—Through its subsidiary Westours, Holland America retains a strong tour profile in Alaska, and with another subsidiary company, Windstar, offers small-ship sailing vacations in Costa Rica, the Caribbean and Mediterranean. Westours celebrates 50 years of Alaska tours in 1997.

—In 1989, Carnival Cruise Lines acquired Holland America and its affiliated companies, but retains HAL's Seattle headquarters and separate management.

Concept . . . .

With its slogan "A Tradition of Excellence," Holland America has always had a reputation for high quality and giving full cruise value for the money, along with a strong program of security and sanitation. Since its acquisition by Carnival, the line has worked to upscale its product and sees itself now firmly entrenched in what is called the "premium" segment of the cruise industry, a notch up from mass-market lines such as Carnival but not in the highest-priced luxury segment.

The line welcomes three new ships to the fleet—the new *Rotterdam VI* in September 1997, and two additional 65,000-ton ships for 1999.

HAL defines its premium status with such details as adding suites with private verandas to its four newest ships, *Statendam, Maasdam, Ryndam* and *Veendam*, along with more elaborate spas and advanced technology showrooms. The new vessels have also been designed to handle both short and long cruises equally well, with generous closet space and more-spacious staterooms.

There's also a strong undercurrent of "politically correct" behavior, consistent with its Pacific Northwest base, from specially packaged, environmentally safe cabin gift toiletries to taking a stand against the proposed Alaska aerial wolf-hunting program several years ago. The company also makes frequent, generous contributions to Alaskan universities and nonprofit organizations such as the Alaska Raptor Rehabilitation Center in Sitka.

Holland America's distinctive logo is painted on the funnels of its ships.

Signatures . . . .

A "No Tipping Required" policy means that while tips are appreciated by crew members, they cannot be solicited. However, very few passengers disembark without crossing more than a few palms with silver.

The line's longstanding tradition of hiring Indonesian and Filipino crew members and training them in its own Jakarta hotel school results in consistently high-quality service.

The continuing use of museum-quality antiques and artifacts from the golden days of Dutch shipping adds dignity and richness to the ship interiors.

The classic ship names, taken from Dutch cities, are always repeated in new vessels, with the present *Statendam, Maasdam* and *Rotterdam* each the fifth to bear the name, the *Veendam* the fourth, the *Nieuw Amsterdam, Noordam* and *Ryndam* the third namesakes, and the *Westerdam* the second in the line with that name.

Gimmicks . . . .

The ubiquitous Holland America bag, a white canvas carry-all embellished with the company's logo and names of all the ships, can be glimpsed all over the world. Each passenger on each cruise is given one of these, so you can imagine how many frequent cruisers manage to amass. They're washable and last forever. "It's the single best investment we ever made," said one HAL insider.

Passport to Fitness, a folded card that has 48 separate areas to get stamped as the holder completes a qualifying activity, from the morning walkathon to aerobics class or a volleyball game. The prizes vary by the number of stamps, but are usually a Holland America logo item such as a T-shirt, cap or jacket. (We heard one eager-to-win passenger ask the librarian to stamp her passport for checking out a book about sports.)

Five Special Touches

1. Beautiful red plaid deck blankets.

2. Toiletries in each cabin wrapped in replicas of period Holland America posters and advertising art.

3. Museum-quality ship and seafaring artifacts in special display cases, along with antique bronze cannons and figureheads.

4. Fresh flowers flown in from Holland all over the ship.

5. Trays of mints, dried fruits and candied ginger outside the dining room after dinner.

Who's the Competition.

Princess is the closest head-on competitor, vying to be top dog in the Alaska cruise market. The two lines can claim the two largest land tour operators, HAL's Westours and Princess's Princess Tours. For the past couple of years, Princess has had more ships in Alaska than Holland America, but Westours claims more tour departures.

Who's Aboard.

While the Alaska market is attracting more and more younger cruisers and families, Holland America's basic passengers can still be defined as middle-aged and older couples who appreciate solid quality in food, surroundings and service. Still, we noted four sets of honeymooners on a *Ryndam* Alaska cruise recently.

The recent reflagging of the fleet to the Dutch flag could also create a resurgence of European passengers, particularly from The Netherlands.

Who Should Go.

More younger couples and families should be aboard Holland America's shorter sailings, especially to Alaska, where the line excels in the scope and variety of its land/cruise packages. Single women and families with children will find HAL is thinking of them—youth counselors coordinate activities for each age group, from an ice cream sundae party for the 5-to-8 set to teen disco parties and contests, and social hosts to dance with unattached women on all cruises 14 days or longer. Physically challenged passengers will find suitable accommodations on board all the new ships, plus extra assistance from the attentive staff, who also lavish special care and attention on the elderly and small children.

Who Should Not Go

Young swinging singles looking to boogie all night or meet the mate of their dreams.

Nonconformists.

People who refuse to dress up.

The Lifestyle

A surprising amount of luxury and pampering go on aboard these ships, with string trios (two of them usually work each ship now) playing at teatime, white-gloved stewards to escort you to your cabin when you board, vases of fresh flowers everywhere, bowls of fresh fruit in the cabins, and most of all, what the Dutch call *gezellig*, a warm and cozy ambiance, defined with curtains in the cabins that can separate the sleeping area from the sitting area, friendly Dutch officers and caring Indonesian and Filipino crew members, who make it a point of pride to remember your name.

In Alaska, naturalists and longtime Alaska residents are always among the lecture staff. Kodak ambassadors are on board designated cruises to assist passengers with photo problems and show examples of good slide photography from the area. Movies are shown at three or four daily screening times, as well as on cabin TV, and shore excursions emphasize sightseeing and flightseeing, with floatplane and helicopter glacier flights, kayaking, raft trips and visits to cultural (Native American) areas and historical city tours.

The line offers three different Alaska itineraries in 1997. The Inside Passage, the Glacier Route and a new combination of the two that adds a visit to Glacier National Park as well as cruising parts of the other two routes.

Wardrobe . . . .

Dress code follows a traditional pattern, with a week usually calling for two formal nights (and they do dress up on these ships, even in Alaska), two informal nights when men are expected to wear a jacket but a tie is usually optional, and three "elegantly casual" nights with no shorts, T-shirts, tank tops, halter tops or jeans permitted. During the daytime, comfortable, casual clothing—jogging outfits, shorts or slacks, T-shirts, bathing suits and cover-ups—are adequate deck wear.

Holland America consistently produces some of the most attractive buffets at sea; here, breakfast aboard the **Maasdam.**

Bill of Fare . . . . .A

"Genteel tradition" is important to Holland America, from a chime master who announces dinner to the Indonesian bellman in the bellboy outfit (similar to the doormen in white at the Peninsula Hotel in Hong Kong) who holds open the doors between the Lido buffet and the deck for every passenger.

Holland America consistently produces some of the tastiest and most appealing buffets at sea, from the lavish Dutch-style breakfasts to wonderfully varied luncheons. In addition to a full hot-and-cold buffet in the Lido restaurants, chefs on deck will grill hot dogs and hamburgers to order, serve up make-your-own tacos, stir-fry-to-order and pasta of the day, plus a very popular make-your-own-ice-cream-sundae counter with a bowl of homemade cookies.

Because of the scope and popularity of the buffet service, dining room breakfast and lunch are served open seating, which means you can arrive within a specified time and sit with whom you wish.

Dinner menus have grown increasingly sophisticated. A typical dinner might include six appetizers (among them warm hazelnut-crusted Brie with apple and onion compote and French bread, bay shrimp coupe with cocktail sauce, smoked king salmon with horseradish cream and herb crostini), two soups (one may be five-onion cream with frizzled onions), three salads (including field greens with smoked duck, Asian pears and toasted pecans), six entrées, from a low-calorie, low-fat sautéed Alaskan snapper teriyaki or fresh halibut with asparagus and lemon pepper mashed potatoes to a Parmesan-crusted chicken breast or a grilled New York steak with baked Idaho potato and onion rings. A cheese and fresh fruit course follows, then a choice of four desserts plus pastry tray, ice creams and frozen yogurts, and sugar-free desserts. Chocoholics will adore the Chocolate Extravaganza late show, served once during each cruise as a midnight buffet.

Children's menus offer four standard entrees—hamburger and fries, hot dog, pizza or chicken drumsticks—plus a nightly chef's special, perhaps beef tacos, fish and chips or barbecued ribs. The more urbane kid may prefer to order from the regular menu.

CHAMPAGNE TOAST

Holland America serves Seattle's famous Starbucks coffee on board all its ships; on the big new liners—Statendam, Maasdam, Ryndam and Veendam—after-dinner espresso is complimentary in the Explorer's Lounge.

Showtime . . . . B+

A more sophisticated level of production shows was introduced recently, with each ship featuring its own specially tailored programs. On the line's long cruises and world cruises, headliner entertainers such as Rita Moreno, Roy Clark, Victor Borge and Vic Damone, plus noted lecturers and even a Las Vegas-style ice skating spectacular, may show up on the program.

Discounts . . . .

Early booking savings can take off 10 to 20 percent for passengers who book and make a deposit on a specified timetable, which may mean anything from one to six months ahead of time. Passengers who book earliest get the lowest prices, and if a new money-saver is introduced after they book, their fare will be adjusted on request and verification. Past passengers also get added discounts and special mail offers on certain cruises.

The Bottom Line

This is an extremely high-quality product with good fulfillment for the money, one that keeps getting better. As much as anybody in the business, Holland America delivers what it promises.

Officers are Dutch, with a no-nonsense attitude about safety and seamanship. The lifeboat drill is thorough and explicit, and cleanliness and sanitation are of an extremely high standard.

When we gave Shirley's parents their first cruise a few years ago for an anniversary gift, Holland America was the line we chose—and they're still saying it was the best vacation they ever had.

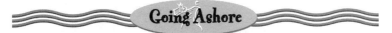

Going Ashore

With its own affiliated tour company Westours, you can expect a wide range of both shore excursions and pre- and post-cruise packages, as well as 35 combination land/sea tours that range from nine to 18 days. Many of them include a rail journey to Denali National Park aboard the deluxe McKinley Explorer rail cars or a motorcoach tour through the rough-and-ready Yukon Territory before or after the cruise. The Westmark chain of hotels throughout Alaska is also an affiliate of Holland America Westours.

Like several other lines, Holland America rates its shore excursions by icon—a single figure means easy activity, sometimes accessible for wheelchairs; a two-figure icon requires moderate activity with some walking over uneven surfaces and climbing staircases; and a three-figure icon designates considerable activity with constant physical movement such as paddling, walking or climbing.

The line offers around 50 excursions, ranging in price from a $16.50 tramway ride to the top of Mount Roberts in Juneau to a $315 combination Skagway Flight and White Pass Summit rail excursion that lasts 8 hours.

Easy Does It

1. Naa Kahidi Theater, Juneau

$16, 1-hour performance, 30 minutes to visit with artists.

A dramatic performance of traditional and contemporary legends of Native Alaska, performed in dance, song and storytelling. Afterwards, mix with the cast and local craftsmen in the Cultural Arts Park.

2. Historic Russian America and Raptor Center, Sitka

$42, 1.5 hours.

The Eagle Center shows how injured birds are cared for from capture to rehabilitation and release back into the wild. Then a local guide takes you on a driving tour of Sitka, including a center where Native Americans are working on totem art forms. The excursion concludes with a performance of Russian folk dancing by the New Archangel Dancers.

3. Ketchikan Waterfront Cruise

$45, 1.5 hours.

A comfortable excursion yacht takes you along the waterfront while you listen to stories of the rough-and-tough old days when Creek Street was the red-light district. You'll cruise past the fishing fleet, float planes and seafood processing plants, and sample Alaskan smoked salmon on the way to see nesting bald eagles and Pennock Island and a distant view of the totem poles at Saxman Totem Park.

For A Moderate Effort

1. Wilderness Lodge Adventure, Juneau

$175, 3 hours, limited participation.

A float plane sweeps you through the wilderness and over glaciers to the Taku Glacier Lodge, where you're welcomed into the rustic lobby by the crackling fireplace, then served a meal of fresh grilled king salmon with various side dishes and soda, beer or wine chilled with glacier ice. After the meal, you can take a nature walk, pitch horseshoes or simply relax in the tranquil surroundings.

2. Sitka Sportfishing

$140, plus a $10 one-day fishing license from boat captain and an additional $10 stamp during King Salmon season, 4 hours, limited participation.

Set out with a knowledgeable local captain into Sitka Sound for halibut or salmon fishing.

3. Orca Beach Nature Hike, Ketchikan

$79, 3 hours, limited participation, hike mostly downhill for 1/5 mile.

Hike through muskeg meadows and old-growth rain forest to a remote beach, where snacks are served, then board a Zodiac landing craft to cruise along the coast to Knudson Cove.

Going All Out

1. Alaska Style Glacier View Golf, Juneau

$49, 3 hours, limited participation, no electric carts.

One of the world's most unusual golf courses is this 9-hole, par-3, hazard-filled course in a glacial valley. The fee includes a bucket of practice balls, greens fees, bag and 8 clubs.

2. "Ski to Sea" Bike Tour, Juneau

$54, 3 hours, 9 miles of biking, limited participation, height limit of over 4'2".

Climb via van to Juneau's Eaglecrest Ski Area, where you board bikes for a tour that begins with five miles downhill through mountain forests and along streams, then four miles of level biking along the Douglas Island Coast, with views of the Mendenhall Glacier and the Chilkat Mountain Range.

3. Keystone Canyon Raft Trip, Valdez

$69, 2 hours, limited participation, rain gear and lifejackets provided but children must weigh at least 40 pounds to fit into lifejackets.

Some 4.25 miles of whitewater rafting takes you into a canyon, through a gap in the Chugach Mountains and past a 900-foot waterfall.

Don't Bother to Book

Juneau City & Mendenhall Glacier Tour

$30, 2.5 hours.

Unless you have mobility problems, you can do a free city walking tour with the well-illustrated maps the city tourist office hands out, then share a 10-minute cab ride with several friends to the Mendenhall Glacier, which has been subtitled America's only drive-in glacier.

Sister ship Maasdam

Ryndam ★★★★★
Statendam ★★★★★
Veendam ★★★★★

The Dutch, or more precisely the Netherlanders, have lent their name to some decidedly unglamorous expressions—in Dutch, Dutch treat, Dutch uncle, Dutch courage. Over the years, they have given us cozy and cliché images of dowager queens in sensible shoes, herrings, Hans Brinker, Gouda and Edam cheese, windmills and respectable burghers staring out at us from museum walls and cigar boxes.

But these ships are not apple-cheeked little Dutch girls in wooden shoes and stiff white bonnets. They're sophisticated and very elegant women of the world who know who they are and what they're doing.

The newest HAL ships are ideal for Alaska, with spacious cabins, each with its own sitting area, and generous closet and drawer space. A variety of lounges, public rooms and outdoor spaces offer enough entertaining alternatives to ensure that passengers won't get bored.

A 26-foot Italianate fountain ornaments the three-deck lobby of the *Statendam*, and a slightly smaller version of the same also decorates the *Ryndam* lobby, while the *Veendam's* centerpiece is a monumental green glass sculpture created by Luciano Vistosi of Murano, Italy, called "Jacob's Ladder."

From the gangway level, a graceful curved stairway and an escalator (convenient but unusual aboard ships) take passengers up one deck to the front office and lobby, the bottom level of the three-deck atrium. Each ship shows off a $2 million art collection, along with dazzling two-deck theaters and showy glass-walled dining rooms, sizable spas and expansive deck areas.

The Brochure Says

"Floating resorts, our ships are our own private islands, destinations in themselves, offering everything you'd expect in a great resort on land. Fine dining. Dazzling entertainment. Activities galore. And it's all included in your cruise fare."

Translation

Holland America seems to be looking to appeal to a new group of passengers, younger, more resort-oriented people who may not have cruised before, by accenting entertainment, cuisine and variety. The previous emphasis on overall cruise value and nearly 125 years of service is still underscored as well.

Cabins & Costs

One of the lavish penthouses on Navigation Deck.

Fantasy Suites: .... A+

Average Price PPPD: $943–$1019 plus air add-ons.

The penthouses on Navigation Deck, one on each ship, are huge—1123 square feet—ideal for entertaining with a living room with wraparound sofa, four chairs, big-screen TV; a large private veranda, dining table that seats eight, butler pantry; separate bedroom with queen-sized bed, built-in dressing table and walk-in dressing room lined with closets. The marble bathroom has double sinks, a whirlpool tub, a steam bath/shower combination and separate water closet with bidet; there's even a custom-tiled guest bath.

Small Splurges: .... A

Average Price PPPD: $533–$752 plus air add-ons.

A deluxe outside double with private veranda in categories A or B measure 284 square feet and have a sitting area with sofa that can be converted into a third bed, a TV with VCR, minibar and a refrigerator, as well as a whirlpool bath. Both categories are identical, but the As are one deck higher than the Bs.

Suitable Standards: ....B

Average Price PPPD: $352–$428 plus air add-ons.

Each large outside double contains twin beds that can convert to queen-sized, a sitting area with sofa and chair, a desk/dresser with stool, coffee table, hair dryer, safe, large closet, and bath with tub/shower combination. Six wheelchair-accessible cabins, outside doubles with shower only, are also available.

Bottom Bunks: ....B

Average Price PPPD: $190–$266 plus air add-ons.

Even the cheapest cabins on the luxurious vessels are pretty good. Inside doubles are 187 square feet with sitting area sofa and chair, twin beds that can convert to queen-sized, a desk/dresser with stool, coffee table, hair dryer, safe, and a four-door closet. Bathrooms have showers only, and a floral privacy curtain between beds and sitting area.

The *Statendam*'s itinerary in Alaska—seven-day Inside Passage cruises from Vancouver that call in Ketchikan, Juneau and Sitka and cruise Glacier Bay and the Inside Passage.

The *Ryndam* repositions to Alaska through the Panama Canal before starting a summer season of seven-day Glacier Route sailings between Vancouver and Seward, calling in Ketchikan, Juneau, Sitka and Valdez. In September the ship is scheduled to return through the canal to the Southern Caribbean to resume its 10-day programs.

The *Veendam* makes its Alaska debut with seven-day Glacier Bay sailings from Vancouver calling at Juneau, Skagway and Ketchikan and cruising the Inside Passage and Glacier Bay.

A musical production show aboard the Statendam *illustrates HAL's younger, more energetic style that has emerged with the newest class of ships.*

Traditionalists as well as luxury loving passengers should like these vessels, which gleam with softly burnished wood and brass, with the added zing of dramatic showrooms that are themed from Dutch masterpieces by Vermeer, Rembrandt, Rubens and Van Gogh.

While the decorous gentility will attract well-heeled older passengers, there's enough spark and energy to appeal to upscale younger couples and singles as well. Almost anyone should feel at home aboard, especially if home were a palatial mansion with a smiling staff.

The message these newest Holland America ships seem to be sending is that the company is aiming in the direction of other luxurious large-ship companies, such as Crystal Cruises. Both hardware (the new ships) and software (the food, service and ambiance) just keep on improving on this very fine line.

Five Spectacular Places

1. The striking two-deck Rotterdam dining rooms on all the ships have a magnificent entry stairway ideal for making a grand entrance, window walls on three sides and a ceiling covered with a thousand frosted Venetian glass morning glories.

2. The Crow's Nest top deck observation lounges offer Alaska-themed decor. On the *Ryndam*, designer Joe Farcus has created crackle-glass "glaciers" as flooring and a ceiling of glass cylinders cut at different angles like glacial ice surfaces.

3. The sumptuous and subdued libraries have plenty of cushy chairs for readers and writers.

4. The full promenade decks on all the ships, covered in teak and lined with classic wooden deck loungers, invite you to stretch out in the shade with a good book.

5. The handsome covered Lido Deck pool area with its retractable sliding glass dome (ideal in Alaska's changeable climate), playful dolphin sculptures, spas and children's wading pools.

Five Good Reasons to Book These Ships

1. Sunbathers will like the blue terrycloth covers fitted to the loungers, much more comfortable for wet or oiled bodies than the usual plastic strips or removable cushions.

2. Buffets galore for nibbling and noshing, from an ice-cream-sundae bar to a make-your-own taco stand, free hot fresh popcorn at the movie matinees in the theater, the Chocolate Extravaganza late-night buffet, the hot hors d'oeuvres at cocktail time in the Crow's Nest, the Royal Dutch Tea, and a glass of fresh carrot juice from the juice bar in the Ocean Spa.

3. A good workout, from the Passport to Fitness program (see Gimmicks, above) to a jog around the *Statendam* or a fast game of deck tennis on the *Ryndam*, with some aerobics, massage, sauna and steam treatments in the expansive Ocean Spa with its Stairmasters, treadmills, bicycles and free weights.

4. You'll have plenty of closet and drawer space to store your wardrobe, no matter how much you've over-packed.

5. The romantic little piano bars on board each ship, especially elegant and intimate.

HOLLAND AMERICA LINE

Ryndam
Statendam
Veendam
★★★★★
★★★★★
★★★★★

Registry	**The Netherlands**
Officers	**Dutch**
Crew	**Indonesian/Filipino**
Complement	**571**
GRT	**69,130**
Length (ft.)	**720**
Beam (ft.)	**101**
Draft (ft.)	**25**
Passengers-Cabins Full	**1613**
Passengers-2/Cabin	**1266**
Passenger Space Ratio	**54.60**
Stability Rating	**Good to Excellent**
Seatings	**2**
Cuisine	**International**
Dress Code	**Traditional**
Room Service	**Yes**
Tip	**No Tipping Required**

Ship Amenities

Outdoor Pool	**2**
Indoor Pool	**0**
Jacuzzi	**2**
Fitness Center	**Yes**
Spa	**Yes**
Beauty Shop	**Yes**
Showroom	**Yes**
Bars/Lounges	**8**
Casino	**Yes**
Shops	**5**
Library	**Yes**
Child Program	**Yes**
Self-Service Laundry	**Yes**
Elevators	**8**

Cabin Statistics

Suites	**29**
Outside Doubles	**485**
Inside Doubles	**148**
Wheelchair Cabins	**6**
Singles	**0**
Single Surcharge	**150%**
Verandas	**200**
110 Volt	**Yes**

HOLLAND AMERICA LINE

Nieuw Amsterdam   ★★★★
Noordam   ★★★★

In May 1984, two new ships, the Noordam and Sitmar's Fairsky (now Princess Cruises' Sky Princess) each made a debut cruise from Los Angeles to the Mexican Riviera a week apart along the same familiar route down to Puerto Vallarta and back. Cruise writers who were aboard both sailings had spirited arguments back and forth about which ship was prettier, the innovative Fairsky, the last big steamship to be built, or the solid, well-crafted and traditional Noordam. There was no decision, no winners or losers, although proponents of each went away certain their arguments had prevailed.

A tile surround on the aft swimming pool aboard the **Noordam** *keeps sunbathers cool.*

The *Nieuw Amsterdam* debuted in 1983, the first new ship for Holland America in nearly quarter of a century, and, like her identical sister *Noordam* a year later, was built in France's Chantiers d'Atlantique yard. Despite some noticeable vibration in certain areas, the ships are classy, traditional and comfortable, with museum-quality artifacts relating to sailing and the sea handsomely displayed.

All the cabins are relatively large with plentiful wardrobe space, from the minimum-priced insides to the deluxe staterooms with sitting areas. There are no large suites or private verandas. Outside cabins have windows on Main Deck and above; the portholes begin on A Deck and get more view-restrictive on B and C Decks. Inside cabins mark the imaginary "window" with fabric draperies that are always closed.

Once on board, passengers relax almost instantly in the spacious public rooms and tasteful, subdued decor. There's no glitz or jingle-jangle to bring in a jarring note, and the smiling, soft-spoken serving staff of Indonesians and Filipinos do nothing to break the mood. A few pockets of activity shelter night owls—the Horn Pipe Club on the *Nieuw Amsterdam*, the Pear Tree on the *Noordam*—but most passengers turn in fairly early, as is typical in Alaska.

The Brochure Says

"Attentive Filipino and Indonesian crew members offer gracious 'Five-Star' service, expecting no reward beyond your smile of thanks—because Holland America sails under a 'tipping not required' policy."

Translation

Note it does not say, Tipping not permitted. If you wanted to press the issue, you could claim tipping is not required on any cruise ship, but very obviously the passenger is expected to supplement the low base salaries on most major vessels with a tactfully "suggested" tip. Holland America does not permit its employees to "suggest" or even "hint" about a tip; instead, they simply provide excellent service the entire time you're aboard the ship, so that only a churl would even consider disembarking without dispensing some largesse.

INSIDER TIP

Happy Hour in the Crows Nest on the Noordam *is from 4:45 to 5:45 p.m. and from 7 to 8 p.m., with the first drink at the regular price and subsequent ones at half price. Drinks are accompanied by a generous assortment of hot and cold hors d'oeuvres.*

Cabins & Costs

Fantasy Suites: .... *C*

Average Price PPPD: $457–$533 plus air add-ons.

While there are no really big elegant suites aboard, the top category A cabins offer a great deal of comfort if not space. The wood furnishings are dark and polished, and all accommodations contain a king-sized bed, sitting area with sofa-bed, armchair, table, desk and double windows, as well as mini-refrigerator, closets with good storage space and bathroom with tub/shower combination. The down side is that every window in the A category cabins has a partially obstructed view from hanging lifeboats. The part you'll see through your window is only the top half, which still lets you see some of the sea.

Small Splurges: ....B

Average Price PPPD: $390–$466 plus air add-ons.

We'd recommend opting for a B or C rather than an A category on these ships, because you'll get the same or even more space, along with tub and shower and sitting area, and may not, depending on deck location, have to look out over hanging lifeboats. The best B cabins are 114 and 115 on Boat Deck, oversized quarters with double bed, and our favorite C cabins are those forward on Boat and Upper Promenade Decks with a captain's-eye view of the sea ahead. On the Boat Deck, cabins #100-103 are wheelchair-accessible quarters with bathroom grip rails, shower seat and low hanging closet rack.

*An inside cabin on the **Noordam** is spacious and comfortable; notice the curtains that suggest a window may be behind them.*

Suitable Standards: ....B

Average Price PPPD: $305–$381 plus air add-ons.

If you could nail down one of two E category Large Outsides (cabins E 711 or 716) you'd find a very big cabin with twin beds, large TV, long desk counter, leather headboards, and plenty of storage; these two cabins are almost double the size of the others in this category. The others are also OK, just not so big.

Bottom Bunks: ....C+

Average Price PPPD: $190–$266 plus air add-ons.

All the lowest-priced inside cabins have two lower beds and are the same size with the same furnishings as most of the other cabins aboard, including color TV, but on a lower deck (C Deck) and forward.

ANNOYANCES

This is really nit-picking, but the friendly, polite servers stand and chat with well-meaning passengers in the dining room, asking questions about their families and home towns, sometimes slowing down the service to a crawl.

INSIDER TIP

One of the best views of the stage is from the five rows of black leather theater seats in the center back of the main level of the show lounge, where latecomers are often put.

On the balcony level of the show lounges, late arrivals have to sit on the outer edges away from the railing in tables and chairs arranged in conversational groupings, and they do just that—make conversation while the show is going on at a volume that competes with the performers.

The *Nieuw Amsterdam* spends summer in Alaska on an Inside Passage seven-day roundtrip itinerary out of Vancouver, calling in Juneau, Sitka and Ketchikan.

The *Noordam* sails a summer seven-day Glacier Route in Alaska between Vancouver and Seward, calling in Juneau, Sitka, Ketchikan and Valdez.

While more than 10 years old, both ships are kept remarkably clean in the traditional Holland America shine-and-polish style. Where the age and wear shows is on the few outer deck areas covered with astroturf, with spots, splotches and patches all too apparent. Inside, however, housekeeping is of the sort our mothers used to describe as, "You could eat off the floor."

We like the glass bowls of fresh fruit in the cabins and batik bedspreads with matching privacy curtains, one of the cozy touches the Dutch call *gezellig*, as well as the comfortable places to sit all around the ship with antiques, ship models and old maps to study.

Five Favorite Spots

1. The Crow's Nest, elegantly cozy forward observation lounges with hot hors d'oeuvres at cocktail time and piano music throughout the evening, as well as period ship models in plexiglass cases.

2. The Lido, where the art of the buffet comes to life; not only does everything look good enough to eat, but it really is. And you can make your own ice cream sundaes for dessert.

3. The Explorer Lounge on the *Nieuw Amsterdam*, with a wall lined with wooden ship figureheads holding lamps; this is where the Rosario Strings play after dinner while bar waiters offer espresso, cappuccino and liqueurs—on a tab, of course.

4.   The Ocean Spa on both ships, with massage rooms, saunas, gym with bikes, rowing, treadmills and weights, and just outside, the pool and spas.

5.   The broad natural teak deck all around both ships on Upper Promenade, with sheltered, covered reading spots and rows of traditional wooden deck loungers reminiscent of ocean-liner days.

Five Good Reasons to Book These Ships

1.   A tempting range of food opportunities, from light and healthful menus and sugar-free desserts to make-your-own-taco or ice-cream-sundae stations.

2.   Hot, fresh popcorn served for movie matinees (but not evening screenings) in the theater.

3.   The Dutch figures in traditional costume in the glass cases at the entrance to the Lido restaurant.

4.   The broad expanse of Lido Deck in natural teak with fresh water swimming pool, wading pool and splash surround, only steps away from the hot dog/hamburger grill and the outdoor Lido Bar.

5.   The classic Holland America tote bag, free to every passenger on every sailing.

Five Things You Won't Find On Board

1.   A well-stocked library; if you want to read a current best-seller, bring it yourself.

2.   A free self-service laundry; you pay $1 to wash your clothes, but soap and the dryer are free.

3.   A bathroom mirror reflection in the designated handicap cabins if you're in a wheelchair; you can easily roll the chair under the sink rim, but can't see your reflection once you're there.

4.   Slot machine gambling when the ships are in port.

5.   A good view of the stage from every seat in the two-deck show lounge, especially in the balcony; you'll have to search to find a good spot from which to see everything.

Nieuw Amsterdam
Noordam

★★★★
★★★★

Registry	**The Netherlands**
Officers	**Dutch**
Crew	**Indonesian/Filipino**
Complement	**566**
GRT	**33,930**
Length (ft.)	**704**
Beam (ft.)	**89**
Draft (ft.)	**25**
Passengers-Cabins Full	**1378**
Passengers-2/Cabin	**1214**
Passenger Space Ratio	**27.94**
Stability Rating	**Good**
Seatings	**2**
Cuisine	**International**
Dress Code	**Traditional**
Room Service	**Yes**
Tip	**No tipping required**

Ship Amenities

Outdoor Pool	**2**
Indoor Pool	**0**
Jacuzzi	**1**
Fitness Center	**Yes**
Spa	**Yes**
Beauty Shop	**Yes**
Showroom	**Yes**
Bars/Lounges	**8**
Casino	**Yes**
Shops	**3**
Library	**Yes**
Child Program	**Yes**
Self-Service Laundry	**Yes**
Elevators	**7**

Cabin Statistics

Suites	**0**
Outside Doubles	**411**
Inside Doubles	**194**
Wheelchair Cabins	**4**
Singles	**0**
Single Surcharge	**150%**
Verandas	**0**
110 Volt	**Yes**

HOLLAND AMERICA LINE

Rotterdam

It's still possible on the Rotterdam, built in 1959, to see how it used to be divided into first and transatlantic classes. A central stairway called "the secret staircase," inspired by stairs in the French chateau of Chambord, makes it possible for two people to go up or down on separate, adjacent stairs without seeing each other, except on the landings when sliding doors are open.

The Dutch say gezellig *for cozy, which describes these booths in the* **Rotterdam's** *Lido Cafe.*

One of the true grande dames of the sea, the elegant *Rotterdam* has been renovated numerous times without losing her original character. The gleam of polished wood interiors, plush and leather lounge furniture will remind you of the splendid ocean-liner days, and the number of intimate bars and lounges around the ship, each with its own dance floor, suggests one of the favorite onboard activities.

But even sun-and-pool fans will enjoy the ship on warm days in Alaska. An extension of the upper promenade deck adds a permanent cover to the Lido pool deck below, and a horseshoe-shaped wooden bar with 16 barstools supplements the white plastic loungers and deck chairs and umbrella-covered tables around the blue-and-white tile pool. A covered grill on the starboard side turns out hot dogs, hamburgers and sandwiches grilled to order. Tea and coffee are served throughout the day in the Lido restaurant.

The flagship of the fleet, the *Rotterdam* is the fifth ship with this name. Its replacement *Rotterdam VI* enters service the day this vessel is retired in September 1997.

EAVESDROPPING

A young Dutch officer just transferred to the Rotterdam*: "I told them, I'll do anything, work long months with a short vacation, just put me on the Rotterdam instead of one of those new hotels with a little hull wrapped around it so it'll float—the* Rotterdam *is a real ship!"*

The Brochure Says

"Holland America's Grand Voyage service begins the moment you step aboard. A string quartet plays. An officer smiles. A white-gloved steward escorts you to your stateroom, where everything has been laid out for your imminent arrival; personalized stationery, fresh flowers, even a plush terry robe to slip into."

Translation

Posh is an understatement on a long voyage aboard the *Rotterdam*, where every day seems to bring another special gift from the line. We'd suggest you carry an extra bag to bring them home in, except that HAL gives you a canvas carry-all as well.

Cabins & Costs

Fantasy Suites: . . . . **A-**
Average Price PPPD: $449–$508 plus air add-ons.
While not as plushly evocative as some of the public rooms, the A category staterooms aboard have king-sized beds, sitting area with sofa, two chairs and oval black granite table, a long dresser with 10 drawers, safe and shelves, mini-refrigerator, built-in dressing table and stool, separate dressing room and bath with tub and double sinks.

Small Splurges: . . . . **B+**
Average Price PPPD: $364–$423 plus air add-ons.
Deluxe outside double cabins in category B provide plenty of room and some of the custom cabinetry from the 1950s, including vanity tables with tall mirrors, built-in drawers and clips to secure bottles of perfume or other toiletries. A separate sitting area has a sofa and chairs with coffee table, and a dresser with nine drawers stores lots of clothing. Bathrooms usually have tubs and heated towel racks. We particularly like the forward-facing cabins on Boat Deck, B 33 and B 34, with three windows each.

Batik fabrics and built-in wood cabinetry decorate this standard outside cabin with portholes aboard the Rotterdam.

Suitable Standards: .... B

Average Price PPPD: $240–$253 plus air add-ons.

Because the original ship was built before modular cabins came into play, standard cabins vary somewhat in size and shape. All the standard doubles have two lower beds or double bed, private bath (some with tubs and heated towel racks), TV, batik bedspreads and curtains, a chair or two, built-in cabinetry with lower drawers and upper shelves, plus sometimes a pullout writing desk or vanity table.

Bottom Bunks: C

Average Price PPPD: $171–$242 plus air add-ons.

The cheapest economy inside doubles are category O, with upper and lower berths and bath with shower only. The ones we've looked at are very small, but still have a chair, dressing table with mirror, dresser with six drawers, some of them with locks, and a tile bath with shower only.

INSIDER TIP

Note that the Rotterdam *also has number of small single inside and outside cabins with one lower bed and bath with shower.*

Where She Goes

The *Rotterdam* will make seven-day sailings along Alaska's Glacier Route between Vancouver and Seward, calling in Ketchikan, Juneau, Sitka and Valdez, followed by a nostalgic cruise from Vancouver to Ft. Lauderdale, her last sailing before retirement in September 1997.

The Bottom Line

This is one of our very favorite ships, and it makes us sad to note a few signs of age, such as the worn teak decking aft on Promenade Deck. Cozy, clean and comfortable cabins and gracious, understated public rooms; an around-the-ship promenade, part of it glassed in, lined with old-fashioned wooden steamer chairs; a plethora of fresh flower arrangements everywhere; a big, bright gym and sun room; the stylish, art deco nightclub and lounges—all add up to a classy and classic shipboard experience that cannot be duplicated. We all bid her farewell in September 1997.

Fielding's Five

Five Classic Places

1. The Ritz-Carlton Lounge, a two-deck nightclub that impeccably recalls the glorious days of ocean liners, with a shimmering 90-foot wall mural from 1959 with Aegean scenes and a grand curved staircase for a movie-star entrance. The furniture is upholstered in jewel-toned velvets in sapphire, emerald and topaz, and the dance floor is incised brass.

Romantic tables for two in the **Rotterdam's** *Odyssey Dining Room.*

2. The two high-domed dining rooms, the La Fontaine decorated with ceramic scenes from the famous fables, and the Odyssey with ceramic scenes from Homer's epic poem.

3. The dual "secret staircase" left over from the days when the ship was divided into two classes, structured so people can go up or down at the same time without seeing each other.

4. The Ambassador Lounge, like a New York bar of the 1950s with its bull's-eye glass, long velvet banquettes, inlaid wood parquet dance floor and tiny red plush barstools for fashion-model derrières.

5. The easy-to-love Ocean Bar, one of the great small bars at sea, with its comma-shaped bar lined with stools and its handful of tête-à-tête cocktail tables.

Five Off-the-Wall Hideaways and Secret Spots

1. The Tropic Bar, a tiny pseudo-tropical late-night drinking-and-singalong spot tucked away behind the Ritz-Carlton night club. It's usually open only on long cruises.

2. An indoor swimming pool down on D Deck with marble benches, saunas and massage rooms nearby, tile fish on the pool bottom and sculptured fish on the walls.

3. The Sky Room, on Bridge Deck above the Sun Room, a little piano bar with overstuffed plush chairs (you can find the stairs leading up there near the Wireless Office).

4. A tiny terrace with tables and chairs outside the Sky Room, where nobody will ever think to look for you.

5. The shuffleboard courts outside the gym and sun room on Sun Deck, where spectators gather on wooden benches during the numerous hotly-contested tournaments.

Five Good Reasons to Book These Ships

1. To experience what the grand days of ocean-liner travel were all about.

2. To make a complete round-the-world cruise for her final season.

3. To admire the one-of-a-kind wood paneling and marquetry, the exquisite restored 90-foot wall mural of the Aegean that adorns the two-deck walls of the Ritz-Carlton nightclub, to seek out (behind the slot machines) the unique tapestry murals created for the 1959 ship in the former card room, now the casino, and the original wood chairs in a 1950s moderne design in the Queen's Lounge.

4. To read or write in the Reading Room with its dictionary stand, writing tables, wing chairs with batik upholstery and dark blue velvet hassocks piped with gold.

5. To get a last sad look at a ship of this type, since the corporate owners in their infinite wisdom decided not to make the sizable investment it would take to bring her up to the new SOLAS (Safety of Life At Sea) standards after her 1997 World Cruise.

Five Things You Won't Find On Board

1. A disco, although there are two piano bars.

2. A wheelchair-accessible cabin, although ramps are available to help get over the doorsills.

3. A children's playroom (don't bring the kids along on this ship).

4. An unobstructed sea view from the cabin windows on Sun Deck; they're partially blocked by hanging lifeboats.

5. A real fire in the fireplace in the casino.

HOLLAND AMERICA LINE

Rotterdam ★ ★ ★ ★ ★

Registry	**The Netherlands**
Officers	**Dutch**
Crew	**Indonesian/Filipino**
Complement	**603**
GRT	**38,000**
Length (ft.)	**748**
Beam (ft.)	**94**
Draft (ft.)	**30**
Passengers-Cabins Full	**1347**
Passengers-2/Cabin	**1065**
Passenger Space Ratio	**35.68**
Stability Rating	**Excellent**
Seatings	**3**
Cuisine	**International**
Dress Code	**Traditional**
Room Service	**Yes**
Tip	**No tipping required**

Ship Amenities

Outdoor Pool	**1**
Indoor Pool	**1**
Jacuzzi	**1**
Fitness Center	**Yes**
Spa	**Yes**
Beauty Shop	**Yes**
Showroom	**Yes**
Bars/Lounges	**7**
Casino	**Yes**
Shops	**4**
Library	**Yes**
Child Program	**Yes**
Self-Service Laundry	**Yes**
Elevators	**8**

Cabin Statistics

Suites	**29**
Outside Doubles	**307**
Inside Doubles	**268**
Wheelchair Cabins	**0**
Singles	**15**
Single Surcharge	**150%**
Verandas	**0**
110 Volt	**Yes**

HOLLAND AMERICA LINE

HOLLAND AMERICA LINE

CRUISE LINE

901 South America Way, Miami, FL 33102
☎ *(305) 530-8900, (800) 645-8111*

History . . . .

Majesty Cruise Line, an upscale spin-off of Miami-based Dolphin Cruise Line, inaugurated its $220 million, 1056-passenger *Royal Majesty* in July 1992 when it was christened in New York by actress/singer Liza Minelli. The new line came up with some fresh ideas, including a totally nonsmoking dining room and a number of nonsmoking cabins and was built in less time than normal because the hull had already been completed for a ship that was never finished at Kvaerner-Masa Yard in Finland.

—The first Miami-based ship in the mini-cruise market to split itineraries between the Bahamas and Mexico, so a passenger could book two back-to-back cruises with different itineraries (1993).

—In April 1997 Majesty assumed operation of the *Cunard Dynasty* and renamed it *Crown Majesty.*

Concept . . . .

After years of sailing the popular *Dolphin IV* from Miami on three- and four-day budget cruises, Dolphin Cruise Line decided to start up a sister company to operate a new, upscale ship offering to an increasingly younger market cruises that were elegant but still affordable, with an emphasis on hospitality and service.

Signatures . . . .

The distinctive crown logo is visible on the ship's superstructure.

The most attention-getting detail about Majesty Cruise Line is the non-smoking rule—no smoking in the dining room, show lounge or in 132 designated cabins, 25 percent of the total.

"It's a unique selling point," commented one of the travel agents on the inaugural sailing. "A few clients out there among the smokers won't like it, but for every one of them you lose, you'll pick up three others that are thrilled to be in a dining room without any smoking."

Gimmicks . . . .

The Hanna-Barbera costumed characters aboard in the Caribbean are equally popular with kids and adults, and when they appear, which they do frequently, video and still cameras pop up all over the ship as loved ones run to be photographed with Fred and Barney.

Who's the Competition.

In Alaska, a ship of this size and style falls in a niche between the small casual ships of Alaska Sightseeing and Clipper and the larger mainstream cruises typified by Princess and HAL.

Who's Aboard.

One can expect a contingent of older, more sedate Cunard passengers who had booked before the changeover plus a younger group of Majesty cruisers from the east coast.

Who Should Go.

It's a good ship for seniors because it's not too large, has a warm atmosphere and a caring cruise staff. Children love the Hanna-Barbera characters, of course, and families have enough options to be together when they wish or apart and still have a good time.

Who Should Not Go

Dowager veterans of the world cruise, and anyone who would be a party-pooper with a lot of families with children, yuppies and singles having a really great time.

The Life-style.

In the Caribbean, it's a young, active ship with exercise classes such as tai chi, aerobics and stretch-and-tone scheduled before 9 a.m., plus quiz, Scrabble and ping-pong competitions, dance and golf lessons, ice-carving demonstrations and art auctions. Besides the daily program for adults, children are issued their own colorful activities booklets with Fred Flintstone on the cover. We would expect a more conservative lifestyle in Alaska.

Wardrobe.

Because there are usually a number of first-time cruisers aboard, some of them group and incentive travelers, dress codes are not as strictly adhered to as on some ships. But the line does observe two formal nights when men are asked to wear "proper attire," and two semi-formal nights that usually call for jacket and tie. Casual-dress evenings call for resort-wear rather than shorts, T-shirts or jeans.

NO NOs
Shorts are not allowed in the dining room after 6 p.m. and bathing suits are never permitted in public rooms without a coverup.

Bill of Fare. .... B+

In the dining room, dinner menus usually offer a choice of four or five main dishes, say, Cornish game hen, steak, veal, grilled fish and a vegetarian pasta dish. A choice of three or four appetizers, two soups, two salads and a range of desserts presented at the table fills out the menu.

The buffet breakfasts are copious, with ready-made omelets, scrambled eggs, bacon, sausage, ham, potatoes, herring, smoked salmon, bagels, fruits, cereals and all kinds of freshly made pastries.

A "Light at Sea" menu lists calories, cholesterol and sodium count (but not fat grams). We tried the low-calorie pita pockets with chicken, cucumber, tomatoes and onions that were delicious. Other lunchtime options that day were a California frittata, sauteed ling cod, mignons of turkey supreme Cacciatore, braised round of beef, plus an onion, tomato and white bean salad garnished with black olives.

Showtime. . . . . .B+

Royal Majesty presents live theatrical productions such as "Star-Spangled Girl" and "Murder at the Howard Johnson's" during each cruise by a resident acting company.

Discounts . . . .

The AdvanSaver promises that the earlier you book, the more you'll save.

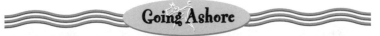

The Bottom Line

Majesty has maintained an efficient and well-run operation in the Caribbean and we would expect the same in Alaska. However, Fred Flintstone may be replaced by Nanook of the North.

Going Ashore

See Alaska scenery from the handsome Midnight Sun Express dome cars.

Crown Majesty 12- and 13-day Cruise/Tours let you add on overland journeys to enhance your Alaska vacation. The most unusual is the Eskimo Country 13-day program ($1595 add-on per person, double occupancy) that takes you on a pre-cruise overland trip. First you fly to Fairbanks, where you spend two nights, take a river cruise on a paddlewheeler and city tour that includes a gold mine visit. Then you board the luxury dome cars of the Midnight Sun Express for a ride to Denali National Park, where you spend the afternoon on a wildlife tour of the park. After overnighting in the park, you reboard the train to continue on to Anchorage, where you'll spend the night. The next day, fly across the Arctic Circle to Kotzebue for a tour of this prosperous Eskimo town, then fly on to colorful Nome, where you'll overnight. Return to Anchorage the next morning by air in time to transfer to Seward and embark the *Crown Majesty* for your seven-day cruise.

Crown Majesty   ★★★★

The former Cunard Dynasty turned into Crown Majesty in 1997. The size is ideal, it's elegantly decorated and under Majesty's operation the food and entertainment should be pleasing to a younger audience for the Alaskan cruise.

The pretty oval pool aboard the Crown Majesty is surrounded by a Palm Beach-style deck with comfy loungers and umbrella-shaded tables.

The *Crown Majesty* is one of three ships built between 1990 and 1993 for Palm Beach-based Crown Cruise Line, owned by the Scandinavia-based Effjohn Group—*Crown Monarch, Crown Jewel* and *Crown Dynasty*. But the owners sold the *Crown Monarch* and the *Crown Jewel* to Asian-based operators, Star Cruises, leaving only the *Crown Dynasty*, to become the *Cunard Dynasty*. In the spring of 1997, Cunard turned over the operation of the *Dynasty* to Majesty Cruise Line and it became the *Crown Majesty*. You can come home again.

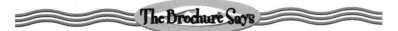

The Brochure Says

"After dining amid magnificent sea views, take your seat for the Broadway-style revue. Dance in our lovely disco or choose your favorite game of chance in the casino. Watch a movie in the comfort of your cabin, or take a moonlight stroll on deck. Then, sample a delicacy or two from the Midnight Buffet."

Translation

It's all happening here, on a lovely ship that you share with fewer than 800 fellow passengers.

Cabins & Costs

Fantasy Suites: .... B+

Average Price PPPD: NA, but Cunard price was $515–$590 including airfare.
Top digs are 10 suites with about 350 square feet of area each, with teak-decked private balconies, separate sitting areas, mini-refrigerator and extra-large closets. (Two other suites have extra-large sitting areas with bay windows instead of private balconies if you prefer.) The two lower beds can be converted to one double, and the bath has a shower only.

Small Splurges: .... B+

Average Price PPPD: NA, but Cunard price was $482–$551 including airfare.
The seven extra-large category A forward cabins on Deck Six give you a captain's-eye view of the sea through big angled glass windows, two beds that can be put together for a double, two chairs, cocktail table, dresser/desk and chair. These are about the same size as the Fantasy Suites above, but without the veranda.

Suitable Standards: ....B

Average Price PPPD: NA, but Cunard price was $401–$471 including airfare.
Category C standard outside doubles are available on three decks, average 140 square feet with two lower beds that can convert to a double, remote-control color TV, safe, mirrored built-in dresser/desk, satellite telephone and bath with shower.

Bottom Bunks: C

Average Price PPPD: NA, but Cunard price was $281–$314 for the G, $235–$261 for the H, including airfare.
The two H category cabins would be so rare to be able to book—they're like the loss leader in a supermarket ad—that we might as well recommend the next category up, a 132-square-foot G inside double with two lower beds, TV, telephone and bath with shower.

Where She Goes

Summer finds the *Crown Majesty* in Alaska sailing between Vancouver and Seward, calling at Ketchikan, Tracy Arm, Juneau, Sitka and cruising Hubbard Glacier. The seven-day return substitutes Skagway and Wrangell for Sitka. There is an optional pre- or post-cruise package to Alaska's interior also available.

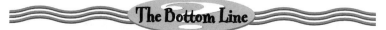

The Bottom Line

While big enough to give a sense of stability, the *Crown Majesty's* public rooms and lounges have an intimate ambience, so passengers can socialize easily. And its staterooms, while not overly spacious, are comfortable and handsomely furnished. There's something for everyone aboard this clean, pretty ship.

Fielding's Five

Five Super Spaces

1. The drop-dead-gorgeous, five-deck atrium with its spiral staircase and trompe l'oeil mural of Italian colonnades with blue skies and clouds beyond, and down at the very, very bottom on a parquet floor, a white piano.

2. The Palm Beach-style deck with comfy loungers covered in blue-and-white striped mattresses, matching umbrellas to shade the tables and pretty oval pool.

3. The Rhapsody Lounge showroom with wood-backed banquettes in dark pink and purple tapestry fabric and matching carpet.

4. The surprisingly lavish Olympic Spa that offers seaweed body wraps, massages, body-composition analysis, makeup and hair styling and full beauty salon services.

5. The Marco Polo Cafe, the casual buffet-service restaurant with wicker chairs and a sunny tropical atmosphere.

An elegant Italian mural dominates the **Crown Majesty's** *five-deck atrium.*

Crown Majesty ★★★★

Registry	Panama
Officers	British
Crew	International
Complement	320
GRT	20,000
Length (ft.)	537
Beam (ft.)	74
Draft (ft.)	18
Passengers-Cabins Full	856
Passengers-2/Cabin	800
Passenger Space Ratio	25
Stability Rating	Fair to Good
Seatings	2
Cuisine	Continental
Dress Code	Traditional
Room Service	Yes
Tip	$8 PPPD, 15% automatically added to bar check

Ship Amenities

Outdoor Pool	1
Indoor Pool	0
Jacuzzi	4
Fitness Center	Yes
Spa	Yes
Beauty Shop	Yes
Showroom	Yes
Bars/Lounges	6
Casino	Yes
Shops	Yes
Library	Yes
Child Program	Yes
Self-Service Laundry	No
Elevators	4

Cabin Statistics

Suites	12
Outside Doubles	268
Inside Doubles	120
Wheelchair Cabins	4
Singles	0
Single Surcharge	175-200%
Verandas	10
110 Volt	Yes

MAJESTY CRUISE LINE

MAJESTY CRUISE LINE

NORWEGIAN
CRUISE LINE

7665 Corporate Center Drive, Miami, FL 33126
☎ *(800) 327-7030*

The sports bar on the **Windward** *underscores NCL's emphasis on active and theme cruises.*

History . . . .

Norwegian Caribbean Lines was founded in 1966 by Knut Kloster and Ted Arison (see Carnival Cruises, "History") to create casual, one-class cruising in the Caribbean in contrast to the more formal, class-oriented tradition of world cruises and transatlantic crossings. That partnership soon broke up, however, leaving Kloster to begin a rapid expansion of the line while Arison went off to found Carnival Cruise Lines.

NCL's first ship was the *Sunward*, but the fleet soon grew to include the *Starward* (1968), *Skyward* (1969), *Southward* (1971) and, also in 1971, a replacement for the original *Sunward* called *Sunward II* (the former *Cunard Adventurer*).

But the real coup came in 1979 when the Kloster family bought French Line's *France*, which had been laid up in Le Havre for five years, made a major rebuilding to convert the former ocean liner into a cruise ship and renamed her *Norway*. From her debut in 1980, she was the flagship

325

of the line, and the other four vessels came to be called "the white ships" for their white hulls that contrasted sharply with the dark blue hull of the *Norway.* (All the original "white ships" have been retired from the fleet, the last in September 1995.)

In 1984, Kloster Cruise Limited, the parent company of Norwegian Cruise Line, bought Royal Viking Line, promising to make minimal changes to the highly respected company. Two years later, Kloster changed the Norwegian registry of the RVL ships to Bahamian, then a year after that closed down the long-time San Francisco headquarters and moved the entire operation to Florida.

In 1987, the former Norwegian Caribbean Lines changed its name to Norwegian Cruise Line with an eye to long-range marketing of Alaska, Bermuda and European cruises, and in 1989 acquired San Francisco-based Royal Cruise Line. This time, however, Kloster left the new acquisition in San Francisco with most of its executive roster intact.

The dismantling and sale of RVL happened in the summer of 1994, with the flagship *Royal Viking Sun* and the Royal Viking name, logo, past passenger list and general goodwill sold to Cunard, who promptly (but only briefly) named the new division Cunard Royal Viking Line (see Cunard, above). The *Royal Viking Queen* was soon transferred over to Royal Cruise Line and renamed the *Queen Odyssey.* Two earlier RVL ships, *Royal Viking Star* and *Royal Viking Sea,* also went to Royal to become *Star Odyssey* and *Royal Odyssey.*

In 1996, Royal Cruise Line was dismantled, the *Crown Odyssey* becoming NCL's *Norwegian Crown,* the *Queen Odyssey* becoming *Seabourn Legend* and the *Star Odyssey* becoming the *Black Watch* for Fred Olson Lines. The corporate name was changed to Norwegian Cruise Line, Ltd. The *Royal Odyssey* was to be turned into the *Norwegian Star* in 1997.

In the late 1980s, Knut Kloster began taking a less-active role in the company in order to pursue his dream of building the world's biggest passenger ship, the 250,000-ton, 5600-passenger *Phoenix World City.* Despite its detractors who say the project's dead, the giant ship may still be a viable possibility, pending funding. Recently, Westin Hotels signed on as hotel manager for the newly named *America World City: The Westin Flagship,* but funding was still not set at press time.

—The first three- and four-day cruises to the Bahamas incorporating a private island beach day.

—First line to restage hit Broadway musicals aboard cruise ships; the *Norway's* first production was "My Fair Lady."

—The official cruise line of the National Basketball Association, the Basketball Hall of Fame and the National Football League Players Association; NCL presents a number of sports theme cruises throughout the year.

—First cruise line to broadcast live NFL and NBA games live aboard its ships.

Signatures.....................................

Theme cruises—especially the annual *Norway* jazz festival, now in its 15th year, and the sports theme cruises that are aboard all the ships.

The "Dive-In" program—the first and perhaps most successful of the watersports packages found on cruise ships combines onboard instruction and equipment rentals with shore excursions to snorkel and dive spots. A Sports Afloat T-shirt is given to participants in designated activities who accrue seven tickets by the end of the cruise.

Gimmicks.....................................

The line's award-winning advertising campaign built around a sexy young couple who look like they might star in lingerie or perfume ads and the slogan, "It's different out here." The campaign itself is great, but it could be argued they're barking up the wrong mast, because we've never seen that couple on an NCL ship.

Who's the Competition ....

The main competitors in all its cruising areas (now that Carnival has entered Alaska) are the ships owned by Kloster's old nemesis Arison and the rapidly growing Royal Caribbean Cruise Line.

Who's Aboard ....

A lot of sports-oriented young couples from the heartland; yuppies and baby boomers; people who want to see a Broadway show without actually having to set foot in Times Square.

Who Should Go ....

Young couples and singles looking for a first-time cruise; couples and families that want to see Alaska by sea.

Young families who will appreciate NCL's "Kids Crew" program for kids 3 to 17, with special kids-only activities onboard and ashore. They're divided into four different age groups: Junior Sailors, 3–5; First Mates, 6–8; Navigators, 9–12; and teens, 13–17.

Who Should Not Go ....

Longtime cruise veterans looking to check out a new line, senior singles, and urban sophisticates who've "been there, done that."

The Lifestyle..............................

"Elegant, yes; stuffy, never," was the way they described themselves a couple of years ago, and it's fairly apt. NCL's ships offer traditional cruising, with themed sailings, international-themed dinners several times a sailing, live music on deck, and something going on around the ship every minute. Not long after boarding, passengers are offered free spa demonstrations, free casino lessons, a rundown on the children's program for the week, a free sports and fitness orientation, dive-in snorkeling presentation for the Ketchikan call and as many as three singles parties—one each at 8 p.m. for college-aged spring break celebrants and over-30 singles (a Big Band dancing session is usually scheduled at the same time for the over-50s set), plus a third at 11:30 p.m. for any singles that couldn't find a friend at the first two parties.

In other words, you'll stay busy aboard—and that's before the dozen or so shore excursions offered in each port of call!

Wardrobe...

NCL calls for less-stringent dress codes than its competitors, good news for guys who hate to wear ties. A seven-day cruise usually calls for two formal outfits, two informal outfits and a "costume" for a theme country/western night if you wish. Short cruises schedule one formal night and two informal nights. Formal garb is described by NCL as "cocktail dresses or gowns for the ladies and the men wear a jacket and tie or tuxedo." On informal nights, "just about anything but shorts is fine." For daytimes, take along some exercise clothing, bathing suits, shorts and jeans, T-shirts and sandals, plus warm clothes and walking shoes for going ashore. NCL also reminds passengers not worry about clothes— if they forget something, they can buy anything they need in the shipboard shops.

Bill of Fare........................... B

The food is big-ship cruise fare with some new cutting-edge options.

The dinner menu usually provides five appetizers, three soups, two salads, a pasta and four main dishes, one of which is fish, along with a full vegetarian menu offered nightly. There are four desserts plus ice cream and fruit, and low-fat, low-calorie dishes are indicated on the menus with an asterisk. Dinners are served in two assigned seatings at assigned tables, with first seating 6:30 p.m. and second seating 8:30 p.m.

A welcome-aboard buffet is typical of lunchtime self-service offerings— a make-your-own taco table and a vegetarian buffet with hot and cold selections, plus carved roast beef, turkey goulash with rice and precooked hamburgers, along with a dessert table and separate beverage service area.

An alternative restaurant called Le Bistro on board requires an advance reservation and a tip to the waiter but makes no surcharge for the food. The menu, described as "South-Beach style" by the Miami-based line (meaning Miami Beach's trendy art deco district), offers for starters a Norwegian seafood medley, escargots, French onion soup or clam chowder, three salads including Caesar and a warm spinach, then a vegetable main course, two pastas and three main dishes—chicken Provençale, pepper steak Madagascar and veal medallions with a wine/herb sauce and polenta. Dessert choices include a warm apple tart, a chocolate dessert and a selection of fruit and cheese.

Showtime................................. A

NCL was the first cruise line to create a buzz about its onboard entertainment, presenting shipboard versions of popular Broadway shows from "My Fair Lady" to the relatively current "The Will Rogers Follies" and the popular revival "Grease." In addition to the Broadway shows, each ship presents a song-and-dance Sea Legs revue as well as variety performers on other evenings.

Also aboard: Q and A sessions with sports stars, several different lounges offering live music for dancing, art auctions, games, dance lessons, and pop psychology lectures about astrology or fashion colors.

Discounts . . . .

Early booking discounts knock off as much as 15 percent of the cruise price.

Children under two sail free; a maximum of two adults and two children per cabin is the limit for this offer.

The Bottom Line

These are good, moderately priced traditional cruises that will particularly appeal to first-time cruisers, honeymooners, couples, families and singles up to the outer perimeters of Baby Boomdom. Filled with nonstop activities, music, very professional entertainment and sports-themed programs for watching or doing, NCL is never boring for middle-of-the-road mainstreamers, although very sophisticated travelers may (despite the "It's different out here" commercials) stifle a yawn now and again.

Going Ashore

With some 65 shore excursions priced from a $26 salmon bake in Juneau to a $214 combination flightseeing and float trip in Skagway, Norwegian Cruise Line aims to show you some serious Alaska for a big, mainstream cruise ship. Perhaps their most unusual option is an Alaskan adaptation of their popular Caribbean Dive-In program in which passengers can go snorkeling or scuba diving in Ketchikan.

Macho Maneuvers for the Fittest

1. Scuba Diving at Mountain Point, Ketchikan

$155, 3 hours, limited to certified divers with card.

Wet suit, tanks and all the other equipment you need is provided, but you should be in excellent shape and capable of moderate dives. In return, you'll see wolf eels, huge sunflower starfish and other unique denizens of Alaska's deep. Water temperatures, they point out, are similar to the California coast.

2. Snorkeling at Mountain Point, Ketchikan

$55, 3 hours.

No previous experience is required but you should be in excellent physical condition for this moderately difficult excursion. Equipment is provided, and your adventure guide will take you along the coast to see unique invertebrate life, followed by a ride on a heated bus to a special Jacuzzi party aboard the *Windward*.

3. Trail Hiking to Herbert Glacier, Juneau

$49, 5 hours.

A rugged 9-mile hike that requires top physical condition takes you along steep muddy trails and through brush to within 400 yards of the glacier, where you stop for a snack and a rest before returning to the trailhead.

Accessible Adventures for the Couch Potato

1. Chilkat Voyager Canoe Adventure, Haines

$84, 3.5 hours, mildly active, for anyone over seven years old.

A dozen paddlers fit into each canoe, and after a little practice, you'll be able to shoot the Chilkat with no sweat (well, maybe a little). You can look for eagles along the way, perhaps even stop by the edge of the river to see animal tracks. Hearty snacks and refreshments are served at the "take out," when the paddling's over.

2. Chilkat Bald Eagle Preserve Jet Boat Tour, Haines

$74, 3.5 hours.
You start with 25 miles of bus tour before relaxing in a jet boat (no paddling) through the Bald Eagle Preserve, with photo ops galore at the eight nests along the river.

3. Juneau Sportfishing Adventure

$149 plus $10 for fishing license and $20 tag if you catch a King Salmon, 5 hours.
Go fishing for salmon on an enclosed 26-foot boat with your own licensed captain. If you catch a fish, you can arrange to have it flash frozen, smoked or canned and shipped back home. (Let's see, that smoked salmon should run about $25 a pound...)

Shopping Ops

Alaska has lots of scenery, history and outdoor adventure, but serious shoppers may find it lacking. These excursions allow some shopping time at the end of the history/scenery/adventure.

1. Walk—Sitka Historic and Nature

$45, 2.5 hours, moderately difficult, equipment provided.
Enjoy an invigorating three-mile guided walking tour through historic Sitka, to Sitka National Historical Park with its flat trails and dozens of totems, then stroll on to the Alaska Raptor Rehabilitation Center to see the birds. A bus takes you back to town with plenty of shopping time before the ship sails.

2. Haines Cultural and City Tour

$34, 3 hours.
See Tlingit Totem carving at the Alaska Indian Art Center, valuable Chilkat blankets at Sheldon Museum and Cultural Center, and a drive around Fort William H. Seward Square, where you have time to shop in the arts and crafts galleries in downtown Haines before returning to the ship.

3. Chilkat Indian Dancers and Salmon Bake, Haines

$52, 3.5 hours.
Fresh local salmon cooked over open alderwood fires, barbecued ribs and a salad bar are followed by a very professionally performed program of Chilkat dancing and storytelling with beautiful costumes. Following the Tlingit custom of potlatch (gifts for guests) you'll get a bright print of a Coho salmon to keep, plus some time to go shopping in the Native art galleries.

Sister ship **Dreamward**

Windward ★★★★★

It was the water curtain on sister ship Dreamward *that really grabbed our attention. On the inaugural sailing, we sat in the front row scribbling notes about traffic "flow" and "splashy" production numbers while watching a dazzling revue staged behind a unique curtain of water. A Gene Kelly-lookalike splashed about in "Singin' in the Rain," marine creatures frolicked "Under the Sea" and not a drop of water fell on the front row. The water spurts from below like fountains or drizzles from above like rain, and the big finale incorporated fireworks, fog and film clips of Esther Williams swimming with cartoon characters Tom and Jerry.*

How do you make a big ship look like a little ship? The answer is clearly illustrated aboard NCL's new *Windward*, one of a pair of ships that carry 1246 passengers but offer so many intimate spaces they actually seem cozy. There are no soaring atriums or double-decker dining rooms; instead, three separate dining rooms that seat from 190 to 282 passengers appear to have more smaller tables seating two to four than big ones seating six to eight. Instead of a vast self-service buffet area, the ships have incorporated quick pick-up breakfasts and lunches into a small snack bar adjacent to the Sports Bar & Grill, with a continental breakfast and lunchtime hot dogs and hamburgers. Salads, desserts and beverages are laid out buffet-style. Many areas, including some of the dining rooms and deck sunbathing spots, have been terraced to give an illusion of smaller space but with more privacy.

INSIDER TIP

If you're not assigned to one of the dramatic terrace restaurants, you can still eat breakfast or lunch in one of them any time you wish, since those meals are served open seating at your choice of restaurant. And the view is even better in the daylight.

NORWEGIAN CRUISE LINE

The Brochure Says

"No matter where you choose to go, you are certain to have a lot of fun getting there: full-court basketball, a jogging track and fitness center, golf driving nets, outdoor hot tubs, a two-story casino, a Sports Bar & Grill with ESPN, NFL and NBA games beamed in live, dozens of top-notch entertainers—they're all here, just waiting for you."

Translation

We're ready for the young and the restless, and double-dare anyone to get bored aboard.

Cabins & Costs

Suite # 20 aboard the **Windward.**

Fantasy Suites: .... A

Average Price PPPD: $649 plus airfare.

Top digs are six 350-square-foot grand deluxe suites with concierge service, all facing forward on three different decks for a captain's-eye view of the world. The living room is sumptuously furnished with a brocade sofa and three chairs, a long desk and dresser with eight drawers and glass coffee table. In the bedroom, you can choose either twin or queen-sized beds. The bathroom has tub and shower, and additional perks include a mini-refrigerator and a private safe.

Small Splurges: .... B

Average Price PPPD: $535 plus airfare.

Penthouses with private balconies are 175 square feet inside plus a veranda that is large enough for two chairs and a table. A separate sitting area with love seat and chairs, floor-to-ceiling windows, twin or queen-sized bed, private safe, TV set, mini-refrigerator and concierge service are included.

Suitable Standards: .... B

Average Price PPPD: $342 plus airfare.

Standard outside staterooms are virtually identical in size (160 square feet) and furnishings—sitting area and twin or queen-sized bed, TV set, built-in cabinetry—with the price varying according to deck location. "I'd advise clients to book one of the lower-category outsides," one travel agent told us, "because the differences in deck and amenities isn't that much." Accordingly, we'd recommend the D category outsides; get any lower on the totem pole and you're facing partial or full obstruction from hanging lifeboats. Six wheelchair-accessible cabins have shower seat and hand rails plus spacious turn-around room and no sills to impede the wheels.

Bottom Bunks: C

Average Price PPPD: $257 plus airfare.

The lowest-priced cabins aboard are category J inside double cabins with two lower beds in 150 square feet of space. Needless to say, you shouldn't expect a sitting area with sofa.

INSIDER TIP

If you want to book a category A outside cabin and value your privacy, opt for those on Atlantic Deck instead of Promenade Deck. While Promenade Deck is considered posh by old-time cruisers, it also means the joggers and strollers are walking around the deck outside your windows day and night, while on Atlantic deck only the gulls and flying fish can look in while the ship's at sea.

Where She Goes

The *Windward* summers in Alaska with seven-day sailings every Monday from Vancouver that alternate Misty Fjords and Glacier Bay as all-day cruising destinations. The ship also calls in Skagway, Haines, Juneau and Ketchikan.

Fall and spring repositioning cruises take the *Windward* on two transcanals and two Pacific Coast cruises.

The Bottom Line

This is a very special pair of ships, stylish enough for frequent travelers but accessible to first-time cruisers as well. They offer everything an active young passenger might wish without appearing intimidatingly huge. While the cheaper cabins are not as spacious as you might wish, they're a lot bigger than many NCL cabins used to be. And the fact that these vessels return to the human scale in contrast to the awesome new megaships is a great plus.

Fielding's Five

Five Fabulous Places

1. The sunbathing deck, not acres of Astroturf lined with sunbathers sprawled everywhere, but lounge chairs arranged in a series of teak terraces separated by low wooden planters filled with clipped boxwoods, rather like an amphitheater.

The aft pool deck has terraced sunbathing.

2.   Sports and Sky Decks include two golf driving areas, ping-pong tables in an enclosed alcove, a volleyball-basketball court and shuffleboard on rubberized mats, plus a full fitness center with sauna and massage.

3.   The big forward Observation Lounge doubles as a late-night disco with marble dance floor and a pair of electronic route maps that show the ship's itineraries.

4.   Le Bistro, originally a fourth dining room, has turned into a 76-seat specialty restaurant with no surcharge, only a request for advance reservations and a tip for the waiter afterwards. It's a good place for a quiet dinner for two, perhaps celebrating a romantic occasion, or a place to get together with other new friends.

5.   The 150-seat Sun Terrace dining room, three levels set high atop the ship and aft, facing a wall of windows to the sea, and one deck below, The Terraces, 282 seats on several levels that also overlook the sea through an expanse of glass with a huge undersea mural on the back wall.

The Sun Terrace dining rooms aboard the **Windward** *offer sweeping views to the sea.*

Five Good Reasons to Book These Ships

1. To meet jocks, both professional and amateur.

2. To sail aboard a ship christened by ex-first lady Barbara Bush (the *Windward*, 1993).

3. To luxuriate aboard a ship that was designed especially for new, younger cruise passengers who want everything a shoreside resort can offer, including an oceanfront room.

4. The Sports Bar & Grill, which brings in live sports telecasts from around the world daily on big-screen TV sets, with small snack bars not far away in a quiet corner if you want a hot dog with your beer or soda.

5. To venture aboard a young-minded ship beyond the Caribbean into Alaska where you can—no kidding—go snorkeling in Ketchikan with a wet suit provided by the ship.

Five Things You Won't Find On Board

1. A single cabin.

2. A self-service laundry.

3. Anyone wearing shorts in the dining room after 6 p.m.

4. A giant atrium with revolving sculpture.

5. A lavish lunchtime deck buffet.

Windward ★★★★★

Registry	**Bahamas**
Officers	**Norwegian**
Crew	**International**
Complement	**696**
GRT	**41,000**
Length (ft.)	**624**
Beam (ft.)	**94**
Draft (ft.)	**22**
Passengers-Cabins Full	**1502**
Passengers-2/Cabin	**1246**
Passenger Space Ratio	**32.90**
Stability Rating	**Good**
Seatings	**2**
Cuisine	**Themed**
Dress Code	**Traditional**
Room Service	**Yes**
Tip	**$9 PPPD, 15% automatically added to bar checks**

Ship Amenities

Outdoor Pool	**2**
Indoor Pool	**0**
Jacuzzi	**2**
Fitness Center	**Yes**
Spa	**Yes**
Beauty Shop	**Yes**
Showroom	**Yes**
Bars/Lounges	**5**
Casino	**Yes**
Shops	**3**
Library	**Yes**
Child Program	**Yes**
Self-Service Laundry	**No**
Elevators	**7**

Cabin Statistics

Suites	**101**
Outside Doubles	**428**
Inside Doubles	**92**
Wheelchair Cabins	**6**
Singles	**0**
Single Surcharge	**150-200%**
Verandas	**48**
110 Volt	**Yes**

PRINCESS CRUISES

10100 Santa Monica Boulevard, Los Angeles, CA 90067
☎ *(310) 553-1770, (800) LOVE-BOA(T)*

A new tradition aboard the newest Princess ships is to stage the captain's cocktail party in the atrium lobby.

History . . . .

While the popular TV series "The Love Boat" catapulted Princess Cruises to worldwide fame, the company had been a household name on the West Coast, at least among cruise aficionados, from the 1960s.

In the winter of 1965-66, Seattle entrepreneur Stan McDonald chartered the 6000-ton *Princess Patricia* from Canadian Pacific Railway and offered cruises along the Mexican Riviera from Los Angeles. From the ship's name came the company name, Princess Cruises. The first season went so well aboard the "Princess Pat," as everyone began to call her, that McDonald soon chartered a newly built Italian ship called the *Italia* and renamed her the *Princess Italia*. In 1968, the *Princess Carla* (the former French Line *Flandre*), then Costa's *Carla C*, was chartered, and in 1971 the *Island Princess* (the only one of these still in the fleet).

Then London-based Peninsular and Orient Steam Navigation Company, better known as P&O, the largest and oldest shipping company in the world, eyed the action and decided to come into the cruise scene with its new *Spirit of London*, which it positioned on the West Coast in the winter of 1972–73 to compete with Princess. There was little competition; McDonald continued to dominate Mexican Riviera cruising, despite one travel writer's comments that aboard the Princess Pat "the standard dessert was canned peaches" and the decor "was on a par with a good, clean $7-a-night room in a venerable but respected Toronto hotel."

So in 1974, P & O acquired Princess Cruises, including its key marketing staff, and set about upgrading the fleet hardware. The *Carla* and *Italia* went back to Costa Cruises in 1974, and the *Island Princess* was purchased outright. P & O's new *Spirit of London* was added to the fleet as the *Sun Princess*, and the *Sea Venture*, sister ship to the *Island Princess*, was acquired to become the *Pacific Princess*.

Things were already going well, but destined to improve even further when TV producer Doug Cramer showed up in 1975 with a new series he wanted to film aboard a cruise ship. *Et voila!* "The Love Boat" was born.

In 1988, continuing its "if you can't beat 'em, buy 'em" strategy, P & O/Princess acquired Los Angeles-based rival Sitmar Cruises, which added three existing ships and one nearly completed new ship, *Star Princess*, to the fleet, to bring it up to nine vessels.

For most of 1997, there are still nine Love Boats cruising the seven seas, with a 10th, the 104,000-ton giant *Grand Princess*, due to arrive in the spring of 1998 to sail the Caribbean year-round. (A prudent move, since the ship is too big to go through the Panama Canal.)

The *Fair Princess*, laid up since October 1995, locates to Australia to replace P&O's retiring *Fairstar*, and in late 1997, the Star Princess moves to parent company P&O to become the *Arcadia*, replacing the retiring *Canberra*.

—Parent company P & O claims it invented leisure cruising in 1844 when British author William Makepeace Thackery sailed around the Mediterranean on a free ticket to publicize the service and wrote a travel book about his cruise—*From Cornhill to Grand Cairo*—under the pseudonym Michael Angelo Titmarsh.

—One of the three largest cruise lines in the world.

—Offers the largest number of world-wide destinations of any major line.

—First to introduce all outside cabins with a high proportion of private balconies (*Royal Princess*, 1984).

—First major cruise line to introduce multimedia musical shows produced in-house.

—First to install a "black box" recorder on each of its ships for additional safety data in case of an incident at sea.

—Introduced easy-to-use phone cards to make local or long distance calls from anywhere in the world with a push-button phone; the card (good for $20 worth of phone time) was originally developed as a convenience for the Princess crew (sold across the fleet, July 1995).

—TV's "The Love Boat" is seen in 93 countries and heard in more than 29 different languages. The title comes from a book written by a former cruise director named Jeraldine Saunders about her life onboard.

DID YOU KNOW?

While the Pacific Princess *is the vessel most associated with "Love Boat" over the years, the pilot episode was actually filmed aboard the original* Sun Princess, *the former* Spirit of London, *now retired from the fleet.*

Concept . . . .

"It's more than a cruise, it's the Love Boat," a beaming Gavin MacLeod said on the Princess commercials.

What does that make you think of? The TV series, of course, with its glamorous, friendly crew, never too busy to intercede in someone's love affair. Luxurious staterooms and elegantly garbed passengers. Nubile nymphs in bikinis. Exotic ports, perpetual sunshine and cloudless blue skies. In other words, the perfect vacation—a cruise.

With its varied fleet of vessels, ranging from the homey, mid-sized 610-passenger *Island Princess* and *Pacific Princess* to the new 1950-passenger *Sun Princess* and *Dawn Princess* and the 2600-passenger *Grand Princess*, the line feels it offers "something for everyone" from "endless activity" to "total relaxation."

Princess' familiar flowing-haired logo atop the funnel of the **Crown** Princess.

Signatures . . . .

The line's distinctive stack logo, the "sea witch" with the flowing hair, provides instant identification when a Princess ship is in port. Just as distinctive, but less well known, is the Princess tradition of furnishing each of its new ships with an exquisite museum-quality million dollar-plus art collections from contemporary artists such as Andy Warhol, David Hockney, Robert Motherwell, Frank Stella, Laddie John Dill, Billy Al Bengston, Richard Diebenkorn and Helen Frankenthaler.

On-board pizzerias with special ovens serve up pizzas and calzone cooked to order.

Gimmicks

Declaring St. Valentine's Day as Love Boat National Holiday aboard all the line's vessels, with renewal of vows ceremonies in which some 4000 couples participate. The holiday also features a poetry contest and reading, romantic feature films, a hearts card game tournament and honeymooner and singles parties.

Who's the Competition.

In Alaska, Princess has been competing head-on with Holland America for some years, and usually outnumbers HAL in ships positioned there for the summer.

Who's Aboard.

Romantic couples of all ages who saw "The Love Boat" on TV; long-time loyals, both couples and singles, over 45; a group of younger couples who've met on board and continue to take vacation cruises together; some families with children, who gravitate toward those ships that have dedicated playrooms and full-time youth counselors (*Sky Princess*, *Sun Princess* and *Dawn Princess*); people with glints of gold from head (hair coloring) to toe (gold lamé sandals or ankle bracelets), neck (gold chains) to fingertips (gold pinky rings, a gold lamé tote).

Who Should Go.

Anyone who wants a very traditional cruise experience with a chance to dance and dress up; admirers of avant-garde Pompidou Center architect Renzo Piano, who designed parts of the *Crown* and *Regal Princess*, families whose teenagers like the pizzeria and the zany fountain drinks aboard the *Crown* and *Regal*; young women who want to meet some Italians; anyone who loves pasta, pastries and cappuccino; fans of the Cirque du Soleil who'll adore the avant-garde shows on the *Crown*, *Regal, Sun, Dawn* and *Star*. More younger passengers should be boarding, because Princess is becoming expert at giving them what they want, at least on the big new ships—a less-structured captain's cocktail party; music for listening and dancing all over the ship; lots of sundeck and water areas with swim-up bars, waterfalls, swimming pools and Jacuzzis. Families with children now that Princess is welcoming them with open arms.

Who Should Not Go

Anyone with children under 18 months of age (babies are not permitted on board); anybody who refuses to wear a tie on any occasion; anyone who would answer "Huh?" to the query, "Fourth for bridge?"

The Lifestyle . . . .

Set in the framework of traditional cruises, a day aboard a Princess ship includes a plethora of activities and entertainment, from an exercise class in the gym or a facial in the beauty salon to language lessons, pool games, bridge classes, aquacise in the ship's pool, indoor and outdoor game tournaments, bingo, golf chipping, feature films in the ship's theater or in the cabin, port lectures, shopping lectures, cooking demonstrations, galley and bridge tours, fashion shows and karaoke singing. Even kids have their own karaoke contests, along with coketail parties, coloring contests and ice cream parties.

Many evenings are relatively formal aboard, with passengers wearing their finest clothes and jewelry and Italian or British officers hosting dinner tables, but other nights, such as the traditional London Pub Night, casual wear is prescribed and beer and pub dishes are on the agenda, along with rowdy music hall songs and dances.

Wardrobe . . . .

Princess passengers usually have two formal nights, two or three semi-formal and two or three casual nights during a week. For formal nights, men are requested to wear tuxedos, dinner jackets or dark suits and women cocktail dresses or evening outfits. Semi-formal evenings call for men to wear jacket and tie, women to wear dresses or dressy pantsuits.

On casual evenings, men may wear open-necked sport shirts, slacks and sports outfits; women, slacks, dresses or skirts. Daytime clothing can be quite casual, but coverups over bathing suits are expected for passengers walking through the ship.

Bill of Fare . . . . .B+

Cuisine is Continental with an emphasis on Italian dishes. A pasta or risotto specialty is featured every day at lunch and at dinner, along with a low-fat, low-calorie selection and a vegetarian dish.

Late-night buffets aboard the Princess ships are themed, with fish and chips following London Pub Night, a pasta party, a pizza party, a champagne fountain and Crepes Suzette on French Night, and a gala buffet among the other offerings.

Meals are served in two assigned seatings, with dinners somewhere between 6-6:30 p.m. for first seating, 8–8:30 p.m. for second seating. Breakfast and lunch are also served at assigned seatings when the ships are at sea, but may be open seating when the ship is in port. Your travel agent should request your seating preference when booking. All Princess dining rooms are smoke-free.

Pizzerias that cook pizzas and calzones to order are aboard most of the line's ships (see "Signatures").

The captain's gala dinner may offer Sevruga Malossol caviar, shrimp cocktail, liver pâté Strasbourg and fresh fruit cup with Triple Sec, following by a choice of three soups, a salad, ravioli with porcini mushroom sauce, rock lobster tail, salmon en croute, pheasant breast flambé or tournedos, along with four desserts plus cheese and fruit. Wine prices aboard are generally reasonable.

Meals in the dining room and pizzeria are usually somewhat better than the buffets, but the latter are improving. The new *Sun Princess* is leading the way to better cuisine throughout the fleet.

Showtime . . . . A

Princess pioneered elaborate multimedia shows with film clips projected onto screens beside the stage and pre-recorded "click track" sweetening to swell the musical accompaniment. As other lines began using many of the same techniques, the company started updating its entertainment to include stylish costumes and contemporary sounds.

The audience gets to participate in the popular "Love Boat Legends," playing on all the line's ships, with 24 passengers selected from volunteers who audition the first day, rehearse all week and join the cruise staff and entertainers in performing the last night of the sailing.

Perhaps the most sensational production is *Mystique*, an innovative and elaborately costumed production with a company of 23 performers, including nine European and Asian acrobats, set under the sea in Atlantis, with inflatable scenery that literally "grows" in front of your eyes; it's remarkable. *Mystique* appears only on board the *Crown Princess, Regal Princess, Star Princess, Sun Princess* and *Dawn Princess.*

Big Band music, a splashy new Caribbean revue, a show-biz production called *Let's Go to the Movies,* a full lecture program, trivia quizzes, "Baby Boomer" theme nights, London Pub Night and A Night at the Races fill out the fun.

On the new *Sun* and *Dawn Princess,* big-name entertainers are scheduled for some sailings.

Discounts . . . .

Love Boat Savers are discounts that take off from $500 to $1150 per person from the cruise-only price, but the offer is restricted to residents of the U.S. and Canada. The lowest fares are for the earliest bookings; discounts may decrease as the sailing date approaches. Discounts vary according to the price and season.

Frequent cruisers who belong to the Captain's Circle are mailed notices on special savings for designated sailings, including deals like two-for-one buys, 50 percent off for the second passenger in a cabin or free upgrades.

The Bottom Line

Princess prides itself on little extra details that make a cruise more luxurious, such as stocking each passenger cabin with robes to be used during the sailing, a bowl of fresh fruit replenished daily, CNN on cabin TV sets, designer toiletries, pillow chocolates and 24-hour room service.

Housekeeping aboard all the ships is excellent and service generally good, particularly in the dining room where Italian waiters and captains really seem to enjoy taking special orders and preparing tableside dishes such as Caesar salad and crêpes suzette.

All in all, these are good cruises for almost everyone.

Going Ashore

Princess Cruises' tour affiliate Princess Tours owns wilderness lodges, luxury glass-domed Midnight Sun Express rail cars and a fleet of motorcoaches, so you can expect a wide range of options to mix and match with your Princess cruise.

There are 41 Cruisetours available that range from 11 to 18 days and cover the Heart of Alaska, Alaska Wilderness and Mt. McKinley, Alaska Wilderness and the Kenai or Yukon Gold Rush country. For a little shoreside sightseeing before or after the tour, there are pre- and post-cruise hotel packages in the cities of embarkation or disembarkation.

Some 54 shore excursions are offered, ranging in price from $15.95 for the Naa Kahidi Theatre performance and the Sealaska Cultural Arts Park to $329 for a fly-in fishing trip.

Some Special Interest Excursions
For Salmon Savorers
1. Authentic Alaskan Salmon Bake, Juneau

$24.50 adults, $16.50 children 12 and under, 1.5–2 hours.
The menu calls for all-you-can-eat alderwood-barbecued salmon and barbecued ribs, salad bar, cornbread, brownies and beverages, cooked and served outdoors by a stream with canopy-covered tables in case of rain. Afterwards, roast marshmallows over a campfire or walk over to see spawning salmon (in season) or visit the Raptor Center which cares for injured birds of prey. Buses return to town every half-hour.

2. A Trip to Taku Glacier Lodge, Juneau

$189 per person, 3 hours, including a 50-minute floatplane ride.
The deluxe version of a salmon bake takes you by floatplane into the wilderness to a rustic lodge, with salmon cooked outdoors over an alderwood fire, along with side dishes, sodas, beer and wine. Afterwards, walk into the rainforest to look for eagle nests or the occasional bear.

3. Mendenhall Glacier Float Trip, Juneau

$99 adults, $65 children 6 to 12, children must be accompanied by an adult.
Smoked salmon snacks, reindeer sausage, cheese and apple cider are the rewards at the end of this splashy whitewater float trip on the Mendenhall River with views of the Mendenhall Glacier.

Flower Children
Beautiful Butchart Gardens, Victoria

$39 adults, $19.50 children, 3.5 hours.
Following a city drive through veddy-veddy British Victoria, you'll arrive at the magnificent Butchart Gardens with two hours to explore 35 acres filled with bright blooms, plus a Sunken Garden, Japanese Garden, Italian Garden and English Rose Garden.

Gold-Diggers
Pan for Gold, Juneau

$37 adults, $23 children 12 and under, must be accompanied by adult, 1.5 hours.
Guaranteed gold in every pan, plus an official-looking Gold Claim Deed from Gold Creek, site of the original Juneau discovery.

Kayakers

Sea Kayaking Adventure, Sitka

$82 adults, $56 children 6 to 12, 3 hours total with 1.5 hours kayaking, rain gear and life jackets provided.

Start with instructions on handling two-person kayaks, then set out in groups of four to six vessels through Sitka Sound.

Anglophiles

Craigdarroch Castle & Anne Hathaway's Cottage

$36 adults, $18 children 12 and under, 3.5 hours.

An architectural tour of Victoria leads to this 39-room Scottish castle built by one Robert Dunsmuir, followed by a tour of a replica of Anne Hathaway's Cottage in Stratford-upon-Avon, plus a visit to the Olde Curiosity Shoppe in a replica English village.

English/Western Saddlers

Horseback Riding, Skagway

$109 adults, $105 children with minimum age 14 and minimum height 4'10", 3 1/4 hours with 1 3/4 hours on horseback, participants must have some riding experience.

Canter through the Dyea Valley as you hear tales of the gold rush in the meadows where the Stampeders massed to climb the infamous Chilkoot Trail. Afterwards, have a snack of fresh smoked Alaska salmon pâté.

Crown Princess ★★★★★
Regal Princess ★★★★★

"Euclid alone / Has looked on beauty bare." Edna St. Vincent Millay

The most beautiful ship interior we ever saw was the Crown Princess *dome when it was under construction at the Fincantieri shipyard in Italy in early 1990. Architect Renzo Piano walked us through the pristine space that from the outside forms the "dolphin brow" of the ship. Inside it resembles what Piano called "the inside of a whale," with polished, rounded bone-colored ribs arching from ceiling to floor framing wide curved glass windows. As Piano talked about metaphor and magic, we stroked the silky, eggshell finish of the glossy plaster ribs.*

When we came back to Europe a few months later to sail on the maiden voyage, the dome was filled with slot machines and potted palms, red leather chairs and cocktail tables. It was never so beautiful again.

This elegant pair of ships, while similar in size to sister ship *Star Princess*, are far from identical to her. They were built in Italy's Fincantieri yard, while *Star Princess* came out of France's Chantiers d'Atlantique.

The *Crown Princess* and *Regal Princess* are unmistakable, even at a distance, because of their sloped, dolphin-like brow and strong vertical funnel. Controversial Italian architect Renzo Piano dislikes too much emphasis on the dolphin-like shape he designed—"A ship is a ship, it's not a dolphin."

The vertical funnel, a bold departure from the broad raked funnels on most of the Love Boats, he terms "a frank, clear, strong statement…and it works beautifully, by the way, to take the smoke away."

If an award were given for spacious cabins, these ships would win hands down. Cocktail lounges on board are lovely, as is a wine-and-caviar bar, a patisserie/sidewalk cafe in the lobby, a wonderful shopping arcade and a well-planned show lounge with fairly good sightlines except from the back of the main lounge.

CHAMPAGNE TOAST

On our most recent visit to these ships, the wood bars at eye level that had once sabotaged the observation facility of The Dome had been removed and lower wooden benches put in their places. Now the area really works as an observation lounge; finally, passengers are using it during the daytime as well as after dark.

The Brochure Says

"Her teak is from Burma, her marble from Carrera, and her fittings were forged by Italian craftsmen in shipyards over 200 years old…a masterpiece of the sea created by one of the world's most gifted architects."

Translation

Just what it says. These ships are the last word in design and decor, luxurious, graceful, stylish and very comfortable, and they whisper about their $200 million-plus price rather than shout it the way Carnival's megaliners do.

Cabins & Costs

Fantasy Suites: .... A+

Average Price PPPD: $621 plus airfare.

Top accommodations are the 14 suites, each with a double-size private veranda large enough for two lounging chairs with a small table between as well as a bigger table with two chairs, ideal for private breakfasts in the sun and sea breeze. A wide wooden doorway divides the living room with its sofa, chairs, tables and mini-refrigerator from the bedroom with its king-sized bed (which has a single mattress top rather than the two divided mattresses one usually gets when two beds are pushed together). Each room has its own TV set. A large dressing room lined with closets and enough storage space for an around-the-world cruise leads to the spacious marble bathroom with separate bathtub and stall shower. The toilet and second lavatory are adjoining, with another door that opens for the living room so it can double as a powder room when you're entertaining.

A prettily furnished deluxe cabin on the **Regal Princess.**

Small Splurges: .... A

Average Price PPPD: $514 plus airfare.

The category A mini-suites with private veranda are a bit smaller on both balcony and interior, but still very comfortable with bed (twins or queen-sized), sitting area with sofa and chairs, TV, mini-refrigerator, bath with tub and shower and spacious closet space.

Suitable Standards: .... A

Average Price PPPD: $346 plus airfare.

Category GG outside double cabins forward on Plaza Deck provide queen-sized beds and a convenient location, but there are only four of them. All the standards contain amenities usually found only in suites—mini-refrigerators, remote-control TV sets, guest safes and walk-in closets. Baths have showers only. Other standards offer two lower beds that can be made into a queen-sized bed.

Bottom Bunks: .... A

Average Price PPPD: $236 plus airfare.

Even the lowest category inside double cabin, the N category forward on Plaza Deck (only steps away from the lobby), measures 190 square feet and contains the same amenities and furnishings as the mid-range standards (see "Suitable Standards," above).

Where She Goes

The *Crown Princess* makes seven-day Gulf of Alaska sailings between Vancouver and Seward, calling in Ketchikan, Juneau and Skagway, and cruising College Fjord, Glacier Bay and/or Hobbard Glacier.

The *Regal Princess* sails Sundays roundtrip from Vancouver, cruising the Inside Passage and Glacier Bay, and calling in Juneau, Skagway and Sitka.

The Bottom Line

This is an exquisite pair of ships, and generally everything runs smoothly. Newly embarking passengers are serenaded by a Filipino string trio and greeted by white-gloved stewards to escort them to their cabins. Everything you need to know is spelled out in the daily "Princess Patter" programs or advance cruise materials mailed ahead of time, making these very good vessels for first-time cruisers. With the improvements in The Dome (see "Champagne Toast"), Piano's vision seems clearer, although a lot of the magnificent view windows between the "whale ribs" are still blocked by slot machines. As for people who worry that there's nothing to do on a cruise, we'd like to take them on a stroll around these ships at almost any hour of the day or night, and they'd never fret again.

Fielding's Five

Five Super Places

1. The chic 1930s-style cocktail lounges on promenade deck, the Adagio on the *Regal*, the Intermezzo on the *Crown*, where you half-expect to see Cary (but not Hugh!) Grant at the next table.

2. The Italian garden ambience in the Palm Court Dining Room on the Regal Princess, with its ivy-patterned carpet, pastoral garden murals and pastel rose and teal decor.

3. The Patisserie in the three-deck atriums, the true gathering spot on the ships; you can get cappuccino and espresso all day long, accompanied by freshly baked pastries, and observe the comings and goings of fellow passengers.

4. The Bengal Bar aboard the *Regal Princess* takes you back to the raj with wicker chairs, ceiling fans and a life-sized Bengal tiger, plus some tiger balm—a menu of rare single malt whiskies or a classic Bombay Sapphire gin martini.

5. The Presto Pizzeria on the *Crown Princess* with its Italian food-and-wine print red tablecloths, red-and-white glazed tile walls and natural teak floors, warm and inviting, serving five types of pizzas including vegetarian, plus calzones, garlic focaccio and Caesar salad, open 11 a.m. to 5 p.m., then again from 9 p.m. to 1 a.m.

Three Off-the-Wall Things to Do

1. Order one of the zany drinks from the boldly illustrated menu in Characters Bar, perhaps the Strip & Go Naked or Ta Kill Ya Sunrise.

2. Converse with the talking elevators, which announce each deck and caution you when you exit to watch your step.

3. Check out the photo of ex-president George Bush on board wearing a *Regal Princess* cap and chatting with Captain Cesare Ditel; you'll find it with other trophies in the corridor between the library and the Stage Door lounge.

Dancing in The Dome on the **Regal Princess.**

Five Good Reasons to Book These Ships

1. To see the spectacular shows, especially *Mystique*, go to the pizzeria afterwards, talk about the performance show with other audience members, then watch the stars come in for an after-show snack.

2. To join in some lively passenger game shows, including Team Trivia and Jeopardy.

3. To attend a captain's cocktail party where you don't have to stand in line for ages to shake hands and be photographed with the captain; on these ships everyone circulates throughout the three-deck atrium, drinks in hand, and anyone who wishes to be photographed can pose on the curved staircase for the ship's photographer.

4. To get fit and trim with the line's exclusive cruisercise program.

5. To get more spacious cabins for the money than almost anywhere else afloat.

Five Things You Won't Find on Board

1. A gym or spa with sea views.

2. Jogging permitted before 8 a.m.

3. Locked bookcases; Princess trusts these passengers not to steal books or games.

4. The best seats for the show in the front row; third row from the back, one level up from the main seating area, is better.

5. Captain Stubing (although his alter ego, Princess spokesman Gavin MacLeod, does show up sometimes).

Crown Princess
Regal Princess
★★★★★
★★★★★

Registry	**Liberia**
Officers	**Italian**
Crew	**International**
Crew	**696**
GRT	**70,000**
Length (ft.)	**811**
Beam (ft.)	**105**
Draft (ft.)	**26**
Passengers-Cabins Full	**1792**
Passengers-2/Cabin	**1590**
Passenger Space Ratio	**44.02**
Stability Rating	**Good to Excellent**
Seatings	**2**
Cuisine	**Continental**
Dress Code	**Traditional**
Room Service	**Yes**
Tip	**$7.75 PPPD, 15% automatically added to bar checks**

Ship Amenities

Outdoor Pool	**2**
Indoor Pool	**0**
Jacuzzi	**4**
Fitness Center	**Yes**
Spa	**Yes**
Beauty Shop	**Yes**
Showroom	**Yes**
Bars/Lounges	**6**
Casino	**Yes**
Shops	**4**
Library	**Yes**
Child Program	**Yes**
Self-Service Laundry	**Yes**
Elevators	**9**

Cabin Statistics

Suites	**14**
Outside Doubles	**604**
Inside Doubles	**177**
Wheelchair Cabins	**10**
Singles	**0**
Single Surcharge	**150-200%**
Verandas	**184**
110 Volt	**Yes**

Sky Princess

The TSS Sky Princess, *constructed in 1984 in France's CNM shipyard near Toulon as Sitmar's* Fairsky, *was the last big steam turbine passenger ship to be built, probably the last that will ever be. TSS means turbine steamship, and while steamships are more expensive to operate than motor ships, they also offer a smoother, quieter ride. "She has an underwater body that is a masterpiece," said one of the officers who oversaw her construction. Smooth-riding but unfinished, she had to slip out of the shipyard in the dead of night, according to some crew members aboard at the time, because shipyard workers, fearful of losing their jobs when the project was done, were sabotaging their own work, building things during the daytime and breaking them again at night. The interior finishing was completed on the long crossing from France to Los Angeles.*

Our welcome-aboard buffet on the Sky Princess *in Alaska was far more lavish than the other Love Boats.*

Sky Princess was one of the early ships to be decorated by a team of designers, some of them noted for hotel rather than naval architecture. As a result, materials such as silk wall coverings, burled blond wood paneling, marble, Venetian glass and glove leather upholstery (instead of the Naugahyde prevalent then on many cruise ships) and subtle, harmonious shades of beige, gray, pale sage greens and soft rose were introduced into a sea of cheerful Scandinavian woolens in coral, marine blue and bright green. A recent refurbishment has kept the original design features virtually intact.

DID YOU KNOW?

When Sitmar operated the ships that became Sky Princess, Dawn Princess and Fair Princess (only the Sky Princess remains in the fleet today) the late Boris Vlasov, who owned the line, insisted that white Swedish rubber rather than carpet lined all the stairwells, so passengers could see how clean everything was kept.

The Brochure Says

"Passengers looking for comfort and understated elegance need look no further than the *Sky Princess*. Ultra-spacious, her casual, easy-going atmosphere pleases everyone from couples to teens."

Translation

Cabins aboard are larger than on the *Island* or *Pacific Princess*, the decor subtle, and the friendly Italian waiters like to joke with passengers. Children and teens find a lot to like aboard, including three pools, a fully supervised youth and teen center and the pizzeria, of course.

Cabins & Costs

Fantasy Suites: ....A

Average Price PPPD: $828 plus airfare.
Book one of the 10 AA category suites and you'll enjoy a private veranda as well as a separate living room with leather loveseat, four leather chairs, glass-and-chrome dining table, long marble-topped desk, stocked mini-bar and mini-refrigerator and TV. In the bedroom is a queen-sized bed (except Malaga and Amalfi suites, which have twin beds), robe and slippers, marble nightstand with four drawers, a dressing room with marble-topped table, three-way mirror, leather chair, big safe, built-in dressers with six drawers each, and two separate hanging closets with safes in each. The marble bathroom has a deep Jacuzzi tub.

Small Splurges: .... B+

Average Price PPPD: $700 plus airfare.
Category A mini-suites on the Lido don't have private verandas but they do have picture windows, a bedroom with twin beds and wooden nightstand with two drawers, and a sitting room with long leather sofa, three leather armchairs, desk/dresser with marble inset, color TV, handsome marble lamp with linen shade, cabinet for bar glasses, mini-refrigerator, plenty of good mirrors, two full-length hanging closets with safe and bath with shower and long marble counter.

PRINCESS CRUISES

Cabin 148 is a Category C outside double.

Suitable Standards: .... C+

Average Price PPPD: $486–$600 plus airfare; price varies depending on deck location.
All the standard inside and outside cabins are similar, with twin beds, nightstand, desk/dresser, two chairs, small table, generous closet space and bathroom with shower. Nearly half also have optional pull-down berths for third and fourth occupants. Six cabins are designated wheelchair accessible, including C 207 and C 208, outsides which are slightly larger than standards, with no lip on the doors, a shower with seat and pull bars, a roll-under sink, lower handles on the closets and a low-hanging rod accessible from a wheelchair; very wide inside with three windows.

Bottom Bunks: .... C+

Average Price PPPD: $414 plus airfare.
The category M inside doubles are the least expensive accommodations on board, but are still fairly spacious and similar to the "Suitable Standards". Two lower beds, TV, very large closets, bath with shower, desk/dresser with chair and a second chair with small table.

INSIDER TIP

Library books must be checked in and out on the Sky Princess, and anyone planning to abscond with an unfinished novel faces a $50 fine added to his cabin account.

DID YOU KNOW?

Don't try this at home! The Love Boat cocktail is a blend of tequila, creme de cacao, Galliano, grenadine and cream.

Where She Goes

Sky Princess makes 11-night roundtrip cruises to Alaska from San Francisco, calling in Victoria, Vancouver, Juneau, Skagway and Ketchikan, and cruising the Hubbard Glacier. On a few designated sailings, Sitka replaces Juneau or Skagway.

The Bottom Line

This ship, one of the most elegant at the time of its inaugural sailing in 1984, has held up very well. The top deck indoor spa, including a whirlpool with raised stairs, was one of the first top deck, glass-walled spas; before that, indoor pools and a modest exercise area were usually found on a bottom deck amidships.

Sky Princess is particularly good for families with children because the cabins with upper berths are spacious enough you won't feel cramped and because the child-care and teen programs on board are so well-arranged. The Youth Center is particularly pleasant, with linoleum floor, lie-down sofas and sturdy play tables. The Teen Center has lots of curved banquettes and game tables with industrial lamps overhead and a video game room with six games. The two dining rooms are light and bright with big windows, so if you're lunching during Alaska whale-spotting, you won't miss much. The buffets on this ship are much more elaborate than most of the others.

Fielding's Five

Five Special Spots

1. Veranda Lounge, the venue for dancing before and after dinner, is a lovely room with its swirl marbleized carpet in gray and teal, with teal leather and fabric chairs, teal glass-topped tables with leather trim, sheer Austrian shades at the windows and pale wood walls.

2. The Pizzeria with its black bentwood chairs with red seats, big tile kitchen decorated with faux salamis, cheeses and hams, big round booths big enough for six or eight, and atop every table jars of crushed red pepper and oregano. For people who want a full lunch, a blackboard promotes a soup of the day and a pizza of the day.

3. The Horizon Lounge, an observation lounge with a forward-facing wall of windows, lots of cushy leather chairs in teal and caramel, and squashy cushions in the window ledges for additional seating with a view.

4. A beautiful library with two separate reading rooms, each with deep black leather chairs and wood-paneled walls, along with curved modern desks in wood and black leather for writing diaries or postcards.

5. The intimate little Melody Bar with its long granite bar lined with black leather swivel barstools, burled wood and mirrors on the walls, a perfect little hideaway for two.

Five Good Reasons to Book This Ship

1. The Pizzeria for its made-to-order pizza.

2. The big, lavish showroom with its thrust stage where you might see comedian Dick Gold, harmonica virtuoso Harry Bee, the juggling Zuniga Brothers and the Love Boat singers and dancers.

3.   To buy some Lladro porcelain in the new Alaska-themed pieces, Eskimos ice-fishing and such; Lladro must sell like crazy on cruise ships if the Spanish are creating whole new groups. What's next? The characters from "The Love Boat"?

4.   To compete in the passenger talent show.

5.   To experience the smooth ride of the last passenger steamship ever built.

Five Things You Won't Find on Board

1.   Alcoholic drinks available for 18-to-21 year-olds.

2.   Silent elevators—the ones on the *Sky Princess* talk to you.

3.   No full promenade deck all around the ship; the green astroturf-covered walking deck (no jogging) says 11 times around its perimeter is one mile and the textured dark red jogging track above the Sun Deck says 15 laps is a mile.

4.   Marble bathroom counters on inside cabins.

5.   Gambling within a three-mile limit of the Alaska coastline.

The Sky Princess's *Video Arcade has a lot of kid appeal.*

Sky Princess ★★★★

Registry	British
Officers	British
Crew	International
Complement	535
GRT	46,000
Length (ft.)	789
Beam (ft.)	98
Draft (ft.)	25
Passengers-Cabins Full	1806
Passengers-2/Cabin	1200
Passenger Space Ratio	38.33
Stability Rating	Good to Excellent
Seatings	2
Cuisine	Continental
Dress Code	Traditional
Room Service	Yes
Tip	$7.75 PPPD, 15% automatically added to bar checks

Ship Amenities

Outdoor Pool	3
Indoor Pool	0
Jacuzzi	1
Fitness Center	Yes
Spa	Yes
Beauty Shop	Yes
Showroom	Yes
Bars/Lounges	5
Casino	Yes
Shops	4
Library	Yes
Child Program	Yes
Self-Service Laundry	Yes
Elevators	6

Cabin Statistics

Suites	10
Outside Doubles	375
Inside Doubles	215
Wheelchair Cabins	6
Singles	0
Single Surcharge	150-200%
Verandas	10
110 Volt	Yes

NOTE: *Star Princess* leaves Princess service in the fall of 1997 to become P&O's *Arcadia*. Prior to that, she makes two Hawaii cruises in October, followed by a Panama Canal transit.

Star Princess ★★★★

> It was a unique experience to tour France's Chantiers de L'Atlantique shipyard in late 1988, to see a ship nearing completion that began life as Sitmar's FairMajesty and by a stroke of a pen was turned into Princess' Star Princess overnight. That's why the Star Princess is not just like its sister ships Crown and Regal. When P&O bought Sitmar in July 1988, it acquired one ship under construction and two others on the drawing board, so because of the long planning and building time—two to three years—all three ships still carry many Sitmar characteristics, including Italian instead of British officers.
>
> Particularly memorable for us was sailing aboard the Star Princess inaugural cruise with her godmother, the late Audrey Hepburn, as a fellow passenger.

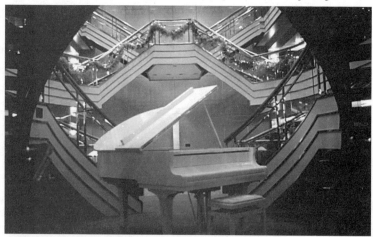

The atrium lobby and piano are framed by a dramatic staircase.

The *Star Princess* has one of the best pool-and-sun decks at sea. It runs most of the length of the vessel and stars two large swimming pools spanned by a raised sun deck. The area is filled out by an aft buffet cafe and a forward bar and pizzeria. Overall, she heralded a "new Princess," bigger, brighter, livelier than her predecessors, with a wider appeal and more accessibility to younger passengers than any of the previous ships from either Princess or Sitmar. A little more than a year after *Star Princess* first entered service, its median passenger age was seven years lower than the line's fleetwide average.

A three-deck atrium with a stainless steel kinetic sculpture dominates the amidships area. This is the vessel that first introduced the very popular La Patisserie cafe and pastry shop in the lobby area.

The spa, beauty salon, gym and massage areas, on the other hand, were relegated to below-decks without windows rather than given a prominent and sunny spot atop the ship as on the *Sky Princess*.

The Brochure Says

"...*Star Princess* also offers some of the largest standard staterooms in the industry. Connoisseurs of fine cruising will be dazzled by this modern-day floating resort."

Translation

An apt description. It's hard to think of anything you'd find at a resort hotel that you can't find on the *Star Princess*, except for sand between your toes.

Cabins & Costs

Fantasy Suites: ....A
Average Price PPPD: $614 plus airfare.
The 14 AA category suites are top-of-the-line, measuring 530 square feet and named for popular Mediterranean ports. Inside the sliding glass doors is an open, L-shaped room divided into sitting and sleeping areas with sofa, two chairs, coffee table, queen-sized bed, nightstands and built-in desk. There's plenty of closet and storage space, two TV sets, a dressing room with mahogany built-in dressing table and large mirror, a spacious marble bathroom divided so the tub, separate shower stall and wash basin can be closed off to let the toilet and second wash basin double as powder room. A minibar is stocked with complimentary beverages, and a mini-refrigerator keeps everything cold.

Small Splurges: ....B
Average Price PPPD: $507 plus airfare.
The 36 category A mini-suites are 370 square feet each, with private veranda, sitting area with built-in desk and counter as well as sofa and chairs, and a large bath with tub/shower combination.

Suitable Standards: ....A
Average Price PPPD: $228–$438 plus airfare.
All cabins aboard have twin beds that can be rearranged into one queen-sized bed, walk-in closet and separate dressing area, refrigerator and mini-bar, guest safe, terrycloth robes, hair dryers and color TV. Both outsides (with picture windows) and

insides are the same size—180 square feet. Ten are designated wheelchair-accessible, and these measure 240 square feet with extra-wide doors and no thresholds.

Bottom Bunks: ....A

Average Price PPPD: $186 plus airfare.
The cheapest cabins are N category with two lower beds, only seven of them, located forward on Plaza Deck. Furnishings are the same as "Suitable Standards."

Where She Goes

Star Princess spends her last summer in Alaska for Princess in 1997, cruising the Glacier Route between Vancouver and Seward (for Anchorage). She sails on Mondays, cruising Glacier Bay, Hubbard Glacier and/or College Fjord, calling in Skagway, Juneau and Ketchikan.

The pool deck on the Star Princess *has a very popular waterfall.*

The Bottom Line

When a ship is this perfect for warm-weather cruising, we're puzzled as to why Princess sends it up to Alaska in the summer. But wherever it goes, it's a natural magnet for families and younger cruisers.

Fielding's Five

Five Great Places

1. The Lido Deck pools have a raised sunbathing deck between the Oasis pool, with its waterfall and in-pool bar, and the Paradise pool, which is flanked by four whirlpool spas.

2. Characters, a colorful Lido Deck bar serving up outrageous drinks, both alcoholic and non-alcoholic, including a margarita big enough for four in a goldfish bowl-sized glass with four straws.

Characters Bar is famous for creating giant, zany drinks.

3. Windows to the World, a circular glass-walled observation lounge above the bridge where The Dome is located on the Crown and Regal, doubles as an observation lounge and after-dark entertainment center with music. The French shipyard workers called it Le Camembert because its round shape reminded them of a cheesebox.

4. The Club House Youth Center and Off Limits Teen Center get a lot of space, making this a good ship for kids and teens.

5. The Sports Deck, with its basketball, volleyball and paddle tennis court, jogging track, state-of-the-art gymnasium and aerobics room.

Five Good Reasons to Book This Ship

1. You can spend all day on the pool deck for optimum fun in the sun.

2. It's a great place for kids, who keep busy with supervised activities from 9 a.m. to midnight, plus a kids-only wading pool.

3. Teens have their own social life on board, with special hours in the adult disco, the chance to film an episode of "Love Boat," Italian lessons, arts and crafts, video games, karaoke talent shows and PG-13 movies nightly.

4. A museum-quality art collection of contemporary works valued at $1 million plus.

5. You'll be traveling with younger passengers who get involved with a more active shore excursion and onboard sports program.

Five Things You Won't Find Aboard

1. A small intimate bar for a quiet getaway for two.

2. Fuddy-duddies.

3. An ocean view from the gym or the disco; they're on a lower deck hidden away for privacy and noise control.

4. Smoking in the dining room or show lounge.

5. The very expensive swan logo commissioned for this ship by Sitmar shortly before Princess bought the company.

Star Princess   ★ ★ ★ ★

Registry	Liberia
Officers	Italian
Crew	International
Complement	600
GRT	63,500
Length (ft.)	805
Beam (ft.)	105
Draft (ft.)	27
Passengers-Cabins Full	1838
Passengers-2/Cabin	1490
Passenger Space Ratio	42.61
Stability Rating	Good to Excellent
Seatings	2
Cuisine	Continental
Dress Code	Traditional
Room Service	Yes
Tip	$7.75 PPPD, 15% automatically added to bar checks

Ship Amenities

Outdoor Pool	3
Indoor Pool	0
Jacuzzi	4
Fitness Center	Yes
Spa	Yes
Beauty Shop	Yes
Showroom	Yes
Bars/Lounges	3
Casino	Yes
Shops	4
Library	Yes
Child Program	Yes
Self-Service Laundry	Yes
Elevators	9

Cabin Statistics

Suites	14
Outside Doubles	570
Inside Doubles	165
Wheelchair Cabins	10
Singles	0
Single Surcharge	150-200%
Verandas	50
110 Volt	Yes

Sun Princess
Dawn Princess

It was love at first sight when we walked aboard the Sun Princess, still under construction in Italy's Fincantieri shipyard. An orchestra was playing, the magnificent marble atrium glowed with polished brass and an Italian barman was handing out cups of freshly made cappuccino. Later, we would see the many unfinished sections of the vessel, but for that one magic moment, it was as if the ship were completed and ready to sail.

The first of the new Grand Class ships for Princess, the *Sun Princess* at her debut was the largest cruise ship in the world. Two sister ships follow, *Dawn Princess* in the spring of 1997 and *Sea Princess* for early 1999, plus, of course, the world's largest cruise ship to date, the 104,000-ton *Grand Princess*, due in 1998. The most remarkable thing about these ships is that when you're aboard, they really doesn't seem as large as they are, 77,000 tons and carrying 1950 passengers. Nobody ever seems to be standing in line; even the captain's welcome aboard cocktail party is held in the soaring four-deck central atrium, allowing passengers to enter immediately at any level from any direction. Sunbathing space on deck is generous, and 410 of the cabins have their own private verandas. A full-time gardener tends to the $1 million-plus worth of plants on board.

The Brochure Says

"We're also taking a great Princess tradition and making the ultimate luxury, a stateroom with a private balcony, affordable for everyone. With up to 80 percent of outside accommodations—over fifteen hundred staterooms—featuring private balconies, (this ship) truly opens up a new world in cruising: Cruising in Grand Style!"

Translation

Princess pioneered the concept of private verandas for more than just penthouse suites when the *Royal Princess* was introduced in 1984. Now, aboard the *Sun Princess*, almost everyone gets a private veranda.

Cabins & Costs

Fantasy Suites: .... A+

Average PPPD: $650 plus airfare.

Six spacious aft suites, each measuring between 536 and 754 square feet, with private balcony, separate bedroom, large living room, dining table with four chairs, wet bar, granite counter, big divided bath with stall shower and Jacuzzi tub, dressing room, desk/makeup area in bedroom, two TV sets, mini-refrigerator.

Cabin B310, a mini-suite with veranda, is listed in the brochure prices at around $543 a day per person, double occupancy

Small Splurges: .... A

Average PPPD: $543 plus airfare.

Thirty-two mini-suites are almost as lavish, with private veranda, sitting area with sofa and chair, queen-sized bed, walk-in closet, two TV sets, bath with tub and shower and mini-refrigerator.

Suitable Standards: .... A

Average PPPD: $421 plus airfare.

The least expensive cabins with private balconies also have twin or queen-sized bed, big closet, desk/dresser with chair, TV and mini-refrigerator.

Bottom Bunks: .... A

Average PPPD: $250 plus airfare.

The smallest inside doubles are a comfortable 175 square feet with two lower beds that can convert to queen-sized, desk/dresser, chair, bath with large tile shower and generous storage space.

Where She Goes

Both *Sun Princess* and *Dawn Princess* sail between Vancouver and Seward (for Anchorage) every Saturday on alternating schedules. When *Sun Princess* is in Vancouver, *Dawn Princess* is in Seward and vice versa. The *Sun's* season starts in early May, the *Dawn's* in late May. Both will cruise Glacier Bay, College Fjord and the Inside Passage and call in Skagway, Juneau and Ketchikan. The season ends in mid-September.

The Bottom Line

While the *Sun Princess* and its technology are cutting edge, traditional touches are everywhere—the Wheelhouse Bar with its ship models from the P&O archives, a "museum" of opera costumes in glass cases outside the theater, Queen Mary deck chairs on the natural teak promenade deck, and handsome real wood laminates in cabins and public rooms. The deck space is broken up into different levels with free-form "islands" of green Astroturf resembling landscaping. The casino is huge, but is not permitted to dominate the ship. While passengers are aware of where it is, they are not forced to constantly walk through it. The ship works extremely well and rides very smoothly. The only lines we experienced aboard were when passengers queued up to be photographed with Gavin MacLeod, Captain Stubing of "The Love Boat."

Fielding's Five

In Verdi's Pizzeria, a choice of made-to-order pizzas served up hot.

Five Favorite Spots

1. Verdi's, an elegant pizzeria that resembles a terraced winter garden with its verdigris wrought iron trim.

2. The Horizon Court, a gala buffet area serving food 24 hours a day, plus a nightly alternative dinner menu with table service and music for dancing from 7:30 p.m. to 4 a.m.

3. The magnificent Princess Theatre, as professional as anything on Broadway or in the West End, with flawless sightlines from every seat.

4. The Vista Lounge, a second show lounge arranged in a cabaret style, again with perfect sightlines from every seat because of a cantilevered ceiling designed without support posts underneath.

5. The elegant Compass Rose piano bar with its wood paneled walls and rich upholstered banquettes and chairs.

Five Good Reasons to Book This Ship

1. To be able to dine in the Horizon Court when you don't feel like dressing up for the dining room.

2. To see brilliant entertainment in a professional theater with red plush row seats from the Schubert Theater in Los Angeles.

3. To participate in the New Waves watersports program with a scuba certification course and snorkeling instruction.

4. To enjoy really delicious pizza baked to order in Verdi's.

The elegant library aboard **Sun Princess** *has several leather "listening chairs" for music or audio books.*

5. To try out the "listening chairs" in the library, the sophisticated golf simulator ($15 for nine holes at Mauna Kea) or browse among the $2.5 million worth of art, all commissioned especially for the ship.

The marble bar at the popular Patisserie in the main lobby on both ships.

Dawn Princess / Sun Princess ☆☆☆☆☆ / ★★★★★

Registry	Italian
Officers	Italian
Crew	International
Complement	900
GRT	77,000
Length (ft.)	856
Beam (ft.)	106
Draft (ft.)	26
Passengers-Cabins Full	2270
Passengers-2/Cabin	1950
Passenger Space Ratio	39.48
Stability Rating	NA
Seatings	2
Cuisine	Continental
Dress Code	Traditional
Room Service	Yes
Tip	**$7.75 PPPD, 15% automatically added to bar checks**

Ship Amenities

Outdoor Pool	4
Indoor Pool	1
Jacuzzi	5
Fitness Center	Yes
Spa	Yes
Beauty Shop	Yes
Showroom	Yes
Bars/Lounges	7
Casino	Yes
Shops	7
Library	Yes
Child Program	Yes
Self-Service Laundry	Yes
Elevators	11

Cabin Statistics

Suites	6
Outside Doubles	597
Inside Doubles	408
Wheelchair Cabins	18
Singles	0
Single Surcharge	150-200%
Verandas	411
110 Volt	Yes

RADISSON SEVEN SEAS
CRUISES

600 Corporate Drive, Suite 410, Fort Lauderdale, FL 33334
☎ *(305) 776-6123, (800) 333-3333*

History . . . .

This hybrid cruise line with four very different ships—what they have in common is superlative quality—came about through a series of marketing agreements. Radisson, of course, is a long-time hotel brand name that entered the cruise industry with the first major twin-hulled cruise vessel, the 354-passenger *Radisson Diamond*, which debuted in 1992. Seven Seas was a San Francisco-based company marketing the elegant little 172-passenger *Song of Flower*, a Sea Goddess-like ship owned by Japan's "K" Line freight and container company under its "K" Line America subsidiary in New Jersey, and the 188-passenger *Hanseatic*, arguably the most luxurious expedition vessel in the world, is owned by Germany's Hanseatic Cruises. Radisson Seven Seas Cruises was launched Jan. 1, 1995, with 500 employees in the Ft. Lauderdale-based offices of the former Radisson Diamond Cruise. The line's newest vessel is the 320-passenger *Paul Gauguin*, scheduled to operate year-round in French Polynesia beginning in early 1998. Only the *Hanseatic* sails in Alaska.

—First cruise ship to be christened in the stern; it has no discernible bow. (*Radisson Diamond*, 1992, Greenwich, England).

Concept . . . .

Radisson Seven Seas says it aims to bring together four ultra-deluxe ships, exotic destinations worldwide and innovative shipboard programming to create four distinct styles of luxury cruising offering excellent service, intimate ambience and strong value for the dollar throughout the fleet.

The *Hanseatic* is notable for its state-of-the-art environment-saving features, including an advanced non-polluting waste disposal system and a pollution-filtered incinerator that enable it to call in remote and environmentally sensitive areas.

Gimmicks . . . .

A "passenger bridge" on the *Hanseatic* is furnished with ocean charts and radar; in addition, passengers are free to visit the ship's real bridge whenever they wish.

Who's the Competition.........................

The *Hanseatic* faces competition only from the *Bremen*, also marketed in North America by Radisson, a state-of-the-art expedition vessel that cruises with a similar mix of Europeans and North Americans. Word of mouth has been the primary factor in attracting more and more passengers to these vessels. Both vessels are owned by Germany's Hapag-Lloyd.

Who's Aboard............................

On all the ships, upscale middle-aged couples are the major passengers, along with older singles and younger, baby boomer pairs. *Hanseatic's* luxurious version of soft adventures attracts a more cosmopolitan crowd than the earnest expedition types who like to rough it.

Who Should Go............................

People who don't like the idea of having to tip—tips are already included in the fares but passengers may offer additional money for special service at their own discretion.

Who Should Not Go ....

The ships reserve the right to limit the number of children on board, but all except very mature teens and well-behaved 10-to-12-year-olds should not be aboard in any case.

The Lifestyle ....

What the ships have in common is a small number of passengers in a relaxed but luxurious atmosphere with impeccable service and very good food. Entertainment, while it is provided, is a minor concern, as are casinos and gift shops, while enrichment lecturers, beauty services, fitness centers and alternative dining options are major onboard pluses.

Tips are included in the basic fares on all the ships, which makes the interrelationship between crew and passenger less forced, and all the ships provide a single open seating at mealtimes, letting passengers sit where and with whom they please.

Wardrobe...............................

All the ships are relatively dressy, except that the publicity people for *Hanseatic* says that only penguins need to wear the tuxedos—male passengers are perfectly fine in a dark suit. That's fine, but they also hint that they want male passengers to be in a jacket, not necessarily with a tie, every night.

Bill of Fare.......................... B+

The *Song of Flower* and *Radisson Diamond* outshine the *Hanseatic* a bit in the kitchen, but perhaps that's because they're dealing with a more homogenous passenger list and don't mind pushing the envelope when they've found something really interesting they want people to taste. The food aboard is varied and tasty, and manages to please both English- and German-speaking passengers.

Showtime. . . . . .B

Even on the *Hanseatic*, there's life after dinner, what with a quartet playing for dancing and an occasional folkloric troupe showing up to perform esoteric routines they learned from a Peace Corps volunteer. But showtime is not bigtime on these smallish ships, and it shouldn't be.

Discounts . . . .

Early booking bonuses of $500 per person off the listed fares are in effect for the *Hanseatic* if you book by designated deadlines, and you get $500 off if you combine two back-to-back cruises.

The Bottom Line

We can think of no other cruise line that has such dissimilar but very comparable ships. They're all small, intimate and upscale, with flawless European service and excellent food, fascinating itineraries and lavish accommodations. More remarkably, they give you a lot of value for the admittedly top-market prices. Strange bedfellows? Perhaps, but what they have in common is more important than how they are different from each other.

Hanseatic ★★★★★, ⚓⚓⚓⚓⚓

"Penguins, whales, seals—we can guarantee you'll see them," the captain says cheerfully. On that autumn stopover in San Diego, he was between a successful transit of the Northwest Passage and the beginning of the Antarctic season, and feeling particularly chipper because he believes the Hanseatic, the largest ship ever to make the transit, has established a new time record for it— 14 days. We find ourselves remembering not only a much longer transit on a less-sophisticated ship a decade before but also the constant wondering about whether we'd make it through at all. Ironically, in the summer of 1996, the ship ran aground in the Northwest Passage and had to transfer passengers to the Capitan Dranytsin to finish the trip. No one was injured but the vessel was out of service for a month or so.

Until the last year or so, the ship was marketed primarily in Germany and still attracts a mixed bag of Europeans and North American passengers who laud the no-tipping policy, polished European serving staff and open bridge rules that allow passengers access to the navigational bridge at all times. Elegant and luxurious, with spacious cabins and beautifully decorated public rooms, the *Hanseatic* seems almost too lavish for an expedition ship, but who says you have to rough it just because you're going into the wilderness?

The Brochure Says

"After a day of observing penguin rookeries, (a passenger) could ease into the glass-enclosed whirlpool or enjoy a relaxing massage and sauna; perhaps snuggle up with a favorite book from the library, order room service and enjoy the view from the picture window of his spacious stateroom. For guests on Bridge Deck, there's the added luxury of private butler service."

Translation

Wake me when the Northern Lights come on, Jeeves.

Cabins & Costs

Fantasy Suites: ....A

Average Price PPPD: $1069 including round-trip airfare.

There are four deluxe suites aboard, each measuring 475 square feet, with walk-in closet, large sitting area with sofa and chairs, twin or queen-sized beds, dining-height table with chairs and butler service plus other furnishings and amenities listed under "Suitable Standards," below.

Suite 104 has a lavish sitting room and separate bedroom.

Small Splurges: .... NA

It's not necessary to splurge on this ship; the standards are more than adequate.

Suitable Standards: ....A

Average Price PPPD: $574 and up, depending on cabin category, including airfare.

Each accommodation, even the least expensive, has twins or queen-sized bed, a marble bathroom with tub and shower, a separate sitting area with chaise or sofa, TV set with VCR, writing desk, hair dryer, mini-refrigerator stocked with non-alcoholic beverages and generous closet and drawer space. The standards measure 236 square feet.

Bottom Bunks: .... NA

N/A

Where She Goes

The *Hanseatic* goes to the ends of the earth—literally. The ice-hardened vessel cruises from the Arctic to the Antarctic, and is as equally at home in Spitsbergen or Patagonia, the Galapagos or the South Georgias. She begins her year in the Antarctic, then sails north. Her Alaska calls for 1997 include Nome, the terminus of the Northwest Passage cruise, followed by a nine-day Sept. 6 Nome to Seward sailing that visits the Russian Far East and a 10-day Alaska and Inside Passage cruise to Vancouver departing Sept. 15.

The Bottom Line

The *Hanseatic* is an elegant and luxurious ship with rich wood-toned paneling in all cabins and public rooms and spacious staterooms; all outside cabins come with windows or portholes. It's also an extraordinarily tough expedition ship with a 1A1 Super ice-class rating, just one notch below the icebreaker classification. A friendly young European staff and a very high crew-to-passenger ratio of one crew member to every 1.4 passengers mean the service is exemplary, and the food, while not cutting-edge contemporary, is quite tasty. A thumbs-up recommendation!

Fielding's Five

Five Record-Breaking Rooms

1. In the Explorer Lounge with its pretty upholstered, wood-framed tub chairs and leaf-patterned carpet, a quartet plays for dancing before and after dinner, and a pianist accompanies afternoon tea.

2. Darwin Hall is a large and comfortable lecture room that doubles as a cinema; this is where the experts tell you about the local wildlife—and we don't mean pub-crawling.

3. Casual breakfast and lunch buffet service takes place in the Columbus Lounge with its rattan chairs and big windows.

4. The Marco Polo Restaurant manages a miracle—it seats all the passengers at once with every chair near enough to one of the big windows to watch the scenery go by.

5. Passengers have their own "bridge" to monitor the ship's route and progress on ocean charts and a radar monitor in the glass-walled observation lounge with its 180-degree view.

Five Good Reasons to Book This Ship

1. Because they leave the tuxedos to the penguins—male guests need only wear a dark suit for formal nights—but it's still the dressiest expedition vessel afloat, with jackets requested for men every night.

2. Because they supply the parkas and rubber boots you need to go ashore in polar regions; you don't have to go and buy bulky gear you'll probably never use again and figure out how to pack it to get it to the ship.

3. Because they carry 14 Zodiacs to take you ashore or cruising around an iceberg.

4. Because you can travel with the ease of knowing you and your vessel are doing nothing to damage the environment.

5. Because shore excursions are included.

Hanseatic   ★★★★★, ⚓⚓⚓⚓

Registry	**Bahamas**
Officers	**European**
Crew	**International**
Complement	**125**
GRT	**9,000**
Length (ft.)	**403**
Beam (ft.)	**59**
Draft (ft.)	**15.4**
Passengers-Cabins Full	**188**
Passengers-2/Cabin	**170**
Passenger Space Ratio	**52.94**
Stability Rating	**Good to Excellent**
Seatings	**1**
Cuisine	**Continental**
Dress Code	**Informal**
Room Service	**Yes**
Tip	**Included in fare**

Ship Amenities

Outdoor Pool	**1**
Indoor Pool	**0**
Jacuzzi	**1**
Fitness Center	**Yes**
Spa	**No**
Beauty Shop	**Yes**
Showroom	**No**
Bars/Lounges	**2**
Casino	**No**
Shops	**1**
Library	**Yes**
Child Program	**No**
Self-Service Laundry	**No**
Elevators	**1**

Cabin Statistics

Suites	**4**
Outside Doubles	**86**
Inside Doubles	**0**
Wheelchair Cabins	**2**
Singles	**0**
Single Surcharge	**150%**
Verandas	**0**
110 Volt	**No**

⚓ROYAL CARIBBEAN

1050 Caribbean Way, Miami, FL 33132
☎ (305) 539-6000, (800) 327-6700

The signature Viking Crown Lounge and RCCL logo.

History . . . .

In 1969, three Norwegian shipping companies, I.M. Skaugen, Gotaas Larsen and Anders Wilhelmsen, founded RCCL for the purpose of offering year-round seven and 14-day cruises out of Miami. Now owned by Wilhelmsen and the Hyatt Hotels' Pritzger family of Chicago, Royal Caribbean Cruises Ltd. is a publicly traded company on the New York Stock Exchange.

The line in late 1996 ordered a 130,000-ton vessel, the largest cruise ship ever built, for delivery in 1999.

The delivery of the *Grandeur of the Seas* at the end of 1996 and the sale of *Song of Norway* to Britain's Airtours brings the line's total to 10 vessels with three more new ships due before the end of 1998. The new *Rhapsody of the Seas* joins *Legend of the Seas* in Alaska in 1997. Just past its 25th anniversary, RCCL is definitely one a handful of major players in the cruise industry.

—First cruise line to commission three new ships expressly for the Caribbean cruise market, *Song of Norway* (1970), *Nordic Prince* (1971) and *Sun Viking* (1972).

—First cruise line to "stretch" a ship, cutting it in half and dropping in a new midsection, then putting it back together (*Song of Norway,* 1978).

—First cruise line to commission a specially designed ship for three- and four-day cruises (*Nordic Empress,* 1990).

—First seagoing, 18-hole miniature golf course (on *Legend of the Seas,* 1995).

—First cruise line to open shoreside hospitality centers in popular ports where passengers can leave packages, make phone calls, bone up on local shopping or sightseeing, get a cold drink and use toilet facilities (1995).

Concept . . . .

Consistency is the key word here. RCCL aims to provide a cruise experience to mainstream, middle-of-the-road passengers that is consistent in style, quality and pricing, with a majority of the ships following a consistent year-round schedule. Rod McLeod, former head of sales and marketing, called it "the doughnut factor" from a travel agent who once commented that what he liked best about RCCL was that all the doughnuts on all the line's ships taste exactly the same.

Signatures . . . .

RCCL ships are easily recognized at a distance because of the Viking Crown Lounge, a cantilevered round glass-walled bar and observation lounge high atop the ships projecting from or encircling the ship's funnel; company executive Edward Stephan dreamed it up after seeing the Seattle Space Needle.

DID YOU KNOW?

When RCCL delivers its Song of Norway *to British-based Airtours, the new owners won't get to keep the Viking Crown Lounge; the cantilevered signature bar will be removed before delivery.*

Lounges, bars and restaurants on board are named for Broadway musicals and operettas, sometimes with unintentionally funny results, as with the *Sun Viking's* Annie Get Your Gun Lounge. (That's also a musical that few of today's RCCL passengers would remember.)

DID YOU KNOW?

We fantasize over musical titles they haven't yet used on the RCCL ships, like a dining room named for Grease or Hair, or a gym called Black and Blue.

Gimmicks . . . .

ShipShape Dollars, given out each time a passenger participates in an exercise or sports activity; with six you get an egg roll. Actually, you get egg-yolk yellow T-shirts proclaiming the wearer ShipShape. Passengers compete wildly for them and proudly wear them for years afterward aboard cruise ships of competing lines.

Who's the Competition . . . .

RCCL competes directly with Carnival and Norwegian Cruise Line in Alaska just as it does in the Caribbean, but it also vies price-wise with lines such as Celebrity and Princess. The line's new megaliners have brought in a more glitzy sheen, with flashy gaming rooms created by a Nevada casino designer instead of a ship designer.

Who's Aboard . . . .

All-American couples from the heartland between 40 and 60, with new clothes, new cameras and nice manners; families with fairly well-behaved children; two or three 30-something couples traveling together; born-to-shop types who find the line's newer ships with their mall-like galleries familiar and comforting; clean-cut young couples on their honeymoons; single 20-somethings on holiday sharing an inexpensive inside cabin, more often females than males.

Statistically, the median age is a relatively low 42, with a household income from $40,000 to $75,000. One-fourth are repeat passengers, half are first-time cruisers. More Europeans, Australians and Latin Americans are also gravitating to the line.

Who Should Go . . . .

These are ideal ships for first-time cruisers because the staff and the signage instruct and inform without appearing to lecture, putting everyone at ease right away. Also for honeymooners, fitness freaks, sunbathers, big families on a reunion and stressed-out couples who want some time together in a resort atmosphere. Baby Boomers and their juniors 25 to 45 years old will always be warmly welcomed: RCCL wants YOU!

Who Should Not Go . . . .

Dowager veterans of the world cruise.

Small-ship enthusiasts.

Anyone who dislikes regimentation.

The Lifestyle . . . .

RCCL's ships follow a traditional cruise pattern, with specified dress codes for evening, and two meal seatings in the dining room at assigned tables for a minimum of four and a maximum of eight or 10; very few if any tables for two are available. A day-long program of games, activities and entertainment on board is supplemented by shore excursions that emphasize sightseeing, outdoor adventures, Alaska's wildlife and flightseeing.

Wardrobe . . . .

RCCL makes it easy for passengers by spelling out dress-code guidelines in the brochure. A normal seven-day cruise has four casual nights where sport shirts and slacks are suggested for men, two formal nights where women wear cocktail dress or evening gowns and men wear suits and ties or tuxedos, and one or more theme nights where passengers may don '50s or country/western garb if they wish. During the day-time, comfortable casual clothing—jogging outfits, shorts or slacks, T-shirts or sweatshirts—is appropriate on deck but sometimes not in the dining room.

NO NOs

No bathing suits, even with coverups, are allowed in the dining room at any time. Shorts, jeans and tank tops are not permitted after 6 p.m.

INSIDER TIP

Tuxedos are for rent on board most RCCL ships; ask your agent to check when booking if you think you may want to rent one.

Bill of Fare. . . . . B+

Non-threatening, special-occasion food is produced by an affiliated catering company on a rotating set menu that is similar but not identical on the different ships. There's a wide variety and good range of choices, and the preparation is capable if not inspired. Dinner includes seven appetizers (four of them juices), three soups, two salads, five main dishes and six desserts (three of them ice creams). On a typical day main dishes may include crabmeat cannelloni, sole Madagascar, pork loin au jus, roast duckling and sirloin steak. In addition, a nightly vegetarian menu, a kids' menu and a ShipShape low-fat, low-calorie menu are offered.

Our very favorite from the latter seems tailored to The Ladies Who Lunch—it starts with a shrimp cocktail without sauce, then consomme, hearts of lettuce salad with carrot curls and fat-free dressing, followed by poached fish and vegetables, then rich, sugary Key Lime Pie with a whopping 12 grams of fat per slice.

Except on cruises of 10 days or longer, when cabin occupants can order from set lunch or dinner menus, 24-hour room service is limited to breakfast and cold snacks such as sandwiches, salads and fruit-and-cheese plates. Breakfast and lunch buffets are served in a self-service caf-eteria with hot and cold dishes available, and early morning coffee, afternoon tea and midnight buffets fill out the legendary eight-meals-a-day format.

Captain Sealy's menu for kids includes fish sticks, peanut butter and jelly sandwiches, tuna fish, pizza, hamburgers and macaroni and cheese, plus chocolate "ship" cookies. On a recent sailing aboard the *Splendour of the Seas*, we felt the food preparation and presentation had greatly improved.

ROYAL CARIBBEAN
CRUISES, LTD.

CHAMPAGNE TOAST

Just like their competitors, RCCL bar waiters on embarkation day are hustling around with trays of brightly colored fancy drinks in souvenir glasses, but unlike some of their competitors, they prominently display signs showing the drink price at $4.95 so an unwary first-timer doesn't assume that they're free.

Showtime..........................A/C

The major production shows produced by the line, complete with Broadway-style playbills and computerized light cues, are sensational on the bigger ships with their state-of-the-art technical facilities. Passengers entertain each other at karaoke nights, masquerade parades and passenger talent shows, and pack appropriate garb for country/western night and '50s and '60s rock 'n roll night.

Discounts ....

A breakthrough rate program allows discounts on many cabins and sailings. Ask your travel agent.

The Bottom Line

Very nice but over priced, especially when the line's consistency of pricing puts its older vessels in the same general range as its newer ones. Cabins are small throughout the fleet except in the newest Project Vision ships, but are very quiet in all the newer ships, thanks to modern soundproofing techniques that provide a 42-decibel reduction in the walls and 40 at the door from hallway noise. RCCL delivers a consistency across the fleet just as it intends to, even though the ships represent four different design groups and sizes.

Going Ashore

As this formerly all-Caribbean cruise company continues to produce new ships, it expands its coverage in far-flung cruising areas. Alaska welcomes two big new RCCL ships, *Legend of the Seas* for its third season, and the new *Rhapsody of the Seas*. The 74 shore excursions offered range from $25 for a city tour of Wrangell to glacier sightseeing flights in Skagway or Juneau for $205.

Not all excursions are offered on both vessels; if you have your heart set on a particular excursion, be sure it's available on the ship you're booking. The level of difficulty for each excursion is rated Mild, Moderate or Strenuous depending on how much physical activity is required.

Below are some suggested excursions for first-time visitors, who should try to budget at least one flightseeing, one water and one land excursion, plus an active adventure such as mountain biking or sea kayaking.

Good Excursions for First-Time Visitors

1. Flightseeing: Combine a flight on a helicopter or float plane with a landing, either on a glacier or at a wilderness lodge.

Flight to Taku Glacier Lodge, Juneau

$172, 3 hours total, 50 minutes flight time.
Fly over five glaciers on the way to the lodge, then enjoy a grilled fresh salmon meal and a flight back to Juneau over the nesting areas of bald eagles.

2. By sea: Choose between active (sea kayaking, canoes, whitewater rafting and float trips) and passive (easy-going jet boat or pontoon boat wildlife tours).

Chilkat Nature Hike & Kayak Adventure, Haines

$89, 4 hours, moderate fitness required for 1.5 mile hike over uneven terrain, 2 miles of paddling in two-person kayak.
Hike through old-growth groves in a temperate rainforest, then board the kayak to paddle back to the dock.

3. By train: The historic narrow-gauge White Pass & Yukon Railway chugs out of Skagway following the same route it carried the Klondike Stampeders during the Gold Rush. For add-on overland journeys before or after your cruise, consider the super-deluxe rail cars of the McKinley Explorer or Midnight Sun Express traveling between Fairbanks and Anchorage with a stop in Denali National Park, or, if you're on a budget, the more utilitarian dome cars of the Alaska Railway.

White Pass Scenic Railway, Skagway

$79 adult, $40 child under 12, 3 hours.
The historic little train climbs past Bridal Veil Falls, Inspiration Point and Dead Horse Gulch to White Pass Summit and returns to the dock.

4. By motorcoach: Every port of call offers its own city tour, but unless your mobility is impaired, you can walk around on your own. In Skagway, take a free walking tour with the rangers from the Gold Rush National Park. Sitka, Juneau, Ketchikan and Haines are small enough to get around on foot, and (sorry, guys) Seward, Wrangell and Valdez have very little of interest. Instead, look for a drive that will take you out of town to a point of cultural or scenic interest to show.

Saxman Native Totem Village in Ketchikan

$41 adult, $21 child under 12, 2 –2.5 hours.
A good introduction to a real Native American village, whose 400 or so residents are Tlingit, Haida and Tshimshian. A huge collection of standing totem poles, more than two dozen, is on display. The Cape Fox Dancers perform in the Beaver Clan House, and there's a carving shed with master carvers at work, a nice gift shop selling crafts and a Native storyteller relating a traditional legend. It's 2.5 miles outside Ketchikan.

Legend of the Seas   ★★★★★
Rhapsody of the Seas   ☆☆☆☆☆

They call it "The Ship of Light" and claim it has more glass than any other ship afloat, more than two acres of windows, from the atrium hotel lobby with its soaring glass elevators to a Roman spa with clear crystal canopy that can be opened to the air or covered against temperature extremes. The two-deck dining room walls are glass, the Viking Crown Lounge wrapped around the ship's funnel is almost all glass, and a glass-walled cafe that doubles as observation area is high atop the ship and forward. People who cruise on glass ships should take along their sunglasses.

Legend of the Seas and sister ships *Splendour of the Seas, Grandeur of the Seas, Enchantment of the Seas* and *Rhapsody of the Seas* are the first five of a projected six vessels in RCCL's Project Vision series, ships that are slightly smaller but considerably faster than the line's giant *Sovereign, Monarch* and *Majesty*. They cruise at 24 knots as compared to the usual 20 or less, allowing passengers a longer time in port or shorter transits between ports.

Despite their size, these ships give the impression of intimacy, particularly in the soaring seven-deck Centrum with its glass skylight ceiling, where each deck level has its own small sitting areas, library or cardroom.

The most talked-about feature on Legend of the Seas *is its eighteen-hole miniature golf course, the first at sea.*

The Brochure Says

"Your accommodations aboard the *Legend of the Seas* are exceptionally roomy and comfortable, with large staterooms, more expansive public areas and more cabins with verandas."

Translation

Cabins are a bit bigger than the previous RCCL norm, although the one we occupied, called a Larger Outside, begged the question, Larger than what? The ship's extra width—with a 105-foot beam, it's barely slim enough to squeeze through the Panama Canal—gives a greater sense of space throughout the ship. The passenger-space ratio of 38.32 is much higher than on the line's megaships.

KEELHAUL

The gaudy casinos with Tiffany stained glass lamps over the tables, tacky carpeting and far too many pinging slot machines and neon lights resemble early downtown Reno.

Cabins & Costs

Fantasy Suites: ....A+

Average Price PPPD: $821 plus air add-on.

The 1148-square-foot Royal Suite with its gleaming white baby grand piano is drop-dead gorgeous, from its private veranda to its sumptuous marble bathroom with separate WC and bidet, three wash basins, stall shower and oval Jacuzzi tub. For entertaining, there's a wet bar, mini-refrigerator, full entertainment center with TV, VCR, CD and the rest of the alphabet. Two sofas, two chairs, a glass dining table for four, separate bedroom with king-sized bed, easy chair and super storage space.

Small Splurges: ....A

Average Price PPPD: $649 each for two, $382 each for four, or $218 each for seven, plus air add-on.

The two family suites, each with two bedrooms, two baths (one with tub and one with shower), private veranda, sitting area with sofa-bed and chair, and a pull-down berth, big enough to sleep seven and certainly comfortable enough for four.

A spacious Category D deluxe outside cabin on **Legend of the Seas** *has sitting area and private veranda.*

Suitable Standards: ....C+

Average Price PPPD: $357 plus air add-on.

Category F Larger Outsides provide twin beds that can convert to queen-sized, a sitting area with loveseat, small glass table with a brass wastebasket fitted underneath, nice built-in cabinetry, desk/dresser with three big drawers on one side, three little ones on the other, two nightstands with two drawers each and floral curtains with sheer drapery underneath. A small TV set, closet with one full-length and two half-length hanging areas, safe, full-length mirror and cabinet with shelves above make the basic unit more spacious and comfortable than on most RCCL ships. Bathrooms have showers only.

Wheelchair Accessible:

Seventeen cabins from Standard Insides to C category suites are designated accessible for the physically challenged; all are near elevators. Doors are an extra-wide 32 inches across; there are no doorway sills; the bathrooms have shower stalls with stools and grab bars, and both bathrooms and passenger corridors are wide enough for a wheelchair to turn around.

Bottom Bunks: .... *C*

Average Price PPPD: $271 apiece for two, $189 apiece for four, plus air add-on.
Even the standard quad insides with two lower and two upper berths have a sitting area with TV and a little space to move around. Storage is adequate, if not overly generous, and you can always take turns sitting on that cute little sofa.

CHAMPAGNE TOAST

For outstanding attention to disabled passengers: the large number of wheelchair-accessible cabins (17); Braille elevator signs; special cabin kits for hearing-impaired passengers with strobe-light door knocker and telephone ringer, mattress-vibrator alarm clock, telephone amplifier and enhancing FM receivers for sound in the show lounge.

Where She Goes

The *Legend of the Seas* spends summers in Alaska cruising the Inside Passage, sailing roundtrip from Vancouver and calling in Skagway, Haines, Juneau and Ketchikan. *Rhapsody of the Seas* arrives in mid-June from San Francisco and sails roundtrip from Vancouver calling in Juneau, Skagway, Sitka and Ketchikan. Both ships cruise Misty Fjords.

The Bottom Line

The Project Vision ships look like moneymakers for the company. They feel like smaller ships than they are, because of the number of intimate areas tucked away here and there.

Cabins are somewhat more spacious than on previous RCCL ships—even another 24 square feet is a bonus. A total of 17 staterooms are designated for the disabled. Practical touches including removable coat hangers, some with skirt clips, along with good mirrors and makeup lighting will be appreciated, too.

Since several different designers created the public areas, there is a pleasurable variety of decorating styles. Deck areas are handsomer than on the line's megaships. There are canvas-shaded seating areas and pools with arcs of water spraying, although the golf course takes up a lot of sunbathing area.

We can already hear the cash registers ringing as this formerly conservative company starts crowding Carnival on the outer edges of Glitz World.

ROYAL CARIBBEAN
CRUISES, LTD.

Five Fabulous Places

1. A spectacular solarium with a "crystal canopy" sliding roof, pool with water jets and spas, Roman marble floors and walls, fountains, even a convivial marble bar; also there—a full spa, gym and beauty salon, steam baths and saunas.

2. The first 18-hole golf course at sea, in miniature, of course, complete with water hazards, sand traps, halogen lights for night play, wind baffles and a clear dome roof in bad weather; reserved tee times, club rentals, $5 a game or $25 for unlimited play throughout the seven-day cruise.

3. The Centrum, the seven-deck, glass-ceilinged heart of the ship with two glass elevators, marble terraces and champagne bar.

4. The two-level dining room, where diners are surrounded by glass walls and a dramatic curving stairway lets well-dressed couples make a dramatic entrance.

5. The theater, the best showroom at sea from an audience point of view because all the seats are good—and comfortable. High-tech professional shows, an orchestra pit and retractable 50-screen video for multimedia productions.

Five Off-the-Wall Fun Facts

1. Sitting in the Viking Crown Lounge on these ships puts you at eye level with the Statue of Liberty.

2. If these two ships sailed through your neighborhood at normal cruising speed, they'd be ticketed for exceeding 30 m.p.h.

3. The steel used in *Legend of the Seas* could build two Eifel towers.

4. The ships are twice as wide as Rodeo Drive in Beverly Hills, and twice as long and three times as high as the Hollywood sign.

5. Passengers on a seven-day cruise on *Rhapsody of the Seas* devour 4200 chickens, 2150 bagels, 3065 pounds of watermelons, 600 cases of beer and 383 cases of soda.

Five Good Reasons to Book These Ships

1. If you've always wanted to play miniature golf at sea.

2. If you like translating basic Latin phrases like those adorning the marble walls of the Solarium—Bene Lava, Omnia Vincet Amor, Genius Loci and Carpe Diem.

3. To enjoy the excellent collection of original art on board—1939 pieces altogether.

4. To hit the steam room and sauna, Jacuzzi and stand-up Solarium Bar.

5. To stargaze from a special deck with state-of-the-art starwheels that rotate on a "star-time" clock mechanism to show where constellations are in synchrony with real time and place. The cruise staff has been trained to explain it.

Five Things You Won't Find on Board

1. A self-service passenger laundry.

2. A golf cart on the 18-hole course.

3. A bad seat (or a smoking seat) anywhere in the show lounge.

4. A lot of space around your dinner table.

5. Public rest rooms in the Viking Crown Lounge.

Legend of the Seas / Rhapsody of the Seas ★★★★★ ☆☆☆☆☆

Registry	Liberia
Officers	Norwegian
Crew	International
Complement	720
GRT	69,130
Length (ft.)	867
Beam (ft.)	105
Draft (ft.)	24
Passengers-Cabins Full	2076
Passengers-2/Cabin	1804
Passenger Space Ratio	38.32
Stability Rating	Good to Excellent
Seatings	2
Cuisine	Themed
Dress Code	Traditional
Room Service	Yes
Tip	$7.50 PPPD, 15% automatically added to bar checks

Ship Amenities

Outdoor Pool	1
Indoor Pool	1
Jacuzzi	4
Fitness Center	Yes
Spa	Yes
Beauty Shop	Yes
Showroom	Yes
Bars/Lounges	7
Casino	Yes
Shops	4
Library	Yes
Child Program	Yes
Self-Service Laundry	No
Elevators	11

Cabin Statistics

Suites	8
Outside Doubles	575
Inside Doubles	327
Wheelchair Cabins	17
Singles	0
Single Surcharge	150%
Verandas	231
110 Volt	Yes

ROYAL CARIBBEAN
CRUISES, LTD.

Night lights of Juneau

Rafting near Mendenhall Glacier, Juneau

SEABOURN
CRUISE LINE

55 Francisco Street, San Francisco, CA 94133
(415) 391-8518, (800) 929-4747

History . . . .

The buzz started in 1987 with a full-color ad in the travel trades depicting the dapper and distinguished Warren Titus, recently retired head of Royal Viking Line, clad in a tuxedo and standing on a pier at night to announce the impending arrival of a new super-luxury cruise line to be called Signet Cruises. But while the new company's first ship was still under construction, it was learned a small Texas-based company had registered the name Signet Cruises, presumably in case they might start a cruise line in the future. So the fledgling new line, owned by young Norwegian industrialist Atle Brynestad, changed its name to Seabourn and—the cliché is inevitable—the rest is history.

On a rainy mid-December morning in 1988 in San Francisco, ambassador and former child star Shirley Temple Black smashed the customary bottle of champagne against the bow of the 200-passenger *Seabourn Pride* with aplomb (to the rhythm of what some of us imagined was "On the Good Ship Lollipop") and later requested a tour of the engine room.

The *Pride* was followed in 1989 by almost-identical sister ship *Seabourn Spirit*, both achieved great acclaim, especially in the luxury travel press. In 1991, Carnival Cruise Lines, having long touted an upscale "Tiffany product" they intended to introduce, purchased 25 percent of Seabourn, and acquired an additional 25 percent in 1996, as well as the former *Royal Viking Queen/Queen Odyssey*, now *Seabourn Legend*.

—First cruise line to implement a timeshare-at-sea program called WorldFare, in which passengers purchase 45, 60, 90 or 120 days of Seabourn cruising and use them over a period of 36 months on any cruises (1993).

Concept . . . .

To offer discriminating passengers all the amenities they expect aboard a full-sized cruise vessel of 10,000 tons carrying 200 in an onboard ambiance that is "casual, but elegant." Service is "warm and friendly, but impeccable. And there is absolutely no tipping."

Signatures . . . .

The blue-and-white shield logo that adorns the double funnels of the ships.

The shore excursions, custom-designed especially for Seabourn passengers, include world-class golf options and noted special lecturers. The Celebrity Chefs series that brings well-known chefs from restaurants around the world to prepare signature dishes or special menus to complement the ship's already superb cuisine. Sampler cruises of three days to attract new passengers.

EAVESDROPPING

Then-mayor of San Francisco Art Agnos, touring the newly christened ship with its godmother Shirley Temple Black and other local officials, quipped, "If the Pilgrims had come over on the Seabourn Pride *rather than the May-flower, they never would have gotten off the ship."*

Gimmicks . . . .

Seabourn Club members (past passengers) get 10 percent off on cruises.

DID YOU KNOW?

You can get a preview of the Seabourn Legend *in the film* Speed 2, *a sequel to the Sandra Bullock hit* Speed, *filmed aboard the ship in the fall of 1996.*

Who's the Competition. . . . .

The usual suspects, of course. Silversea Cruises gives Seabourn a good run for the money-passengers with its present high quality product (which, unlike Seabourn, includes all beverages in a less-pricey base fare). And of course, the one and only Sea Goddess, which had a four-year head start on Seabourn.

Who's Aboard. . . . .

Veteran cruisers from Royal Viking and Sea Goddess, first-time cruisers who only want the best and can afford it, a few families traveling in three-generational groups with interconnecting suites, ranging in age from thirtysomething two-income professional couples to retired CEOs. About half the passengers on any cruise are under 50. On our several cruises with Seabourn, we've met English country squires, San Francisco restaurateurs, Hong Kong journalists, a young California-based New Zealand executive, a romance novelist, a noted jazz musician, and numerous doctors, dentists, lawyers, financiers and psychoanalysts. They're more often old money rather than nouveau riche. Passengers are always falling into small-world conversations, finding they have close mutual friends or children attending the same schools. It's a small world in that tax bracket.

Who Should Go

Anyone who books a suite at the Pierre, lunches at The Club in Pebble Beach, has a house in Vail or a condo in Deer Valley. Clubby and very posh, these ships are for couples who are rich and successful. If you want to see a cross-section of typical passengers, ask the line to send you a copy of their pretty publication for repeat passengers called *Seabourn Club Herald*. There, on several back pages, are color photographs of recent passengers—Stirling Moss, the legendary British motorcar racer; actress Rhonda Fleming; Teddy Roosevelt's granddaughter Sarah Gannett—along with a number of the rich and unfamous.

Who Should Not Go

Children or even restless teenagers would not find places to go and things to do on these ships. Anyone unwilling to dress for dinner would be out of place. And anyone who doesn't know what "out of place" means should certainly not go.

The Lifestyle

The ships are large enough to give passengers a sense of privacy when they wish but with a variety of indoor and outdoor spaces to be social or be secluded. Obviously the luxuriously comfortable cabins with seating areas, TV/VCR and full meal service entice passengers to spend more time inside. Days are casual, with many passengers lounging on deck in bathing suits reading a book, but evenings get much more formal. There are not many organized activities on board since passengers prefer to plan their own time, but they will attend outstanding lecturers.

Wardrobe

While daytimes may be spent in casual, but never sloppy, garb, people dress up in the evenings, not because a dress code tells them they must, but because they like to, and because they are at ease in tuxedos and dressy gowns, silk or linen suits and top-label sportswear.

Bill of Fare . . . . .A+

Sophisticated contemporary cuisine prepared a la minute (when it's ordered) and served in small portions to encourage passengers to try the suggested menu rather than simply one or two dishes. We remember one chef's suggestion menu from Stefan Hamrin that we followed all the way through—an avocado fan with jumbo shrimp and scallion sauce, followed by creamy onion garlic soup with croutons, then a field salad of arugula and radishes, roast rack of spring lamb Dijonnaise, and hot macadamia nut soufflé with Tia Maria sauce. The food was light enough and the portions small enough that we were satiated but not stuffed at the end of the meal.

The Veranda Cafe on the Seabourn Spirit is a delightful place to have breakfast on a sunny morning.

Mornings you can breakfast on deck under the shade of a canvas canopy or inside the jade green-and-white marble Veranda where the fresh fruits are arranged on the buffet like gemstones and the thinly sliced smoked salmon and gravlax are draped like silk with caper beading.

Murals depicting the classic days of cruising adorn the lobby of the Seabourn Legend.

Showtime............................A

When the ships began operation, the evening's entertainment was done by the Styleliners, a quartet of singers who perform music by Sondheim, Porter, Berlin, Gershwin and other notables in a choreographed concert style. The ships still offer musical cabaret shows on the modest stage using the variety of principal artists performing during the cruise, as well as bringing in regional entertainers from the ports of call. Lecturers from celebrity chefs to contract bridge teachers, jazz artists, pianist-humorist Victor Borge and other celebrities. TV personality Dick Cavett, actress Brenda Vaccaro, Paris-based food writer Patricia Wells and astronaut Wally Schirra were among the recent guests.

Discounts ....

Seabourn never allows the "D" word to creep into a discussion, but a rose by any other name can still save some money on a cruise. Repeat passengers in The Seabourn Club get "savings on the cruise tariff" of 10 percent from having made a previous cruise, plus 5 percent off the fare for friends they bring along who occupy a separate suite. Cumulative days of cruising with the company also brings "substantial fare reductions," and anyone who completes 140 days aboard the ships gets the next cruise of up to 14 days free. An "early payment program" means if you book and pay for your cruise 12 months ahead of time you save 10 percent, six months ahead of time and you save 5 percent. A "single traveler savings option" on certain cruises reduces the normal 200 percent surcharge to only 110, 125 or 150 percent.

The standard suite-like cabins aboard are large enough to have friends in for cocktails.

The Bottom Line

When the *Seabourn Pride* had been running for a year and the *Seabourn Spirit* just introduced, we asked Warren Titus about the difference between operating Seabourn and operating Royal Viking. "It's much easier for us to cater to a single strata of people...They basically come form the same background and tastes...and it's so much easier to satisfy people on this ship than on a Royal Viking ship with a variety of cabins and prices."

Seabourn ships are the ultimate in patrician elegance without ever being stuffy. Your dinner table partner might turn out to have a title preceding his name, but he's unlikely to ever mention it. Everything works on these ships from the food to the service to the ambiance. You get, quite simply, a superbly satisfying cruise experience.

Going Ashore

In keeping with its posh image, Seabourn never fills its motorcoaches on shore excursions, leaving plenty of leg room for tour participants. For the same reason, groups are kept small. Altogether, the line usually offers around 25 excursions in Alaska and Western Canada. Some are complimentary, and some may require a 30-day advance booking to ensure the tour will operate. In Alaska, the Misty Fjords Flightseeing ($160) requires advance booking.

The line also performs concierge service on board for passengers who wish to make private arrangements, whether booking a rental vehicle or guide, or chartering a special tour.

Seabourn's Signature Series is a set of optional excursions that are usually exclusive to the company and not available to the average traveler, but you won't find any of these in Alaska. Most of the shore excursions offered here by Seabourn are similar to those offered by most of the other cruise companies. The exceptions are noted below.

Special Excursions

1. Grand City Drive and Tea at the Empress Hotel, Victoria

$58, 4 hours.

We've seen many shore excursions that promise an English tea, but nobody else guarantees the classic, ivy-covered Empress, built in 1905, as the venue. You'll start with a driving tour of town, then a visit to Craigdarroch Castle, built in the 19th century by a homesick Scot. Tea at the Empress is the big finale of the excursion.

2. Little Norway, Petersburg

Complimentary, 1 hour.

The big ships don't call at little Petersburg, founded and populated by Norwegian fishermen and still more unspoiled by tourism than the other towns along the Inside Passage. This tour takes you to the Sons of Norway Hall for some Norwegian pastries and folk dancing, followed by a school bus tour of the waterfront and its busy port. The town is particularly friendly to Seabourn passengers because you're aboard a Norwegian ship.

3. Anan Wildlife Observatory Flightseeing Adventure, Ketchikan

$220, a minimum number of participants required.

Only two other lines, Holland America and World Explorer, offer a tour similar to this one and, oddly enough, both are more expensive than Seabourn's. The excursion takes you by float plane into the wilderness of the Tongass National Forest and sets you down on Anan Bay, where you hike a half-mile to the wildlife observatory. You'll see spawning salmon, soaring bald eagles, seals and sea otters, and have a fairly good chance of spotting black and brown bears catching the salmon in transit.

Sister ship Seabourn Pride

Seabourn Legend ★★★★★★

> *Day after day, time after time, we find ourselves agreeing that there is no-where else on earth we would rather be than right here, right now, aboard the* Seabourn Pride *listening to Page Cavanaugh at the piano playing "Rainy Day" at cocktail time in the understated elegance of The Club.*
>
> *Notes from the inaugural sailing*
> *December 1988*

Nothing makes the folks at Seabourn madder than to hear their 10,000-ton cruise ships called "small," "little" or "yacht-sized." They have, as Warren Titus pointed out on the first sailing of the *Seabourn Pride*, "all the amenities and facilities of a full-sized cruise ship but only for a few people." Everything here is scaled to the human passenger rather than cruise industry statistics, and they spent a lot of time determining what the experienced cruise passenger who books the upper end of the market would like. Suite-rooms are a spacious 277 square feet with very lavish bathrooms and sitting areas large enough to host six people comfortably at cocktail time. There are all sorts of beautiful public rooms and deck spaces, along with, at one time, a mysterious flying saucer-like device called the Star Observatory, where passengers could climb in and lie back on cushy leather seats to star-gaze through a telescope; that's not easy on a moving ship, which is why we've never saw anyone try it.

The Brochure Says

"To some, a Seabourn cruise may be expensive; but it is not overpriced. In fact, the authentic Seabourn experience is an extraordinary value."

Translation

Even at $1000 a day, you can reassure yourself you're getting your money's worth. (Actually, Alaska tariffs on the Legend are lower than the fleetwide average.)

Cabins & Costs

Fantasy Suites: ....A+

Average Price PPPD: $1420 including airfare.

Owner's Suite Type E (there are two per ship) are 575 square feet with veranda, large living room with curved sofas, chairs and coffee table plus a dining table with four chairs, a marble bath with tub and twin sinks plus a second half-bath for guests, and a separate bedroom with all the amenities listed below (see Suitable Standards).

Small Splurges: ....A+

Average Price PPPD: $1300 including airfare.

Each of the 16 Regal C suites is 554 square feet with a small private veranda, queen-sized bed in a separate bedroom, curved sofas and chairs in the living room and lots of built-ins, plus all the amenities listed below (see Suitable Standards) and two bathrooms, one with tub and one with shower.

Suitable Standards: ....A+

Average Price PPPD: $820 including airfare.

The standard suite-rooms are 277 square feet each with a five-foot picture window placed low enough on the wall that you can lie in bed (either twins or queen-sized) and watch the sea. A tapestry-print sofa, three chairs and two round stools provide plenty of guest seating, along with a mini-refrigerator, full array of crystal and a fully stocked liquor cabinet. The coffee table can be raised to dining table height if you want to dine in, and there's a walk-in closet with lots of storage, a built-in dresser/desk with drawers and mirror, and a marble bathroom with tub, twin sinks set in a marble counter and a mirrored storage area for toiletries.

Bottom Bunks: .... NA

There's no such thing on Seabourn ships.

EAVESDROPPING

Famous Last Words Department: A quartet of San Francisco travel agents, invited for the christening-day tour of the Seabourn Pride, walked from the gangway into the reception hall and turned up their noses at the last-minute touch-ups of artificial greenery to replace plants damaged in the stormy crossing, accepted a glass of champagne from a white-gloved waiter and flounced into the Magellan Lounge, where they sat at the back table just long enough to empty their glasses. "Hmph," one sniffed, "I don't like this room; it's too dark." "Well, this ship'll never touch the Sea Goddesses," her friend commented. "I've seen enough—ready to go?" And away they went, back down the gangway without looking at anything else.

DID YOU KNOW?

We have had innumerable conversations with heads of certain ultra-deluxe cruise lines about why they don't include as largesse the relatively inexpensive duty-free bar drinks (even if it's house brands only) and dinner wines like Song of Flower, Silversea *and* Sea Goddess *ships do, and the answer we invariable get is, "The passengers who don't drink don't want to subsidize those that do."*

Where She Goes

The *Seabourn Legend* starts the Alaska summer season in 1997 with a 17-day roundtrip from San Francisco that calls in Victoria, Petersburg, Juneau, Skagway, Haines, Sitka, Ketchikan, Seattle and Eureka, and cruising Misty Fjords, Wrangell Narrows, Tracy Arm, Endicott Arm and the Inside Passage. A 14-day sailing from San Francisco to Vancouver follows a similar itinerary. Other summer sailings cruise between Seattle and Vancouver, San Francisco and Vancouver or San Francisco and Seward (for Anchorage). The season ends in August when the ships sails from Seward via the Aleutians and Russian Far East to Tokyo on a 19-day voyage that includes two days of cruising the Kuril Islands.

The Bottom Line

Yes, it's expensive, but not even the worst nit picker could find anything to complain about with the food, service and accommodations. And there are really exotic and interesting itineraries, calling at some rarely visited ports, along with appealing mix-and-match cruises that can be combined for a sizable savings. Go for the standard suite-rooms unless you want to splurge to get a veranda. When you head for the deck, there's a steward in white shirt and tie to turn your deck chair toward the sun hourly or spritz you with mineral water. In the evening, you can slip away for cocktails in the club while the pianist plays your favorite sentimental song, or don something dazzling for dinner dancing between courses in the restaurant. Or enjoy breakfast in bed while gazing at the sea through a five-foot picture window with its own automatic window washing system.

Fielding's Five

Five Unforgettable Places

1. A watersports marina that can be thrust out from the ship when it's at anchor, letting passengers swim in a giant submersible steel mesh tank with its own teak deck around it, or go windsurfing, sailing or waterskiing.

2. Forward on the top deck is the Horizon Lounge with wrap-around glass windows, cushy blue leather chairs and couches, a polished granite bar, a radar screen for passengers to play with and a computer-animated wall map of famous historic voyages as well as itinerary information.

3. The Sky Bar, a wooden bar with a circle of barstools around it plus wooden tables and lower stools fixed on the teak decking, is a popular gathering spot.

4. The Club, cool white and beige with wood, marble and woven textures, is equally handsome in the daytime with sunlight streaming in its glass dome or in the evening with the shades lowered and a pianist playing Duke Ellington compositions.

5.   The Restaurant, with quiet, comfortable tables placed well apart, tapestry-patterned chairs and silky curtains; a pianist plays during dinner and there's a small dance floor for those evenings when dinner dancing is scheduled.

Five Good Reasons to Book These Ships

1.   Because service is so good you don't have to lift a finger; you can let things come to you, rather than having to go fetch them.

2.   Because you can buy an air/land program that includes economy-class airfare or optional upgrades, premium hotel accommodations, hospitality desks at the hotels and transfers to and from the ship.

3.   Because tipping is not only not requested, but not permitted.

4.   The little extras that mean a lot—bathrobes, hair dryers, combination safes, walk-in closets with four different kinds of hangers, personalized stationery, a sewing kit with the needles already threaded, a 24-hour room service menu that includes everything from sandwiches to grilled steaks, complete sets of bathroom towels in two colors, peach and pewter gray, and exquisite almond-scented toiletries.

5.   Instead of aspic-encased show buffets and parades of baked Alaska, you can find sevruga caviar whenever you want to order it, fresh broiled sea bass, sautéed pheasant breast with Calvados sauce, chocolate truffle cake.

Five Things You Won't Find On Board

1.   A lap swimming pool; the smallish pool is adequate but wedged between the Veranda Cafe and a stairwell. The Jacuzzi is more popular than the pool.

2.   A view of undersea life in the underwater viewing room on the bottom deck when the ship is moving; all you see are bubbles.

3.   A delay on getting your laundry and dry cleaning back; same-day service is available.

4.   A surprise when you get to the dining room; copies of the menus are delivered daily to the cabins so you can plan ahead.

5.   Bar drinks and dinner wine included in the fares; you'll pay extra for those.

Seabourn Legend ★★★★★

Registry	**Norway**
Officers	**Norwegian**
Crew	**European**
Complement	**140**
GRT	**10,000**
Length (ft.)	**439**
Beam (ft.)	**63**
Draft (ft.)	**16.4**
Passengers-Cabins Full	**208**
Passengers-2/Cabin	**200**
Passenger Space Ratio	**50**
Stability Rating	**Good**
Seatings	**1**
Cuisine	**Contemporary**
Dress Code	**Traditional**
Room Service	**Yes**
Tip	**No tipping allowed**

Ship Amenities

Outdoor Pool	**1**
Indoor Pool	**0**
Jacuzzi	**3**
Fitness Center	**Yes**
Spa	**Yes**
Beauty Shop	**Yes**
Showroom	**Yes**
Bars/Lounges	**3**
Casino	**Yes**
Shops	**1**
Library	**Yes**
Child Program	**No**
Self-Service Laundry	**Yes**
Elevators	**3**

Cabin Statistics

Suites	**104**
Outside Doubles	**0**
Inside Doubles	**0**
Wheelchair Cabins	**4**
Singles	**0**
Single Surcharge	**110-150%**
Verandas	**6**
110 Volt	**Yes**

SEABOURN CRUISE LINE

Society Expeditions

2001 Western Avenue, Suite 710, Seattle, WA 98121
☎ *(206) 728-9400, (800) 548-8669*

Passengers aboard an expedition cruise in the Bering Strait on the World
Discoverer *go birdwatching in a Zodiac.*

History . . . .

Seattle adventurer and entrepreneur T. C Swartz founded Society Expeditions in 1974 under the name Society for the Preservation of Archeological Monuments, dedicated to saving the giant *moai* statues on Easter Island, and got into the cruise business when he chartered the 138-passenger *World Discoverer* in 1979 for a five-year series of museum and university charters and independent expeditions to exotic areas of the world.

In 1984, when that charter was up, the owner of the vessel, Heiko Klein, head of a German travel company called Discovery Reederei, leased the ship to a short-lived cruise company called Heritage Cruises, which had also chartered the sailing yacht *Sea Cloud*. Heritage hired the famous decorator Carleton Varney to turn the doughty expedition vessel into a chic luxury ship that would offer exotic expeditions with music and entertainment (i.e., life after dinner).

When Heritage went out of business at the end of 1984, Klein again chartered the *World Discoverer* to Swartz. Society also acquired the *Lindblad Explorer* in 1985 when Lindblad Travel went out of business. Klein ultimately ended up buying out Swartz in 1988 to become the owner of Society Expeditions. The company ordered a new expedition ship called the *Society Adventurer*, to be built in Finland and delivered in 1991. Then Klein entered into a marketing agreement with Abercrombie & Kent to promote the two existing expedition ships and the new one coming up.

When the *Society Adventurer* was almost completed, Society Expeditions refused to accept delivery of the $68 million vehicle and started a contractual dispute with the shipyard. In January 1992, Society filed a Chapter 11 reorganization plan bankruptcy. The *Explorer* was acquired by business associate Abercrombie & Kent and the *World Discoverer* leased to Clipper Cruises, which operated the vessel through the end of April 1995. Society Expeditions came back into business in 1994.

—First line to offer a seven-continent world cruise (1982).

—First company to attempt commercial marketing of a tourist space ship cruise into outer space (1984).

DID YOU KNOW?

The erstwhile Society Adventurer *languished in the shipyard another two years before making its 1993 debut as the* Hanseatic, *now marketed by Radisson Seven Seas Cruises and owned by Hapag-Lloyd.*

Concept . . . .

To offer expedition cruises to a loyal coterie of repeat passengers, along with "the opportunity to visit small, out-of-the-way ports that are inaccessible to larger ships and the delight of traveling with like-minded individuals with whom you share common interests."

Signatures . . . .

The soaring bird logo over the blue-and-white D with the globe inside; the Zodiacs, inflatable landing craft, carried aboard and used almost daily; the inclusion in basic rates of all shore excursions, lectures and special programs; the largesse of throwing in small unadvertised "surprises" during the cruises; the strict environmentally responsible onboard program of waste management.

Gimmicks . . . .

The Ship's Log from every cruise, compiled by the captain and naturalists aboard and mailed to passengers long after they have returned home, reminding them afresh of what a good time they had. On Antarctic cruises the line sends each passenger a bright red parka, so he or she won't get lost in the ice and snow.

Who's the Competition. . . . .

There was a time when Society Expeditions and Lindblad Travel virtually dominated the upscale expedition market in the United States, but while Society was away the newcomers began to play, many of them former associates and/or employees of the two leaders. Now we have Quark Expeditions, which took up the Lindblad/Salen Lindblad banner; Zegrahm Expeditions, founded by a group of ex-Society Expeditions executives and expedition leaders; and the two new luxury expedition ships, the *Bremen* and the *Hanseatic*, originally everyone's hope for the future growth of expeditioning but both operated by companies that are more upscale-mainstream than expedition-oriented.

DID YOU KNOW?

The late Lars-Eric Lindblad of Lindblad Travel also had chartered the World Discoverer *briefly but let it go because regulars on his 80-passenger* Lindblad Explorer *thought the 138-passenger ship was "too big."*

Who's Aboard . . . .

Mostly well-traveled, well-read, upper-income couples and singles over 45—weeellll, over 65 in most cases, but who's counting? On the *World Discoverer's* historic first Northwest Passage west-to-east crossing, one of the youngest of our fellow passengers was celebrating his 50th birthday. They are alert, curious, quizzical, argumentative, politically conservative but environmentally active, warm, friendly and loving.

Who Should Go . . . .

Perhaps the cost and the length of the cruises have been deterrents to younger passengers in the expedition field, but the last under-35 passenger we can recall was a stowaway on the *World Discoverer's* 32-day transit of the Northwest Passage in 1985.

DID YOU KNOW?

The young stowaway, who got aboard by wearing a Society Expeditions membership pin he had cajoled from a disembarking passenger in Nome and said he was "desperate" to be among the first to transit the Northwest Passage from west to east, was mentally noted by all the other passengers who averaged 50 years his senior but not remarked on, until crew members found him sleeping in a lifeboat (the usual hideaway for a stowaway) the first night out.

Captain Heinz Aye, a stickler for rules, put him off at the first port of call, Little Diomede Island, Alaska, in the Bering Strait three miles from Siberia. The local tribal chief promised the young man could stay for the two weeks until the next plane arrived but "would have to work for his keep." We never saw him again and have often wondered what happened after that day we sailed away and left him on Little Diomede.

Who Should Not Go . . . .

Stowaways, obviously (although Captain Aye is now master of the *Bremen*). Infants and small children, because there are no facilities for them aboard. Wheelchair passengers because there are no easily accessible cabins. Anyone looking for life after dinner.

The Lifestyle ....

Almost everyone becomes obsessed with observation and record-keeping, scribbling in journals, making photographs and sketches, even videotaping with murmured commentary into the side of the camera. We hunt the ship's library for books about the area, flock to 25-year-old documentary films and attend rambling discourses on anything having faintly to do with the subject at hand. Dress is casual in the extreme, the food is good to excellent, and life aboard becomes more comfortable and insular day by day.

Wardrobe ....

Comfortable, sensible clothes that do not need a lot of care, practical shoes for walking and hiking, rain gear and rubber boots, spare walking shoes to replace the pair you got wet on the last Zodiac landing.

Bill of Fare .... B+

In the Arctic and Antarctic, passengers always feel a pang of guilt when they hear about the deprivations of the early explorers, then step on the scales to find they've gained another pound or two from the excellent cuisine on board. Fresh fruits and vegetables are air-lifted, by charter plane, if necessary, into some of the most remote airports of the world to keep *World Discoverer* passengers happy and well-fed.

Showtime .... N/A

Unless watching ancient Film Board of Canada documentaries like "Group Hunting on the Spring Ice, Part III" with a soundtrack entirely in the Netsilik Eskimo dialect is your cup of tea, you'll go to bed after dinner with a good book.

Discounts ....

Previous cruisers with Society Expeditions frequently get direct-mail brochures with early booking discounts on upcoming journeys. Call and ask to get on their mailing list, even if you're not a previous passenger; it just may work.

Explorers meet seals.

The Bottom Line

Out of the 200+ cruises we've made during the past 15 years or so, we've spent more days at sea aboard the *World Discoverer* than any other ship—something like 109 days in the Arctic, the Antarctic, Burma, India, Singapore, Indonesia, Fiji, Alaska and Siberia—more than three months altogether, under the auspices of at least three different cruise lines. Obviously we like the ship and its programs very much, but at the same time, we feel the improvements that have been made in expedition cruising with the introduction of the *Bremen* and the *Hanseatic*—private verandas, elegant dining rooms and lounges, state-of-the-art lecture halls—should not be disparaged in the reverse snobbery of the old-time expeditioners. The new ships are more environmentally correct, and they have the opportunity of attracting a larger, younger international market who might appreciate a cabin TV set that receives satellite news or a trio playing for dancing after dinner. We haven't heard the Germans or Japanese on these new ships complaining about "too much luxury."

World Discoverer ★★★, ⚓⚓⚓⚓⚓

Along the horizon, as far as the eye could see, shimmering cliffs of ice towered, as if Dover had frozen over. It was a surrealist fantasy. The Beaufort Sea was calm and the sky was blue. Our little blue-and-white ship World Discoverer *seemed trapped between the icy cliffs on one side and the glittering sand-colored skyscrapers of an Arctic Metropolis twinkling with lights and belching flames on the other. Fire and ice in a vast, flat sea. We were five days north of Nome, looking at something no map had prepared us for, one of the Arctic's more devious tricks, a mirage called "looming." The flames and towers to our starboard side were part of the oil equipment at Prudhoe Bay. The stark icy cliffs to our port side were illusions, the flat ice cap of the Beaufort Sea reflect-*

ing against itself in the morning sunlight. How many explorers desperately searching for the Northwest Passage during the past 400 years had seen a similar wall of ice ahead and turned back?

Icebergs off the coast of Greenland during a Northwest Passage transit.

Her dark blue hull, which still reduces pre-1984 passengers into fits of muttering, "But it was always red!" came courtesy of Heritage Cruises' decorator Carleton Varney ("The blue looks more nautical, don't you think?"). There are three decks with passenger cabins, all of them fairly small with basic furnishings and baths with showers only, plus a lavish owner's suite on the Boat Deck and two smaller suites on A Deck. A restaurant and two lounges, one forward and one aft, plus a film/lecture hall on the topmost deck, make up the basic layout. There is a small swimming pool aft on deck and access to the forecastle forward on Boat Deck to see whales, Northern Lights and icebergs.

The Brochure Says

"The *World Discoverer* is a small cruise ship accommodating only 138 passengers in a relaxed and casually elegant atmosphere. On board, a genuine camaraderie prevails among travelers. Her attentive staff presents every comfort. Each cabin has an outside view, lower beds, private bathroom and individual comfort control."

Translation

Everything is on hand to please the people "who want their adventure and their dry martini too!," as the late Antoinette DeLand, first author of the Fielding cruise guides, observed.

Cabins & Costs

Fantasy Suites: . . . . B+

Average Price PPPD: Owner's suite $602, other suites $582 plus airfare.
Although there are three suites on board, the owner's suite on Boat Deck is the largest, a big cabin with large sitting area, king-sized bed, a wall of storage closets

and a spacious bath. If that's spoken for, the two 2-room suites on A Deck will do very well, each with two lower beds, dresser and nightstands in the bedroom, sofas and cabinets in the living room, and a bathroom with tub and shower.

Small Splurges: .... *C*

Average Price PPPD: $547 plus airfare.
The deluxe double cabins are a bit bigger than the others and conveniently located on Odyssey Deck. They contain two lower beds, window and bathroom with shower. Closet space is barely adequate.

Suitable Standards: .... *C-*

Average Price PPPD: $434 plus airfare.
The category 4 cabins on Voyager Deck are where we've spent many of those 109 days; we can still see them in our sleep. There are two lower beds, one of which folds into the wall during the daytime, and one of which makes up as a day sofa. We draw straws to see which one has to sleep in the pulldown bed. Two of them have a third pulldown bunk, which takes up even more of the limited space. Then you have a desk/dresser with mirror, chair and three drawers, one of which locks, a space where clothes are hung back to front rather than the more standard side by side, a couple of storage shelves with wire baskets and a tiny bath with shower.

Bottom Bunks: .... D

Average Price PPPD: $332 plus airfare.
Although the eight forward cabins in Category 1 on Discoverer Deck have two lower beds, they also have those washing-machine portholes with the sea splashing against the glass—when you're lucky enough not have them covered because of rough seas. Baths have shower only, of course, and the rest of the furnishings approximate those in Suitable Standards, above.

Where She Goes

In Alaska the *World Discoverer* offers four expeditions. In May and June, two 15-day sailings between Seward (for Anchorage) and Petropavlovsk in the Russian Far East include calls in the Aleutians, Fox Islands, Andreanof Islands, Rat Islands, Near Islands and Commander Islands. A nine-day sailing roundtrip from Seward calls at Kodiak, Russia's Katmai Peninsula and the Kenai Peninsula on a Gulf of Alaska cruise. Two "Bridging the Bering Strait" itineraries in July cruise between Seward and Nome, visiting the Kenai Fjords, Kodiak Island, the remote Pribilofs, Shumagin and Semidi Islands. In August, a 13-day Gulf of Alaska and Inside Passage cruise sails between Seward and Prince Rupert, Canada, along the Inside Passage.

The Bottom Line

The peripatetic *World Discoverer* offers single-seating meals (you can sit where and with whom you please, but tables for two are grabbed up quickly) with fairly sophisticated cuisine, along with top-notch lecturers and wildlife experts to help passengers identify seabirds, spot and identify whales, or look for lichens. Late-night activities run more to aurora borealis gazing than disco dancing. There are no casinos or dance bands aboard— there used to be a pianist who doubled as a Zodiac driver, or was it a Zodiac driver who doubled as a pianist?—so entertainment is usually limited to lectures, films and passenger accounts of discoveries from the latest shore explorations, which on a slow day in the high

Arctic sometimes deteriorated into a show-and-tell of desiccated animal droppings. It's expensive but rewarding; you should know after reading this whether it's right for you.

Five Favorite Spots

1. The Crow's Nest, a tiny forward observation area higher than anything else on the ship, situated about where the crow's nest would have been on a sailing ship, with standing room only for half a dozen people at most, a rail to get a firm grip on, and a view into the crashing, churning sea that is more exciting than any roller coaster ride in any amusement park in the country, especially when you're rounding Cape Horn.

The lovely lounge aboard the World Discoverer proves you're not exactly roughing it.

2. The Discoverer Lounge, scene of the nightly "recaps" and once home to the long-gone brass palm trees, a nightclub touch decorator Varney borrowed from Los Angeles' Cocoanut Grove and added to the structural support posts around the room. He wrapped them in brass strips, then hung a cluster of brass "palm fronds" from the low ceiling like foliage on a tree. Unwary dancers ran the risk of getting maimed when they waltzed under them, and the captain pruned them regularly until one day they were entirely gone.

3. The Marco Polo Restaurant, once pretty in pink with chairs that used to be too big and heavy to pull up under the tables, has been trimmed down but still looks lovely, and offers open seating.

4. The lecture hall is the most popular after-lunch nap spot on the ship, especially if the documentary of the day is a couple of decades old.

5. The Lido Lounge, a big comfortable aft lounge with banquettes, tables and chairs, used all day long from buffet breakfast and lunch through needlepoint, reading, postcard writing and chatting.

Five Good Reasons to Book These Ship

1. To go to Kodiak Island and see the bears.
2. To visit the captain and navigator on the open bridge.

3. To have the optimum opportunity for spotting marine mammals—this ship detours for whales.

4. To land in the remote Pribilof Islands.

Birdwatchers gather on the beach on a cool, sunny day in the Pribilof Islands.

5. To explore the Russian Far East.

Five Things You Won't Find On Board

1. A room key; passengers leave their cabins unlocked during the day, bolting them from the inside when they go to bed.

2. Room service (unless you're sick).

3. Cabins designated wheelchair accessible; but there is an elevator aboard, albeit a small one.

4. An inside cabin.

5. Frivolous reading in the library.

World Discoverer ★★★, ⚓⚓⚓⚓

Registry	Liberia
Officers	German
Crew	International
Complement	75
GRT	3153
Length (ft.)	285
Beam (ft.)	50
Draft (ft.)	15
Passengers-Cabins Full	138
Passengers-2/Cabin	129
Passenger Space Ratio	24.44
Stability Rating	Good
Seatings	1
Cuisine	Continental
Dress Code	Casual
Room Service	No
Tip	$8 PPPD

Ship Amenities

Outdoor Pool	1
Indoor Pool	0
Jacuzzi	0
Fitness Center	Yes
Spa	No
Beauty Shop	Yes
Showroom	No
Bars/Lounges	2
Casino	No
Shops	1
Library	Yes
Child Program	No
Self-Service Laundry	No
Elevators	1

Cabin Statistics

Suites	3
Outside Doubles	59
Inside Doubles	0
Wheelchair Cabins	0
Singles	0
Single Surcharge	140%
Verandas	0
110 Volt	No

SPECIAL EXPEDITIONS

123 South Avenue East, Third Floor, Westfield, NJ 07090
☎ *(908) 654-0048, (800) 348-2358*

History . . . .

Launched in 1979 as a travel company offshoot of Lindblad Travel by
Sven-Olof Lindblad, son of the late expedition pioneer Lars-Eric Lindblad, Special Expeditions has also carved out its own very special niche
in expedition cruising. Sven bought the division in 1984 and acquired
the line's first ship, the 80-passenger *Polaris*, the former *Lindblad
Polaris*, in 1987, followed by the *Sea Lion* in 1989 and the *Sea Bird* in
1990. With wife Maria, Sven co-owns the *Swedish Islander*, a 128-foot
ship that carries 45 passengers around the Stockholm Archipelago for a
program called "Impressions of a Swedish Summer," putting them up
overnight in small country inns. Special Expeditions also owns the *Caledonian Star.*

Concept . . . .

The logo for Special Expeditions, a giant eye in dark blue, "stands for a
different way of looking at the world, with more of an in-depth perspec-
tive," says Lindblad. Many of the places his expeditions visit are fresh
and fascinating, not always as gee-whiz name-dropper stops but visited
rather for their own unique environments, and the company's excellent
expedition leaders and naturalists devote considerable time and attention to interpreting them for passengers.

Signatures . . . .

The blue eye logo on the stack of the line's *Polaris* and *Caledonian Star*
and the sides of the smaller *Sea Lion* and *Sea Bird*.

Zodiacs, inflatable rubber landing craft used to explore ashore or venture in close to icebergs and cliffs of nesting seabirds.

Allowing a serendipitous flexibility in the schedule when something
special occurs.

Including all shore excursions and sightseeing, as well as some transfers
and shore meals, in the basic fares.

A generosity of spirit in refusing to exploit on-board revenue—visits to the ship's doctor are free and the staff frequently offers free drinks or beer and wine with meals.

Gimmicks

Publishing individual brochures for each sailing or series of similar sailings rather than an entire catalogue of cruises by the year.

Who's the Competition

The line's classic competitors in the expedition field are the *Explorer* from Abercrombie & Kent, once its Lindblad Travel stablemate, and Society Expeditions' *World Discoverer*. In Alaska and the Pacific Northwest, the *Sea Lion* and *Sea Bird* come head-to-head with Alaska Sightseeing/Cruise West's very similar small vessels, which offer fewer expeditioning extras than Lindblad.

Who's Aboard

Mostly seniors and retirees who have the time and money for expeditioning and the thirst to learn more about the world around them.

Who Should Go

Birdwatchers of the world—these are some of the most fantastic voyages for birding we've ever been aboard; whale watchers and wildlife spotters; photographers; more young people who enjoy hiking and eco-tourism.

Who Should Not Go

Families with very young children—there's no program for children and no place for them to play.

People with wheelchairs or walkers—these ships have no elevators but do have numerous steep stairs and gangways to negotiate.

The Lifestyle

The overall ambiance is one of fun and discovery, due in part to the energetic young naturalists and expedition leaders. Dress is casual, and single-seating meals are served at unassigned tables. Don't expect a swimming pool, cabin TV set, casino, slot machines or after-dinner entertainment. You may, however, go ashore on an uninhabited island for a barbecue dinner or set out in a glass-bottomed boat while drifting over luminous seas sparkling with rainbow-colored fish, or go swimming or snorkeling from empty beaches in clear turquoise waters. You'll also go back to school if you wish—and everyone does—attending lectures, reading supplementary materials and watching films and slides when not actually ashore or in a Zodiac exploring.

Wardrobe

Very casual, sturdy expeditioning clothes—jeans, twills, shorts and T-shirts, swimsuits, sweaters, depending on the climate, plus sturdy shoes for deck wear and hiking ashore and rain gear in some climates. Most passengers take along one sort of dress-up outfit, not black tie and sequins but more on the order of bolo tie and knit dress.

Bill of Fare . . . . .B

Food is not an obsession with Sven-Olof's passengers—most require only that it be healthful, substantial and digestible with no strange seasonings or ingredients a lifelong New Englander can't recognize. The chefs do a nice job in spite of the guests. Meals are served at a single open seating, allowing passengers to sit where and with whom they please. They do, however, as we have observed over the years, tend to stake out the same table and tablemates for most of the cruise.

Showtime. . . . . N/A

Unless you count the nightly 7 p.m. "recap"—the recapitulation of what happened today and the forecast of what may or may not happen tomorrow—as entertainment, these ships have none.

Passengers explore islands offshore by Zodiac.

The Bottom Line

Special Expeditions has moved ahead carefully and cautiously, concentrating on its strong suits rather than trying to spread itself too thin and offer too many different options to its dedicated repeaters, many of whom sailed with Sven's father before him. It is a solid, predictable cruise product of very high quality and dignity, worth every penny of the sometimes substantial price.

Rather than offer optional shore excursions, Special Expeditions includes them in a seamless, free-form program that takes advantage of serendipity.

Sea Bird   ★★, ⚓⚓⚓⚓

Sea Lion   ★★, ⚓⚓⚓⚓

Both ships cruise the Sea of Cortez in winter, where sea lions sunning them-selves on rocky ledges slide off into the creamy foam to swim over to our rub-ber craft for a closer look. They show great curiosity, playfully swimming and rolling about and deliberately splashing us, then swimming away again. One large dominant male, who felt our presence threatened his harem, followed us doggedly, bellowing loudly and showing his teeth in the most aggressive dis-play he could summon. Overhead, the tropic birds darted around gossiping shrilly with each other, and the blue-footed boobies honked hoarsely across the guano-covered rocks. This is the noisiest island in the unspoiled group that are North America's equivalent of the Galapagos.

This pair of sturdy little American-built expedition vessels have been re-configured since their days with now-defunct Exploration Cruise Lines, when they sailed as the *Majestic Explorer* and *Great Rivers Explorer*. Now they carry only 70 passengers instead of the 92 they used to handle. Meals are single-seating. Cabins are all outsides, but instead of windows or port-holes, the four lowest-priced accommodations on the lower deck have portlights located high up in the walls, which let in a little light but don't allow a view. The ships carry Zodiacs, inflatable rubber landing craft, in order to take passengers exploring ashore or in the sea. A shallow eight-foot draft permits these small vessels to get into small ports and visit uninhabited islands in Alaska and British Columbia.

The Brochure Says

"Your voyage is led by historians and naturalists rather than conventional tour guides, specialists who share their enthusiasm for the area with informal talks, slide presentations, and anecdotes over drinks at the end of the day. You join them for frequent trips ashore, and on forays in Zodiac landing craft to explore remote areas."

Translation

This is not a cruise, this is a learning expedition that will enrich a part of your life, or at least teach you how to recognize a frigate bird in flight.

Cabins & Costs

Fantasy Suites: .... NA

There are no cabins on board in this category.

Small Splurges: .... B

Average Price PPPD: $612 plus airfare.

The Category 4 aft cabins on Upper Deck, #216 and #219, are large and comfortable and only steps away from the deck when you want to run out and see the (choose one: bear, whale, porpoises, sea lions, pelicans). They have twin beds or double beds, depending on which cabin you select, a desk/dresser/table and large window. The bathrooms throughout the ship are quite compact with shower only.

Suitable Standards: .... C-

Average Price PPPD: $527 plus airfare.

Upper Deck category 2 cabins are a bit smaller than the category 4 (see Small Splurges, above) but contain twin beds and a big window.

Bottom Bunks: .... D

Average Price PPPD: $427 plus airfare.

The four cheapest category cabins are on the lowest passenger deck with portlights instead of windows, meaning you have a little daylight but don't get to look outside. One double bed and a single that converts to a couch in the daytime round out the furnishings, and there is a small bathroom with shower.

Where She Goes

Both *Sea Lion* and *Sea Bird* cruise the coastal waterways of Alaska and western Canada, and spend spring and fall cruising from Portland along the Columbia River and Hells Canyon, Idaho, "In the Wake of Lewis and Clark."

"Exploring Alaska's Coastal Wilderness" sailings depart throughout June, July and August, sailing between Juneau and Sitka on eight-day itineraries, exploring Point Adolphus and the Althorp Rocks, where humpback whales often feed; spending a full day in Glacier Bay; calling in Haines; and exploring the areas around Admiralty Island, Le Conte Bay and Tracy Arm. An optional seven-day excursion to Denali, Fairbanks and Anchorage is available for $2,980 per person, double occupancy.

During May and late August/early September, the vessels sail between Sitka and Seattle, calling in Juneau and Ketchikan and cruising British Columbia's Inside Passage, Alert Bay and Johnstone Strait, as well as visiting the San Juan Islands in Washington. Passengers disembark the 11-day sailing in Seattle.

September offers departures of a seven-day "Coastal Waterways of the Pacific Northwest" that includes the San Juan Islands, Victoria, Princess Louisa Inlet, Johnstone Strait and Alert Bay, disembarking in Vancouver.

The Bottom Line

Shore excursions and non-alcoholic beverages are included in the basic fare. Most of the cabins open directly onto an outer deck, which could be a nuisance in cold rainy weather like you get sometimes in Alaska. To avoid this, book one of the cheaper Category 1 or Category 2 cabins on a lower deck. While dress is casual, bring along a change of sneakers, since you often get wet feet on Zodiac landings.

A rare spotting of a black bear provides great photo ops.

Fielding's Five

Five Familiar Places

1. The dining rooms, big enough for everyone in one open seating with passengers free to sit where they please, have round and rectangular tables for five to eight.

2. In the observation lounges, the furniture is arranged in conversational groupings with swivel chairs and fixed small tables; lectures, "recaps" and social gatherings take place here.

3. The Sun Deck makes a good place for lounging and reading between wildlife spotting and bird-watching.

4. The upper deck forward is where to gather to look for whales or eagles.

5. Despite their modest sizes, *Sea Bird* and *Sea Lion* have full around-the-ship promenade decks for inveterate walkers who don't mind a double-digit number of laps to make a mile.

Five Good Reasons to Book These Ships

1. To learn how to identify frigate birds, tropic birds and blue-footed boobies in flight.

2. To explore the rivers, deltas, fjords and seas of the American west.

3. To look for furry sea otters, puffins and guillemots.

4. To take a comfortable, affordable expedition close to home in little more than a week.

5. To venture into places such as Princess Louisa Inlet looking for black bears and Point Adolphus, where the humpback whales feed.

Sea Bird *and* **Sea Lion** *take passengers for close-up looks at Alaska.*

Five Things You Won't Find On Board

1. A children's program.

2. Cabins designated wheelchair-accessible.

3. Room service.

4. Spa and beauty shop.

5. Elevators.

Sea Bird
Sea Lion

★★, ⚓⚓⚓⚓
★★, ⚓⚓⚓⚓

Registry	**Bahamas**
Officers	**Swedish**
Crew	**Filipino**
Complement	**22**
GRT	**99.7**
Length (ft.)	**152**
Beam (ft.)	**31**
Draft (ft.)	**8**
Passengers-Cabins Full	**76**
Passengers-2/Cabin	**72**
Passenger Space Ratio	**NA**
Stability Rating	**Good**
Seatings	**1**
Cuisine	**American**
Dress Code	**Casual**
Room Service	**No**
Tip	**$7 PPPD, 15% automatically added to bar check**

Ship Amenities

Outdoor Pool	**0**
Indoor Pool	**0**
Jacuzzi	**0**
Fitness Center	**No**
Spa	**No**
Beauty Shop	**No**
Showroom	**No**
Bars/Lounges	**1**
Casino	**No**
Shops	**1**
Library	**Yes**
Child Program	**No**
Self-Service Laundry	**No**
Elevators	**0**

Cabin Statistics

Suites	**0**
Outside Doubles	**36**
Inside Doubles	**0**
Wheelchair Cabins	**0**
Singles	**0**
Single Surcharge	**150%**
Verandas	**0**
110 Volt	**Yes**

WORLD EXPLORER CRUISES

555 Montgomery Street, San Francisco, CA 94111-2544
☎ *(415) 393-1565, (800) 854-3835*

History . . . .

San Francisco-based World Explorer Cruises was a division of the wide-spread C.Y. Tung family shipping interests, marketing the *Universe* for many years on summer Alaska sailings when the vessel was not in use as a floating university.

The Seawise University concept had been a passion in this family since the late Mr. Tung acquired the *Queen Elizabeth 1* for the purpose of creating a university that would sail around the world. Unfortunately, that poor ship never got out of Hong Kong harbor, where she burned and sank during the refitting in 1972.

Concept . . . .

Education, eco-tourism and a close-up, first-hand look at Alaska are the main aims of the summer sailings. The slogan, "a 14-day adventure for the heart, mind & soul" seems to be the company's concept. The new *Universe Explorer* has also added winter Latin America and Caribbean sailings.

Signatures . . . .

Classical music instead of production shows, a full audience listening to lecturers instead of playing blackjack, hands-on crafts lessons.

Gimmicks . . . .

Fitness class hearts—12 laps around the deck net you one heart, and 20 hearts gets you a T-shirt that says Sound Mind, Sound Body, Universe.

Who's the Competition . . . .

Nobody really offers a cruise like this one—14 days hitting more ports in Alaska than any other ship, and promoting the educational and cultural level of the cruise.

Who's Aboard . . . .

The entire membership of Elderhostel, families with children, staffers from the University of Pittsburgh (who accredit the Semester-at-Sea program), grandparents bringing their grandchildren on a cruise, one family with several children including an infant. Many, many repeaters. According to one longtime staffer, "Our passengers are those that have never taken a traditional cruise and didn't want the glitz."

Who Should Go.....................................

People interested in getting a close-up look at Alaska and a lot of lectures; people who don't want to dress up.

Who Should Not Go ....

Anyone fussy about food and service; anyone who usually books a suite on a cruise ship; anyone who likes to dress up.

The Lifestyle ....

While the educational and eco-tourism aspects of the voyage are emphasized almost constantly, they still get passengers stirred up with typical cruise ship frivolities including bingo, singalongs, horse racing, mileage pools, a masquerade parade, passenger talent shows, bridge competitions and dancing gentlemen hosts. This is not exactly Mensa on vacation.

INSIDER TIP

Unlike expedition ships, the Universe Explorer *does not include shore excursions in its fare; passengers pay from $12 for a botanical walk in Wrangell to $280 for a flightseeing excursion to Mt. McKinley or $475 for mountain biking tours in eight ports of call.*

Bill of Fare.................................C

Breakfast usually offers a blackboard special of the day, with one fresh fruit, one egg dish, and side dishes that include oatmeal, blueberry pancakes and such.

A typical lunch starts with three appetizer choices—perhaps fresh asparagus, fruit or a cheese plate, a smoked chicken risotto soup, a salad bar, and a choice of pan-fried fillet sole of lemon butter and almonds; Seafood Louie salad; beef Stroganoff over noodles; or the "light" selection of the day. There is also a continental self-service breakfast served on the enclosed promenade deck.

Dinners also feature several appetizers, one soup, the salad bar and a choice of several main dishes, perhaps salmon, barbecued chicken and steak, along with a vegetarian main dish.

Showtime.................................C

Longtime musicians Peggy Wied and the Voyagers bill themselves as "seniors playing for seniors." Classical concerts are interspersed with folk singers and a belting country, blues and pop singer who also leads singalongs.

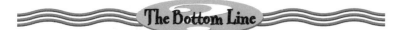

This is the favorite Alaska cruise for a great many people, but we were amused to find the passengers being so self-congratulatory—"Aren't we clever not to be on some tacky cruise ship that doesn't really show you Alaska?"—every time a more handsome ship passed us along the Inside Passage. We restrained ourselves from pointing out that they're taking the same optional, land-operated shore excursions in Alaska that, say, Princess and Holland America passengers do. They just sometimes cost more with World Explorer.

This small, one-ship, soft-adventure company has a plethora of shore excursions during its 14-day programs, some 52 that range from a $22 Wrangell city tour to a $280 overflight of Mt. McKinley. They are sold on board the ship only. As noted above, we were surprised to see that with this moderately priced cruise line, many of the same excursions are priced higher than aboard mainstream ships. The following are some special splurges to consider:

Go for Broke

1. Alaska Bike & Cruise package

$475 for the full cruise, with eight days of cycling; $285 for a half-cruise with four days of cycle use; or $90 for one day at a time.

Bikes are mountain bikes or Trek hybrids with gel saddles, racks and cyclometers. A helmet is required and is rented by surcharge fee.

2. Kayak Games and Mini-Tour, Skagway

$47 for adult or child, 1.5 hours.

This lighthearted approach to kayaking is tailored especially for kids and teens. Passengers must be 8 years or older and travel with a parent or guardian in their kayak. Paddling is in smoother water than other kayak tours, with an obstacle course, races, and kayak surfing.

3. Stikine River Jet Boat, Wrangell

$142, adult or child, no passengers under 11, 3 hours.

Wet gear and life jackets are provided at the dock before your jet boat tour around icebergs and up close to glaciers.

4. Mt. McKinley Peak Experience, Seward

$280 for adult or child, 3 hours, flies when weather permits.

Take a motorcoach to Anchorage, then take off from Lake Hood, flying over the Susitna Valley to McKinley's south face.

5. A Day in Anchorage, Seward

$95 adult, $48 child, all day.

Take a motorcoach to Anchorage with free time to do your own city tour, go shopping, to a restaurant or to the fine Museum of History and Art.

Universe Explorer   ★★, ⚓⚓⚓

The weary, sagging old *Universe*—still sentimentally recalled by both Semester-at-Sea students and Alaska cruisers—has been sent to the breakers in India and replaced with Commodore's *Enchanted Seas*, which carries a new name, *Universe Explorer*, the 12th name change this ship has had in its 39-year-history. During the years, a second swimming pool was added on deck and the casino and boat deck stern extended so the latter could house a disco. For World Explorer sailings, the casino has been turned into the library, complete with all the former Universe's 12,000 volumes, and a computer room has been added. Sadly, on a 1996 Alaska cruise, a laundry room fire killed five crew members.

The Brochure Says

"Since the SS Universe Explorer carries a maximum of only 739 passengers, you're really able to get to know your fellow travelers...And on most sailings, carefully screened hosts provide unescorted ladies with welcome companionship for dining, dancing and ship and shore activities."

Translation
You can always find a fourth for bridge if you want to duck out on the glacier tour.

Cabins & Costs

Fantasy Suites:..N/A
None.

Small Splurges: . . . . *C*

Average Price PPPD: $285 plus airfare.
Four cabins of different shapes and sizes are designated suites, and are larger than most but not all the other cabins. Two of them, #618 and #628, also have bathtubs. Furnishings are trim and attractive if hardly glamorous, but a striking improvement over the old *Universe.*

Suitable Standards: . . . . *C*

Average Price PPPD: $249 plus airfare.
A large percentage of the cabins on board are standard or deluxe outside doubles, many with twin beds that can be converted to queen-sized. A desk/dresser, TV set, chair or small sofa/bed for a third cabin occupant are the usual furnishings. Some accommodate a third and fourth occupant at a flat rate of $995 for the cruise.

Bottom Bunks: . . . . *C*

Average Price PPPD: $164 plus airfare.
The cheapest beds aboard are in the category 9 insides with upper and lower berths, but there are only nine of these.

The *Universe Explorer* sails roundtrip from Vancouver on 14-day itineraries from mid-May to late August, calling in Ketchikan, Juneau, Skagway (with optional shore excursions to Haines), Valdez, Seward (for Anchorage), Sitka, Wrangell and Victoria, and cruising B.C.'s Inland Passage, Glacier Bay, Yakutat Bay and Hubbard Glacier.

For the money and the numbers of ports, this is one of Alaska's best buys for travelers who are destination-oriented. An added attraction is the new ship. Although built 40 years ago, the *Universe Explorer* is a tremendous improvement over the line's dowdy *Universe*, offering more indoor and outdoor areas for passengers to explore, along with much larger, nicer cabins and baths.

Universe Explorer ★★, ⚓⚓⚓

Registry	**Panama**
Officers	**European/American**
Crew	**International**
Complement	**330**
GRT	**23,500**
Length (ft.)	**617**
Beam (ft.)	**84**
Draft (ft.)	**28**
Passengers-Cabins Full	**739**
Passengers-2/Cabin	**726**
Passenger Space Ratio	**32.36**
Stability Rating	**Good**
Seatings	**2**
Cuisine	**International**
Dress Code	**Casual**
Room Service	**No**
Tip	**$8.50 PPPD, 15% automatically added to bar check**

Ship Amenities

Outdoor Pool	**1**
Indoor Pool	**0**
Jacuzzi	**1**
Fitness Center	**Yes**
Spa	**No**
Beauty Shop	**Yes**
Showroom	**Yes**
Bars/Lounges	**6**
Casino	**No**
Shops	**2**
Library	**Yes**
Child Program	**No**
Self-Service Laundry	**Yes**
Elevators	**3**

Cabin Statistics

Suites	**4**
Outside Doubles	**286**
Inside Doubles	**74**
Wheelchair Cabins	**2**
Singles	**2**
Single Surcharge	**130%**
Verandas	**0**
110 Volt	**Yes**

OTHER CRUISE COMPANIES

The following are cruise marketing companies that represent various lines or charter various vessels seasonally over a period of years. They specialize in expedition cruises, with some sailings in Alaska, Northern Canada and the Arctic.

13 Hazelton Avenue, Toronto, Ontario, Canada M5R 2E1
☎ *(416) 964-9069, (800) 263-9147*

This fast-growing Canadian expedition company, founded in 1992, claims it cruises "to the ends of the earth" with its active, moderately priced cruises to the Arctic in summer and the Antarctic in winter (austral summer in the Southern Hemisphere).

It uses six chartered Russian and Estonian ice-rated research vessels manned by Russian and Estonian crews with a North American and European cruise staff. Ships currently in the fleet include the 120-passenger *Marine Discovery* (the *Alla Tarasova*), the 38-passenger *Marine Challenger* (the *Livonia*), the 44-passenger *Marine Spirit* (the *Professor Shuleykin*), the 44-passenger *Marine Intrepid* (the *Professor Multanovsky*), the 80-passenger *Marine Adventurer* (the *Akademik Ioffe*), and the 80-passenger *Marine Voyager* (the *Akademik Sergey*).

Cabins aboard are generally small, with portholes or windows, and some in the bottom categories have shared bathroom facilities. One, two or three suites with sitting area, two lower beds and private bath facilities with shower are available on all the vessels except the *Marine Discoverer.* Furnishings are basic, with bunks, a table and a chair. Food is served family-style and consists of "basic comfort food," as one recent passenger described it. Dinners usually offer a soup, salad, hearty casseroles or pasta dish and fruit for dessert, while lunches may be soup and cheese sandwiches or fried chicken and French fries.

Passengers are most often veteran expeditioners or independent adventurers of various ages from the late 30s to the 70s. Excursions ashore are made by Zodiac, inflatable rubber landing craft. Lecturers who specialize in the flora, fauna or geology of an area are aboard, and a comprehensive handbook is provided about each region.

Marine Expeditions emphasizes controlled tourism and adheres to all international environmental regulations, frequently participating in programs with international scientific groups.

In the summer, Marine Expeditions cruises part of the Northwest Passage from Sondre Stromfjord, Greenland, to Nanisivik/Arctic Bay, Canada, on a nine-day itinerary; sails from Sondre Stromfjord to Churchill, Canada on a 12-day program; sails from Vladivostok, Russia, to Nome through Kamchatka Peninsula and the Kuril Islands on a 13-day cruise that includes roundtrip airfare from Anchorage beginning at $4795 per person, double occupancy; sails the Aleutians on a 17-day program from Prince Rupert to Nome, with calls in Kodiak, the Semedi and Shumagin Islands, Unimak Island, the Fox Islands, Dutch Harbor and Unalaska, the Pribilofs, St. Matthew and St. Lawrence in the Bering Sea, the Chukotskiy Peninsula, Yttygran Island and Providenya in the Russian Far East, with a connecting flight to Nome; fares start at $4795 per person, double occupancy.

QUARK
EXPEDITIONS

980 Post Road, Darien, CT 06820
☎ *(203) 656-0499, (800) 356-5699*

Quark Expeditions was founded in 1990 by veteran expeditioners of countless Arctic and Antarctic programs who were able, thanks to the thaw in U.S./Russian relations, to charter former Soviet atomic fleet icebreakers to cruise not through balmy oceans but pack ice as thick as 16 feet. Many of the nuclear powered vessels were built in Finland's Wartsila shipyard in the early 1980s, during the period when we were there observing construction of more traditional cruiseships like the *Royal Princess* and Carnival's *Fantasy.*

Voyages to the geographic North Pole aboard the icebreaker *Yamal* usually set out from Murmansk or Pevek in Russia's Arctic (after a connecting flight from Helsinki), sail the Barents Sea and crunch through ice to Franz Josef Land before reaching the Pole where a celebratory barbecue is held on the ice, along with a brief plunge into the Arctic Ocean for anyone who wishes. A pair of onboard helicopters extends the sightseeing possibilities, and lecturers and expedition leaders tell everything you ever wanted to know about the biology, geology and history of the Arctic.

Quark's Russian icebreakers sail both polar regions.

The fleet employed by Quark includes the *Kapitan Dranitsyn, Kapitan Khlebnikov, Alla Tarasova, Yamal, Professor Khromov* and *Professor Molchanov.* The because-it's-there adventurers will need big bankrolls though— most of the North Pole sailings run into five figures sans decimal point, starting around $16,900. Arctic journeys are more modestly priced, beginning around $6000 for a 10-day cruise through the high Arctic.

The only nuclear icebreaker we've seen first-hand is the *Yamal*, which was briefly disabled and awaiting repairs off the Siberian coast, when we met up with them while we were on another, more traditional expedition vessel. It was filled with wanna-be North Pole adventurers champing at the bit to get moving, passing their days with Zodiac explorations of the Russian Far East.

1414 Dexter Avenue N # 327, Seattle, WA 98109
☎ *(206) 285-4000, (800) 628-8747*

This small Seattle-based expedition company, made up of experienced expedition veterans from pioneer outfits such as Lindblad Travel and Society Expeditions, has grown by leaps and bounds since its debut in 1991. Over the years, Zegrahm has offered some of the most exotic and far-out cruises you could take around the world.

On Aug. 3, 1997, it attempts the first-ever passenger-ship circumnavigation of Baffin Island aboard the icebreaker *Kapitan Khlebnikov*, 17 days of cruising, sometimes through pack ice, in search of the rare, one-horned narwhal, walrus, beluga whales and polar bears. Company founder Werner Zehnder says it has been a dream of his to make this journey since 1985, when he, along with the authors, was aboard the first west-to-east transit of the Northwest Passage with the late Captain Tom Pullen, an icemaster who knew intimately all the waterways of the Canadian Arctic. This journey is a culmination of years of planning and dreaming. Fares range from $7650 to $10,750 per person, double occupancy, plus airfare to and from Toronto, with ongoing air lifts to Resolute to embark and disembark the vessel.

Aboard the same vessel, Zeghram offers a Canadian Arctic and Greenland itinerary, and, in 1998, a cruise through the Aleutians and the Pribilofs to the beautiful Kamchatka Peninsula in the Russian Far East aboard the *World Discoverer* (see Society Expeditions, page 399).

ALTERNATIVE CRUISES

Author Harry Basch photographs nesting murres in Sireniki in the Russian Far East.

The captain of the *QE2* is not likely to give you a turn at the wheel, and you won't be wading ashore in Skagway from the gigantic Sun Princess. Big cruise ships are like seagoing deluxe hotels, lavishly appointed, self-contained cities.

But just as travelers seek out little country inns and bed-and-breakfast establishments in off-the-beaten-track locations, cruise passengers sometimes look for alternative cruises aboard smaller vessels that sail to out-of-the-way corners.

You'll never see these ships in TV commercials. They don't have glittering casinos and Las Vegas-type shows, glamorous passengers dolled up in sequins and satins, miles of midnight buffet and cruise directors organizing fun and games.

Not all of them sail the ocean blue, and few of them boast sleek, streamlined curves and acres of teak decks. Some of them, in fact, are downright funny-looking—beetle-browed Russian icebreakers capable of moving through six inches of pack ice with a solid crunch-crunch-crunch sound. Some will take you fishing or exploring a day or two where no one else goes, and some make eco-tourism expeditions on research vessels.

Adventure and Eco-tourism Sailings

The following are some companies that offer expedition and eco-tourism cruises in Alaska and Northern Canada:

Canadian River Expeditions Ltd.

3524 W 16th Avenue, Suite 1A, Vancouver, BC, Canada V6R 3C1, ☎ *(604) 738-4449.*
A family operation making river expeditions into the Queen Charlotte Islands, the Yukon and coastal British Columbia.

Captain Al Parce

X-Ta-Sea, PO Box 240250, Douglas, AK 99824, ☎ *(907) 364-2275.*
Takes four people at a time out in his 49-foot vessel into Tracy Arm, Frederick Sound and Admiralty Island on various itineraries from one to six nights.

The Explorers Club

46 East 70th Street, New York, NY 10021, ☎ *(800) 856-8951.*
Makes adventure expeditions, including occasional sailings on the Russian icebreaker *Kapitan Khlebnikov.*

Glacier Bay Adventures

PO Box 68, Gustavus, AK 99826, ☎ *(907) 697-2442.*
Makes eco-tour explorations of Alaska's Glacier Bay Country aboard the *Stellar*, a research vessel built for the Alaska Department of Fish and Game.

InnerAsia Expeditions

2627 Lombard Street, San Francisco, CA 94123, ☎ *(800) 777-8183.*
Once again offering Alaska coastline cruises on its little 12-passenger *Discovery* after several years of inactivity while the vessel was under charter during the Exxon oil spill cleanup.

Lifelong Learning, Inc.

101 Columbia, #150, Aliso Viejo, CA 92656, ☎ *(800) 854-4080.*
Programs in the Antarctic, Costa Rica, the Amazon, North Africa, Asia Minor, the Yucatan, Japan, Europe, Canada and the U.S.

NWT Marine Group

17 England Crescent, Yellowknife, N.W.T., Canada, X1A 3N5, ☎ *(403) 873-2489.*
A family-run company that cruises Canada's Arctic along the Great Slave Lake and MacKenzie River aboard the 20-passenger *Norweta.*

TCS Expeditions

2025 First Avenue, Suite 830, Seattle, WA 98121, ☎ *(800) 727-7477.*
Veteran expeditioner T.C. Swartz, former head of Society Expeditions, provides adventure cruises to Iceland, Greenland, the Canadian Arctic and the North Pole.

Zegrahm Expeditions

1414 Dexter Avenue N., #327, Seattle, WA 98109, ☎ *(800) 628-8747.*
Longtime expedition leader Werner Zehnder and his team of experts explore the Arctic and Antarctic, and offer dive excursions to Galapagos, cruises of the Seychelles aboard the *Caledonian Star* and catamaran explorations of Australia's Kimberley Coast. (See Zegrahm under Other Cruise Companies, page 426)

ALTERNATIVE CRUISES

Vehicle and Passenger Ferries

Travelers with their own vehicles may wish to look into the excellent vehicle and passenger ferry system in Washington, Alaska and British Columbia. If you're traveling with a vehicle of any sort, but especially a motorhome or camper, you'll want to make reservations as early as possible. A year in advance is not unusual, especially if you want vehicle space and a cabin aboard one of the Alaska Marine Highway ferries in the Inside Passage.

Alaska Marine Highway System

P.O. Box 25535, Juneau, AK 98802-5535, ☎ *(800) 642-0066, Ext. 9505, (907) 465-3941.*
The smart blue-and-white ferries cruise throughout Alaska's Southeast, including Ketchikan, Sitka, Prince of Wales Island, Juneau, Haines and Skagway.

B.C. Ferries

1112 Fort Street, Victoria, B.C., Canada V8V 4V2, ☎ *(604) 386-3431.*
Offers year-round vehicle and passenger service, including a "Gateway to Alaska" sailing from Port Hardy to Prince Rupert which cuts out 934 miles of roadway.

Victoria Line Ltd.

1112 Fort Street, Victoria, B.C., Canada V8V 4V2, Canada, ☎ *(800) 668-1167, U.S. (800) 683-7977.*
Sails mid-May through mid-October from Seattle's Pier 48 daily at 1 p.m. Departs Victoria's Ogden Point at 7:30 a.m. daily. Carries passenger cars, bicycles, motorcycles, buses, RVs and commercial vehicles. Sailing time is 4.5 hours, and the vessel, *Royal Victorian*, offers excellent crafts in a duty-free shop as well as the ubiquitous Starbucks Coffee Bar, outdoor beer garden on deck, buffet dining room, bar and lounge, children's play room and video game room.

ALTERNATIVE CRUISES

WHERE ARE THEY NOW?

A Work in Progress

We all wonder whatever became of our favorite ships when they seem to have dropped off the planet or at least out of the travel agencies. Too many times cruise lines either never mention them again or say they "retired" them. That doesn't necessarily mean the ships are sent out to pasture, mothballed or sent to the breakers; it may mean they've been sold or leased to another cruise company. So we set out in chase of recently familiar ships, the vintage vessels which are changing hands rapidly these days because of the 1997 SOLAS (Safety of Life at Sea) and IMO (International Maritime Organization) safety requirements that will be difficult and expensive to implement. Here's where they were and what they were doing in late 1996. To be continued...

Achille Lauro

This ship was little-known in the United States until the dramatic events on board in October 1985, when terrorists took control of the vessel as it was sailing between Suez and Alexandria, while most of the passengers were on an overland excursion, and killed an American passenger. The bad-luck ship was built as the *Willem Rhys* in Holland, with its keel laid in 1939 but the vessel not launched until 1946 and delivered in 1947, for service between Rotterdam and Indonesia. She sailed around the world with two-class service for Rotterdamsche Lloyd until she was sold to Flotta Lauro, renamed the *Achille Lauro*, and rebuilt in Palermo in 1965. The work was delayed by an explosion and fire. She made her first voyage under the new name in 1966, then suffered another fire in 1972 during a refit in Genoa. In 1975, she collided with the livestock carrier *Yousset* in the Dardenelles, which sank with the loss of one life (plus some of the livestock, presumably). In 1982 she was impounded in Tenerife because of unpaid repairs, and then laid up the following year. In 1984 she returned to Mediterranean service. Despite being engulfed in world-wide publicity after the terrorist attack, the ill-fated ship continued cruising for Lauro; by then the line was renamed *StarLauro*. We passed her in the Bosphorus Straits in the summer of 1990, rusty, weary, and listing heavily to port. A disastrous fire aboard when she was off the Horn of Africa in 1994 totally destroyed the ship. She sank as rescuing tugs came in sight of her.

American Adventurer

The kids' cruise line ship spent only a year in extra-heavy duty with high-density family cruises before returning to Genoa to revert to its previous identity as *CostaRiviera*.

Aurora I, Aurora II

Sold to Singapore-based Star Cruises to become the *MegaStar Taurus* and the *MegaStar Aries*.

Boheme

Once a popular budget cruise ship sailing the Caribbean. Since 1985, it's the *Freewinds*, owned by the Church of Scientology. According to insiders, members get a free cruise if they make a donation of $5000 to the church.

Britanis

At this writing, the beloved old American-built *Britanis* is laid up.

Caribbean Prince

Now sailing as the *Wilderness Explorer* for Glacier Bay Tours and Cruises.

Carnivale/FiestaMarina

Carnival's short-lived *FiestaMarina* version of its longtime "fun ship" *Carnivale* directed at the Latin American market fizzled, despite the high quality product, and with running mate *Mardi Gras*, was sold to Epirotiki during another short-lived marketing agreement that ended with the Greek company, in effect, buying the two ships from Carnival.

Constitution

The *Constitution* has been retired by American Hawaii, who said it would be too expensive to renovate the ship and bring it up to new SOLAS standards.

Crown Monarch

Now sailing in Asia as the *Nautican* for Singapore-based Lines International.

Cunard Crown Jewel

Sold to Singapore-based Star Cruises to become the *SuperStar Gemini*.

Cunard Countess

Sold to the Awani Cruise Line of Indonesia for $23 million.

Cunard Dynasty

Now sails as Majesty Cruise Lines' *Crown Majesty*.

Cunard Princess

Now sails as the *Rhapsody* for Mediterranean Shipping Cruises.

Danae

After being burned and scuttled in Venice harbor, the ship was resurrected as the *Baltica* for Sunshine Cruises (a.k.a. Greek-based Festival Shipping) and subsequently renamed *Danae Princess* by new operators Italia Cruise Lines.

Dapne

Sold to Swiss-run Leisure Cruises, a new company, for $11 million.

Dawn Princess

The former *Fairwind* for now-defunct Sitmar, the *Dawn Princess* reverted to Vlasov's V.Ships in Monaco, its former owners, and was leased to a German travel company, which renamed her *Albatros*, with one "s."

Dolphn IV

Sold to a central Florida shipping company named Kosmas, a.k.a. Canaveral Cruise Line Inc. in July 1995, the vessel makes two-night cruises out of Port Canaveral. The company has been accused of misrepresenting themselves as members of Cruise

Lines International Association (CLIA) and of alleged deceptive acts and practices through a telemarketing subsidiary.

Emerald Seas

Last seen sailing in the Mediterranean as the *Sapphire Seas*.

Enchanted Seas

Now sailing as *Universe Explorer* for World Explorer.

EnricoCosta

Now sailing as the *Symphony* for Mediterranean Shipping Cruises.

EugenioCosta

Sold to Bremer Vulkan Shipyard for May 1997 delivery.

Fair Princess

After a potential sale to now-defunct Regency Cruises fell through, Princess towed the *Fair Princess*, the former *Fairsea*, to Mazatlan where the ship was laid up awaiting purchase. In mid-1996, it was promised to P&O Australia to replace the aging *Fairstar*.

Festivale

The former Carnival ship is now sailing as Dolphin's *IslandBreeze*.

Kazakhstan II

Sold to the Lady Lou/Sea Delfin Shipping Ltd., Malta, renamed *Delfin* and reflagged in Malta.

Majestic

Leased by Premier Cruises to London-based CTC Cruises for a four-year period.

Mardi Gras

After being leased out for a year as *Pride of Galveston*, the ship was renamed *Apollo* by owner Epirotiki. It was reported to be leased to Takis Kiriakidis' Royal Venture Cruise Line but that never materialized.

Mermoz

The ships remaining from the trio of cruise lines owned at the end of 1994 by the French-based Accor Group went to Costa. The *Mermoz*, at press time is still marketed to European cruisers and music lovers (for its annual classical music festival at sea).

Monterey

It's been nearly five years now that the U.S.-built *Monterey* has been sailing as flagship of the former StarLauro Cruises, now Mediterranean Shipping Cruises. It was picked up at bank auction for a song by a Panamanian company called Cia Naviera Panocean SA in Honolulu after parent company Aloha Pacific filed for bankruptcy in 1989.

Nordic Prince

Sold by Royal Caribbean Cruises Ltd. in early 1995 to Airtours, a British travel company, who renamed it *Carousel*.

Ocean Islander

This trim, mid-sized vessel that sailed for Ocean Cruise Lines in Europe, the Caribbean and South America, is now the *Royal Star* for Star Line Cruises in Mombasa.

Ocean Princess

Ran aground and was badly damaged in South America in 1993; we had gone aboard her only a couple of days before in Rio. Two decks were partly flooded and she was declared a total loss. Ellice Navigation in Piraeus bought her and towed her to Greece, where she was reconstructed as the *Sea Prince*. A subsequent sale to Louis Cruise Line of Cyprus has netted still another new name— *Princesa Oceanica*.

Odessa

The recently refurbished vessel from Black Sea Shipping was impounded in Italy a year ago, joining a number of other Black Sea vessels being detained by creditors in various ports of the world.

Pearl, Pearl of Scandinavia, Ocean Pearl

Poor pitiful *Pearl* had a lot of names during her illustrious career. Now she's the *CostaPlaya*, marketing cruises to Cuba from the Dominican Republic, sold only to Europeans and Latin Americans by parent company Costa Crociere in Genoa to circumvent U.S. trading-with-the-enemy restrictions.

Regent Star, Regent Sun

After bankruptcy of Regency Cruises, this pair of ships was reportedly leased to Takis Kiriakidis' Royal Venture Cruise Line in Tampa.

Sagafjord

Cunard decided to retire this prestigious and beloved ship after an engine room fire off the Philippines interrupted her 1996 world cruise. She had previously been scheduled to leave the fleet at the end of her 1996 Alaska season, but has been sold to Saga Holidays to sail as *Gripsholm*.

Sea Princess

The *Sea Princess* was renamed *Victoria* in mid-1995, in order to free the name for a new Princess ship due in 1998.

Song of Norway

Sold to Britain's Airtours, who previously bought its former RCCL running mate *Nordic Prince*. Her new name is *Sundream*.

Southward

The longtime Norwegian Cruise Line vessel was sold to Airtours to become the *Seawing* for the British-based travel company.

Star Princess

Transferred to P&O to become the *Arcadia*, replacing the *Canberra* in late 1997.

Starward

The last of the Norwegian Cruise Line "white ships" to leave the fleet, the *Starward* has been turned into the *Bolero* for Greek-based Festival Shipping's Azur-Bolero Cruises.

The Victoria

Now at Louis Cruise Line in Cyprus as the *Princesa Victoria*.

Ukraina

In the spring of 1996, this former Black Sea Shipping vessel briefly sailed as the *Royal Seas* for Royal Seas Cruise Line on two- and five-day cruises out of Tampa.

Universe

The doughty old *Universe*, which served for years as the Semester-at-Sea ship and made summer Alaska sailings for World Explorer Cruises, was sent to the breakers. She has been replaced by the *Universe Explorer*, the former *Enchanted Seas*. See World Explorer Cruises.

Vasco De Gama

The schizophrenic, dual-named vessel—its other moniker and present legal name is *Seawind Crown*—was finally officially renamed and able to sail under only one name, thanks to its purchase in July 1995, by a group of New York investors called Capital Holiday.

World Renaissance

Sold in August 1995, by Epirotiki (it was the line's flagship) to an Indonesian travel company.

GETTING READY
TO GO

If you have a special occasion to celebrate, let the line know ahead of time and they'll bake you a cake, as Cunard did for this couple.

Timetable

Two Months or More Ahead of Time:

—Get a passport (see Appendix, page 457) or get your old one renewed if it's within six months of expiring. For Canada, Americans need a passport or a birth certificate or voter registration, along with pohto ID such as a driver's license. Non-U.S. or non-Canadian citizens will need a passport.

When Your Tickets Arrive:

—Sit down and examine carefully everything in the package, because there may be forms you need to fill out and mail or fax back to the line. At the very least, there are forms that you should fill out at home before leaving rather than at the check-in counter at embarkation, when you may be holding up a long line. And there will be valuable information dealing with life aboard the ship, wardrobe and how to communicate with you on the ship for those at home.

—Give a copy of the satellite communications telephone number for the ship to whomever should contact you in an emergency, and threaten violence if they call when there is no emergency. (There's nothing scarier than to be relaxing aboard a ship miles from land and have the radio officer ring your cabin with a call from home.)

—If you're traveling independently to the ship, take with you the name and telephone number of the port agent for the city of embarkation, because sometimes a ship isn't where it's supposed to be when you arrive.

The Day or Night Before:

—Pack your bags, being sure to affix to each one the baggage tags the cruise line has sent, with your name and cabin number clearly written on each.

The Day of Your Flight or Transfer to the Ship:

—Get to the airport (or the ship) comfortably early in case there's a traffic delay. Pay careful attention to boarding time and sailing time instructions. If you're too early, you'll sit around on a folding chair in a large terminal waiting until you can board.

Stewards aboard Princess Cruises' Sky Princess *await boarding passengers in Vancouver.*

Eleven Tips To Lighten Your Luggage

1. Lightweight Bags: We carry soft-sided but durable bags in small to medium sizes, tucking in an empty folding bag to bring dirty laundry or souvenirs back home. Try never to carry more than you can handle yourself, since you may arrive in some primitive place where there are no baggage carts. While a ship doesn't care how much baggage you bring on board, the airline that gets you there can be sticky about overweight luggage. Also, cabin closet and drawer space may be limited on smaller ships or in lower category accommodations.

2. List: Work out a wardrobe list in advance to avoid those just-in-case clothes that get thrown in at the last minute and never worn. Remember that separates multiply, you can wear an outfit more than once, and sticking to basic color combinations means fewer shoes and accessories to coordinate.

3. Laundry: Virtually every cruise ship has a laundry, either self-service or send-out. Daytime clothes are casual and if they're washable as well, you don't need to take many. Dry-cleaning is available on most of the newer ships, and you'll often find irons and ironing boards in self-service laundries or from the housekeeping department for last-minute touch-ups.

4. Layering: Bulky garments add weight and take up space; instead, layer lightweight garments for cool mornings on deck. You'll have more wardrobe variety as well. Wear your bulkiest clothing and shoes to the ship to save having to pack them.

5. Lightweight fabrics: Carry more light natural fibers such as cottons and woolens to layer in Alaska's cool climate; avoid synthetics, which tend to cling and don't breathe. Silks are nice for dressy evenings and can be layered.

6. Location purchasing: Since you're going to be tempted by clothing in ports of call—T-shirts, sweaters, logo sweatshirts—you might as well plan for it. Take fewer casual items and shop with a clear conscience.

7. Little sizes: No, we don't mean clothing but toiletries; save those samples that come in the mail or buy the smallest possible tubes and containers before leaving. All but a few ships have complimentary toiletries in the cabins; we've tried to point out those that don't. (See Five Things You Won't Find Aboard under the cruise ship you're sailing aboard.)

8. Less is more: We've long ago limited gifts and souvenirs for friends back home to small, unbreakable, easily packed items such as scarves, flat placemats, leather goods including wallets or belts, rather than outsized, fragile items that have to be hand-carried.

9. Libraries: Don't carry a collection of hardbound best-sellers to read aboard; every ship has a library of some sort, from the *Universe Explorer's* 20,000 volume collection to a small group of dog-eared paperbacks on an expedition vessel. Tuck a paperback or two into your luggage and then trade with someone else when you've finished.

10. Logic: Carry essentials including passport, tickets, traveler's checks, cash, extra glasses, cameras and prescription medications in hand baggage you always keep with you; never put them in a suitcase that may be checked.

11. Leave it out when in doubt: We've never yet come back from a cruise without at least one garment we carried and never wore. Other passengers usually don't notice if you're wearing the same thing several times; it's the pleasure of your company, not your wardrobe, that counts.

For many people, dressing up for formal night is a special part of the cruise.

Wardrobe Tips: Sequins Don't Wrinkle

Chances are, everything you need to pack for your cruise is already in your closet—(we know this doesn't make a good argument for someone using the cruise as an excuse to buy some smashing new clothes)—because people on ships wear the same clothes as people on land, regardless of what some department store fashion buyers seem to think.

In the daytime, casual jeans and sweatshirts or jogging suits pass muster all over the ship, and in the evening, dress-up clothes of the sort you'd wear to a dinner party or nice restaurant will do just fine.

On the most classic and elegant ships, the dreaded words "formal night" do mean a tuxedo, dinner jacket or dark suit for a man, and a cocktail outfit or evening dress for women, but a blazer or sports jacket and tie for men, a dress or pantsuit for women, will be acceptable.

Five Essentials to Pack in Your Hand Baggage

1. Prescription medications in their original containers.

2. Sunblock, a hat and an umbrella.

3. An extra pair of prescription eyeglasses or contact lenses.

4. A sweater to combat overzealous air conditioning on board.

5. Proof of citizenship—passport, copy of birth certificate or voter registration card; a driver's license is not acceptable.

Nice to Take Along

1. Camera and film (if you're a novice, practice at home with a roll or two before you leave).

2. Lightweight binoculars.

3. Small, packable guidebooks for the area.

> ### INSIDER TIP
>
> *It's a good idea not to pack anything firm whether valuable or not in your checked baggage. In several major airports that handle a lot of cruise traffic (including New York's JFK) cameras and jewelry have a way of disappearing between the time the bag comes off the plane and when it gets into the baggage area. Soft-sided bags are easily 'frisked" by unscrupulous baggage handlers.*

Air/Sea Packages

If you've bought an air/sea package, the travel agent or cruise line has forwarded your air tickets to you a distressingly short time before departure. Nevertheless, take a moment and double-check the departure times and other details to be sure they coincide with the date and departure time of the cruise. If you're traveling with a spouse, you may or may not be seated together on the plane, since the block of tickets is run through a computer that couldn't care less about your marital bliss. If this happens to you, see if another member of your group will change seats with one of you if you're all clumped together.

Your route between home and the port may also be circuitous because of the airline hub system. If there's a long way to get there, you can count on that being your route. Should you have plenty of frequent flyer miles, you could book the cruise at the cheaper cruise-only price and use your mileage to get to and from the port. The only downside there is if your cruise is cancelled at the last minute, the cruise line would probably not refund you the value of your lost mileage.

Arriving at the Airport of Your Port City

With an air/sea package, you will find somewhere in the arrival airport a uniformed meet-and-greet holding a sign with the name of your ship or cruise line on it. She may be at the gate or in the baggage area. She will tell you to claim your luggage and then mill about with the rest of your group until everyone has his or her bags, or until the couple whose bag was lost go to the baggage window and fill out the lost luggage forms.

Then you'll all be led as a group to your vehicles, and the meet-and-greets will supervise loading you and your baggage into the same or different vehicles. It's not a bad idea for a couple traveling together for one to get into the bus and get a seat for the two of you and the other watch the baggage until it is actually put into a vehicle.

Arriving at the Pier

The porter will ferry your baggage from the taxi to the baggage-loading area for the ship, or, if you've arrived by transfer on an air/sea package, the meet-and-greets will see to its transfer. Again, it's a good idea to keep an eye on your bags as they're transferred.

You'll be ushered into a large hall where a lot of people are milling about or standing in line. In Vancouver, most departures are from the Canada Place pier, and each cruise line has its own area within the hall. Find them first. There will be from one to 10 counters with letters of the alphabet above them. Queue up under the letter for your surname; if you are a couple with different surnames, as we are, select the shorter of the two lines. You will turn in your cruise tickets, passports, and (please, please, please) your already-filled-out forms, give them a credit card to imprint for onboard charges, and they in turn will give you a boarding card, perhaps a cabin key and part of your ticket. You will then be directed to the security point where you'll put everything through the machines again, just as you did at the airport. (If you're carrying 1000 ASA film for your cameras, this second X-ray dose could damage the film.)

Security

Cruise passengers have gotten accustomed to the same security drills as airline passengers, running baggage through the X-ray devices and showing a boarding pass to reboard the vessel. The newest precautionary safety measure introduced on some lines recently is the requirement of a photo ID to back up the usual boarding card for passengers boarding and reboarding the ship.

Visitors who have not made previous arrangements are not permitted to board most ships in port. If you want to invite a friend on board for lunch or a drink, be sure to ask well ahead of time at the purser's desk if it can be arranged.

Shipboard security officers like this Holland America stalwart stand at the gangway when ships are in port to enforce the "No Visitors" rule.

Boarding

You will follow a long line of people carrying their hand baggage along an interminable gangway, perhaps up some stairs or an escalator, perhaps along a covered walkway, to the point where a strip of tape has been stuck across the floor and a man with a camera will order you to stop by a life ring and smile. Try to look as cheerful as you can, because this photograph will be put on display the next day for everyone on the ship to see.

When you cross over the threshold from the gangway into the ship, you will be simultaneously greeted with a smile, handed some sheets of paper that you don't have anywhere to put, told to watch your step and watch your head, and have a white-gloved steward try to wrestle your hand baggage off your shoulder while asking you your cabin number. He'll lead you to your cabin, where you may or may not be greeted by your cabin steward or stewardess, who introduces himself or herself politely and explains how to turn on the TV and flush the toilet.

Check to see that your dining table assignment card is waiting in your cabin; if not, go immediately to the maitre d'hotel and arrange it. The Rotterdam *dining room here shows the variety of table sizes available.*

The First Five Things to Do After Boarding

1. Check the shipboard program to see when the lifeboat drill is held and what time the welcome-aboard buffet lunch service shuts down.

2. Be sure your dining table assignment is set. If not, hie yourself to the maitre d's table and get one.

3. Go to the spa or beauty salon in person to book all upcoming appointments for hair, nails, massage and facials.

4. Hurry to the library to check out that new best-seller or videotape you want to see; if the library is not staffed and things are locked up, make a mental note of what you want and check the shipboard program for the first opening time.

5. Unpack.

On Board

—Establish credit for your shipboard account.

On check-in or after boarding, you'll be asked to leave a credit card imprint to establish your shipboard charge account. Most ships make it impossible to spend cash until check-out time. (On a few small vessels without a completely computerized billing system, you may find that sales revert to cash at midnight the night before disembarkation to facilitate billing.) The purser's office slips a bill under your cabin door the last night of the cruise, usually long after bedtime, and you don't need to stop by the desk at all unless you have a question about it.

Every ship sailing today has some sort of gym and fitness center, as well as indoor and outdoor pools where water exercises are held.

Spas

Almost every ship today sails with some sort of gym or fitness center; a jogging or walking track, either a specially surfaced ring around an upper deck or the passenger promenade deck; a daily exercise program that includes aerobics and other energetic activities; and a menu that includes designated low-fat, low-salt, low-calorie dishes. In addition, most have a full range of beauty, hair, nail and spa services, including manicures, pedicures, massage, steam baths, hydrotherapy, facials, herbal wraps and even mud/steam baths. The bigger the ship, the more the facilities.

Like most casinos, shops and photographic services, spas and beauty shops at sea are operated by concessionaires. Steiner of London, which dates back to 1903 when the company got its first royal warrant for hairdressing, has the lion's share of ship contracts, some 104 vessels at last count.

Passengers are urged to book massage and beauty services as quickly as possible after boarding, since the best times go quickly. Busiest days are when the captain's formal welcome aboard and farewell parties are held.

Five Ways to Get Invited to the Captain's Table

1. Occupy the most expensive cabins aboard.

2. Be a many-time repeat passenger.

3. Be rich and/or famous, a travel agent or a member of the media.

4. Be an extremely attractive blonde, preferably Norwegian.

5. Have your travel agent make the request, describing you as a rich, famous, beautiful, Scandinavian, blonde travel writer.

The Lifeboat Drill

A mandatory lifeboat drill for all the ship's passengers and crew will be called within 24 hours after sailing from the port of embarkation. You will be told to go to your cabin and get your life jacket, then report to your lifeboat station as designated on a sign affixed to your cabin wall or door. Sometimes you report to a public lounge on the ship, sometimes directly to your boat station on deck. Crew members will be posted in each stairwell and hallway to direct you to your station. It is requested that you not use the elevators since in a real emergency, they might be disabled. The signal to gather for the lifeboat drill is seven short and one long blast on the ship's whistle. You stay at your station until released by the crew member in charge. Don't worry about struggling into your life jacket in the cabin; a crew member will help you at the boat station if you need assistance. Smoking and drinking during lifeboat drill is prohibited.

Steer clear of the ship's casino as well as the bingo games, if you're on a tight budget.

Five Money-Saving Tips On Board

1. Take along your own soft drinks, wine or liquor (or buy them along the way in port) for pre-dinner libations in your cabin (but don't take your own drinks into the ship's public areas—that's a no-no). A few lines state that bringing your own liquor to your cabin is not allowable, but we've yet to see it enforced.

2. Ask the shore excursion staff about ways of doing your own sightseeing program ashore instead of buying a costly shore excursion; a group of four can sometimes

negotiate a tour with a local cab driver for less than the cost of four excursions, and a couple can walk around a town in Alaska on their own and catch the highlights, using the shore excursion booklet as a guide.

3. If you have kids along, persuade them to participate in the youth programs and activities rather than hang out in the video arcades, where quarters have a way of melting away quickly.

4. Steer clear of the casino and bingo games on board if you're on a tight budget, or set aside the amount of money you can afford to lose and don't dip any deeper.

5. If your shopping resistance is low, concentrate on sightseeing instead; otherwise you'll end up with bulky shopping bags full of things that are not as irresistible as you thought when you get them home.

INSIDER TIP

To get better service than the other passengers doesn't cost a thing; just read a crew member's name tag, look him in the eye, call him by name, smile and say thank you and show an interest in him as an individual. And remember the name next time without having to look at the name tag.

KEELHAUL

Many cruise lines now offer "port lecturers" who hand out maps to what they call "recommended" shops where the merchandise is "guaranteed." All this means is that the shops listed on the maps have paid to be listed and give commissions to both the "lecturer" and the cruise line. Most promise a 30-day opportunity to return or exchange defective merchandise, but any legitimate shopkeeper should promise the same. Too many passengers read these maps without realizing they are commercial ventures, and become fearful of going into a "non-guaranteed" shop and getting ripped off. While this practice is more common in the Caribbean, it's beginning to slip into Alaska as well.

Shore Excursions

A few cruise lines, primarily expedition vessels, include shore excursions in the base price, but aboard most ships, you'll be offered a variety of optional group port tours that may range from an inexpensive walking tour of a small town such as Skagway to a costly helicopter flight over a glacier.

Early in the sailing, the shore excursions director will hold one or more sessions to describe the tours as well as shopping pointers and ways to tour on your own. You're usually given a printed form with the excursions and prices on them, which you fill out and turn in to the shore excursions office. The excursions are then charged against your shipboard account, and the tickets or vouchers delivered to your cabin. Take care of your tickets and remember to have them along with you, "ripped and ready" as one shore excursions manager used to say, when you go ashore to take the tour. No ticket, no tour.

If you're on a budget, you'll want to weigh carefully which excursions to take and which to skip. Consider taking your own walking tour in a small port rather than getting on a bus or in a van with the others. The shore excursions manager can usually give you some advice.

Remember too that certain excursions have limited participation, so if there's something you can't live without, get to the shore excursions office as soon as possible after that tour is open for booking. Some cruise lines will let your travel agent book a tour for you ahead of time so you're guaranteed a spot.

The usual shore excursions offered in each port will be described under the name of the port, starting on page 83.

Scoping Out Seasickness

The recent removal of the Transderm Scop seasickness "patch" from the market was a better-late-than-never move for this often-dangerous drug perceived as innocuous by its users because it resembled the harmless and familiar Band-Aid. Over the years we've encountered numerous serious medical incidents because of the patch, whose main medical ingredient was scopolamine. The former prescription-only medication carried a lengthy cautionary sheet in fine print inside each package that we are confident few if any of its users ever read. Adverse reactions ran from dryness in the mouth (two-thirds of its users) to disorientation and loss of memory, particularly in older users.

There are much safer and equally effective treatments for seasickness, as well as some unusual remedies, included in the following roster:

1. Sea Band or Travel Garde bracelet-like knit bands worn around the wrist at acupressure points to relieve symptoms of nausea.

2. Ginger root capsules, available in health food stores or Asian pharmacies, taken before meals.

3. Nonprescription antihistamine remedies such as Dramamine, Antivert or Bonine can be taken one or two hours before sailing but may cause drowsiness.

4. Some shipboard doctors recommend a Dramamine injection, which works more quickly than an ingested tablet for a sudden or severe onset of seasickness.

Sidestepping Seasickness

But we have a more revolutionary cure for seasickness—a malady we must confess we've never suffered, but we do have sympathy for its victims. Here are three things to do if you're worried about a little *mal de mer*.

1. Select the right ship.

2. Sail the smoothest waters.

3. Sleep in the steadiest beds.

Ships with a deeper draft (the measurement of the ship's waterline to the lowest point of its keel) usually perform better in rough seas than ships with shallow drafts.

Destinations and itineraries can make a big difference for passengers concerned about ship motion. Plan to sail in sheltered waters such as Alaska's Inside Passage or along one of the great rivers of the world, where land is in sight and waters are calm. Conversely, in areas where two seas meet—Cabo San Lucas, Mexico, where the Sea of Cortez meets the Pacific, for instance, or South Africa's Cape of Good Hope or South America's Cape Horn—are notorious waters. Areas with powerful currents that have a speed greater than 0.8 knots an hour—the Falklands, South Indian Ocean, Bay of Bengal,

Bay of Biscay, Solomon Sea, Java Sea, Bering Strait, Spitsbergen and the Angulhas Current along the southern tip of Africa—can really stir up the water.

Other rough sea reliables include the North Atlantic, the South China Sea, the Aegean in summer, the Shetlands and west coast of Scotland. In our experiences over the years, areas that stand out dramatically are an April crossing on the North Atlantic, Cape Horn and the Drake Passage on a January Antarctic sailing, a November sailing along the coast of West Africa off Namibia, and the seas around Nome, Alaska, anytime.

The smoothest ride on most ships is on a lower deck in an amidships cabin. The higher-priced sun and boat deck cabins give more bounce and roll. But book a cabin too close to the bow or stem, and you may feel every swell. Taking an outside cabin near the waterline bothers some cruisers, because the seas slosh across the little round window like a washing machine in the laundromat.

Take your camera manual and spare batteries with you on your cruise, especially if you're going into severe weather areas to photograph icebergs from the deck of the **World Discoverer.**

Ten Tips for First-Time Photographers

1. Take your camera manual with you on the cruise so if you have problems, a more experienced photographer on board can help you figure it out.

2. Always take a set of spare batteries and have them along with you when you go ashore.

3. When photographing people on deck or ashore against bright backgrounds, use your flash to fill in extra light on their faces.

4. Don't rest your elbows or camera against the ship's rail to steady it; the ship's vibrations will make your photo blur.

5. If you want to shoot pictures through the window of a tour bus, put your camera as close as possible to the glass without touching it; be aware tinted windows can cut down on your light and alter the colors of the subject. And using the flash will give you a beautiful picture of a white light in the bus window.

6. On deck, in small boats and Zodiacs, carry a plastic bag to slip over your camera to keep the salt spray from splashing it.

7. If you're traveling with a borrowed camera, get it far enough in advance so you can shoot a practice roll and develop it before leaving home.

8. When photographing lounge shows or lecturers indoors on a cruise ship, be aware how far the light from your flash will carry; it may be necessary to move forward into a better position to get your shot, but do it quietly and don't block anyone else's view. Some ships do not allow flash pictures during a show and almost all ban the use of video cameras.

9. If you hold your camera firmly in both hands, push your elbows against your rib cage, begin mentally counting backwards from 10 to 1 and midway squeeze the camera button strange as it may sound, you can get a steadier shot in a low light situation.

10. Think in terms of telling a story with your cruise photographs—photograph the life ring with the ship's name on it, your cabin, your waiters and stewards, even yourself in the mirror dressed for the captain's dinner.

The purser's or hotel manager's desk, usually in the main lobby is the place to take your complaints in most cases.

Where to Complain

Cruises score higher on passenger satisfaction surveys than any other form of leisure travel. But if things go wrong, the worst thing you can do is seethe silently and complain to your travel agent after you get back home, or mutter about it to fellow passengers. That only aggravates the annoyance.

Instead, when you have a specific problem during your cruise, take it immediately to the person responsible for that area of service, speak calmly and explain the situation in a reasonable tone of voice.

—Cabin or cabin service complaints should go to the housekeeper; if it doesn't work out, go to the hotel manager.

—Dining room complaints should be taken up with the maitre d'hotel or the dining room captain responsible for your table area; if you don't get satisfaction, go to the hotel manager or chief purser.

—Ship charges or procedures should be discussed with the purser's desk or information desk.

—Always point out any problems or complaints on the questionnaire you're given at the end of the cruise. Everyone up to and including the chairman of the board and the ship owner read these whenever there is a serious complaint. And don't be coerced by an anxious waiter or steward to give an excellent rating when not warranted just because he says he may lose his job as a result.

KEELHAUL

We give a punishing Keelhaul Award to those litigious passengers who threaten to sue cruise lines because there happened to be a hurricane or storm at sea that spoiled their vacation. When was the last time they sued Holiday Inn or Marriott under similar circumstances?

THE END OF THE CRUISE

Despite the highly polished service, Seabourn's cadre of dining room stewards does not accept gratuities.

Tipping

It used to be that any article on shipboard tipping—"shipboard gratuities," as the cruise line brochures like to call it—dealt simply with whom, how much and when. At some point in his disembarkation lecture, the cruise director would say, "So many passengers have asked us about whom and how much to tip..." and launch into an easy-to-compute per-person-per-day figure for the waiters and the cabin stewards.

Then you would go back to your cabin and figure out how much to tip each, get some change and slip that amount into the little envelopes that had a way of appearing in your cabin just when needed. You might put a little extra cash in for someone who was extra solicitous, knock off a little from someone else who had done less than you expected.

That was the way it used to be.

In the late 1970s, Holland America Line, which trains its own employees at special hotel schools in Indonesia and the Philippines, implemented a "no tipping required" policy. "We don't say tipping is not permitted," a line spokesman explained, "simply that it is not required. A passenger is free to tip any of our serving personnel if he wishes, but those personnel are not permitted to solicit tips in any fashion."

Then in 1984, Sea Goddess Cruises came along with an even more explicit rule—"If you are concerned about tipping, the Sea Goddess concept is quite simple: gratuities are discouraged."

Seabourn went them one further in 1990; the company "strictly prohibits all staff for any solicitation or acceptance of gratuities."

In 1996, Cunard also eliminated tipping on board the *QE2*, *Royal Viking Sun* and *Vistafjord*.

Even more astonishing is that we were getting excellent service on all three lines, erasing that notion that the word "tip" was an acronym "to insure promptness."

Well, if that isn't the case, what is a gratuity? Is it a voluntary reward for extra-special service, or is it, as in most European hotels and restaurants, a percentage charged for service and as routine a part of the bill as taxes? And if that's so, why couldn't it be added into the base cruise fare?

An automatic up-front payment would eliminate the problem crew members face called "stiffing"—a passenger leaving no tip whatsoever on a cruise where tipping is expected.

Aboard some ships, tips are automatically calculated and added to the passenger's shipboard account. And on most ships, bar service charges of 15 percent are automatically added to the drink tab. Cunard established a policy a couple of years ago of letting passengers who were uncomfortable with the matter of tipping pay the usual amount up-front.

On Crystal's ships, you can even charge your tips on your shipboard account and receive in exchange small printed cards to sign and present to your waiters and cabin steward, who later turn them in for cash. This relieves you of adding and multiplying chores and the necessity of going down to the purser to get change.

Some of the confusion about tipping comes from ships with open-seating policies. Since you may have a different waiter each time, how do you know whom to tip?

The Greek stewards' union requests each passenger set aside a prescribed amount that is pooled and divided among the crew under a prescribed formula. The usual argument that a crew member will work harder if he's hoping for a tip doesn't apply here, since everyone's going to get the same. (Insiders say peer pressure shapes up any lazy stewards on a Greek ship.)

Some of the smaller American ships and expedition vessels also use the pool system for tips.

Anytime we mention tipping in our newspaper columns, the mail is fast and furious, very little if any of it defending the practice of tipping. The most audible complaints come not from first-timers but veteran cruisers.

Here are some of the questions raised—Should the person who eats breakfast and lunch from the self-service buffet and goes ashore for dinner when the ship is in port be expected to leave the same amount as the passenger who shows up in the dining room for all three meals every day? And should the couple in the small inside cabin on the lower decks give the same steward's tip as the couple in the big boat deck suite?

These are questions for which there are no easy answers. In the meantime, to find out the recommended tip amounts for each ship, check that ship's listing in the guide.

The Last Day: Don't You Love Me Any More?

Everyone at your table has hugged goodbyes the night before, after each has discreetly handed out the tips in their proper little envelopes and expressed a heartfelt thanks to the dining room stewards. The evening is always long and loud after a short cruise, with everyone getting in their last few hours of drinking and gambling and dancing, and quiet and downbeat after a long cruise, when the difficult transition to going home has to be made.

Bags go into the hall at midnight or sometime before 6 a.m. They'll be gathered up and ferried to a central area on the ship and transferred ashore after the ship has been secured the next morning.

No passengers are permitted to disembark until all the luggage has been unloaded and put ashore.

> ### INSIDER TIP
> *Obvious as this may seem, you must be scrupulously careful setting aside the clothing you need to travel in the next day, all the items including shoes and underwear, before putting your bags outside your door for collection. You won't see them again until you're back on shore. Pajamas are not proper debarkation attire.*

Breakfast service is more limited on disembarkation day, with the added aggravation in American ports that the tea is terrible because there's so much chlorine in the water in case the kitchen has a surprise public health inspection, and there are no poached eggs because for some mysterious reason, the kitchen cannot poach eggs if the public health inspectors are aboard.

If your waiters are friendly but a little withdrawn, it's because, on many ships, they're the same busy beavers that spent the night lugging luggage down the halls and so have had maybe two hours of sleep maximum. Your tablemates, your best friends for life during the past week or so, may seem inordinately concerned with airport and getting home details, but you all exchange addresses and phone numbers.

You say goodbye a dozen times to everyone while you're milling about waiting for the ship to be cleared by customs and immigration and for your group's turn to depart.

Getting Off

You have been given color-coded baggage tags depending on aircraft departure times or ongoing arrangements, and your baggage will be waiting in the customs hall in the color-coded group. Do not panic; it is probably there somewhere. Gather it up, getting a porter if you need one or lugging it out by yourself if you don't.

You will have been given a U.S. customs form to fill out, which you will turn in at the gate as you leave. Most cruise ships arriving in U.S. ports have customs and immigration officials on board who have precleared your passport and customs forms before you disembark the ship.

INSIDER TIP

It's a good idea to take a close look at your bag before setting it out in the hall. When you get on the dock, you'll see a dozen just like it. The idea is to pick up the one belonging to you. We have seen passengers wandering around with no idea of what their bags actually look like.

Going Home

If you're on the air/sea package, your return to the airport and home will be very similar to your arrival, with the meet-and-greets on hand with their signs and advice. Sometimes, after you claim your baggage and clear customs at the port, you can trundle it right over to the airline's baggage truck at the pier and check it in there, trusting it will arrive in your home airport when you do. It usually does.

APPENDIX: THE NUTS AND BOLTS

How to get a passport:

Apply in person at one of the 3500 clerks of court or post offices which accept applications, or at one of the 13 passport agencies in the United States.

Present two passport photographs (go to a photographer who specializes in these), a photo ID with your signature such as an active driver's license, and proof of citizenship or nationality—a certified copy of a birth certificate, a Certificate of Naturalization or an expired U.S. passport.

Pay $65 if you're over 18, $40 if you're under 18, and turn in or mail in the completed printed form you were given to fill out. If you're renewing your passport, pay $55.

How to select a travel agent:

Take as much time and care with your choice as when choosing a mate, looking for intelligence, warmth, patience, friendliness and diligence. A knowledge of basic geography is helpful too.

Look for professional associations; the agent should be a member of ASTA (American Society of Travel Agents), ARTA (Association of Retail Travel Agents), CLIA (Cruise Lines International Association) and/or NACOA (National Association of Cruise Only Agents). The latter specialize in cruises, but it does not mean they are more qualified on the subject than "full service" agents, only that they are specialists.

Whenever you book a cruise ticket through an agent, the agent receives a commission from the cruise line, not from you. There may be surcharges on other agency services, however, with the recent airline caps restricting the commission an agent can make from booking an air ticket.

How to go through immigration:

Have your passport ready and in your hand.

Be sure you're in the correct line; signs often indicate certain lines are restricted to airline crews, nationals of that country or members of European Community nations only.

When you near the immigration officer, be sure to remain behind the taped or painted line on the floor until the person ahead of you has finished and left.

Answer any questions asked, but don't volunteer comments, and don't fidget while he's examining your passport.

How to go through customs:

Have ready any receipts for large purchases you may have made on the trip.

Fill out the requisite form honestly.

Be prepared to open any bags or suitcases if requested, but never hesitate or ask the officer if he wants it opened, even when the man in front of you has had to open his.

Trip cancellation insurance:

This covers you if you have to cancel your cruise at the last minute, after the full fare has been paid and the cancellation penalties kick in, because of illness, death in the family or business emergencies.

Travel agents usually recommend a client take this insurance; some of the more cautious even ask a client who refuses it to sign a form indicating they were offered the insurance. Cruise lines, while not wanting to appear heartless, point out that while an emergency of this sort may happen once in your lifetime, it happens to them every sailing.

Vaccinations and medications:

If you are going to exotic areas of the world, check with your doctor or public health authorities about any medications or vaccinations recommended for travelers to that region. Remember that if you eat and sleep only aboard the cruise ship you will not be taking the same risks as someone on a trek or a safari.

Port Taxes:

Those friendly tropical islands who love tourists also love slapping on huge port taxes, also sometimes called "head taxes," for visitors. The highest one we've encountered in North American waters is Bermuda's $60 a passenger.

Some sharp-eyed cruisers may note that the cruise line's port fees may actually exceed the total of the individual ports' actual taxes. The usual explanation for this is administrative costs, whatever that means.

Pre- and post-cruise packages:

Most cruise line brochures have add-on pre- or post-cruise packages for the cities of embarkation and disembarkation. If you're interested in such a package, discuss it with your travel agent to be sure the hotel being used is one you would like and that the price is less than you could get on your own. The upside of these packages is that they usually include transfers, which could save a lot of money in some cities.

INDEX

Order Your Guide to Travel and Adventure

Title	Price	Title	Price
Fielding's Alaska Cruises and the Inside Passage	$18.95	Fielding's Las Vegas Agenda	$14.95
Fielding's The Amazon	$16.95	Fielding's London Agenda	$14.95
Fielding's Asia's Top Dive Sites	$19.95	Fielding's Los Angeles	$16.95
Fielding's Australia	$16.95	Fielding's Malaysia & Singapore	$16.95
Fielding's Bahamas	$16.95	Fielding's Mexico	$18.95
Fielding's Baja	$18.95	Fielding's New Orleans Agenda	$16.95
Fielding's Bermuda	$16.95	Fielding's New York Agenda	$16.95
Fielding's Borneo	$18.95	Fielding's New Zealand	$16.95
Fielding's Budget Europe	$17.95	Fielding's Paris Agenda	$14.95
Fielding's Caribbean	$18.95	Fielding's Portugal	$16.95
Fielding's Caribbean Cruises	$18.95	Fielding's Paradors, Pousadas and Charming Villages	$18.95
Fielding's Disney World and Orlando	$18.95	Fielding's Rome Agenda	$14.95
Fielding's Diving Indonesia	$19.95	Fielding's San Diego Agenda	$14.95
Fielding's Eastern Caribbean	$17.95	Fielding's Southeast Asia	$18.95
Fielding's England	$17.95	Fielding's Southern Vietnam on 2 Wheels	$15.95
Fielding's Europe	$18.95	Fielding's Spain	$18.95
Fielding's European Cruises	$18.95	Fielding's Surfing Indonesia	$19.95
Fielding's Far East	$18.95	Fielding's Sydney Agenda	$16.95
Fielding's France	$18.95	Fielding's Thailand, Cambodia, Laos and Myanmar	$18.95
Fielding's Freewheelin' USA	$18.95	Fielding's Vietnam	$17.95
Fielding's Hawaii	$18.95	Fielding's Western Caribbean	$18.95
Fielding's Italy	$18.95	Fielding's The World's Most Dangerous Places	$19.95
Fielding's Kenya	$16.95	Fielding's Worldwide Cruises '97	$19.95

To place an order: call toll-free 1-800-FW-2-GUIDE
(VISA, MasterCard and American Express accepted)
or send your check or money order to:
Fielding Worldwide, Inc., 308 S. Catalina Avenue, Redondo Beach, CA 90277
http://www.fieldingtravel.com
Add $2.00 per book for shipping & handling (sorry, no COD's), allow 2–6 weeks for delivery

Fielding's
Worldwide Cruises

"Recommended without reservation."

—Philadelphia Inquirer

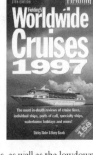

This totally new, encyclopedic volume is the definitive guide for choosing the perfect cruise. It's really two books in one, with ratings of 178 ships and profiles of 58 cruise lines, as well as the lowdown on the 220 most visited ports around the world. Written by Shirley Slater and Harry Basch, a husband-and-wife travel-writing team whose work has been published internationally, the text is both urbane and engaging and packed with valuable insider information.

Reviews of 178 ships, and 220 ports of call, with 200 b/w photos and 23 helpful maps.

$19.95

Fielding's
Caribbean Cruises

Frank, in-depth reviews of every major ship that sails the Caribbean.

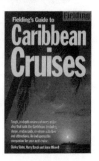

The most comprehensive guide to the ships that ply the Caribbean and all 35 ports of call. Written in a descriptive, entertaining style, it contains all the facts the reader needs to choose the right ship and the right destinations.

Filled with hundreds of helpful hints, loads of charts and tables, plus 43 maps, 150 b/w photos and 868 restaurant and attraction listings.

$18.95

Fielding's
European Cruises

The indispensable guide to Europe's most popular cruises.

As many as 80 ships and 74 ports of call are covered, enabling readers to make the best choices in touring Europe this elegant and hassle-free way! This highly informative handbook is written in an engaging style by Shirley Slater and Harry Basch, the husband-and-wife travel-writing team, called "America's premier cruise specialists" by the Chicago Sun Times.

Loads of charts and tables and helpful hints, plus 74 maps and 50 b/w photos.

$18.95

Fielding's
Freewheelin' USA

The Fielding way to discover America's back roads.

Authors Shirley Slater and Harry Basch have logged more than 50,000 miles traveling around the U.S. In this entertaining guide, the renowned husband-and-wife travel-writing team tells readers everything they ever wanted to know about RVs and the freewheeling lifestyle. Extremely readable and filled with amusing anecdotes from the authors' road diary, it is the perfect handbook for a weekend getaway or a tour across the country!

With 125 b/w photos and 70 helpful, detailed maps.

$18.95

NEW FIELDINGWEAR!

Now that you own a Fielding travel guide, you have graduated from being a tourist to a full-fledged traveler! Celebrate your elevated position by proudly wearing one of these heavy-duty, all-cotton shirts, selected by our authors for their comfort and durability (and their ability to hide dirt). Choose from three styles—radical "World Tour," politically correct "Do the World Right," and elegant "All-Access."

Important note: Fielding authors have field-tested these shirts and found that they can be swapped for much more than their purchase price in free drinks at some of the world's hottest clubs and in-spots. They also make great gifts.

WORLD TOUR

Hit the hard road with a travel fashion statement for our times. Visit all 35 of Mr. D.P.'s favorite nasty spots (listed on the back), or just look like you're going to. This is the real McCoy, worn by mujahadeen, mercenaries, U.N. peacekeepers and the authors of Fielding's *The World's Most Dangerous Places*. Black, **XL**, heavy-duty 100% cotton. Made in the U.S.A. $18.00.

DO THE WORLD RIGHT

Start your next adventure wearing Fielding's politically correct "Do the World Right" shirt, complete with freaked-out red globe and blasting white type. A shirt that tells the world that within that high-mileage, overly educated body beats the heart of a true party animal. Only for adrenaline junkies, hard-core travelers and seekers of knowledge. Black, **XL**, heavy-duty 100% cotton. Made in the U.S.A. $18.00.

Name:

Address:

City:

State: Zip:

ALL-ACCESS

Strike terror into the snootiest maitre d', make concierges cringe, or just use this elegant shirt as the ultimate party invitation. The combination of the understated red Fielding logo embroidered on a jet-black golf shirt will get you into the snobbiest embassy party or jumping nightspot. An elegant casual shirt for those who travel in style and comfort. Black, **XL** or **L**, 100% preshrunk cotton, embroidered Fielding Travel Guide logo on front. Made in the U.S.A. $29.00.

Telephone:
Shirt Name:
Quantity:

For each shirt, add $4 shipping and handling. California residents add $1.50 sales tax.
Allow 2 to 4 weeks for delivery.
Send check or money order with your order form to:

Fielding Worldwide, Inc.
308 South Catalina Ave.
Redondo Beach, CA 90277

Or
order your shirts by phone:
1-800-FW-2-GUIDE
Visa, MC, AMex accepted

International Conversions

TEMPERATURE

To convert °F to °C, subtract 32 and divide by 1.8.

To convert °C to °F, multiply by 1.8 and add 32.

Fahrenheit | **Centigrade**

Fahrenheit	Centigrade	
230°	110°	
220°		
210°	100°	Water Boils
200°		
190°	90°	
180°	80°	
170°		
160°	70°	
150°		
140°	60°	
130°		
120°	50°	
110°		
100°	40°	
90°	30°	
80°		
70°	20°	
60°		
50°	10°	
40°		
30°	0°	Water Freezes
20°	-10°	
10°		
0°	-20°	
-10°		
-20°	-30°	
-30°		
-40°	-40°	

WEIGHTS & MEASURES

LENGTH		
1 km	=	0.62 miles
1 mile	=	1.609 km
1 meter	=	1.2936 yards
1 meter	=	3.28 feet
1 yard	=	0.9144 meters
1 yard	=	3 feet
1 foot	=	30.48 centimeters
1 centimeter	=	0.39 inch
1 inch	=	2.54 centimeters

AREA		
1 square km	=	0.3861 square miles
1 square mile	=	2.590 square km
1 hectare	=	2.47 acres
1 acre	=	0.405 hectare

VOLUME		
1 cubic meter	=	1.307 cubic yards
1 cubic yard	=	0.765 cubic meter
1 cubic yard	=	27 cubic feet
1 cubic foot	=	0.028 cubic meter
1 cubic centimeter	=	0.061 cubic inch
1 cubic inch	=	16.387 cubic centimeters

CAPACITY		
1 gallon	=	3.785 liters
1 quart	=	0.94635 liters
1 liter	=	1.057 quarts
1 pint	=	473 milliliters
1 fluid ounce	=	29.573 milliliters

MASS and WEIGHT		
1 metric ton	=	1.102 short tons
1 metric ton	=	1000 kilograms
1 short ton	=	.90718 metric ton
1 long ton	=	1.016 metric tons
1 long ton	=	2240 pounds
1 pound	=	0.4536 kilograms
1 kilogram	=	2.2046 pounds
1 ounce	=	28.35 grams
1 gram	=	0.035 ounce
1 milligram	=	0.015 grain